Strengthening the National Institute of Justice

Committee on Assessing the Research Program of the
National Institute of Justice

Charles F. Wellford, Betty M. Chemers, and Julie A. Schuck, *Editors*

Division of Behavioral and Social Sciences and Education

NATIONAL RESEARCH COUNCIL
OF THE NATIONAL A(

THE NATIONAL ACADEMIES PRESS
Washington, D.C.
www.nap.edu

THE NATIONAL ACADEMIES PRESS 500 Fifth Street, N.W. Washington, DC 20001

NOTICE: The project that is the subject of this report was approved by the Governing Board of the National Research Council, whose members are drawn from the councils of the National Academy of Sciences, the National Academy of Engineering, and the Institute of Medicine. The members of the committee responsible for the report were chosen for their special competences and with regard for appropriate balance.

This study was supported by Contract No. 2007-IJ-CX-0001 between the National Academy of Sciences and the U.S. Department of Justice. Any opinions, findings, conclusions, or recommendations expressed in this publication are those of the author(s) and do not necessarily reflect the views of the organization or agencies that provided support for the project.

International Standard Book Number-13: 978-0-309-15635-6
International Standard Book Number-10: 0-309-15635-1

Additional copies of this report are available from the National Academies Press, 500 Fifth Street, NW, Lockbox 285, Washington, DC 20055; (800) 624-6242 or (202) 334-3313 (in the Washington metropolitan area); Internet, http://www.nap.edu.

Printed in the United States of America

Suggested citation: National Research Council. (2010). *Strengthening the National Institute of Justice*. Committee on Assessing the Research Program of the National Institute of Justice, C.F. Wellford, B.M. Chemers, and J.A. Schuck, Editors. Division of Behavioral and Social Sciences and Education. Washington, DC: The National Academies Press.

THE NATIONAL ACADEMIES

Advisers to the Nation on Science, Engineering, and Medicine

The **National Academy of Sciences** is a private, nonprofit, self-perpetuating society of distinguished scholars engaged in scientific and engineering research, dedicated to the furtherance of science and technology and to their use for the general welfare. Upon the authority of the charter granted to it by the Congress in 1863, the Academy has a mandate that requires it to advise the federal government on scientific and technical matters. Dr. Ralph J. Cicerone is president of the National Academy of Sciences.

The **National Academy of Engineering** was established in 1964, under the charter of the National Academy of Sciences, as a parallel organization of outstanding engineers. It is autonomous in its administration and in the selection of its members, sharing with the National Academy of Sciences the responsibility for advising the federal government. The National Academy of Engineering also sponsors engineering programs aimed at meeting national needs, encourages education and research, and recognizes the superior achievements of engineers. Dr. Charles M. Vest is president of the National Academy of Engineering.

The **Institute of Medicine** was established in 1970 by the National Academy of Sciences to secure the services of eminent members of appropriate professions in the examination of policy matters pertaining to the health of the public. The Institute acts under the responsibility given to the National Academy of Sciences by its congressional charter to be an adviser to the federal government and, upon its own initiative, to identify issues of medical care, research, and education. Dr. Harvey V. Fineberg is president of the Institute of Medicine.

The **National Research Council** was organized by the National Academy of Sciences in 1916 to associate the broad community of science and technology with the Academy's purposes of furthering knowledge and advising the federal government. Functioning in accordance with general policies determined by the Academy, the Council has become the principal operating agency of both the National Academy of Sciences and the National Academy of Engineering in providing services to the government, the public, and the scientific and engineering communities. The Council is administered jointly by both Academies and the Institute of Medicine. Dr. Ralph J. Cicerone and Dr. Charles M. Vest are chair and vice chair, respectively, of the National Research Council.

www.national-academies.org

COMMITTEE ON ASSESSING THE RESEARCH PROGRAM OF THE NATIONAL INSTITUTE OF JUSTICE

CHARLES F. WELLFORD (*Chair*), Department of Criminology, University of Maryland
GEORGE F. SENSABAUGH, JR. (*Vice Chair*), School of Public Health, University of California, Berkeley
CHARLES E. ANDERSON, JR., Engineering Dynamics Department, Southwest Research Institute, San Antonio
ROBERT D. CRUTCHFIELD, Department of Sociology, University of Washington
JOEL S. ENGEL, JSE Consulting, Armonk, New York
JOHN L. HAGAN, Department of Sociology, Northwestern University
ADELE V. HARRELL, Independent Consultant, Washington, DC
DAVID D. JENSEN, Knowledge Discovery Library, University of Massachusetts, Amherst
TRACEY L. MEARES, Yale Law School
EDWIN MEESE III, Heritage Foundation, Washington, DC
DANIEL S. NAGIN, H.J. Heinz School of Public Policy, Carnegie Mellon University
ALEX R. PIQUERO, College of Criminology and Criminal Justice, Florida State University
CHARLES H. RAMSEY, Philadelphia Police Department
MARY ANN SAAR, Independent Consultant, Baltimore
JAY A. SIEGEL, Department of Chemistry and Chemical Biology, Indiana University–Purdue University, Indianapolis
CAROL H. WEISS, Harvard Graduate School of Education, Harvard University

BETTY M. CHEMERS, *Study Director*
CAROL PETRIE, *Director, Committee on Law and Justice*
JULIE ANNE SCHUCK, *Research Associate*
JACQUELINE R. SOVDE, *Program Associate*

COMMITTEE ON LAW AND JUSTICE

JAMES Q. WILSON (*Chair*), University of California, Los Angeles
PHILIP J. COOK (*Vice Chair*), Sanford Institute of Public Policy, Duke University
CARL C. BELL, Community Mental Health Council, Inc., Chicago
ROBERT D. CRUTCHFIELD, Department of Sociology, University of Washington
GARY LaFREE, National Consortium for the Study of Terrorism and Responses to Terrorism, University of Maryland
JANET L. LAURITSEN, Department of Criminology and Criminal Justice, University of Missouri, St. Louis
GLENN C. LOURY, Department of Economics, Brown University
CHARLES F. MANSKI, Department of Economics, Northwestern University
TRACEY L. MEARES, Yale Law School
TERRIE E. MOFFITT, Department of Psychology and Neuroscience, Duke University
RUTH D. PETERSON, Department of Sociology, Criminal Justice Research Center, Ohio State University
ROBERT J. SAMPSON, Department of Sociology, Harvard University
JEREMY TRAVIS, John Jay College of Criminal Justice, City University of New York
DAVID WEISBURD, Department of Administration of Justice, Center for Evidence Based Crime Policy, George Mason University
PAUL K. WORMELI, IJIS Institute, Ashburn, Virginia

JANE L. ROSS, *Acting Director*
BETTY M. CHEMERS, *Senior Program Officer*
LINDA DEPUGH, *Administrative Assistant*

Preface

Experience strongly suggests that few people or organizations seek public assessments of their performance. This is especially true for government agencies, for which the consequences of such reviews can be painful and seldom seem to result in agency enhancements. It was therefore both surprising and exciting when the National Institute of Justice (NIJ) asked the National Research Council (NRC) to conduct an assessment of its operations, research, and impact. Although NIJ was prompted to seek this review by the requirements of the Office of Management and Budget's Program Assessment Rating Tool (PART) process and the results of some assessments by the Government Accountability Office, the agency's genuine interest in having a comprehensive and objective assessment impressed me as well as the other members of the committee. Having worked at NIJ for a year following completion of my graduate work and in a number of different capacities over the years since then, I knew how important the decision of the NIJ leadership to seek this review was to the committee's ability to conduct the assessment.

While the committee received admirable cooperation from NIJ and other components of the U.S. Department of Justice, the reader will see that our assessment was at times limited by the absence of basic data describing NIJ's work and accomplishments. Time and again, information that any effective agency would be expected to maintain as part of its review of its operations was difficult to access or not available. We detail these problems in the report and call for changes in management and record-keeping that, if implemented, will mean that future assessments will not face this problem.

A vibrant and effective federal research agency addressing issues of crime and justice continues to be vital to an improved ability to reduce crime and increase justice. The committee concluded this after a careful review of NIJ and a consideration of the role that other federal, state, and nonprofit organizations can and do play in advancing knowledge about crime and justice. Nothing in this report should be construed to suggest otherwise. We expect there will be debate about some of our recommendations, but there should be no debate on whether an NIJ is important to facing the "challenge of crime in a free society."

This report is the product of collective contributions. We could not have completed our work without the assistance of the NRC staff who provided wise counsel as well as invaluable support in drafting our report, and of numerous scholars, practitioners, policy officials, and program mangers who met with the committee and provided the information, data, and research necessary for our assessment.

We are grateful for the involvement of staff from NIJ. The director, deputy directors, and division chiefs briefed the committee on their programs and fielded numerous questions. These staff included David Hagy, director; Marc Caplan, chief, Operational Technologies Division; Christine Crossland, acting chief, Violence and Victimization Research Division; Thomas Feucht, executive science advisor and previous director of the Office of Research and Evaluation; William Ford, acting chief, Information and Sensor Technology Division; Nancy Merritt, chief, Justice Systems Research Division; John Morgan, director, Office of Science and Technology; Winifred Reed, chief, Crime Control and Prevention Research Division; Mike Sheppo, chief, Investigative and Forensics Sciences Division; Cindy Smith, chief, International Center, Office of the Director; and Edwin Zedlewski, senior science advisor. We also recognize the NIJ staff that assisted the committee in assembling documents and data on the agency and clarifying information on their programs. These included Portia Graham, associate director, Office of Operations; Jolene Hernon, director, Office of Communications; Angela Moore Parmley, acting director, Office of Research and Evaluation; John Picarelli, social science analyst; and George Tillery, associate director, Office of Science and Technology. A special note of thanks goes to Patrick Clark, senior social science analyst, and Karen Stern, social science analyst, who served as the NIJ liaisons to the committee.

We also thank the many individuals who served as presenters and discussants at our meetings and provided perspective on NIJ from the field as well as inside the Department of Justice. These included Richard Thornburgh, former U.S. Attorney General (1988-1991); Janet Reno, former U.S. Attorney General (1993-2001); Alfred Blumstein, J. Erik Jonsson university professor, urban systems and operations research, Carnegie Mellon

University; Charles Bostian, alumni distinguished professor, electrical and computer engineering, Virginia Polytechnic Institute and University; Ronnie Earle, district attorney, Travis County, Texas; Michael J. Farrell, deputy commissioner, New York City Police Department; Jeff Frazier, global justice and public safety director, Cisco Systems, Inc.; Bruce Goldberger, professor, toxicology, University of Florida College of Medicine and ex officio trustee of the American Academy of Forensic Sciences; Martin F. Horn, commissioner, Corrections and Probation, New York City; Gary LaFree, professor, criminology and criminal justice and director of the National Consortium for the Study of Terrorism and Responses to Terrorism, University of Maryland; John M. Pellegrino, director, Sensors and Electron Devices Directorate, U.S. Army Research Laboratory; Richard Rosenfeld, professor, criminology and criminal justice, University of Missouri; David G. Ross, former circuit court judge, Seventh Judicial Circuit, Maryland; and Howard Silver, executive director, Consortium of Social Science Associations.

We are particularly grateful that several former Department of Justice officials took time out of their schedules to meet with committee members. We thank former NIJ directors Sarah Hart, James K. Stewart, and Jeremy Travis for their perspectives on challenges facing NIJ as well as NIJ's role in priority setting and dissemination, and former assistant attorneys general, Office of Justice Programs (OJP), Deborah Daniels and Laurie Robinson for their perspectives, respectively, on the need for a criminal justice research institute and on transition activities of the new administration and their effect on NIJ. Laurie Robinson, at the time she briefed the committee, was director, Master of Science in Criminology Program at the Jerry Lee Center of Criminology, University of Pennsylvania, and has since been reappointed as assistant attorney general, OJP.

We also received briefings from agency directors and program division directors of several federal research agencies. We thank those individuals who provided perspective on the roles and responsibilities of a research agency: Wilson Compton, director, Division of Epidemiology, Services and Prevention Research, National Institute of Drug Abuse; Rolf Dietrich, deputy director, Research Division, U.S. Department of Homeland Security; Christopher Doyle, director, Infrastructure and Geophysical Division, U.S. Department of Homeland Security; Naomi Goldstein, director, Planning, Research and Evaluation, Administration for Children and Families, U.S. Department of Health and Human Services; Wayne Goodman, director, Division of Adult Translational Research, National Institute of Mental Health; Patricia Gruber, director of research, Office of Naval Research; Susan Haire, project officer, Law and Science Program, National Science Foundation; Ralph Hingson, acting director, and Vivian Faden, deputy director, Division of Epidemiology and Prevention, National Institute on Alcohol Abuse and Alcoholism; David Lightfoot, assistant director, Social,

Behavioral, and Economic Sciences Directorate, National Science Foundation; Richard Nakamura, deputy director, National Institute of Mental Health; Kevin Neary, deputy assistant secretary for research, Office of Research, Evaluation, and Monitoring, U.S. Department of Housing and Urban Development; Lynn Okagaki, commissioner, National Center for Education Research, U.S. Department of Education; Georgeanne Patmios, assistant director, Division of Behavioral and Social Research, National Institute on Aging; Norka Ruiz Bravo, director, Office of Extramural Research, National Institutes of Health; Eric Steel, director, Program Office, National Institute of Standards and Technology; and Grover (Russ) Whitehurst, director, Institute of Education Sciences, U.S. Department of Education.

In addition to these public briefings, we reviewed published literature and legislation, documents assembled by NIJ, as well as reports prepared for the committee. We were thankful to have the opportunity to review a report on the National Archive of Criminal Justice Data submitted by Kaye Marz, archive manager, and Christopher D. Maxwell, associate research scientist, from the Inter-university Consortium for Political and Social Research at the University of Michigan. We are also grateful to Nicola Smith, University of Maryland, who prepared a report on NIJ's graduate research and W.E.B. Du Bois fellowship programs and assisted the committee in our citation analyses. We thank Scott McBride and Donna Kenly from Hollander Cohen & McBride Marketing Research for conducting a web-based survey of criminal justice researchers and practitioners and assembling and summarizing the data in a report for the committee.

On behalf of the committee, staff conducted site visits to some of NIJ's technology centers and interviewed 26 current and former NIJ staff to learn more about its processes, programs, and achievements. We are grateful to those who helped make the site visits informative including Troy Krenning, director, National Law Enforcement and Corrections Technology Center, Rocky Mountain; Kevin Lothridge, director, Forensic Science Center of Excellence; Andy Mazzara, director, Weapons and Protective Systems Technology Center of Excellence; Raj Nanavati, director, Sensors, Surveillance, and Biometric Technologies Center of Excellence; Joe Peters, director, Border Research and Technology Center; and Brian Regli, former director, Communications Technologies Center of Excellence.

We are also thankful to the current and former NIJ staff that agreed to be interviewed. The interviews included staff from every division within the Office of Research and Evaluation, two of the three divisions within the Office of Science and Technology, and every function (administration, special advisors, international crime, and communications) within the Office of the Director and as a whole covered the scope of NIJ's operations from the 1970s to present. Each interview consisted of three parts: (1) employee history and professional background; (2) questions related to grant processes and roles; and (3) questions on NIJ's mission and impact. Since our invitation to the interviewees indicated that responses would remain anonymous and all names would be kept confidential, we do not recognize them by name here. However, we acknowledge that without their candor and insight into agency processes we would not have gained as complete an understanding of NIJ.

This study and its report have also benefited from the valuable assistance of many NRC staff within the Division of Behavioral and Social Sciences and Education. Betty Chemers was the study director. As such, she organized meetings, identified sources of information and conducted analyses, and worked tirelessly with the committee to integrate their ideas, writings, and conclusions into a sound report. Julie Schuck, as research associate, assembled background documents, created databases of award histories when none was available, and assisted in drafting and editing this report. Carol Petrie, director, Committee on Law and Justice, provided perspective on NIJ's history and helped us integrate our work with prior NRC studies. This study also benefited from the counsel and experience of Barney Cohen, Anne-Marie Mazza, and Daniel Cork, NRC staff who oversaw relevant assessments of other federal agencies and research programs. Jacqui Sovde, program associate, made sure meetings were organized and conducted in a professional manner and assisted in the editing and formatting of this report. Several others provided administrative support as needed including Barbara Boyd, Linda DePugh, and Anthony Mann. We greatly appreciate the efforts undertaken by Eugenia Grohman, Christine McShane, Jane Ross, Kirsten Sampson Snyder, and Yvonne Wise to complete the review and editing processes and bring this report to fruition.

This report has been reviewed in draft form by individuals chosen for their diverse perspectives and technical expertise, in accordance with procedures approved by the NRC's Report Review Committee. The purpose of this independent review is to provide candid and critical comments that will assist the institution in making its published report as sound as possible and to ensure that the report meets institutional standards for objectivity, evidence, and responsiveness to the study charge. The review comments and draft manuscript remain confidential to protect the integrity of the deliberative process. We thank the following individuals for their review of this report: Todd R. Clear, Department of Law, Police Science and Criminal Justice Administration, John Jay College; Max M. Houck, Forensic Science Initiative, West Virginia University; Rick Kern, Office of the Director, Virginia Criminal Sentencing Commission; Janet Lauritsen, Department of Criminology and Criminal Justice, University of Missouri, St. Louis; Michael D. Maltz, Department of Sociology, Criminal Justice Research Center, Ohio State University; Stan Orchowsky, Office of the Research Director, Justice Research and Statistics Association, Washington,

DC; Robert J. Sampson, Department of Sociology, Harvard University; Robert Santos, Statistical Methods Group, The Urban Institute, Washington, DC; Joan C. Weiss, Office of the Executive Director, Justice Research and Statistics Association, Washington, DC; Chuck Wexler, Office of the Executive Director, Police Executive Research Forum, Washington, DC; Tara Wildes, Office of the Chief, Jacksonville Sheriff's Office, Jacksonville, Florida; and Paul Wormeli, Office of the Executive Director, IJIS Institute, Ashburn, Virginia.

Although reviewers listed above have provided many constructive comments and suggestions, they were not asked to endorse the conclusions or recommendations, nor did they see the final draft of the report before it was released. The review of this report was overseen by John C. Bailar III, Department of Health Studies (emeritus), University of Chicago, and Gary LaFree, National Consortium for the Study of Terrorism and Responses to Terrorism, University of Maryland. Appointed by the NRC, they were responsible for making certain that an independent examination of this report was carried out in accordance with the institutional procedures and that all review comments were carefully considered. Responsibility for the final content of this report rests entirely with the authoring committee and the institution.

Charles F. Wellford, *Chair*
Committee on Assessing the Research Program
of the National Institute of Justice

Contents

Appendixes

Tables, Figures, and Boxes

TABLES

FIGURES

BOXES

Acronyms

AAG	Assistant Attorney General
ABA	American Bar Association
ACA	American Correctional Association
ADAM	Arrestee Drug Abuse Monitoring system
AG	Attorney General
AHRQ	Agency for Healthcare Research and Quality
APM	Analysis, Planning and Management
ASA	American Sociological Association
ASC	American Society of Criminology
ASCLD	American Society of Crime Lab Directors
ATF	Bureau of Alcohol, Tobacco and Firearms and Explosives
BIS-WDS	Brijot Imaging Systems–Weapons Detection System
BJA	Bureau of Justice Assistance
BJS	Bureau of Justice Statistics
BLS	Bureau of Labor Statistics
BPI	OJP Business Process Improvement
BRTC	Border Research and Technology Center
BRTD	U.S. Border Patrol Technology Demonstrations
BSR	Behavioral and Social Research
BTC	NIJ's Breaking the Cycle Program
CAPRAD	Computer Assisted Pre-Coordination Resource and Database System
CAPS	Chicago Alternative Policing Strategy

CBO	Congressional Budget Office
CBRN	Chemical, biological, radioactive, nuclear
CBRNE	Chemical, biological, radioactive, nuclear, and high-yield explosives
CDC	Centers for Disease Control and Prevention
CLAJ	Committee on Law and Justice
CLIP	Crime Laboratory Improvement Program
CMS	Community Management Staff
CNSTAT	Committee on National Statistics
CODIS	Combined DNA Index System
COE	Center of Excellence
COMPSTAT	the name given to a strategic problem-solving process or "strategic control system" first implemented by the New York City Police Department; short for computer statistics or comparative statistics
COPS	Community Oriented Policing Services
COSSA	Consortium of Social Science Associations
COTR	OJP Contracting Officer's Technical Representative
COTS	commercial-off-the-shelf
COV	Committee of Visitors
CPTED	Crime Prevention Through Environmental Design
CRISP	Computer Retrieval of Information on Scientific Projects
CRS	Congressional Research Service
CSR	Center for Scientific Review
DARE	Drug Abuse Resistance Education
DARPA	Defense Advanced Research Projects Agency
DEA	Drug Enforcement Administration
DEPR	Division of Epidemiology and Prevention Research
DHS	U.S. Department of Homeland Security
DMA	Drug Market Analysis Program
DOC	U.S. Department of Commerce
DoD	U.S. Department of Defense
DoEd	U.S. Department of Education
DOJ	U.S. Department of Justice
DOL	U.S. Department of Labor
DPCPSI	Division of Program Coordination, Planning, and Strategic Initiatives
DRP	Data Resources Program
DUF	Drug Use Forecasting system
EPA	U.S. Environmental Protection Agency
ESIP	Equipment Systems Improvement Program

FBI	Federal Bureau of Investigation
FDA	U.S. Food and Drug Administration
FOIA	Freedom of Information Act
GAO	U.S. Government Accountability Office
GIS	geographic information systems
GMS	Grant Management System
GPA	Grant Progress Assessment Program
GPRA	Government Performance and Results Act
GRF	Graduate Research Fellowship
GS	general schedule or grade service (refers to pay level)
HHS	U.S. Department of Health and Human Services
HRSA	Health Resources and Services Administration
HUD	U.S. Department of Housing and Urban Development
IAA	Interagency Agreement
IACP	International Association of Chiefs of Police
ICAM	Information Collection for Automated Mapping project (Chicago PD)
ICP-OES	inductively coupled plasma-optical emission spectroscopy
ICPSR	Inter-university Consortium for Political and Social Research
IES	Institute of Education Sciences
IPT	Integrated Product Team
IRB	Institutional Review Board
JAG	Justice Assistance Grants
JD	Juris Doctor
JRSA	Justice Research and Statistics Association
JUSTNET	Justice Technology Information Network
LAPD	Los Angeles Police Department
LEAA	Law Enforcement Assistance Administration
LECTAC	Law Enforcement and Corrections Technology Advisory Council
LEEP	Law Enforcement Education Program
LESL	Law Enforcement Standards Laboratory
MAPS	Mapping and Analysis for Public Safety Program
MD	Maryland
MMW	millimeter wave
MOA	memorandum of agreement

MOU	memorandum of understanding
MPD	District of Columbia Metropolitan Police Department
NACJD	National Archive of Criminal Justice Data
NAS	National Academy of Sciences
NCJRS	National Criminal Justice Reference Service
NDIS	National DNA Index System
NFC	National Finance Center
NFSIA	Paul Coverdell National Forensic Sciences Improvement Act
NFSTC	National Forensic Sciences Technology Center
NIA	National Institute on Aging
NIAAA	National Institute on Alcohol Abuse and Alcoholism
NIBIN	National Integrated Ballistic Information Network
NIDA	National Institute of Drug Abuse
NIH	National Institutes of Health
NIJ	National Institute of Justice
NILECJ	National Institute of Law Enforcement and Criminal Justice
NIMH	National Institute of Mental Health
NIST	National Institute of Standards and Technology
NLECTC	National Law Enforcement and Corrections Technology Center
NPR	National Performance Review
NRC	National Research Council
NSB	National Science Board
NSF	National Science Foundation
NYC	New York City
NYPD	New York City Police Department
OASH	Office of the Assistant Secretary of Health
OCFO-BD	Office of the Chief Financial Officer-Budget Division
OCOM	Office of Communications
OERI	Office of Educational Research and Improvement
OGC	Office of the General Counsel
OIG	DOJ Office of the Inspector General
OJARS	Office of Justice Assistance, Research and Statistics
OJJDP	Office of Juvenile Justice and Delinquency Prevention
OJP	Office of Justice Programs
OLES	Office of Law Enforcement Standards
OLETC	Office of Law Enforcement Technology Commercialization
OLP	Office of Legal Policy

OMB	Office of Management and Budget
ONDCP	Office of National Drug Control Policy
ONR	Office of Naval Research
ORE	Office of Research and Evaluation
OST	Office of Science and Technology
OVC	Office for Victims of Crime
OVW	Office on Violence Against Women
PAR	Performance and Accountability Report
PART	Program Assessment Rating Tool
PBMA	Planning, Budget, Management and Administration Office
PD	police department
PHDCN	Project on Human Development in Chicago Neighborhoods
PI	principal investigator
POSC	Program Office Solicitation Coordinator
PREA	Prison Rape Elimination Act
PSN	Project Safe Neighborhoods
RAC	Regional Advisory Council
R&D	research and development
RDT&E	research, development, testing, and evaluation
RFP	request for proposal
RSAT	Residential Substance Treatment Programs
SACSI	Strategic Approaches to Community Safety Initiative
SAMHSA	Office of Substance Abuse and Mental Health Services
SBE	Directorate of Social, Behavioral & Economic Sciences
SES	Senior Executive Service
SES	Social and Economic Sciences
SETA	Systems Engineering and Technical Assistance
SME	subject-matter expert
SRG	Scientific Review Group
SSCI	Social Science Citation Index
S&T	science and technology
STOP	(Services, Training, Officers, and Prosecutors) Violence Against Women Formula Grants
SVORI	Serious Violent Offender Re-entry Initiative
TAPAC	Technology Assessment Program Advisory Council
TAPIC	Technology Assessment Program Information Center
TATP	triacetone rriperoxide

TSWG	Technical Support Working Group
TWG	technical working group
USAFRL	U.S. Air Force Research Laboratory
VAWA	Violence Against Women Act

Summary

The National Institute of Justice (NIJ) is the nation's primary resource for advancing scientific research, development, and evaluation on crime and crime control and the administration of justice in the United States. Headed by a presidentially appointed director, it is one of the major units in the Office of Justice Programs (OJP) of the U.S. Department of Justice (DOJ). Under its authorizing legislation, NIJ awards grants and contracts to a variety of public and private organizations and individuals.

At the request of NIJ, the National Research Council (NRC) appointed a committee to assess the operations and quality of the full range of its programs. These include social science research, science and technology research and development, capacity building, and technology assistance. The committee was requested to examine and make recommendations regarding NIJ's role in supporting and sustaining the nation's scientific infrastructure of crime and criminal justice research. We were asked to consider what kinds of research were reasonable and appropriate for NIJ to support and the appropriate structure and scope for its short- and long-term planning and budgeting processes. We were also asked to consider the adequacy of its budget, its current organizational structure, and its mechanisms for translating research into policy and practices and whether these are appropriate for fulfilling its science mission.

The committee concludes that a federal research institute such as NIJ is vital to the nation's continuing efforts to control crime and administer justice. No other federal, state, local, or private organization can do what NIJ was created to do. Forty years ago, Congress envisioned a science agency dedicated to building knowledge to support crime prevention and control by developing a wide range of techniques for dealing with individual offenders, identifying injustices and biases in the administration of justice, and supporting more basic and operational research on crime and the criminal justice system and the involvement of the community in crime control efforts. As the embodiment of that vision, NIJ has accomplished a great deal. It has succeeded in developing a body of knowledge on such important topics as hot spots policing, violence against women, the role of firearms and drugs in crime, drug courts, and forensic DNA analysis. It has helped build the crime and justice research infrastructure. It has also widely disseminated the results of its research programs to help guide practice and policy. But its efforts have been severely hampered by a lack of independence, authority, and discretionary resources to carry out its mission.

The committee considered two basic approaches for how best to achieve the appropriate level of independence for NIJ: (1) moving NIJ out of OJP and (2) retaining NIJ in OJP and giving it a level of independence similar to other federal research agencies. In considering these options, the committee reviewed other federal research agencies, consulted with former directors of NIJ and OJP, and raised the issue with many others who offered guidance to the committee.[1] In its deliberations, the committee considered the recommendations of two other NRC committees that issued reports on related topics: the report on the needs of the forensic science community (National Research Council, 2009c) and the report on the Bureau of Justice Statistics (National Research Council, 2009a). After careful consideration of the evidence, the committee concludes that keeping NIJ in OJP but with substantially increased levels of independence secured by Congress and greater involvement of the research and practitioner communities has a better chance to result in an agency that can gain the trust and confidence of Congress, the administration, and the criminal justice community.

Increased independence is essential if NIJ is to function as a viable federal research agency with full responsibility for the quality of its research. Only Congress can provide the requisites of increased independence and the necessary oversight to ensure that specific authorities cannot be easily retracted or eroded. Without the independence, opportunities may arise for others to inappropriately influence NIJ's programs. If the changes we recommend in this report to improve NIJ's independence and authority are not implemented within 5 years, or if they are and the problems we have identified persist, then we recommend carefully revisiting the idea of moving this research function.[2]

---

[1]Most instructive were the views of Jeremy Travis and James K. Stewart, former directors of NIJ (Travis, 2008; Stewart, 2009).

[2]Congress is currently considering establishing a national crime commission. If it is formed, then it would be the natural body to conduct this review.

Our report makes clear that fundamental reforms are necessary. In order to foster public safety, the nation needs research on the causes and correlates of crime and on what policies and practices work for whom, when, and under what circumstances. NIJ is uniquely placed to do this but currently lacks essential tools: a strong management structure, a scientific staff, a budget to support long- and short-term goals, and protections from political shifts.

To address these problems, the committee makes five recommendations that call for ensured independence and improved governance, a strong science mission, a bolstered research infrastructure, scientific integrity and transparency of its operations, and a culture of self-assessment.

INDEPENDENCE AND GOVERNANCE

Recommendation 1: The committee recommends that Congress provide for the requisite independence and authority of the National Institute of Justice (NIJ) while retaining its organizational placement within the Office of Justice Programs and the U.S. Department of Justice. Among the key issues to be considered in pursuit of this goal are a statutory advisory board, a set term of office and minimum qualifications for the NIJ director, and clear authority for NIJ to make awards and control its budget and resources.

An effective research organization needs to have the independence to conduct its work. The key components of independence include control of the grant-making processes at all steps, from solicitation through grant approval; ultimate authority to establish research and evaluation priorities; authority to make budgetary recommendations at the highest level of the department's budget process; authority for staffing decisions; and authority over its reports and other dissemination products. The history of NIJ reflects diminishing authority and resources, not only as a result of congressional action, but also from actions taken by its oversight agency, OJP.

Also contributing to a weakened NIJ has been its unstable governance. For most of its existence, it has experienced frequent turnovers in leadership, directors whose backgrounds and experience did not reflect its science mission, and advisory boards that have never functioned as a scientific advisory board should—setting agendas, reviewing the integrity of the research operations, and assessing accomplishments of the agency.

In the committee's view, significant improvements will not occur without clear and specific changes in NIJ's independence and authority. We call for the NIJ director to have had experience in directing crime and justice research, be recognized as a highly qualified authority in the fields of crime and justice research (including evaluation research), and have demonstrated success in managing substantial crime and justice research efforts. The NIJ director should be appointed for a fixed renewable 6-year term. We call for an advisory board that reports directly to the NIJ director, whose members are composed predominantly of experienced researchers and whose powers and responsibilities support the research mission. NIJ should be given sign-off authority for its grants. In the past, this authority has not always been recognized by the OJP leadership. The committee also stresses the importance of giving NIJ the authority to present its budget to DOJ and for NIJ to have its own budget line item in the departmental budget that is considered by the Office of Management and Budget and Congress. Unlike other science agencies, NIJ does not have its budget separately reviewed or discussed by congressional appropriators.

NIJ should also have authority to recruit and hire staff. One way to exert political interference is to control the numbers of authorized staff, grade levels, and the ability to fill vacancies. NIJ needs to strengthen the scientific and technical qualifications of its staff. By having greater authority for its staffing, including recruitment, it will be able to determine its needs and attract and hire and retain talented and scientifically trained people.

A STRONG SCIENCE MISSION

Recommendation 2: To strengthen its science mission, the National Institute of Justice (NIJ) should direct its efforts toward building a body of cumulative knowledge that will assist the criminal justice field in its effort to prevent and control crime and improve the criminal justice system; sponsoring research that will improve and upgrade current scientific methods used to study crime; and supporting new areas that have heretofore been neglected due to NIJ's incapacity to commit resources required to support projects of long duration, great complexity, and substantial expense. To improve NIJ's ability to support research, the committee recommends that Congress remove responsibility for forensic capacity-building programs and reinstate them in other U.S. Department of Justice and Office of Justice Program agencies, such as the Bureau of Justice Assistance and the Community Oriented Policing Services office, that have a clearly defined technical assistance mission, are closely linked to state and local criminal justice agencies, and have larger financial reserves to draw on.

NIJ has succeeded in developing a body of knowledge in important areas that are critical to preventing and controlling crime and improving the administration of justice.

For the most part, however, these efforts have been heavily dependent on congressionally mandated programs or the transfer of funds from other OJP or DOJ offices to support their specific programs. These requirements have often been made without a strong science foundation. This situation has particularly impacted NIJ's evaluation research portfolio. Its outcome evaluations are extremely diverse in terms of topic, theory, focus, and method and reflect a lack of programmatic focus on systematic knowledge building or problem solving. One reason for this is that NIJ frequently has limited control over decisions of what programs to evaluate. A second and related reason has been NIJ's failure to engage in long-term strategic planning.

Congressional earmarks and mandates require NIJ to fund programs that are at best minimally related to research. Funds for forensic laboratory capacity-building and forensic training activities, such as the Paul Coverdell, DNA Backlog Reduction, Solving Cold Cases, and Forensic DNA Unit Efficiency Improvement programs, swamp the NIJ research program. Management of these programs diverts a considerable fraction of NIJ's time and resources away from its research mission. More importantly, they diminish its stature as a research agency by not allowing it to set its own priorities and requiring it to undertake activities or to fund organizations that are not appropriate for a research agency.

As a science agency, NIJ should play a central role in defining the type of research and evaluations that make sense. Its primary mission is not to evaluate OJP programs, to be a policy-serving arm of OJP and DOJ, to build the capacity of line agencies, or to disseminate information that is not science based. While research focused on improving the status quo of the criminal justice system is important, it will not point the way to new directions or approaches—it will only suggest what we can do more or less of. Building knowledge for the future will require the agency to make longer term commitments of funds and staff to solving problems in specific areas of criminal justice practice, to engage more actively with the research community in selecting priority areas and testing the feasibility of ideas as they develop, and to make multiyear commitments to researchers to work through the development process.

The committee was charged with recommending a research agenda for NIJ. We have not specified a specific research agenda but instead have described a science-based process that we think should be followed to do this. In large part, this is because we became convinced that proper governance and transparent processes need to be established first within the agency in order to set the agenda and to resolve such issues as the proper balance between basic and applied research. An NIJ with the autonomy and type of leadership we propose will use a strong advisory board and the many research recommendations it has already received (see for example the recommendations from other NRC reports in Appendix E) to set both its long- and short-term agenda and priorities.[3]

NIJ should be provided with the authority and resources necessary to devote sustained attention to more long-term research activities appropriate for a research institute. It needs to structure a research agenda that will advance theory, research methods, science, and practices for the purpose of improving the nation's capacity to prevent and control crime and fairly administer justice. Such an agenda should address such topics as crime control theory with a specific emphasis on the role of police, courts, and corrections in preventing and controlling crime, the fair administration of justice, the etiology of criminal behavior, factors that influence desistance from criminal behavior and the emergence of new opportunities for crime, as well as crime prevention. With more resources and a structured research agenda, NIJ will also be in a better position to justify and support research to improve scientific methods and other kinds of studies, such as surveys and longitudinal studies that have been neglected because of their duration, complexity, and expense.

BOLSTERED RESEARCH INFRASTRUCTURE

Recommendation 3: The National Institute of Justice should undertake efforts to nurture and grow the pool of researchers involved in criminal justice research as well as activities that support the research endeavor itself. These efforts should include increasing the resources devoted to supporting graduate education for persons pursuing a career in criminology and criminal justice studies and other disciplines engaged in research and teaching on criminal justice topics, such as the Graduate Research Fellowship Program and the W.E.B. Du Bois Program, and enhancing the Data Archive Program.

NIJ's efforts to build the research field and support the research endeavor include support of fellowship programs and the criminal justice data archive. In the past three decades, NIJ has developed and sustained a number of fellowship programs. The recipients of NIJ doctoral and young faculty fellowships have made scholarly contributions to the criminal justice literature or to NIJ's research programs and many have remained in the criminal justice field. NIJ's support for graduate students and rising

[3]In setting its research priorities, NIJ will also need to consider future actions of Congress. For example, should Congress adopt the recent recommendation of the NRC (2009c) and establish a new independent federal entity responsible for forensic science activities, NIJ's future role in sponsoring forensic science research and development would need to be defined accordingly.

academics has been effective but modest. The need for new and diverse researchers studying crime and justice issues is as critical today as it was when NIJ was founded. Expanded fellowship programs and the consideration of a robust postdoctoral program in crime and justice are needed.

Currently, NIJ lacks the resources or administrative oversight to effectively expand these programs. The committee observes that, over the years, there has been inaccurate documentation of basic and relevant information regarding the fellowship recipients. In addition, no external formal assessments of NIJ's fellowship programs have been conducted to date.

Similarly, there has been no formal assessment of its program to archive and disseminate crime and justice research data. Nonetheless, we recognize that the Data Resources Program and the resulting data archive at the National Archive of Criminal Justice Data are unparalleled and have provided the community with valuable research and information resources. However, too many grantees continue to ignore requirements for submitting data generated by NIJ grants to the data archive. Contributing to the problem, NIJ has failed to monitor compliance with its requirements that research grantees submit their data sets or risk nonpayment of funds or to develop a strategy that would provide the necessary support to produce quality data sets for the archive.

Although the committee recognizes NIJ's achievements in developing and sustaining these programs and the resource limitations under which it has labored, we recommend that NIJ provide better oversight and management of these programs and conduct formal assessments of them.

SCIENTIFIC INTEGRITY AND TRANSPARENCY

Recommendation 4: The National Institute of Justice (NIJ) should revise its research operations to allow for greater transparency, consistency, timeliness, and appropriate involvement of the research and practitioner communities. In particular, NIJ should make information about its research operations and activities publicly available, easily understood, and consistent with the highest standards found in other high-quality federal research agencies.

Improvement is needed in NIJ's internal operations for selecting and managing its programs to bring them in line with the practices of other federal research agencies. An overriding theme is the need for greater transparency in processes and decisions. Planning activities are not well documented, the signaling of research priorities is haphazard, peer-review feedback to applicants is limited, grant award decisions are not in line with announced intentions, and report review is handled inconsistently by different units. Insufficient transparency contributes to the opinions expressed by practitioners and researchers that NIJ decisions are not made on the basis of scientific criteria. From early announcement of award cycles, to greater information on proposal reviews and decisions, to increased availability of data on awards and award completion, NIJ needs to be better understood by the research and practitioner communities.

Improving NIJ's internal processes can be achieved through good leadership. However, one process that is not under its authority is peer review. Currently, the peer-review process is centralized and administered through OJP. Peer review is fundamental to the scientific process, and NIJ should have complete authority to manage and assess all aspects of it.

Transparency of information cannot be achieved without good record-keeping, and in some instances NIJ is dependent on the centralized grant management information system of OJP. NIJ should take responsibility for documenting its decision-making processes, and in instances in which essential information is not being generated by OJP, it should develop its own documentation and records.

Another theme throughout the committee's deliberations on operations is the need to clarify the important but separate roles that the research and practitioner communities should play in the research program. These roles are reflected in the proposed composition of the NIJ advisory board, in the qualifications of the NIJ director, and in the improvements that the committee is recommending regarding NIJ's research and development management processes. NIJ should increase its efforts to involve researchers and to seek their advice in the development, implementation, and assessment of its research activities. Their advice is critical to identifying and shaping the kind of science needed to accumulate enough knowledge to answer critical policy questions. Practitioners also have an important role to play and, through their training and expertise, can provide broad policy direction to address research concerns. As consumers of research, practitioners can also advise as to its need and relevance.

CULTURE OF SELF-ASSESSMENT

Recommendation 5: NIJ should measure the influence of its programs on research and practice and assess the quality of operations and program-level technical and managerial matters.

NIJ's efforts to assess the quality of its research as well as the many processes that support the research enterprise have been extremely limited. With the exception of the 1977 NRC study and this current one, there has been no other independent review of its entire program. NIJ does not have an advisory board infrastructure to provide oversight to the agency as a whole, to the individual offices, or to large multiyear research projects.

To our knowledge, NIJ does not conduct formal, periodic assessments of planning, peer review, or report review processes—activities that involve substantive judgments regarding the quality of proposed or completed research. These kinds of assessments are urgently needed.

NIJ will not be able to conduct these assessments without better records and procedures that provide access to information. NIJ should take responsibility for creating record systems that will allow for detailed analyses of program funding, administrative and personnel matters, and improved information on programmatic activities. More critically, NIJ needs to track the usage and influence of its funded research in scholarship and practice. Like other well-managed federal research agencies, NIJ should establish self-assessment as an ongoing activity and use it to constantly improve the quality of its research and operations. Furthermore, to ensure transparency, it should make results of such assessments publicly available.

Many advances in the understanding of crime and the criminal justice system during the modern era have been influenced in part by the work of NIJ. It has also promoted the use of scientific methods in evaluations of criminal justice programs to produce evidence-based practices. However, the potential of NIJ has been undermined by the lack of a robust scientific culture. Our analysis strongly suggests that if the improvements we recommend are implemented, NIJ can be the great leader that Congress originally intended.

1

Introduction

The National Institute of Justice (NIJ) is the nation's primary resource for advancing scientific research, development, and evaluation on crime and crime control and the administration of justice and public safety. Headed by a presidentially appointed director, it is one of the major units in the Office of Justice Programs (OJP) of the U.S. Department of Justice (DOJ). Established by the Justice Assistance Act of 1984 and led by an assistant attorney general, OJP is responsible for the overall management, coordination, and oversight of the bureaus and offices under its control, including NIJ.

NIJ derives its principal authorities from the Omnibus Crime Control and Safe Streets Act of 1968, as amended (see 42 USC § 3721-3723), and Title II of the Homeland Security Act of 2002. Under this legislation, it awards grants and contracts to public agencies, private organizations, institutions of higher education, and individuals for the support of research, demonstrations, behavioral studies, program evaluation, technology research and development, and the dissemination of research findings.

In 2004, using its Program Assessment Rating Tool (PART) to assess program performance, the Office of Management and Budget concurred that NIJ should seek an independent assessment of its programs, organization, and processes. This review by the National Research Council (NRC) was requested by NIJ in response to the PART assessment. In 2006, the Committee on Assessing the Research Program of the National Institute of Justice was established by the NRC with a broad charter to review the full range of NIJ programs.

There is wide recognition that NIJ can play a critical role in efforts to better understand crime, improve abilities to prevent and control it, and to use the knowledge gained to foster a criminal justice system that better achieves principles of justice. In a survey of practitioners and researchers conducted for the committee, nearly all respondents (99 percent) stated their belief that it is important to have a government agency dedicated to funding and disseminating research on crime control and criminal justice issues, with a majority believing it has become more important in recent years. This sentiment was also reflected in statements made to the committee by former attorneys general, congressional staff, and leaders of research and professional organizations. As the primary source of federal funding in criminal justice research, NIJ has become a central element in the nation's efforts to control crime and improve justice. The committee agrees that a robust and effective NIJ is a critical element in the federal research structure.

CHARGE TO THE COMMITTEE

The charge to the committee is as follows:

An ad hoc panel will review the programs of NIJ, DOJ. The panel will examine the full range of NIJ programs in order to assess and make recommendations for NIJ's short- and long-term strategic planning and budgeting processes and its organizational structure. A comprehensive review of NIJ must consider NIJ's research and dissemination priorities based on the needs of important stakeholders and the limitations imposed by budget constraints.

Such a review would address key fundamental issues:

1. What is the role of NIJ in supporting and sustaining the nation's scientific infrastructure of crime and criminal justice research? How should the Institute's work relate to the missions of DOJ and OJP? How does the DOJ utilize NIJ as a research and development resource for its assistance programs and its operational components? What questions of policy and public importance should be addressed by NIJ research? What questions should not be addressed?
2. What is the appropriate balance between basic and applied research in both social science and technology development? What levels and types of research are reasonable and appropriate for NIJ to support?

3. What is the appropriate structure and scope for NIJ's short- and long-term planning and budgeting processes given the limits on its funds?
4. What metrics are appropriate for measuring the overall impact of NIJ research and dissemination programs and in what areas and on which topics does NIJ research have the most impact?
5. To what extent does the current federal budget for NIJ limit the agency's ability to develop appropriate research priorities and to provide appropriate levels of funding for the success of research programs?
6. Is the current organization of NIJ appropriate to fulfilling its mission? Does it reflect requirements laid out in its enabling legislation? Does the current organization have the flexibility it needs to accumulate knowledge on important justice system issues and also to respond to more immediate needs?
7. What are the most appropriate and effective mechanisms for translating NIJ research into policy and practice on the ground? Are these mechanisms different for social science and science and technology development?

The study will be conducted over a 27-month period and will result in a published report. The committee may include budget recommendations in its report.

The committee set out to answer these questions after determining that a federal research institute on crime and justice is vital to continuing efforts to control crime and improve justice. The examples in this report, both in regard to NIJ's successes and the country's need, support this view of NIJ's value. Accordingly, we then focused on examining NIJ's efforts in the past, to consider what it has and has not been able to accomplish and to determine what will be necessary for it to reach its potential in the future.

In the course of this study, the committee determined that NIJ is funded insufficiently to carry out its research functions. As a result, we considered, particularly in regard to question 3 above, the appropriate structure and scope for NIJ's short- and long-term planning and budgeting processes without regard for its present funding. We focused our efforts on understanding what research agendas NIJ has put forth to better understand crime and crime prevention and to develop the necessary tools and technologies; what programs NIJ has developed to cultivate the national criminal justice research infrastructure; and what activities it has undertaken to translate research knowledge to policy and practice. We also examined how NIJ currently functions to set agendas, make awards, monitor awardees, disseminate research, build knowledge, and grow the field of criminal justice research, and how these functions can be improved. In addition, we considered whether NIJ's current location in OJP is the most appropriate and effective place to carry out these functions.

In this report we discuss all of these issues and make recommendations to enable NIJ to better achieve the goals set for it by Congress. We have not specified a specific research agenda but instead have described a process that we think should be followed to do this. In large part, this is because we became convinced that proper governance and transparent processes should be established first within the agency in order to set the agenda and to decide the proper balance between basic and applied research. We strongly argue that NIJ should be first and foremost a research agency, and that assistance activities designed to help individual agencies without generalized benefit to the field are best managed elsewhere.

AGENCY ROLE

NIJ's mission is to advance scientific research, development, and evaluation to enhance the administration of justice and public safety.[1] The agency aims to provide objective, independent, evidence-based knowledge and tools to meet the challenges that crime and justice professionals face, particularly at the state and local levels.

NIJ funds research on crime control and prevention, which includes policing, drugs and crime, justice system operations, and behavioral research. NIJ also supports research and development of operational technologies such as forensic tools, protective equipment, communication and information systems, and sensor and surveillance technologies. In addition, it administers capacity-building assistance and training for forensic science practitioners and technology assistance centers for law enforcement and corrections agencies.

NIJ communicates with its constituents and the public through a broad range of conferences, interagency partnerships, and media tools. This includes sponsoring major conferences, workshops, and training programs; providing direct technology assistance to state and local criminal justice agencies; and offering a wide range of publications (hard copy and electronic) to criminal justice system executives and their employees, researchers, and the public. NIJ collaborates with a wide range of other federal agencies and private organizations in the funding of research. In the past, for example, partners have included the U.S. Departments of Defense, Education, Health and Human Services, Homeland Security, and Labor.

[1]See http://www.ojp.usdoj.gov/nij/ [accessed March 17, 2010].

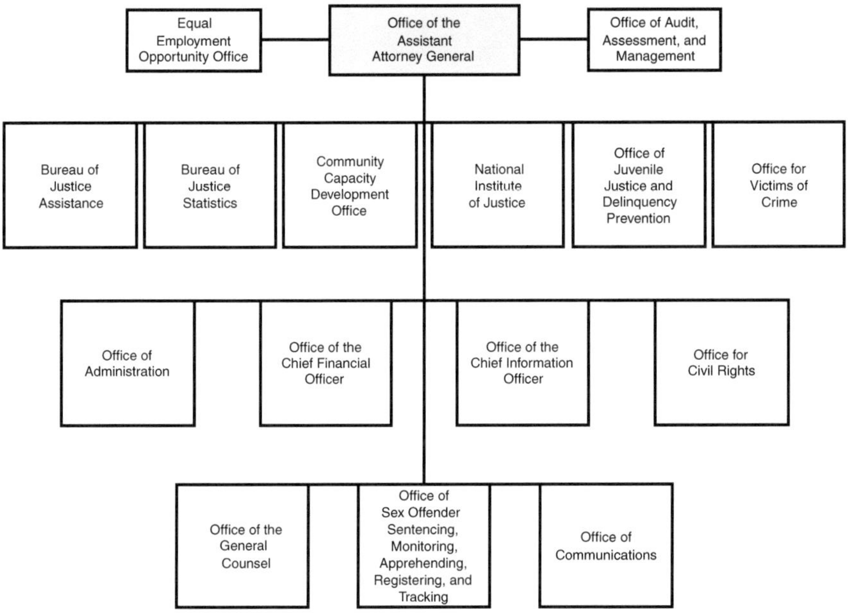

FIGURE 1-1 Office of Justice Programs organizational chart.
SOURCE: Redrawn from Office of Justice Programs website.

AGENCY ORGANIZATION

NIJ is one of a number of bureaus and offices overseen by OJP, which include the following: Bureau of Justice Assistance, Bureau of Justice Statistics, Community Capacity Development Office, Office of Juvenile Justice and Delinquency Prevention, Office for Victims of Crime, and Office of Sex Offender Sentencing, Monitoring, Apprehending, Registering, and Tracking (see Figure 1-1). Through its bureaus and offices, OJP works in partnership with the state and local justice community to identify the most pressing crime-related challenges, to disseminate state-of-the-art knowledge and practices, and to provide grants for the implementation of crime-fighting strategies.

NIJ is organized into three offices: (1) Office of the Director, (2) Office of Research and Evaluation (ORE), and (3) Office of Science and Technology (OST) (see Figure 1-2). The NIJ director, appointed by the president and confirmed by the Senate, establishes the institute's objectives, guided by the priorities of OJP, DOJ, and the needs of the field. Within the Office of the Director is the Planning, Budget, Management, and Administration Division, which is responsible for the agencywide development of strategic

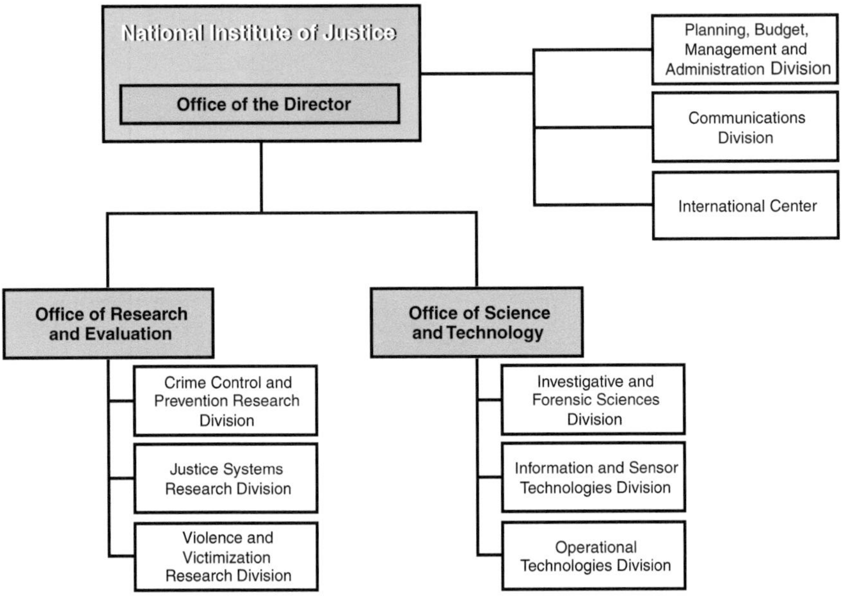

FIGURE 1-2 Organization of the National Institute of Justice.
SOURCE: Adapted from an NIJ presentation to the committee March 27, 2008.

plans and budget; the Communications Division, which is responsible for all outreach and dissemination; and the International Center, which facilitates transnational crime research and strengthens the bonds of the worldwide criminal justice community. Also housed in the Office of the Director are positions for two evaluation research specialists, an executive science advisor, and a senior science advisor.[2]

ORE and OST are each headed by a deputy director. ORE oversees all of the institute's social science research and evaluation studies and has three divisions: (1) Crime Control and Prevention Research, (2) Justice Systems Research, and (3) Violence and Victimization Research. OST manages science and technology research and development, the creation of technical standards, equipment testing, forensic capacity building, and technology assistance to state and local law enforcement and corrections agencies. It also has three divisions: Investigative and Forensic Sciences, Information and Sensor Technologies, and Operational Technologies.

[2]OJP approved the organizational plan dated February 14, 2008. NIJ was reorganized in January 2010 and the three offices remain, but programmatic responsibilities were redistributed.

In 2007, NIJ's total base appropriation was $54 million.[3] Of this, approximately $12 million and $35 million were allocated to ORE and OST, respectively. In addition, NIJ receives nearly $200 million in separate appropriations and outside reimbursements, which support several legislated programs. The following examples include some of these legislated programs as well as a few special initiatives for which funds are set aside each year:

- The Data Resources Program, which ensures the preservation and availability of research and evaluation data collected through NIJ-funded research.
- The Mapping and Analysis for Public Safety Program, which advances the spatial analysis of crime.
- The President's DNA Initiative, which ensures that forensic DNA analysis reaches its full potential to solve crimes, protect the innocent, and identify missing persons.
- The National Law Enforcement Corrections Technology Center system, which supports the transfer and adoption of technology into practice, assists in developing and disseminating technology guidelines and standards, and provides technology assistance and information to law enforcement and corrections agencies, courts, and crime laboratories.
- The Body Armor Safety Initiative, which addresses the reliability of body armor and examines the future of bullet-resistant technology and testing.
- The Violence Against Women/Family Violence Research and Evaluation Program, which advances research and evidence-based policy and programming to protect women and children from violence and abuse.

NEED FOR ASSESSMENT

To fully understand the need for an assessment of NIJ's programs, it is useful to look at the impact of the first assessment of the agency by the NRC. In 1976, in response to a request by the administrator of what was then the Law Enforcement Assistance Administration, now OJP, the NRC undertook an evaluation of NIJ programs. The institute had been in existence for only eight years. That report, *Understanding Crime: An Evaluation of the National Institute of Law Enforcement and Criminal Justice*

[3]Here and throughout the report we present financial figures in constant 2008 dollars in order to adjust for inflation as we compare NIJ's funding over the years. The figures represent program monies and do not include NIJ staff salaries.

(National Research Council, 1977), resulted in major changes in the way NIJ prioritized its research areas, developed its programs, and managed its research award and dissemination processes. These changes in turn made possible, in part, the broad array of research programs and partnerships supported today.

Today NIJ is faced with increasing demands for research findings to support the ever-growing needs of criminal justice agencies and other stakeholders, yet its discretionary budget has been reduced. The balance between investments in social science research and investments in technology has shifted dramatically in favor of technology, but unencumbered resources are too limited to support either research enterprise commensurate with need.

Major changes in the crime and justice environment since the 1977 NRC evaluation of NIJ make the demand for research greater now than it was in the 1970s. Some examples follow:

- During the 1990s, the crime rate dropped dramatically in all major crime categories from homicides to auto thefts, producing the longest and deepest crime decline in the United States since World War II (Zimring, 2007). The number of homicides, the most accurate barometer of serious crime, remains at levels below those experienced in the early 1970s. The homicide rate in 2005 was half of what it was in 1980 and the same as it was in 1966 (Bureau of Justice Statistics, 2007).
- The country has more than twice as many full-time police and correctional personnel as it did in 1980 (a period in which population grew by 33 percent).
- The rate of incarceration has increased from 139 per 100,000 in 1980 to a rate of 509 per 100,000 in 2008.[4]
- Between 1982 and 2003, expenditures for operating the nation's justice system increased from almost $36 to $185 billion, an increase of 418 percent. These expenditures continue to rise.
- In 1977, there were very few empirical studies of crime, and virtually no cohesive research community that studied crime. Between 1977 and 2006, the research on crime and justice issues has grown more sophisticated yet remains quite limited. There are some very strong empirical studies on policing and on criminal behavior. A smaller but still significant body of empirical research exists on corrections. There is still very little research on prosecution and courts.

[4]See http://bjs.ojp.usdoj.gov/content/glance/tables/incrttab.cfm [accessed March 23, 2010].

- The movement to improve the role and treatment of victims of crime in the criminal justice system began to receive federal support in the 1980s and has grown into a major separate stakeholder in the criminal justice system. Research on crime victims is fragmented and strong empirical studies are sparse.
- The upsurge in rates of incarceration has led to a new phenomenon—the release back into mostly urban communities of approximately 650,000 former prisoners each year and an estimated 12 million releases from jails representing 9 million individuals annually.
- In 1977, little was known about the link between illegal drug use and crime. The nation now spends approximately $50 billion a year in the war on drugs, a substantial portion in criminal justice system costs.
- Since 1977, the trends in drug use among the general population age 12 and older declined sharply initially but have slowly increased in the last decade (Office of National Drug Control Policy, 2002; Substance Abuse and Mental Health Services Administration, 2007).
- Transnational organized crime and terrorism have grown exponentially since the 1970s.
- Advances in science and technology have created new tools with the potential to revolutionize the crime and justice environment. These include advances in body armor, automated fingerprint information systems, DNA analysis, and other forensic automated tools.
- Computer technology, including large criminal justice database systems, in-car technologies, and computerized fingerprint databases have revolutionized the identification and investigative capacities of law enforcement and security agencies in the United States and abroad.
- Other technologies, such as less lethal weapons, biometrics, video and other surveillance technologies, and digital communications, may be emerging into practice without sufficient research and development to ensure that they work as needed and are safe.
- Crime involving technology (such as identity theft and online fraud), child exploitation, and the use of computers to conduct illegal transactions and facilitate violent or organized crime (including terrorism), has grown exponentially and become a critical challenge for law enforcement.

A more effective and efficient research response is required to meet the challenges posed by these problems in the coming decades.

STUDY METHODS

The committee reviewed multiple sources of information in order to understand the various programs and operations of NIJ and to evaluate them with respect to quality, limitations, and impact on the criminal justice field (both research and practice). The availability of information necessarily focused this assessment primarily on the period from 1995 to 2007. When more recent data are available, the report does note figures and statistics from 2008 and 2009.

The committee held several public information-gathering meetings, heard presentations, and engaged in discussions with current NIJ staff, including the director, deputy directors, and program chiefs. We were also briefed by leading researchers to gain a better understanding of the current context and nature of social science research in the criminal justice area and of technology development for law enforcement and related purposes. We were also briefed by commissioners, district attorneys, and judges as well as representatives of criminal justice professional associations to gain an appreciation of the effect of NIJ's research and programs on the criminal justice community. We also heard from former attorneys general and former assistant attorneys general who headed OJP.

In an effort to explore the larger question of how federal research agencies operate, the committee received briefings from agency directors and program division directors of several federal research agencies, including the U.S. Department of Health and Human Services, the Department of Homeland Security, the Department of Housing and Urban Development, the Institute of Education Sciences (U.S. Department of Education), the National Institute of Mental Health, the National Institute of Standards and Technology, the National Institute on Aging, the National Institute on Alcohol Abuse and Alcoholism, the National Institute on Drug Abuse, the National Science Foundation, and the Office of Naval Research. We heard detailed information on how advisory boards are used, how priorities are set, and how research portfolios and grants are planned, selected, and assessed. The committee also compiled comparative information on these agencies from their websites.

The committee reviewed public documents related to NIJ, such as authorizing and appropriations legislation, annual reports to Congress, its online award archive, final grant reports, and related articles and reports. The committee also examined a report on NIJ's Data Resources Program at the National Archive of Criminal Justice Data (NACJD). A provision of NIJ awards requires researchers to submit the data collected in their projects to this archive, and NIJ also solicits proposals to use or reanalyze the data archived there. The NACJD report provided descriptions of the history and growth of the archive, its oversight activities, efforts to encourage submission of NIJ-sponsored data, data submission requirements, and efforts to improve data quality. The report also presented statistics on use and user profiles as well as projections for future directions.

The committee requested records that would detail information on NIJ's budgetary and organizational history, current staffing and vacancies, strategic planning activities, and composition of advisory groups. Information on peer review, grant awarding, grant monitoring, and dissemination was also solicited. We received a number of documents from NIJ with useful information—most of them currently in the public domain. In addition, we identified specific program areas that we were interested in learning more about—the program histories as well as an understanding of the scope of work that has been done. For each program area, we asked NIJ to prepare a briefing paper that would outline needs being addressed, investment strategies, portfolio description, current states of knowledge, future plans, and challenges. In all requests, we called for records from the present back 10 years or more in an effort to assess the research program since the 1977 NRC evaluation (National Research Council, 1977) and across more than one administration.

The information we received from NIJ had significant shortcomings. Often the information submitted applied only to the present. If data did extend back for a period of time, it was usually only for 3-4 years. This, the committee was told, was because the current grants management system was instituted in 2003 and because of turnover in staff. We did receive some data (such as meeting summaries, funding histories, and lists of awards and resulting publications) for a period from the early 1990s to the present for a small number of programs; this was a result primarily of the work of individual staff who had maintained their own records. Of critical importance is the fact that the committee was not allowed access to grant applications or peer-review documents. In some cases we were told the information either was proprietary and could only be provided with expressed approval was only accessible through a Freedom of Information Act (FOIA) request, was not available even under FOIA, or did not exist. In some cases, inertia was responsible for us not receiving the information. As a result of the inability to access some types of data, we were limited in our ability to analyze and assess the quality of NIJ's grant award process, funding decisions, and award monitoring. In addition, the limitations in the data we received curtailed our ability to examine the historical trends of NIJ's funding sources, programs, and accomplishments. See Appendix A for a listing of requested materials that were met in part or not met at all.

Because the extant literature and available programmatic information did not provide the committee with a complete understanding of NIJ's current management mechanisms, of the criminal justice community's use of

NIJ's resources, or of the effect of NIJ-funded efforts on criminal justice research and practice, we turned to other sources of data.

Since the National Law Enforcement and Corrections Technology Center (NLECTC) system has represented a large portion of the budget of the Office of Science and Technology for the past 20 years or more, the committee was interested in learning more about this system and in particular the 2007 awards to establish four new centers of excellence. To become better acquainted with the system, several committee members and staff conducted a number of site visits, which included

- the four centers of excellence: (1) the Communications Technologies Center of Excellence in Camden, New Jersey; (2) the Forensic Science Center of Excellence in Largo, Florida; (3) the Weapons and Protective Systems Technologies Center of Excellence in State College, Pennsylvania; and (4) the Sensors, Surveillance, and Biometric Technologies Center of Excellence in New York City;
- one regional center (NLECTC–Rocky Mountain in Denver); and
- one specialty center (the Border Research and Technology Center in Austin, Texas).

The NLECTC system administers advisory councils, which funnel the needs of law enforcement and corrections to both NIJ and the technology center system. These consist of (1) a national council, (2) regional advisory councils, and (3) technical working groups that represent special technology areas. Committee staff attended a meeting of the national council and a few technical working group meetings to gather information. The site visits provided an opportunity to gain practical information that was otherwise lacking from solicitations, program descriptions, meeting summaries, and final reports. They also gave the committee a better understanding of how this major effort is managed as part of the overall portfolio.

Committee staff also conducted interviews of 26 current and former NIJ staff to learn more about the processes used to plan, research, select, and monitor grantees, and to assess performance. The interviews provided perspectives on major changes that occurred throughout NIJ history, its mission, and its impact on the criminal justice community, as well as consideration of its potential in the future. In attending meetings and conducting interviews, the staff was bound by privacy certificate and institutional research board guidelines to protect personal information. Reports prepared for the committee contained only information already available to the public, generalized descriptions, and comments and findings summarized in the aggregate.

The committee hired a marketing research firm to survey criminal justice researchers and practitioners in an effort to assess the broader awareness and image of the work of NIJ. A summary of the survey findings appears in Appendix B. The web-based survey was designed to find out how familiar researchers and practitioners are with NIJ, what services they have used, what they think about the quality of its research, and what impact its programs have had on research and practice.

The committee also reviewed a report prepared on NIJ's graduate research and W.E.B. Du Bois fellowship programs. From information provided by NIJ on fellowship recipients and descriptions that included goals, selection criteria, and management of the programs over the years, the report summarized demographic characteristics of both sets of fellows as well as the works published postfellowship and examined the degree to which these publications were related to their fellowship projects.[5]

REPORT ORGANIZATION

Following this introduction, Chapter 2 contains important background information on the history of NIJ, as well as trends in budget, organization, authority, and operations. Chapter 3 introduces ORE and OST and describes the character and accomplishments of each office's research portfolio as well as the recent decline in their research programs. Chapter 4 examines how NIJ administers and manages its research portfolio and other activities and provides an overview of its staffing resources over time. Chapter 5 examines to what extent NIJ has enhanced research use through its efforts to build research capacities, use research to guide policy and practice, and disseminate research findings to the research and practitioner communities and to what extent these activities have dominated NIJ's research mission. In Chapters 3-5, as NIJ's programs and processes are described, the committee critiques NIJ's practices for monitoring and assessing its own efforts. Chapter 6 examines the value of systematic assessment and provides initial guidance on improving practices for self-assessment. Chapter 7 makes recommendations for improving the federal criminal justice research enterprise.

In addition to the main chapters on the committee's findings, conclusions, and recommendations, six appendixes supply background information on this study and NIJ's programs. Appendix A outlines some of the documents and records the committee requested but was unable to get from NIJ. This allows the reader to understand the limitations on the committee's analyses. Appendix B summarizes the results and demographics of respondents from a November 2008 survey of criminal justice researchers and practitioners conducted for the committee. Appendix C identifies key legis-

[5]Report prepared by Nicola Smith for the committee meeting January 8-9, 2009, on NIJ Fellowship Programs.

lation and summarizes their impact on NIJ's programs and operations and documents changes in its mission statements over time. Appendix D identifies the types of materials NIJ publishes. Appendix E provides a summary of relevant recommendations from previous NRC reports. This is provided to offer NIJ and others ripe areas of needed research on criminal justice issues that have been previously vetted by experts in the field. Appendix F presents biographical sketches of committee members and staff. A list of acronyms used in this report is presented in the front matter.

2

The Federal Role in Research on Crime and Justice

Much has changed since 1968, when the National Institute of Law Enforcement and Criminal Justice, the forerunner to the National Institute of Justice (NIJ), was created. To illuminate these changes and the current context in which NIJ operates, the committee discusses NIJ's history in terms of four major time periods: (1) the first decade following its creation (1968-1978); (2) the second decade, beginning with the passage of the Justice System Improvement Act of 1979 (1979-1993); (3) the period following the passage of the Violent Crime Control and Law Enforcement Act of 1994 (1994-2000); and (4) the current time period, which commences with the decline of Crime Act funding and the change in administration. Across the four decades, we examine NIJ's governance, mission, and budget, make observations about the current programmatic focus and relationship with its oversight agency, the Office of Justice Programs (OJP), and conclude with a description of the 1977 National Research Council (NRC) study of NIJ, which forms a useful backdrop to this report.

HISTORICAL PERSPECTIVES

Although dealing with crime has historically been a state and local issue in the United States, federal involvement in crime control has a long history as well, beginning with efforts to control the opium trade and other drug use in the early part of the 20th century and the long fight against the mafia, which began during Prohibition and was at its height in the 1950s and 1960s. Direct federal assistance to state and local crime-fighting efforts emerged during the social upheaval of the 1960s. Newspapers and other media reported that crime was the number one domestic issue in the minds of the public (Loo and Grimes, 2004). Whether this was in fact the case remains open to scholarly debate, because at the time it was almost impossible to know how bad the crime problem really was. Virtually no national data that could reliably compare crimes across jurisdictions existed.

For policy officials, the media, and the public, the riots and civil rights protests that erupted in major American cities between 1962 and 1968 served as a proxy for crime and created an atmosphere of fear. In response to these problems, in 1965, President Lyndon Johnson created the President's Commission on Law Enforcement and the Administration of Justice, known as the Katzenbach Commission. The commission's 1967 report (President's Commission on Law Enforcement and the Administration of Justice, 1967) called for a revolution in the way America thinks about crime and for greater involvement by the federal government in that revolution.

The Katzenbach Commission called for new initiatives in crime prevention, the development of a wider range of techniques for dealing with individual offenders, the elimination of injustices and biases in the administration of justice, the recruitment of more qualified personnel in every criminal justice system component, more operational and basic research on crime and the criminal justice system, the infusion of funds into every domain of justice system administration, and the involvement of the community in crime control efforts.

The report was prescient about the ways in which technology would revolutionize law enforcement. With regard to research, the commission noted in its report that "every segment of the system of criminal justice [should] devote a significant part of its resources for research to insure the development of new and effective methods of controlling crime" (President's Commission on Law Enforcement and the Administration of Justice, 1967, p. x). Even in the face of the overwhelming operational needs of the criminal justice system at the time, the commission stated that the greatest need in criminal justice was the need to know (President's Commission on Law Enforcement and the Administration of Justice, 1967). The commission's recommendations fit with the policy approaches of President Johnson's Great Society and provided a blueprint for the Omnibus Crime Control and Safe Streets Act of 1968 (President's Commission on Law Enforcement and the Administration of Justice, 1967; Woolley and Peters, 2010).

At the time the commission was doing its work, no national research enterprise on crime and justice with federal leadership existed. There were a handful of organizations—the Vera Institute, the American Bar Foundation, the National Council on Crime and Delinquency, and the California Institute for the Study of Crime and Delinquency—that were conducting research projects, but there was no federal research leadership. The commission recommended a broad range of research efforts to address the information needs of the criminal justice system, including organizing research units in criminal justice agencies and providing public and private support to research institutes, foundations, and universities across the country. It also called for the establishment of a national foundation for research on crime and justice. It recommended that such a national foundation be established as an independent agency; it also acknowledged that there were obvious advantages to having a research agency within the U.S. Department of Justice (DOJ). It reasoned that the simultaneous establishment of a new research and a new aid program would result in competition for scarce resources and present other complications. Given the need for timely and useful information, it might be better to locate this agency within DOJ and defer the idea of an independent research agency (President's Commission on Law Enforcement and the Administration of Justice, 1967).

Omnibus Crime Control and Safe Streets Act of 1968

Following the recommendations of the Katzenbach Commission, Congress passed the Omnibus Crime Control and Safe Streets Act of 1968, establishing the Law Enforcement Assistance Administration (LEAA) (P.L. 90-351, Title I, Part A). The role of the new agency was to assist state and local law enforcement and other criminal justice agencies and to improve law enforcement training and education. Almost all of its funding and programs were geared toward improving the functioning of the criminal justice system at the local and state levels.

The National Institute of Law Enforcement and Criminal Justice (NILECJ) was established in LEAA on June 19, 1968, to develop new techniques and systems to strengthen law enforcement and criminal justice. Its mandate then and over the years has been much broader than state and local assistance, however. Under the original 1968 legislation, it was authorized "to carry out programs of behavioral research designed to provide more accurate information on the causes of crime and the effectiveness of various means of preventing crime, and to evaluate the effectiveness of correctional procedures" (section 401(b)2). It was authorized to conduct demonstrations or special projects pertaining to the purposes of the legislation; to undertake continuing studies and programs of research to develop new or improved approaches, techniques, systems, equipment, and devices to improve and strengthen law enforcement; to evaluate federal programs and demonstrations; to make recommendations for action that can be taken by federal, state, and local governments and by private persons and organizations to improve and strengthen law enforcement; and to carry out a program of collection and dissemination of information pertinent to crime and justice issues. See Box 2-1 for the complete legislative language. The institute's mandate also called for the development of a national and inter-

BOX 2-1
Legislative Language of Omnibus Crime Control and Safe Streets Act of 1968

Sec. 402. (a) There is established within the Department of Justice a National Institute of Law Enforcement and Criminal Justice (hereafter referred to in this part as "Institute"). The Institute shall be under the general authority of the Administration. It shall be the purpose of the Institute to encourage research and development to improve and strengthen law enforcement. (b) The Institute is authorized-

(1) to make grants to, or enter into contracts with, public agencies, institutions of higher education, or private organizations to conduct research, demonstrations, or special projects pertaining to the purposes described in this title, including the development of new or improved approaches, techniques, systems, equipment, and devices to improve and strengthen law enforcement;

(2) to make continuing studies and undertake programs of research to develop new or improved approaches, techniques, systems, equipment, and devices to improve and strengthen law enforcement, including, but not limited to, the effectiveness of projects or programs carried out under this title;

(3) to carry out programs of behavioral research designed to provide more accurate information on the causes of crime and the effectiveness of various means of preventing crime, and to evaluate the success of correctional procedures;

(4) to make recommendations for action which can be taken by Federal, State, and local governments and by private persons and organizations to improve and strengthen law enforcement;

(5) to carry out programs of instructional assistance consisting of research fellowships for the programs provided under this section, and special workshops for the presentation and dissemination of information resulting from research, demonstrations, and special projects authorized by this title;

(6) to carry out a program of collection and dissemination of information obtained by the Institute or other Federal agencies, public agencies, institutions of higher education, or private organizations engaged in projects under this title, including information relating to new or improved approaches, techniques, systems, equipment, and devices to improve and strengthen law enforcement; and

(7) to establish a research center to carry out the programs described in this section.

national clearinghouse for the exchange of criminal justice information, a task that had been accomplished by 1974.

This broad mandate did not reflect earlier thinking on the part of legal scholars that a national institute of justice should be focused on the investigation, analysis, and solution of legal and law-related problems rather than on social science (Early and Burger, 1972). In 1972, the American Bar Association created the Commission on a National Institute of Justice, which sponsored a 3-day conference attended by more than 150 lawyers, judges, scholars, and citizens to discuss the concept. Conference recommendations revolved around the need for independence from political interference, the need to create an advisory board, and a role of "making recommendations and providing support for changes in the nation's justice system" (Anonymous, 1979, p. 298). Despite these early deliberations, however, legal analysis never became a serious part of the institute's portfolio and was partly taken up instead by the Office of Legal Policy within DOJ.

Justice System Improvement Act of 1979

NILECJ, and subsequently NIJ, has been reauthorized or redefined over the years in nine major pieces of federal legislation spanning the period 1979-2005 (see Appendix C). Under the Justice System Improvement Act of 1979, NILECJ functions were redefined and absorbed by NIJ. Under the 1979 statute, several new areas of research were added to the new institute's portfolio, including identifying alternative programs for achieving system goals, analyzing the causes and correlates of juvenile delinquency, and developing improved methods for combating white-collar crime and public corruption. NIJ was also authorized to conduct research on civil justice matters. However, its total budget declined through the decade from a high of $53 million in 1975 to a low of $20 million in 1981. Its total annual budget remained below $25 million through 1988.[1] Because NIJ's limited appropriations were not increased to support the new provisions, most were never carried out. These provisions were removed from subsequent legislation, and new mandates were added over the years.

The institute's mandate under the original 1968 legislation and the 1979 reauthorization clearly gave it a national scope and focus. The inclusion in 1968 of the original program of justice statistics to develop the nation's information systems on crime and justice reflected that role. Under the reauthorization, NIJ made grants to public agencies, colleges and universities, and private organizations; conducted individual studies and

[1]The figures presented are nominal values. When adjusted for inflation, the declining trend in the institute's budget is further discouraging: in constant 2008 dollars, the 1975 total budget was $210 million; in 1981, $47 million; and in 1988, $45 million.

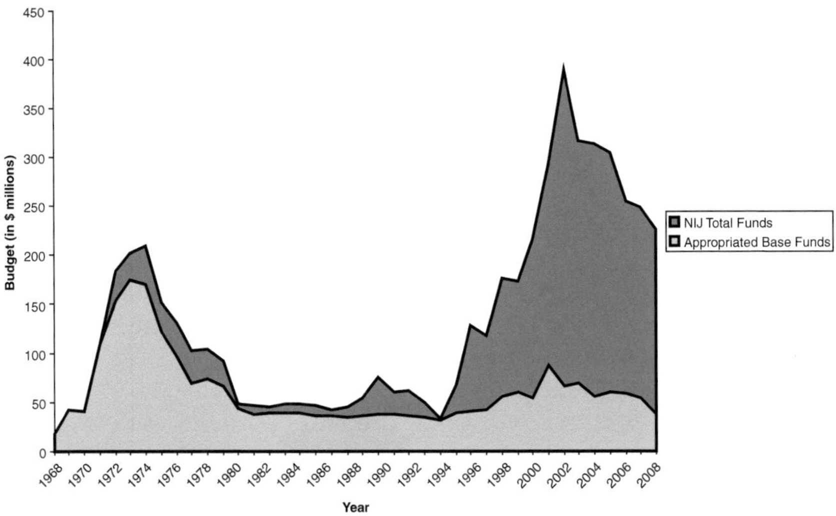

FIGURE 2-1 NIJ funding history, 1968-2008 (converted to constant 2008 dollars).
SOURCE: Adapted from figures in a presentation by NIJ to the committee, July 2008.

programs of research on the causes and correlates of crime and on corrections, police science, public administration, and law; and began planning national statistics programs.

Although the mandate in the 1979 legislation was in many senses broader than that of the Omnibus Crime Control and Safe Streets Act, NIJ's appropriation remained the same or decreased between 1979 and 1994 (see Figure 2-1). Nevertheless, important science programs were initiated during this period, including a major longitudinal study on the development of criminal behavior, the first systematic, federal data collection program on drug use by arrested persons, a multisite experimental study of domestic violence, the testing of geocoding or crime mapping in police departments, and the development of experiments for analyzing crime in places, or "hot spots" (Sherman and Weisburd, 1995; National Research Council, 2004b).

Crime Act of 1994

By 1993, violent crime, particularly youth homicide, had reached an all-time high in the United States. To address this problem, Congress passed the Violent Crime Control and Law Enforcement Act of 1994 (P.L. 103-322, referred to here as the Crime Act). The Crime Act addressed the violent crime problem through a number of major provisions:

- A federal ban on assault weapons, which banned the manufacture of certain semiautomatic firearms, any semiautomatic rifle with certain combinations of specific features, and the possession of newly manufactured magazines holding more than 10 rounds of ammunition. The ban was allowed to expire in September 2004.
- The addition of some 60 offenses to federal death penalty statutes.
- The elimination of student loans (Pell grants) for inmate education.
- The Violence Against Women Act and the creation of the Office on Violence Against Women (OVW).
- The hiring of 100,000 police officers and the creation of the Office of Community Oriented Policing Services (COPS).
- "Truth-in-sentencing" provisions and other correctional reforms.

Congress appropriated over $4.5 billion per year for 5 years to carry out the provisions of the law.

But as Congress and DOJ worked together to develop the sweeping changes in the criminal justice system described above, no plans for expanding the research enterprise to support these new activities were included in the law. NIJ was reauthorized, but the research endeavor was not highlighted nor its relevance or usefulness noted.

References in the legislation to research are limited to listing it (a) as one of seven purposes for which block grant funds may be used; (b) in various places under "limitations of data use" when collecting data on individuals; (c) in encouraging state and local program grantees to comply with any national "research" effort; and (d) in descriptions of specific studies. The specific research studies authorized in the act include an NRC study to develop a research agenda on violence against women; research on drug addiction and antidrug technologies to be conducted by the Office of National Drug Control Policy in consultation with the National Institute of Drug Abuse and the Defense Advanced Research Projects Agency; and the study of family support to police officers by awarding research grants to state and local agencies.

Governance and Mission

Leadership. Prior to 1979, the institute director was selected by the U.S. attorney general. After 1979, the director became a presidential appointee, in part to protect the independence of the institute and its programs. Over the past four decades, NIJ has had 19 directors or acting directors (see

BOX 2-2
List of NIJ Directors

Kristina Rose, acting 2009
David W. Hagy, 2006-2009 (confirmed 2008)
Glenn R. Schmitt, acting 2005-2006
Sarah V. Hart, 2001-2005
Julie Samuels, acting 2000-2001
Jeremy Travis, 1995-2000
Carol V. Petrie, acting 1994
Michael J. Russell, acting 1993-1994
Charles B. DeWitt, 1990-1993
James K. Stewart, 1982-1990
W. Robert Burkhart, acting 1982
James Underwood, acting 1981-1982
Harry Bratt, acting 1979-1981
Blair Ewing, acting 1977-1979
Gerald Caplan, 1973-1977
Martin Danziger, 1971-1973
Irving Slott, acting 1970-1971
Henry Ruth, 1969-1970
Ralph Siu, 1968-1969

Box 2-2). None of these had experience in directing crime and justice research, was recognized as a highly qualified authority in the fields of crime and justice research, or had demonstrated success in managing crime and justice research efforts. Of these, 10 were politically appointed, and 13 served for 2 years or less. Only three directors served for 5 or more years and as a result, the years 1973-1977, 1982-1990, and 1995-2000 were the only real periods of stability in terms of leadership.

The constant change in directors made scientific progress complicated. It was extremely difficult, for example, to establish and maintain the kind of stable scientific planning and awards process called for in the report *Understanding Crime* (National Research Council, 1977). It was almost impossible to accumulate knowledge on any given topic. Not one long-range research plan and very few programs developed during the tenure of a specific director survived the appointment and tenure of his or her successor.

Advisory Boards. In the 1970s and 1980s, the institute had advisory boards to guide its overall program. Although NILECJ and NIJ advisory boards had several incarnations during this period, the original focus was on policy issues rather than on research priorities and activities. Various iterations of the NIJ advisory board focused more on research in later years, but they had limited success in shaping a coherent research program and the idea was abandoned after 1986.

The Institute's first advisory board was called the National Institute Advisory Committee. Although it is unclear exactly when it was constituted, it is mentioned in the first NILECJ annual report in 1974. It was not required by the authorizing legislation but was established by the NILECJ director, who appointed its 19 members, drawn primarily from the medical, education, public policy, and law fields. Three members were practicing law enforcement, courts, and corrections officials and two were researchers. Over the next few years, as members rotated off the committee, they were replaced by prominent researchers. By 1978, researchers constituted a third of the advisory committee's membership.

The original purpose of the advisory committee, according to Gerald Caplan, the former NILECJ director who established it, was to insulate NILECJ from any political interference regarding how it could spend its money. Caplan also wanted it to be a sounding board and to promote research that the staff might not otherwise consider; to provide an additional level of expertise and judgment that staff did not have; and to serve as a source of feedback on general practices. Finally, he hoped that an advisory board would strengthen relationships with prominent individuals as well as collectively create a group of allies.[2]

However, the advisory committee did not play the expected role in shaping the program, and the potential for interference with the research program from others in LEAA never materialized. But as the membership changed and was more heavily researcher based, there was a shift in the deliberations from broad policy issues to advising on research priorities and strategies.

The 1979 Justice System Improvement Act created the National Institute of Justice Advisory Board. The law called for a 21-person board appointed by the president with responsibility for recommending the policies and priorities of the institute; creating, when necessary, formal peer review procedures; recommending to the president at least three candidates for the director's position in the event of a vacancy; and performing additional tasks as necessary. The initial members of the advisory board were appointed by President Jimmy Carter in 1980 but were dismissed in June 1981 by the newly elected President Ronald Reagan, who appointed a new board in its place. This sparked a lawsuit by several members, who petitioned the

[2]Interview with Gerald M. Caplan, a former NILECJ director and former dean of the McGeorge School of Law in Sacramento, December 4, 2008.

federal government unsuccessfully that they had been deprived of their appointments (*Martin v. Reagan*, 525 F. Supp. 110, 1981).

The membership of the new advisory board was almost evenly divided between business entrepreneurs, representatives of not-for-profit organizations, legal and security experts, and criminal justice practitioners. No researchers were appointed. From 1981 to 1984, it held meetings regularly and produced a report based on public hearings in four cities. The report, *Too Much Crime, Too Little Justice* (President's Advisory Board, National Institute of Justice, 1983), dealt exclusively with serious violent crime and included research recommendations in a number of broad areas: law enforcement; costs and fear of crime: response to career criminals; community involvement in crime control; criminal justice management; improving adjudication programs; victims, jails, and prisons; probation and parole; and federal and state local cooperation. It was published but never distributed to the public by the agency. The explanation to NIJ staff regarding the department's refusal to disseminate the report was that it presented too gloomy a picture of the state of affairs in crime and justice, particularly given its timing after the 1984 election. After 1984, meetings of the NIJ advisory board became irregular until its existence was terminated with the passage of the Justice Assistance Act of 1984, which repealed the provision for an agencywide group of advisers. NIJ's lack of an advisory infrastructure is discussed further in Chapter 4.

Mission. The mission of NIJ is to "advance scientific research, development, and evaluation to enhance the administration of justice and public safety."[3] In 1968, as NILECJ was being created, the planners stated that "the basic purpose of the overall program . . . is fostering successful innovation in all our efforts to control crime, especially those of the criminal justice system" (Starnes, 1969). It is clear that the official mission of the agency has changed little over the years, although the implementation of that mission has looked very different in the hands of different directors and under the aegis of different organizations. Once LEAA was abolished in 1979 and NIJ was placed first under the Office of Justice Assistance Research and Statistics and then under the assistant attorney general for OJP, independence became ever harder to maintain as its mission became more and more tied to the state and local assistance mission of OJP through the strategic planning process of the assistant attorney general's office.[4] For

[3]See http://www.ojp.usdoj.gov/nij/about/welcome.htm [accessed March 17, 2010].

[4]See OJP Strategic Goal 4.2: "OJP will reposition statistical, research, and evaluation activities so that they can be more fully leveraged across a wide range of OJP activities and to ensure that programs are addressing the most critical problems in the most effective manner" (Office of Justice Programs, 2006b, p. 20).

example, in the late 1980s and again in the late 1990s, NIJ's programs had to fit the program priorities established by OJP, placing constraints on its ability to develop cumulative knowledge in areas outside these priorities (Office of Justice Programs, 1999). NIJ's research has subsequently focused more on improving standard criminal justice administration and programming than on pursuing and testing new theories about what kinds of justice system responses might have the greatest crime reduction effects.

The effect of all this is that over time the emphasis of NIJ's research program has swung back and forth between basic and applied research. But the two kinds of research activities do not have to be mutually exclusive. Basic research undertaken by NIJ has frequently had implications for policy and practice, and applied research has often pointed out the need for basic research.

One issue that has been neglected is research on what appear to be success stories. A prominent example is the dramatic decline in crime, especially violent crime, since the early 1990s. Many have speculated on this decline, but NIJ has not provided the leadership to provide comprehensive research to address this issue. While others have considered the role of the New York City Police Department's COMPSTAT management system in this reduction (see Kelling and Sousa, 2001) as well as contrary evidence (Harcourt and Ludwig, 2007), NIJ has not developed a comprehensive research program to assess the full range of plausible explanations for the decline in crime.

When added to the institute's inadequate resources (described below), the ever-expanding and changing OJP program priorities over the years have resulted in a scattershot approach by the institute to the development of knowledge on crime and justice, despite the best intentions of staff and new directors to develop a strong and sustainable program.

Post Crime Act Period

In the years immediately following the passage of the Crime Act of 1994, NIJ was impacted in several ways. First, it received an infusion of funds from program offices that were either newly established or authorized to carry out the law's mandates, such as the Violence Against Women Grants Office, COPS, Weed and Seed, the Drug Courts Office, and the Corrections Program Office. While many of these early initiatives undertaken by NIJ at the request of the program offices were modest, later they became much larger in terms of scope and funding. As described in Chapter 3, much of this money went to support large-scale evaluations of Crime Act programs. For the first time in its history, NIJ had the opportunity to expand its work in various target areas, such as corrections, courts, community policing, and drugs. NIJ staff size also grew to meet the demand.

But within 5 or 6 years, many of these funding streams dried up and, with them, NIJ's opportunity to continue its research in specific areas. But one change occurring in this period that did not go away was the shift to a focus on science and technology.

Focus on Science and Technology

Changes in justice assistance[5] legislation have led to a more concentrated focus on research related to justice system operations and less emphasis on research on national and international crime and violence issues. This is particularly evident in the expansion of NIJ's science and technology portfolio, administered through its Office of Science and Technology (OST). NIJ's funding of science and technology activities grew exponentially after the passage of the Violent Crime Reduction Act of 1994 (National Institute of Justice, 1996). Technology research and development had been pursued by NIJ from its earliest days through a small office called the Advanced Technology Division. During the mid-1970s, the office's functions were divided among NIJ's major divisions: a technology assessment program in the Division of Development, Testing, and Dissemination, mostly devoted to developing standards for soft body armor through an interagency agreement with the National Institute of Standards and Technology, and a small program office in the Office of Research Programs that handled forensic science and some development programs, such as automated fingerprint systems and concealed weapons detection programs. When the immediate predecessor to OST, the Division of Science and Technology, was created in 1992, it had a small budget of between $2 and $4 million annually and a staff of four employees, including the division director.

Prior to the Crime Act, NIJ's most notable accomplishments in the area of science and technology were the development and testing of soft body armor for police, support for research on forensic DNA testing and automated fingerprint systems, and development of modern protocols in death investigations. Nearly half of the office's annual budget was spent developing standards for soft body armor, which had become commercially available to police and sheriff's departments.

The first expansion of the OST budget grew out of congressional earmarks. A few members of Congress were interested in technology development to improve law enforcement. OST also enhanced its budget in those early years by developing a formal partnership with the U.S. Department of Defense to transfer and adapt technology related to defense to law en-

[5]Justice assistance is used in this context to refer to LEAA, the Office of Justice Assistance, Research and Statistics, and OJP, the three agencies under which NIJ and its predecessors have been organizationally located.

forcement settings. Over the ensuing years, OST received large transfers of funds through interagency agreements and, in many cases, through the appropriations process.

In 1995, the budget for OST nearly tripled over 1994 levels, and over the ensuing 8 years the office received over $1 billion through a combination of DOJ appropriations and the reimbursement of funds from other federal agencies whose projects OST had agreed to administer (U.S. General Accounting Office, 2003b). In 1994, the total OST budget represented 18 percent of NIJ's overall budget. In 2008, the budget for OST represented more than 80 percent of NIJ's overall budget.

This stands in stark contrast to what has happened to the social science research budget. Once around two-thirds of NIJ's base appropriation prior to 1994, it has remained relatively stagnant in the past decade, representing less than 10 percent of NIJ's overall budget by 2008. However, as this report makes clear, neither OST nor the Office of Research and Evaluation (ORE) has had much discretion over its funds in the Post Crime Act period.

Relationship with OJP

In the past decade, NIJ's identity as an independent research agency has been challenged by efforts of OJP to provide more oversight and centralize activities being undertaken by its various units. OJP's leadership role is described as one of promoting coordination, but, in fact, the assistant attorney general wields a great deal of authority and power that goes beyond coordination. This control has been most evident in OJP's assumption of sign-off authority for all grants and contracts emanating from its five bureaus. See for example solicitation language "all final grant award decisions will be made by the Assistant Attorney General (AAG)" (National Institute of Justice, 2009c, p. 16).

Congress did grant sign-off authority to NIJ on its awards, although interpretation of that authority has varied over the past decade. For example, the 1999 appropriations (P.L. 105-277) authorized OJP to exercise authority over and approve grants and contracts. The 2000 appropriations (P.L. 106-113) renewed the authority but denied OJP authority to approve grants for NIJ, the Bureau of Justice Statistics (BJS), and a few programs of the Office of Juvenile Justice and Delinquency Prevention (OJJDP). Those limitations were repeated in the 2001 appropriations bill language (P.L. 106-553). However, in 2002, the Patriot Act removed those limitations (Doyle, 2001) and, during the period 2002-2008, all funded research required sign-off by the assistant attorney general for OJP. During the transition period in early 2009 and prior to a permanent assistant attorney general's being named head of the Office of Justice Programs, OJP's general counsel affirmed in a meeting on March 17, 2009, and in a follow-up email that NIJ has sign-off authority on grants.[6]

OJP also wields control through oversight of the budget and control of the various offices that support the work of the bureaus. In addition to the Office for Administration, these include the Office for Audit, Assessment, and Management, the Office for Civil Rights, the Office of Communications, the Office of the Chief Financial Officer, the Office of the Chief Information Officer, and the Office of the General Counsel. While these offices had existed under predecessor agencies, the individual bureaus, including NIJ, had either been given or had maintained responsibility for many activities relating to budgeting, staffing, grant awarding, dissemination, and various administrative resources.

Beginning around 2005, in an effort to improve coordination and reduce inefficiencies and overlap, the OJP leadership undertook efforts to reorganize and to centralize many of the functions and activities undertaken by the individual offices. For example, both the peer review process and dissemination activities carried out by the National Criminal Justice Reference Service are managed centrally through contracts administered by OJP. Various documents, such as solicitations, adhere to an OJP-wide template, go through numerous OJP offices during review, and must be approved by the assistant attorney general. NIJ is also dependent on OJP offices for information and administrative services, such as record maintenance and tracking of various grant-related activities. Since 2003, OJP has conducted most of its grant-related operations through its electronic grants management system, and NIJ's capacity to track information relevant to its own operations is very dependent on whether OJP approves such modifications to the system or provides operational support through the Office of the Chief Information Officer. For example, a deficiency of this system is its failure to include names of project directors or principal investigators. Consequently, this information is not publicly available when information on grant activities or products is sought.

Various decisions associated with the hiring of employees are also controlled by OJP. For example, OJP's Human Resources Division screens the

[6]In a meeting on March 17, 2009, chaired by Laurie Robinson, acting assistant attorney general, OJP, and attended by Todd Clear, president of the American Society of Criminology, Richard Rosenthal, and Howard Silver, executive director, Consortium of Social Science Agencies, the OJP General Counsel, Rafael Madden, informed them that the language in the Patriot Act did not restrict NIJ's sign-off authority on its grants. In a subsequent email to Dr. Silver, Mr. Madden explained that this had always been the department's interpretation of the language but that "some, perhaps unaware of the significant body of internal administrative legal opinion with the Department that effectively puts a practical gloss on various terms used in section 108, have expressed a different impression of the meaning of the language, but that does not disturb the Department's consistent official understanding of the practical effect."

initial group of candidates and then forwards the names to the appropriate bureau. An NIJ manager commented that this practice of having nonresearch staff screen for relevant educational and employment backgrounds had resulted in unqualified persons being considered. Most importantly, the assistant attorney general can prevent a bureau such as NIJ from filling its vacancies. Chapter 4 discusses these issues in more detail.

Relationship with Other OJP and Department of Justice Agencies

NIJ research activities are intertwined in various ways with the activities of its six OJP sister agencies as well as agencies within DOJ like COPS, the Federal Bureau of Investigation, the Drug Enforcement Administration, and others. The activities take many forms: participating on DOJ-wide task forces and OJP committees and working groups; providing findings and relevant research information on specific issues; obtaining funding support from these agencies for research and evaluations of interest to them; and advising on program development. NIJ also regularly communicates with its sister agencies to solicit information on the needs of the field and to provide them with information on research findings of use to the field. On its website, it prominently declares that "partnerships with other government agencies and professional associations are critical to determining what works."

NIJ is described as the research, development, and evaluation agency of DOJ but other agencies (BJS, OJJDP) have functions that are spelled out in their legislation that are overlapping or similar to those of NIJ. For example, BJS has a mandate to collect, analyze, publish, and disseminate information on crime and to provide assistance to state and local governments to improve their statistics programs. While BJS has lead responsibility for statistical activities, NIJ is not precluded from undertaking surveys or studying the feasibility of collecting particular kinds of data or the use of such data. Similarly, OJJDP has research as part of its mission and other OJP and DOJ agencies are not necessarily precluded from funding grants that include a research focus or research activities. Historically, this has created a situation in which issues arise over whether certain activities are research and should be appropriately within NIJ's bailiwick, whether funds will be provided to NIJ to support research activities, and what should be the modus operandi for monitoring those studies by both NIJ and the sponsoring agency. Specifically in the case of OJJDP, during the past 10 years, there has been continuing discussion over the question of whether responsibility for all juvenile justice research should be moved to NIJ. Efforts to do so have not been successful. As in the past, NIJ and OJJDP have worked out a modus operandi at the staff level to determine what kinds of research topics will be handled by each office. But this agreement and others like it depend on the willingness and ability of NIJ and the various offices to maintain good relationships with each other.

RISE AND FALL OF RESOURCES

Growth in Funding to State and Local Areas

During the past two decades, an unprecedented level of federal funding was made available to help state and local jurisdictions around the country fight crime. According to its annual reports, between 1990 and 2000 the budget of OJP for state and local assistance grew in constant fiscal 2000 dollars by 610 percent, from about $640 million in fiscal year (FY) 1990 to $3.9 billion in FY 2000, and the OJP budget remained at that level through 2003 (Office of Justice Programs, 1990, 2001). In addition, some $8 billion was available to state and local jurisdictions through COPS in DOJ during the period 1996-2002. These increases supported a vast array of criminal justice system activities, improvements, and new program efforts, including joint federal-local task forces to combat drug-related crime, antigang, and antiterrorism programs.

Funding Comparison

Although some observers have compared NIJ's funding to the funding of other government research institutes that study different but equally important problems (see Blumstein and Petersilia, 1994), the committee thinks the more appropriate comparison is the funding for research and funding for direct federal support of justice programs and functions. Despite the breadth and far-reaching scope of the Crime Act of 1994, there was no expansion of the mandate for conducting research on crime and justice. No additional funds were appropriated for NIJ to carry out research to support the purposes or programs of the new law. This does not appear to be an oversight, but rather seemed at the time to stem from a consensus on the part of the legislation's many authors that enough was known from research, that the correct course of action was clear, and that whatever additional research might be needed to improve operational strategies should be embedded in the programs themselves or conducted by NIJ at the request of program staff.

The NIJ appropriation, which had been a stable 3-5 percent of the LEAA overall appropriation (Armbrust, 1978), was by FY 2000 approximately 1 percent of the funding of OJP and the COPS office combined and approximately half of that consisted of restricted funds. Figure 2-2 shows the trend of appropriations increases for OJP and the COPS office for the period 1984-2003 compared with appropriations for NIJ.

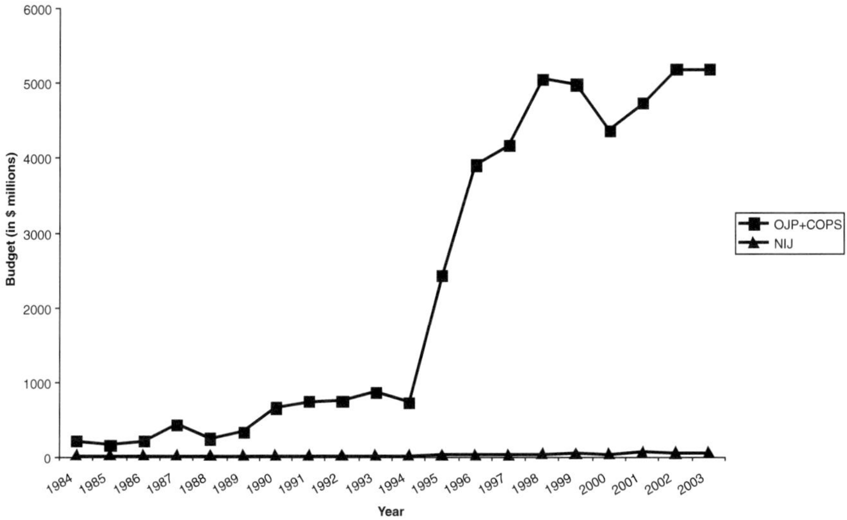

FIGURE 2-2 Budgets by fiscal year, OJP and COPS combined and for NIJ.
NOTES: COPS = Community Oriented Policing Services, NIJ = National Institute of Justice, OJP = Office of Justice Programs.
SOURCE: Created from OJP and COPS figures available from an Office of the Inspector General report (2002) and NIJ base appropriations supplied by NIJ.

In 2008, NIJ's overall appropriations, including restricted funds, were 2 percent of overall OJP funding and 0.002 percent of the overall appropriations of DOJ. We do not include in these calculations the billions of dollars spent at the state and local level for criminal justice system programs and functions.

In contrast, the annual budget of the National Institutes of Health for research (about $28.5 billion) is well over one-third of the discretionary funding of the U.S. Department of Health and Human Services and 7 percent of the total annual departmental budget when one includes the entitlement programs. The Environmental Protection Agency research budget is also around 7 percent of the total annual budget for the agency. The Department of Education appropriation for research and statistics is a much smaller percentage of its overall appropriations but is still close to $500 million each year (Boisseau, 2009).

Discretionary Funds

NIJ's base appropriation, in constant 2008 dollars, hovered between $38 and $41 million between 1984 and 1996, and rose to a high of

$87 million in 2001. However, its total budget grew from $48 million in 1984 to $293 million in 2001. Of this latter amount, the share in 2001 for discretionary research awards was around $22 million in ORE and $14 million in OST. The balance for that year was allocated to earmarked research and development efforts and nonresearch areas, such as forensic capacity building, technology support assistance, program support, and dissemination. As NIJ's budget grew, an increasing portion of its funds were directed to specific recipients or projects by public law, subject to guidance in congressional committee reports or directed though reimbursable agreements. In the period 1995-2003, approximately 72 percent of OST expenditures were predetermined (U.S. General Accounting Office, 2003b). In the subsequent 5 years, OST has continued to lose discretion over its own budget. In 2008, according to the OST deputy director, $2 million of its $209 million budget was discretionary—that is, funds that were not received for specific, predetermined purposes. ORE is in a similar but less oppressive position, because it has had discretion over roughly 20-50 percent of its total budget for the past decade, depending primarily on the amount of transferred funds through reimbursable agreements for a given year. However, its total budget has been one-eighth to one-fourth the size of the OST total budget in the Post Crime Act period. Figure 2-1 illustrates how NIJ's total budget has compared with its discretionary base budget since its inception.

1977 NATIONAL RESEARCH COUNCIL ASSESSMENT

In 1977 an NRC study assessed the operations of NIJ's predecessor agency. *Understanding Crime: An Evaluation of the National Institute of Law Enforcement and Criminal Justice* was undertaken at the request of the administrator of LEAA in an attempt to strengthen scientific processes and improve the quality of the institute's awards and their results. This study is mentioned frequently in this report because several of its conclusions remain as strikingly valid today as they were in 1977. For example, a major criticism was that the results of the institute's research activities were not reaching or being used by practitioners. Another criticism was that the institute made no attempt to build a body of knowledge on crime or criminal justice system problems. That earlier report concluded that there is a need for a program of research on crime problems that is national in scope and should be supported by the federal government. It was most concerned with identifying a style of research and a mode of work that would be effective and sustainable over time (National Research Council, 1977).

The major conclusions in *Understanding Crime* address five areas: (1) the institute's mission to develop reliable, generalized knowledge about crime, criminal behaviors, and the effectiveness of crime control methods and policies; (2) the expansion of resources, including ideas from a wide range of sources, research skills among staff from a variety of disciplines, and more and better data; (3) broadened access to program development, improved mechanisms for quality control, and improved measures to insulate the institute from destructive pressures; (4) a strong advisory system to assist with priority setting and to provide quality control over the research process; and (5) insulation from destructive pressures emanating from unrealistic congressional demands to perform a direct service function, with the committee noting that such demands create impossible conditions for the development of a constructive research program (National Research Council, 1977). Virtually all of these areas are again being addressed in this report, some 30 years later.

CONCLUSIONS

From this brief review of NIJ's history, several important conclusions begin to emerge. First, it is clear that Congress intended NIJ to conduct a broad program of research related to crime causation and prevention, but, through the years, this mandate has shifted to a focus on improving criminal justice administration that is of more immediate benefit to state and local criminal justice agencies. This has played itself out to the extent that NIJ's social science agenda, once predominant, is now dwarfed by technology research, dissemination, and technology assistance activities. Second, despite some early and notable successes in social science and technology research, NIJ resources have never kept up with the mandates imposed on it. Even as increased federal dollars have flowed to state and local criminal justice agencies, NIJ's proportion of those dollars has declined. Third, NIJ has experienced unstable governance for most of its existence, with frequent turnover in leadership, directors whose backgrounds and experience did not reflect NIJ's science mission, and the lack of an advisory board to play a role in supporting and shaping its research activities. Finally, OJP oversight and the centralization of functions among its offices and bureaus have had, over the years, an uneven impact on NIJ's authority over its planning and awards processes, its dissemination processes, its ability to maintain its identity as a research agency, and the overall resources available for research.

3

The Research Program Offices

The National Institute of Justice (NIJ) is still described as "the research, development and evaluation agency of the U.S. Department of Justice (DOJ),"[1] as it was at its inception, yet its program looks a great deal different today. Two of the changes, mentioned in Chapter 2, are the shift from a broad program of research to research that is more heavily focused on criminal justice administration and short-term solutions to crime prevention and reduction. The second change is reduced resources for social science research and greater support for technology research and technology assistance.

This chapter is an overview of the research portfolios of the two main program offices in NIJ, the Office of Research and Evaluation (ORE) and the Office of Science and Technology (OST). We start by analyzing funding support for NIJ's research activities overall and then move on to separate discussions of ORE and OST. For each office we review the major areas of research, the context in which these areas developed, and their current status. Chapter 1 details the sources of information the committee was able to gather. See Appendix A for a listing of requests that could not be met or were met only in part.

As mentioned in Chapter 1, obtaining information on NIJ's research portfolio and presenting it in an organized way proved to be a difficult task. Although a great deal of information on NIJ research is presented on its website, research activities are not always easily differentiated from

[1]See for example NIJ overview, http://www.ojp.usdoj.gov/ or http://www.ojp.usdoj.gov/nij/about/welcome.htm [accessed August 31, 2009].

technology assistance or capacity-building activities. The financial data provided to the committee were often not broken down by research area or were incomplete. For example, some data were available for only a limited number of years, and some data relating to the use of contracts or interagency agreements, known sources of funding for research in certain areas (e.g., body armor), often were not provided as part of the financial history submitted to the committee or available publicly. Although we were able to construct a broadly representative picture of NIJ's funding history, we are aware that it is at best an approximate picture.

RESEARCH PORTFOLIO

NIJ undertakes numerous activities designed to carry out its science mission, and foremost among them is funding research studies. NIJ is authorized to make research grants and contracts with individuals, agencies, institutions of higher education, industry, and private organizations. The planning and monitoring of these awards are undertaken at the staff level through the two program offices and their respective divisions. ORE supports social science research to advance knowledge and shape best criminal justice practices. The research portfolio of OST can be broadly described as applied research aimed at developing technologies that serve criminal justice needs. Substantive areas for both offices are listed in Box 3-1.

Analysis of Awards

The committee's programmatic and financial description of NIJ's research portfolio is based on a database of NIJ awards for the period 1995-2008 that we assembled for this purpose. The database was created from an archive of awards available on the NIJ website.[2] Nearly 5,000 awards are listed online, organized by topical areas and identified with award title, principal investigator (until 2004), institution, and award amount. The topics assigned by NIJ are relatively similar across the years, although some categories have shifted from those reflecting program goals to those describing criminal justice functions and issues. Also, NIJ modified its categories in years when it received allocated funds for specific work, such as violence against women and DNA backlogs and research. (For example, see Box 3-2 for a comparison of topics in 1995 and 2006.) Seeking a consistent set of topics for the 14-year period, the committee chose to organize the awards around the following four categories:

[2]See http://www.ojp.usdoj.gov/nij/awards/welcome.htm [accessed December 10, 2009].

1. social science research—including research awards in the areas of law enforcement (policing), corrections, courts, crime and criminal behavior, crime prevention, drugs, juvenile justice, victimization, and violence against women, family violence, and violence against the elderly;
2. science and technology research and development (R&D)—including research awards in the areas of DNA analysis, forensic sciences, biometrics, communications and information technologies, policing technologies, counterterrorism technologies, less lethal technologies, and sensors and surveillance;
3. technology assistance and program support—including funds for the National Law Enforcement and Corrections Technology Center (NLECTC) system (described later in this chapter) as well as testing and evaluation and standards development and technology-related training and other awards to support or supplement staff, equipment, meeting, or dissemination costs for existing programs, such as criminal justice centers, institutes, or organizations; and
4. forensic capacity-building efforts—including awards to reduce the DNA backlogs and improve forensic laboratories as well as training and outreach efforts in forensic science.

To construct the research portfolio, the committee started with NIJ's categorization of topics, reviewed the award titles and other available information, and attempted to separate the program support and technology assistance awards from the research awards. The awards to reduce the DNA backlog and improve forensic laboratories[3] were identified as such and easily separated from the research awards. All duplicate entries (same award, same year, but categorized under multiple topics) were removed from the database, but continuation awards for subsequent years (to the extent they were available in the online archive) were left in.

Although we recognize that, for a number of reasons, the total figures from this database of awards may not be complete and accurate, we think they present as accurate a picture of trends in NIJ funding of research in different criminal justice areas as can be estimated given the available data. Figures 3-1 and 3-2 illustrate the amounts awarded and the number of awards, respectively, over the last 14 years in the four categories identified above.

The funding trends show that, over this period, NIJ allocated less to research (about $870 million) than to capacity-building efforts (about

[3]Such awards include the Forensic Casework DNA Backlog Reduction Program Formula Grants, the Paul Coverdell Forensic Science Improvement Grants, and the DNA Capacity Enhancement Program Formula Grants.

BOX 3-1
ORE and OST Research Areas

RESEARCH AREAS OF INTEREST MANAGED BY ORE

Violence and Victimization Research Division
- Hate crime
- Responding to domestic violence offenders
- Stalking
- Intimate partner violence
- Sexual Violence Research Program
- Child maltreatment
- Victims and victimization
- Teen dating violence
- Identity theft
- American Indian and Alaska Native crime and justice
- Research and evaluation
- Drugs and crime
- Elder mistreatment research program

Crime Control and Prevention Division
- Police operations
- Police organization
- Gangs and violence
- Firearms and violence
- Juvenile delinquency/juvenile justice
- Forensic policy research
- Mapping and analysis for public safety
- Situational crime prevention
- Data Resources Program
- Police use of force
- Eyewitness identification
- Response in Indian Country and the Southwest border

Justice Systems Research Division
- Prison re-entry
- Prisoner substance abuse treatment
- Community corrections
- Mental health and corrections
- Prison rape
- Women offenders
- Children whose parents are under criminal justice supervision
- Corrections health care (medical)
- Inmate work and ex-offender employment/re-entry

- Criminal justice systems
- Courts

International Center*

- Exploratory topics in global crime
- Rule of law and international justice
- Terrorism
- Cyber crime
- Trafficking in human beings
- Drugs and crime

TECHNOLOGY INVESTMENT PLATFORMS MANAGED BY OST

Within OST, these investment portfolios are administered through three divisions: (1) Investigative and Forensic Sciences Division; (2) Information and Sensor Technologies Division; and (3) Operational Technologies Division.

- Aviation (sensor platforms)
- Biometrics
- Body Armor
- Communications
- Community corrections
- Court technologies
- DNA forensics
- Electronic crime
- Explosive device defeat
- General forensics
- Information led policing
- Institutional corrections
- Less lethal technologies
- Modeling and simulation
- Operations research
- Personnel protection equipment
- Pursuit management
- School safety
- Sensors and surveillance

SOURCE: Pulled from presentations by Thomas Feucht and John Morgan made to the committee at a meeting on December 20, 2007.

---

*During the course of this study, responsibility for the international crime research portfolio shifted to the Director's Office.

BOX 3-2
Comparison of Award Topics, 1995 and 2006

NIJ Awards in Fiscal Year 1995

Section 1: 1994 Crime Act Awards
- Boot Camps
- Community Policing
- Violence Against Women

Section 2: Extramural Research
- Goal 1: Reduce Violent Crime
- Goal 2: Reduce Drug- and Alcohol-Related Crime
  - The Drug Use Forecasting (DUF) Program
- Goal 3: Reduce the Consequences of Crime
- Goal 4: Improve the Effectiveness of Crime Prevention Programs
- Goal 5: Improve Law Enforcement and the Criminal Justice System
  - Corrections
  - Policing
  - Prosecution/Adjudication
  - Systemwide Issues
- Goal 6: Develop New Technology for Law Enforcement and the Criminal Justice System

Section 3: Intramural Research
- Crime Control and Prevention
- Criminal Behavior
- Criminal Justice System

Section 4: Development, Dissemination, and Research Support

NIJ Awards in Fiscal 2006 by Topic
- Communication and Information Technologies
- Computer Crime

$1190 million)[4] and that funding for research, NIJ's primary function, is currently on the decline compared with other functions. Funds available for social science research have been declining almost steadily since 1998 and now constitute the smallest funding category. OST funding for research

[4]All figures have been converted to constant 2008 dollars. The committee thinks that adjusting for inflation presents a more accurate picture of the NIJ budget and the net increase and decrease in funding levels. All figures represent program monies and do not include NIJ staff salaries.

- Corrections
- Courts
- Crime Prevention
- Criminal Justice Research
- Drugs and Crime
- Evaluation
- Forensics, General
- Forensics, Research and Development
- Forensics and Investigative Sciences
    - Convicted Offender DNA Backlog Reduction Program
    - DNA, Missing Persons
    - DNA, Research and Development
    - DNA Capacity Enhancement Program Formula Grants
    - Forensic Casework DNA Backlog Reduction Program Formula Grants
    - Paul Coverdell Forensic Science Improvement Grants
- Less-Lethal Incapacitation
- Policing
- Schools
- Sensors and Surveillance
- Technology, National Law Enforcement and Corrections Technology Centers
- Terrorism and Critical Incidents
- Victimization and Victim Services
- Violence
    - Firearms
    - Sexual Assault
    - Violence Against Women and Family Violence
- Youth
    - Gangs

has undergone several increases and decreases and received the greatest support in fiscal year (FY) 2002, right before the legislative establishment of OST in the Homeland Security Act of 2002. But in 2008, OST funding for research also declined.

A similar picture emerges when one looks at the number of research grants each office funded during the same period. In general, a decline in funds allocated for research grants is reflected in a decline in actual grants awarded. But this decline has not occurred across the board in all catego-

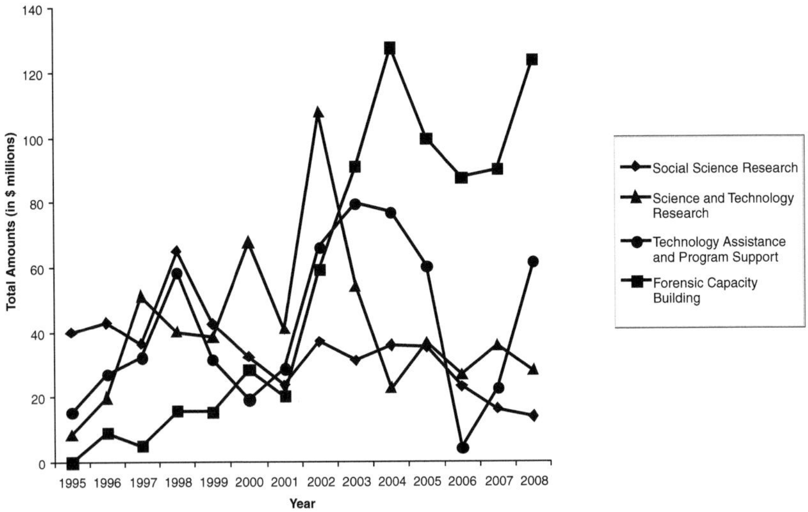

FIGURE 3-1 NIJ award funding history, 1995-2008 (in constant 2008 dollars).
SOURCE: Generated from information in NIJ's online award archive (available http://www.ojp.usdoj.gov/nij/awards/welcome.htm [accessed May 26, 2010]).

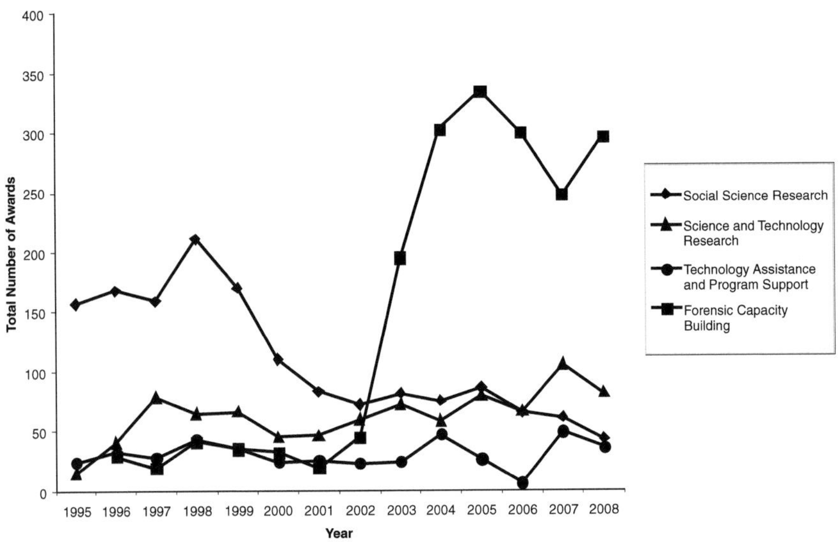

FIGURE 3-2 Number of awards by category, 1995-2008.
SOURCE: Generated from information in NIJ's online award archive (available http://www.ojp.usdoj.gov/nij/awards/welcome.htm [accessed May 26, 2010]).

ries of funding. One can see the dramatic increase in funding and number of awards in the forensic capacity-building category. In fact, since 2002 the number of forensic capacity-building awards has exceeded every other category. In 2008 there were more than seven times the number of forensic capacity-building grants awarded than all social science research grants, and there were 2.5 times the number of forensic capacity-building grants compared with all NIJ research grants.

Analysis of Solicitations

NIJ funds proposals submitted in response to the research solicitations it issues each year. The solicitations issued between 1996 and the present reflect trends similar to those outlined above both in funding levels and in the shift away from research and toward other kinds of activities. This shift is particularly striking after 2005. Prior to this time, the number of solicitations is fairly consistent around 21 (except for a brief addition of 10 solicitations in 1999 and 2000).

The pre-2005 solicitations generally included 3-4 different fellowship programs, 2-3 open investigator-initiated solicitations for both social science research and technology-related proposals, forensic capacity-building solicitations that grew from 1 to 4 different programs, and numerous targeted social science and program evaluation solicitations. The latter category made up the largest share of solicitations.

In 2005 the number of annual solicitations issued by NIJ doubled from 21 to 40. The increase in solicitations reflects the growth of the OST program, in particular the increased emphasis on technology development[5] as well as a doubling of the forensic capacity-building solicitations from 4 to 8. In addition, there are increases in solicitations for social science research and program evaluations of legislative initiatives, such as the solicitation for *Social Science Research on Emerging Issues in Forensic Science*, with ties to the President's DNA Initiative.

Numbers of solicitations and their titles do not present an accurate picture of NIJ funding priorities. For example, in FY 2007 of the 43 solicitations, 18 involve social science research or program evaluation, 16 relate to technology development, and 6 promote forensic capacity-building programs. A review of the solicitations indicates an emphasis on research, development, and evaluation activities. However, actual awards and funding amounts for the period 2005-2008 paint a different picture.

---

[5]In 2005, the open *NIJ Science and Technology* solicitation gave way to a number of solicitations targeting technology development in specific areas, such as communications, corrections, less lethal and pursuit management, electronic crime, personal protective equipment, and sensor, surveillance, and biometric technologies.

The majority (75 percent) of solicitations for social science research, program evaluation, and technology development generated 3 awards or fewer a year, for a total average of 100 awards annually. However, the 6 forensic capacity-building solicitations, combined, generated a total of over 300 awards a year. The forensic capacity-building solicitations resulted in award funds totaling over $300 million for the period 2005-2008. In the same period, the research, development, and evaluation solicitations combined resulted in award funds totaling less than $110 million. The committee views these trends with concern and discusses them in greater detail as part of the description of the specific research portfolios of ORE and OST that follow.

OFFICE OF RESEARCH AND EVALUATION

Overview of the Total Budget

In the past 14 years, the total ORE budget has ranged from approximately $18 to $54 million. Figure 3-3 illustrates the considerable year-to-year fluctuation in funding levels as well as the decline in total funding after 2005. These funding fluctuations can be expected to contribute to difficulties in sustaining continuing programs of research.

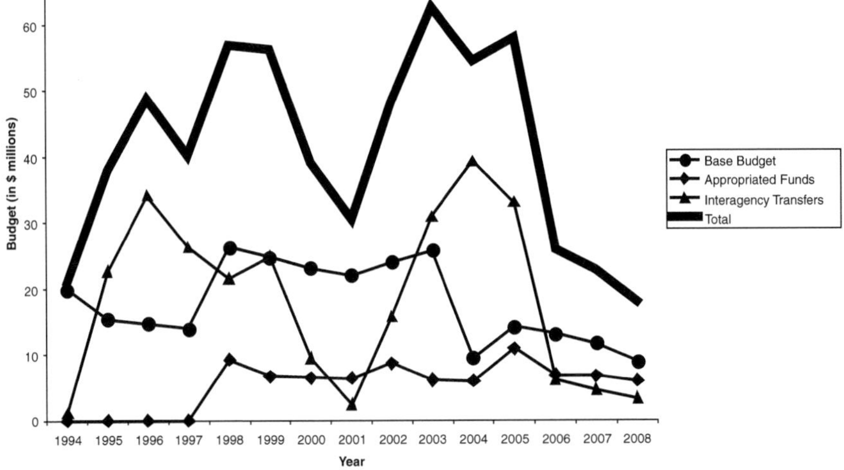

FIGURE 3-3 ORE funding history, 1994-2008 (in constant 2008 dollars).
SOURCE: Adapted from figures provided by Edwin Zedlewski during a presentation to the committee on July 10, 2008.

Even more challenging to ORE's ability to plan and execute a systematic research agenda are the shifts in its discretion over how the funds could be used. The figure illustrates the changes in the three categories of ORE funding: (1) base budget, (2) appropriated funds, and (3) interagency transfers. The base budget—the funds Congress specifically appropriates to NIJ to carry out its mission—generally allows NIJ the most discretion in funding a broad range of research topics. These funds have sharply declined in recent years. In 2004, while overall program funds for ORE dropped from its 2003 budget of $63 million in constant 2008 dollars to $55 million, its base budget funds dropped from $26 to $9.5 million. The base budget funds increased slightly in 2005 to $14 million; however, in 2008 ORE was allocated only $9 million for its discretionary base budget.[6]

The second source of funds comes from other appropriations—funds that Congress appropriates to other agencies but designates them to be used by NIJ for a specific purpose. The funds are then transferred to NIJ to be used in designated research areas. One of the largest sources of transferred funds from separate appropriations is the funding from the Violence Against Women Act (VAWA) appropriation. These funds have been quite significant over time and have been heavily relied on by the Violence and Victimization Division of ORE to support its work.

The third category of funds includes monies transferred to NIJ from other units of the Office of Justice Programs (OJP), the Department of Justice, and occasionally other federal agencies for studies, usually evaluations, related to programs these agencies are sponsoring. Only rarely are these funds available for general research purposes. For example, the increase in transferred funds to NIJ between 2004 and 2006 in part reflects funds from the Office of Juvenile Justice and Delinquency Prevention (OJJDP) and the Bureau of Justice Assistance (BJA). These two OJP bureaus received approval to use a percentage of the funding designated for earmarked programs to support outcome evaluations. Other examples of large research efforts funded with transferred funds include multiyear evaluations of the Serious and Violent Offender Reentry Initiative, the Residential Substance Abuse Treatment program, and adult and juvenile drug courts.

The net effect of these trends has been to erode the discretion of ORE in allocating funds, to reduce the level of funding available for many research areas, and to change the type of studies funded.

---

[6]It is important to note that the director of NIJ determines how much ORE will receive in NIJ base funds. Base funds are used to support other activities, such as dissemination and special projects, and ORE must advocate for its share of these funds. In FY 2003, congressional appropriators designated how much of the base funds should be allocated to OST; this practice was discontinued in 2006.

Social Science Research Portfolio

The ORE research portfolio of the past 15 years is extremely diverse. NIJ research on policing includes not only the nature of policing (police administration, organizational structure, personnel practices) and policing activities (community policing, police behavior) but also the effectiveness of policies, activities, and technologies on specific kinds of crimes, on different populations, and places. Research on violence includes but is not limited to crime trends and rates; the effects of violent crime on children, women, and the elderly; research on specific crimes—homicide, sexual assault, aggravated assault, burglary, and robbery; and the impact of guns and other weapons. Research on drugs and crime includes not only the relationship between the two but also research on drug crime prevalence, drug treatment, and drug markets. The courts and corrections portfolios include pretrial, sentencing practices, special courts, boot camps, correctional populations, sexual assault in prisons, the impact of treatment, and recidivism. The portfolio also includes research on international crimes, such as terrorism and human trafficking, as well as emerging crimes, such as identity theft and computer crime.

The 1977 evaluation of NIJ by the National Research Council (NRC) noted the absence of a cumulative research program in important aspects of crime and justice. To determine whether NIJ has responded to this concern and because of the extreme diversity of its research portfolio, the committee decided to focus on selected research areas for our overview. Our selection started with areas NIJ specifically identifies either in its annual reports or on its website. We then narrowed these down to areas in which multiple projects were funded over a number of years: policing; drugs and crime; violence against women; firearms and violence; and crime mapping. We also picked a single study, the Program on Human Development in Chicago Neighborhoods, because it is the largest longitudinal study ever funded by NIJ, both in terms of dollar value and the length of time it was supported. Some large areas of research—courts, corrections, juvenile justice—are not included in our descriptions because work on particular topics in these areas was less sustained over time. Neither did we examine the broader category of victims and victimization but instead chose to focus on violence against women, a more easily identifiable area that has had considerable funding over time. The research areas we selected are those we determined, with some assistance from NIJ, offered the most promise for understanding the evolution of the ORE research portfolio and its current research endeavors. It is important to note that the areas of research described below do not represent formal programs of research that one might associate with systematic planning but rather collections of projects that have common subject matter.

For each individual portfolio, the committee did not conduct in-depth reviews of the studies, nor did it assess their methodological or policy value. Specific research studies are highlighted to give an overall sense of the work and their contributions to building a body of knowledge. The descriptions also indicate when lines of inquiry ceased or certain research topics were not carried forward or explored. These are offered as examples of opportunities NIJ either was unable to pursue or chose not to do so and do not reflect the committee's recommendations of research activities to be pursued in the future.

Policing Research

The largest single category of research grants is in the policing area. For much of NIJ's history, the policing research portfolio has been its strongest and most visible part of its program. For purposes of this discussion, policing research includes research aimed at improving law enforcement policies and operations. It includes research on community policing but not research on specific crime issues, such as firearms and drugs. These issues have been treated as distinct programs on the NIJ website and in its annual reports, both sources of information for the committee's work. Research associated with the development and use of various law enforcement technologies is also treated separately by NIJ and is discussed separately in the section on the Office of Science and Technology.

Research History

A recent paper by Braga and Weisburd (2006) identified eight major innovations in American policing during the 1980s and 1990s, and NIJ has supported important work on each of them: community policing (Moore, Trojanozicz, and Kelling, 1988), problem-oriented policing (Goldstein, 1979), "broken windows" policing (Kelling and Wilson, 1982), "pulling levers" policing (Kennedy, 1997), third-party policing (Roehl, 1998; Maxson et al., 2005), "hot spots" policing (Sherman and Weisburd, 1995), evidence-based policing (Blumstein and Petersilia, 1994), and COMSTAT (Weisburd et al., 2003). See Box 3-3 for a brief description of these innovations.

NIJ's research on traditional police practices, such as preventive patrol, police response time, and criminal investigations in the late 1970s helped lay the groundwork for the beginning of what has been described as a "quiet revolution in policing" (Kelling, 1988). This important body of research demonstrated that neither crime rates nor citizens' perceptions of their safety were significantly affected by changes in preventive patrols (Kelling et al., 1974); that police response time was unrelated to the probability of making an arrest or locating a witness (Harris, 1978; Kansas City

BOX 3-3
Policing Innovations During the 1980s and 1990s

- **Community policing** is characterized by (1) a larger vision of the police function that may include fear reduction, quality service, both prevention and crime control activities; (2) decentralization of problems and responsibility for dealing with them; (3) community engagement; and (4) identification of priority problems (National Research Council, 2004b).
- **Problem-oriented policing** relies on analytic methods to develop highly localized responses to crime problems with a focus on traditional crimes identified by police information systems (National Research Council, 2004b).
- **Broken windows policing** is a police strategy first put forward in a 1982 *Atlantic* article by George L. Kelling and James Q. Wilson who theorized that a disorderly environment sends a message that no one is in charge, thus increasing fear, weakening community controls, and inviting criminal behavior. It further maintains that stopping minor offenses and restoring greater order can prevent serious crime.
- **Pulling levers policing** includes the strategy of "lever pulling" meetings used in the Boston Cease Fire Demonstration Program in which high-ranking government officials (e.g., Assistant U.S. Attorney, FBI, local police homicide commander) met with people and youth from

(Missouri) Police Department, 1980); and that it was the work of the patrol officer and not detective work alone that increased the probability of an arrest (Greenwood, Chaiken, and Petersilia, 1977).

Police departments changed their arrest practices in domestic violence calls in part as a result of NIJ-sponsored work with the Minneapolis Police Department (Sherman and Berk, 1984), and criminal justice practitioners gained greater understanding of the complexities of those kinds of interventions following seven replications of the original study that NIJ sponsored in 1986 (Blumstein and Petersilia, 1994).

Building on that early foundation, NIJ policing research has contributed to a body of knowledge around what has come to be known as the "focused model of policing." In this model, police strategies are tailored to specific kinds of problems rather than across-the-board reliance on the community and told them that if violence occurred, they would prosecute gun crimes to the full extent of applicable State or Federal law, and would lock up probation or parole violators or those who had outstanding warrants (Kennedy, 1997; National Institute of Justice, 2008b, fn 16).

- **Third-party policing** refers to police insistence on the involvement of nonoffending third parties (usually place managers) in the control of criminal and disorderly behavior, creating a de facto new element of public duty and a sharing of crime control responsibility with a wide range of organizations, institutions, and individuals (Buerger, 1998).
- **Hot spots policing** is a strategy in which police attack chronic concentrations of crime (National Research Council, 2004b).
- **Evidence-based policing** calls for basic police practices based on scientific evidence about what works best to guide practice and evaluate police actions. It is a systematic effort to identify experience as the basis for police work and then to refine practice and policy by ongoing testing of various explanations (Sherman, 1998).
- **COMSTAT** is a process developed by the New York Police Department in 1994 that involves putting resources to emerging crime problems on a timely basis. The responsibility resides with precinct and district commanders who closely monitor crime in their area, identify crime problems, devise and implement solutions and then follow through to determine impact (National Research Council, 2004b).

random patrol, rapid response to calls for service, follow-up investigations by detectives, and unfocused enforcement efforts (National Research Council, 2004b, p. 5). Of particular importance has been research on hot spots, which examines the effectiveness of highly focused and well-managed policing efforts in a variety of environments in which crime is heavily concentrated (Eck, 1993; Sherman and Rogan, 1995; Sherman and Weisburd, 1995; Braga et al., 1999). NIJ research is largely credited for important conclusions emerging from this line of research, including the finding that directed patrols, proactive arrests, and problem solving at high-crime hot spots can be effective in preventing crime in both the hot spot and in the surrounding area (Sherman et al., 1997).

NIJ was able to greatly expand its policing research portfolio with the passage of the Crime Act of 1994. During 1995-1998, it awarded more than 150 research policing grants, totaling approximately $41.2 million in Crime Act funds.[7] Funds, however, did not come directly but were the result of negotiations between the NIJ director and other OJP and Justice Department agency heads who had received direct appropriations. The largest dollar investment ($12.6 million) received by NIJ went for evaluations of programs closely related to these agencies' interests and initiatives.

In 2004, an NRC committee reviewed research on police policy and practices and concluded that, despite the large investment in research on community policing, the evidence as to its effectiveness was equivocal. Acknowledging the difficulties in conducting this kind of research, the report recommended that it should focus on the key elements of community policing and problem-oriented policing. It went on to conclude that there were many important subjects on which no scientific research had been done and pointed out the need for stable, long-term research funding to address the significant gaps in the research. The report recommended that NIJ support a research agenda that was balanced between questions of police lawfulness, legitimacy, and crime control effectiveness (National Research Council, 2004b).

Current Portfolio

According to NIJ, the theme of its current policing research is improved decision making by police with the goal of addressing the needs of law enforcement executives.[8] To that end, ORE supports a mixed and limited number of policing studies, although its continued reliance on transferred funds makes long-term planning difficult. These studies include grants on police use of force, police fatigue and officer performance, performance measures for multijurisdictional task forces, evidence-based model programs for cold case units, an evaluation of multijurisdictional task forces, a randomized experiment of license plate recognition technology, and homicide clearance initiatives. According to NIJ, this mixed portfolio is a result of heavy reliance on the investigator-initiated *Crime and Justice* solicitation and the *Research on Policing and Public Safety Interventions*, the latter a targeted policing solicitation. Both provide wide discretion to researchers in topic selection. With the exception of the work on police use of force and homicide clearance rates, there is little evidence that there is much carryover of research topics from the Crime Act grants. In particular, the committee

[7]Program review memorandum to Jeremy Travis, director, NIJ, January 15, 1999. For the period 1995-2001, "the COPS funded research allocation . . . totaled $46,639,165" (National Research Council, 2004b, p. 30).

[8]Briefing paper on policing portfolio prepared for the NRC Committee on Law and Justice by NIJ.

notes the absence of research to shed light on the impact of policing activities on reducing crime.

Research on Drugs and Crime

Much of NIJ's drug research has focused on identifying drug-using offenders, reducing their drug use, and controlling access to drugs. A guiding thesis behind this research has been that drug users are disproportionately likely to engage in criminal activity and that criminal justice agencies can reduce crime by identifying and treating drug abusers.

Identifying Drug-Using Offenders

Beginning in 1984, NIJ-sponsored urinalysis research on pretrial releasees in Washington, DC, showed high usage of drugs and high recidivism rates (Toborg and Bellassai, 1988; Toborg, Yezer, and Bellassai, 1988) and laid the groundwork for comprehensive pretrial drug-testing programs that sprang up nationwide. In 1987 NIJ launched its Drug Use Forecasting (DUF) system in 10 sites and quickly expanded to 23. DUF showed early on that the levels of drug use among persons arrested for felonies in cities were between 50 and 85 percent, much higher than previously thought (National Institute of Justice, 1990).

Hair analysis, introduced into DUF in 1990, proved to be simpler and relatively less invasive than urinalysis for detecting illegal drugs (Mieczkowski, 1995). It was also shown to have a wider window for detecting opiates and cocaine but to be ineffective for detecting recent cocaine use. NIJ replicated early studies showing that hair analysis detected cocaine more frequently than did urinalysis (Mieczkowski, Mumm, and Connick, 1995; Mieczkowski, 1997). DUF results in later years provided new insights into gun use by those arrested (National Institute of Justice, 1997) and new data on the extent of methamphetamine use in major cities (Feucht and Kyle, 1996).

In 1997, DUF was succeeded by the Arrestee Drug Abuse Monitoring (ADAM) system, and in 2000 numerous methodological improvements were made to it, including a scientific sampling strategy and a new data collection instrument. ADAM data provided useful information about the location of drug purchases (National Institute of Justice, 2000, 2003a) and identified very large variances from city to city in the use of particular drugs (Tonry and Wilson, 1990).

NIJ's funding of ADAM ended in 2001 when Congress reduced its appropriation and it was unable to afford what had become an annual expenditure of $16 million. The Office of National Drug Control Policy revived the program in 2007, and NIJ is consulting with that office on ADAM II.[9]

Reducing Drug Use

The drugs and crime portfolio reflects a heavy investment in activities to evaluate ways to reduce drug use among offenders, thereby reducing recidivism. NIJ research shows that treatment while under criminal justice supervision has been important because many of those receiving it were unlikely to seek treatment on their own (Lipton, 1995). Treatment supervised within the criminal justice system could reduce drug use and a reduction in drug use decreases criminality, even among chronic drug abusing offenders (Lipton, 1996). NIJ research on treatment also shed important light on the characteristics of successful drug treatment programs (Falkin, Strauss, and Bohen, 1999).

The largest investment in research in the drugs and crime area has been directed toward evaluating four major kinds of programs aimed at treating the drug behavior of offenders: (1) drug courts (National Institute of Justice, 2006a), (2) residential drug treatment corrections programs (Inciardi, 1996; Harrison and Martin, 2000; Guerin, 2002), (3) intensive probation supervision (Petersilia and Turner, 1993), and (4) a systemwide approach known as Breaking the Cycle (see Box 3-4). NIJ-sponsored studies have provided critical information on the positive impact of these programs on recidivism and substance abuse relapse (Bureau of Justice Assistance, 2010). NIJ's process evaluation of the Breaking the Cycle demonstrations identified the difficulties of program implementation, while the impact evaluation confirmed that efforts to reduce drug use among all felony defendants under supervision did produce public safety benefits, even when imperfectly implemented (Harrell et al., 2003).

Controlling Drug Markets

A third important area of concentration in the drugs and crime portfolio has been research on the control of drug markets. In 1990, NIJ initiated the Drug Market Analysis (DMA) Program and conducted evaluations of five demonstration sites to determine whether innovative drug enforcement strategies were effective. One project in Jersey City, New Jersey, found consistent and strong effects of a strategy that used intensive crackdowns and coordinated efforts involving local government agencies to close down drug activity (Weisburd and Green, 1995). Another study of rental properties

[9]Briefing paper on drugs and crime portfolio prepared for the committee by NIJ in July 2008.

BOX 3-4
Drug Treatment Programs

- **Drug Courts.** Since 1989, more than 1,500 courts with program support from the Bureau of Justice Assistance (BJA) have implemented or are planning to implement a drug court. In a drug court, court officers (judges, prosecutors, defense counsel) work with substance abuse treatment specialists, probation officers, education and vocational experts, and community leaders to pressure offenders to face their drug problems.
- **Residential Substance Abuse Treatment Programs (RSAT).** Residential Substance Abuse Treatment (RSAT) programs are congressionally mandated (as are drug courts). Operated as a formula grants programs administered by BJA, these programs can be located in jails or prisons or as part of an after-care program. All 56 states and territories have RSAT programs and each state may have more than one.
- **Intensive Supervision Programs.** Intensive supervision is a form of release into the community that emphasizes close monitoring of convicted offenders and imposes rigorous conditions, including random and unannounced drug testing and stringent enforcement of court-ordered conditions.
- **Breaking the Cycle.** Breaking the Cycle was designed to resolve problems that arise at a particular stage of criminal justice processing, only to find that an offender has moved on and the consistency of the intervention cannot be maintained. The key system reforms were early intervention, judicial oversight, graduated sanctions and incentives, and justice and treatment system collaboration. The program was to apply research suggesting that treatment outcomes would improve when reinforced by the coercive power of the justice system.

with drug dealing in San Diego concluded that improved onsite management resulting from targeted police action in the form of Drug Abatement Response Teams did affect drug and crime activity—even 30 months after the initial police intervention (Eck and Wartell, 1999).

NIJ research has also focused on understanding how drug use responds to changes in price in an effort to understand how enforcement affects drug consumption (Caulkins, 1995; Rhodes et al., 1995; Riley, 1997). Research on drug markets is continuing, with one study focusing on methamphetamine use in New York City and another on the impact of policing and community strategies on open air drug markets in three sites in North Carolina.

Current Portfolio

Much of NIJ's research funding has come from congressionally mandated programs, particularly in the drug treatment and drug court areas. But ORE has also consistently supported drugs and crime research with its own base funds, either through a specific drugs and crime solicitation or through the investigator-initiated *Crime and Justice* solicitation. In FY 2008, the drug and crime portfolio consisted of 33 active grants covering 10 areas, including some new ones such as the Chinese drug trade, alcohol and drugs, sentencing, American Indian drug and crime issues, drug investigations, and drugs and rape.

NIJ research in this area has accomplished a great deal. But lack of stable funding has inhibited its ability to fund more long-term research in several important areas. The ADAM system had been intended for use as a research platform, and, with its demise, a rich source of data was eliminated. Research on drug market operations, which includes ethnographic studies and drug market research, has not been supported, nor has research on the life course of drug use careers, especially among arrestees (National Research Council, 2001b). The instability and inadequacy of NIJ funding, coupled with inadequate program direction, have precluded the kinds of longitudinal studies and research platforms that are needed for better understanding of the nexus between drugs and crime.

Research on Violence Against Women

NIJ research on violence against women preceded the passage of the Violence Against Women Act of 1994[10] by several decades. From the mid-1970s through early 1980s, NIJ funded research to analyze and interpret sexual assault evidence and the translation of this information into protocols for victim examination (Schram, 1978). The protocols in current use owe a debt to this work. In the 1980s, NIJ sponsored research on the difficulties faced by women who were victimized and showed that victim involvement often compounds the harm they received (Finn and Lee, 1987). These findings provided the rationale for victim assistance programs and guidelines for improving criminal justice policies related to treatment of rape victims (Blumstein and Petersilia, 1994).

The passage of the Crime Act of 1994, incorporating the Violence Against Women Act of 1994, provided a big boost to research on violence against women. In FY 1995, NIJ issued its first solicitation and awarded nearly $1 million to 6 projects selected from 61 proposals submitted. One

[10]Title IV, Violent Crime Control Act of 1994, P.L. 103-322; 108 Stat. 1902; 42 U.S.C. § 13701, Sections 1206-1208, 1303-1304. This law called for reducing violence against women, which included sexual assault, stalking, and domestic violence. In FY 2005, teen dating became the fourth area of focus under the Violence Against Women Act.

of them was a congressionally mandated national evaluation of the implementation of programs funded by the Violence Against Women Grants Office, now called the Office on Violence Against Women. This office was established to fund improvements in the response of police, prosecutors, and service providers to victims of domestic violence. Early research funding was limited to specific areas, with the objective of evaluating projects funded by the legislation. Other studies examined coordinated responses to domestic violence by prosecutors, courts, and other criminal justice agencies.

Funding for a full-fledged research program came after an NRC study panel proposed a long-range research agenda on causes, prevention, education, and legal strategies (National Research Council, 1996b). This report provided a focus and gave direction to the program, making useful recommendations on substantive issues, as well as to how best to conduct research and create a research infrastructure.[11] In the Violence Against Women Act of 2000, NIJ was mandated by Congress to develop a research agenda in line with the NRC recommendations and to conduct studies on four specific topics: (1) insurance discrimination against victims of domestic violence, (2) workplace effects of violence against women, (3) unemployment compensation for women who are victims of violence, and (4) parental kidnapping (Laney, 2005).

A great deal of what is known today about violence against women is based on NIJ research. A subsequent NRC review of its research in the period 1995-2000 notes support of studies in many of the areas recommended by the 1996 NRC report (National Research Council, 2004a):

- Studies to evaluate measurement instruments
- Studies to examine the context of violence
- Studies on service-seeking behavior
- Evaluation studies of primary prevention programs
- Studies of incidence and prevalence of perpetuation of violence
- Studies that describe current services and evaluate their effectiveness
- Studies that examine the discretionary processes in the criminal and civil justice systems
- The Violence Against Women Survey
- The Judicial Oversight Demonstration, a large demonstration program that tested the effectiveness of court-led coordinated community responses to violence against women. (This very expensive project, funded collaboratively with the Violence Against Women Office, had combined costs of over $25 million.)

[11]Briefing paper on violence against women portfolio prepared for the committee by NIJ in July 2008.

The National Violence Against Women Survey deserves special mention. Beginning in 1998, NIJ collaborated with the Centers for Disease Control and Prevention (CDC) on a 5-year effort to understand why violence against women occurs, how to prevent it, and how to improve legal and health care interventions. The survey was the vehicle for carrying out this effort, and the results have been published in a series of reports on violence against women, intimate partner violence, stalking, and rape. CDC, with support from NIJ and the U.S. Department of Defense, is currently in the process of planning to launch a second national survey on violence against women.

NIJ research has produced a great deal of evidence on the dimensions and characteristics of violence against women, particularly intimate partner violence, a major focus. Research revealed the high percentage of murders of women by their husbands and intimate partners (Campbell et al., 2003; Brock, 2004; Fox and Zawitz, 2004) and the heavy role of alcohol and drugs (Sharps et al., 2003), prior abuse, and gun ownership (Campbell et al., 2003).

NIJ also supported groundbreaking research on the prevalence of stalking, showing it was a much larger problem than had been supposed (Tjaden and Thoennes, 1998, 2000, 2006). Research identified the limited responses of the nation's colleges and universities to student allegations of rape or sexual assault (Fisher, Cullen, and Turner, 1999). NIJ's evaluation of STOP, a major program to improve prosecutorial and police handling of violence against women, found that the funding was a successful way to improve criminal justice services to woman (Burt et al., 2001). The report raised important issues for college administrators, such as making victims' needs a priority in the process.

Funding History

In the past 15 years, approximately $70 million has been expended on research on violence against women.[12] Of this amount, approximately $50 million came from dedicated research funds from the Violence Against Women Act. NIJ base funds and transfers from other Justice Department agencies as well as CDC and the National Institutes of Health have made up the $20 million balance. Also, the Violence Against Women Office has from time to time transferred funds in addition to the appropriated monies to NIJ for special studies.

Of the $70 million expended, the largest amount of funding has gone

[12]NIJ maintains an online compendium of all research on violence against women funded in the period 1993-2008. See http://www.ojp.usdoj.gov/nij/pubs-sum/vaw-compendium.htm [accessed December 10, 2009].

to research on criminal justice system processes as well as treatment and victim services ($20.4 million). Another $18.6 million has been expended on research on the social and cultural context in which violence against women occurs. This category of funding includes such subtopics as specific populations, violence against women and welfare, domestic violence and children, commercial sexual exploitation of children, drug and alcohol use and criminal histories, and context and life course. The third most highly funded category is program evaluations ($17.1 million).

Current Portfolio

The research portfolio demonstrates how a steady source of funding, coupled with a research roadmap in the form of two NRC reports, has enabled NIJ to conduct a sustained and coherent research program. However, the main focus of the research has been and continues to be short-term examinations of interventions and improved practices of immediate assistance by agencies dealing with women victims.

It is worth noting that the 2004 NRC report identified several important research areas that have not received attention. These include information on prevalence and incidence (rates of new cases) and longitudinal studies of U.S. populations to examine the causes and consequences of violence against and by women. It also pointed out the importance of including men and women in any surveys of violence against women (National Research Council, 2004a).

The committee realizes that this kind of data collection effort requires a sizeable investment of funds sustained over time. What is not known is the influence of these data on policy makers, from members of Congress to the Office of Justice Programs to local community agencies.

Research on Firearms and Crime

Strategies to develop and sponsor studies addressing firearms violence began in the late 1970s as part of NIJ's program on research on violent crimes. Early studies on homicide, robbery, and robbery-murder pointed to the central role of firearms. Around 1980 NIJ convened a research symposium to discuss firearms issues and identify questions for future study.

Several important studies emerged from this initial symposium, including (1) a large-scale literature review and issue analysis, (2) a study of firearms acquisition and use by adult felons (Wright and Rossi, 1986), (3) a study of incarcerated juveniles and high-risk high school students regarding their gun-related attitudes and behavior (Sheley and Wright, 1998), and (4) an evaluation of a hot spot firearms seizure experiment conducted in Kansas City as part of a larger Weed and Seed Program (Sherman and

Rogan, 1995). In 1993, with increased federal interest in the study of gun violence arising out of the peak of the drug-violence-crime problems in the United States, NIJ was able to expand the size and scope of its firearms violence research and to use a more systematic and comprehensive set of investment strategies, which included partnering with other federal agencies.

Between the initial foray into firearms research (around 1980) and 2000, NIJ was involved in funding basic descriptive research on key issues regarding firearms. Most NIJ-funded research has delved deeply into the design and implementation of programs aimed at reducing firearm violence through enhanced enforcement strategies. For example, a program evaluation of the Boston Gun Experiment indicated some effectiveness toward reducing juvenile homicide following implementation of a multiagency supply and demand reduction program targeting illegal firearms markets to gangs (Kennedy, 1997; Braga et al., 1999; Tita et al., 2005). An experimental traffic stop and search gun program in Indianapolis, modeled after a similar one in Kansas City (Sherman and Rogan, 1995), was found to be effective in one experimental neighborhood but had no effect in another, probably because of differences in community characteristics and program implementation (McGarrell et al., 2009). Evaluation studies of the assault weapons ban showed that, in the short term, criminal use of the banned guns declined after the law went into effect and the gun murder rate and murders of police officers with assault weapons decreased (Roth and Koper, 1999). However, the long-term evaluation studies indicate that, given the grandfathered nature of the provisions of the ban, overall use of the banned weaponry had not yet declined and thus had no effect on the levels of gun injuries and death (Koper, Woods, and Roth, 2004).

NIJ has also funded other gun deterrence studies. One looked at the impact of an educational intervention that targets first-time offenders for carrying concealed weapons (Roth, 1998). Another conducted an analysis of secondary markets, finding that there are very different types of illegal markets and acquisition patterns in different cities, thus providing evidence that prevention and intervention efforts need to be locally based (Pierce et al., 2003). In addition, gun tracing data studies have been used proactively to map patterns of illegal gun acquisition; these have started to inform the design of intervention strategies by local law enforcement (Haile, 2006). Information gleaned from the Youth Crime Gun Interdiction Initiative indicated that 90 percent of traced guns used in crimes changed hands at least once before recovery by law enforcement and that many of the traced guns were recovered soon (within several years) after their initial purchase (Bureau of Alcohol, Tobacco and Firearms, 1997).

Between 1993 and 1999, NIJ sponsored 32 studies, totaling approximately $8 million, that addressed firearms and violence (bearing in mind that weapons issues were also included as part of many broader violence research efforts). During this period, NIJ firearms research was closely coordinated with firearms initiatives and interests of other agencies including CDC, OJJDP, the Bureau of Justice Statistics (BJS), the Treasury Department/Bureau of Alcohol, Tobacco, Firearms and Explosives (ATF), the Office of Justice Programs, COPS, and the Executive Office for United States Attorneys.

Current Portfolio

Since 2000, amidst reduced funding for firearms-related research, NIJ has been involved in several collaborative efforts:

1. cofunding (with CDC and several private foundations) of an NRC panel on improving research and data on firearms (National Research Council, 2005b);
2. funding of a University of California, Davis, study on firearms markets and firearms violence (Wintemute, 1998);
3. cofunding (with ATF) of the 2001 Youth Crime Gun Interdiction Initiative demonstration and evaluation solicitation on gun tracing expansion and program implementation (Ridgeway et al., 2008);
4. contributions to a Brookings Institution Conference on Gun Violence and Gun Policy;
5. funding of projects (Cohen and Ludwig, 2003) that evaluate an intensive policing patrol program aimed at reducing illegal gun carrying in high-crime areas of Pittsburgh;
6. funding of a project evaluating the long-term impact of the federal assault weapons ban; and
7. a cooperative agreement to provide research-based training and technical assistance to the Justice Department–ATF Project Safe Neighborhoods initiative to reduce gun violence in all 93 U.S. attorney districts.

The current research portfolio on firearms has shifted somewhat from its earlier emphasis on evaluations of police interventions. Current firearms research is being carried out as part of the Project Safe Neighborhoods (PSN) initiative, and NIJ's role is now advisory. PSN grew out of an earlier program, which was a multiagency, multidisciplinary effort targeted at homicide, youth violence, or firearms violence in nine sites and on reducing rape and sexual assault in one site (National Institute of Justice, 2008b).

Moving ahead, there are several challenges and obstacles that continue to plague this area of research as well as NIJ's commitment to it. The retirement of a key staff person working on the firearms and violence portfolio has created a vacuum that has yet to be addressed by NIJ. Financial resources are limited as funding and research priorities are shifted away from violence and toward terrorism. In the research field, there continues to be methodological difficulties of measuring the impact of national gun violence reduction programs, such as PSN, as well as inadequate data. In addition, the issue of firearms will probably always be surrounded by a challenging and difficult political and social context.

Crime Mapping

NIJ's efforts to support R&D of crime mapping technologies began in 1995. The Crime Mapping Research Center, established in 1996, was replaced in 2002 by the Mapping and Analysis for Public Safety (MAPS) Program. Its intent, according to NIJ, is to "increase the integration of spatial statistics and traditional mapping analysis."[13]

The program supports intramural projects and extramural grants as well as sponsoring visiting fellows. In 1996, NIJ published a case study of the Chicago Police Department's Information Collection for Automated Mapping (ICAM) project. Described as user-friendly, it has been used to provide information about crime patterns to beat police officers, residents, businesses, and community groups. Also, Chicago Police Department dispatchers used it to link calls to the nearest available units. The intent of the case study was to promote such technologies to other departments. It is not known if this effort was successful, but the subsequent widespread consideration of hot spots policing, described earlier, suggests that the technology has become increasingly popular in law enforcement. The combination of this technology and hot spots policing is credited as an important driver of innovation in policing (National Research Council, 2004b).

NIJ has increased the number of extramural crime mapping projects that have been supported each year, from two in 2003 to seven in 2007. By far the largest of these grants is the result of an earmark ($3 million to Georgia State University to continue work to improve the collection and dissemination of criminal justice data across jurisdictions). Several funded projects are aimed at improving the performance of law enforcement via the use of crime mapping and data collection technologies. For example, a 2005 grant supported an analysis to determine the optimal search areas for a suspected serial criminal. Another was to the Police Department of Redlands, California, to develop the capacity to share data among regional

[13]Information for this section was drawn from an NIJ briefing paper on crime mapping research (July 2008) and a crime mapping paper prepared for the Committee on Law and Justice (May 9, 2009).

agencies. NIJ funded several grants for simulation studies as well as grants for technological development.

A striking feature of the portfolio is the limited support that has gone to universities where important spatial research is being conducted. NIJ's efforts have run parallel to advances in spatial analyses by criminologists, geographers, sociologists, and other social scientists. However, it is not clear that NIJ has been a substantial direct supporter of many of those social science efforts, but its support of infrastructure, in particular by archiving data at the National Criminal Justice Data Archive at the University of Michigan and by developing the capacity of local police agencies to geocode data, does advance this work.

From its inception, a major objective has been to build an infrastructure to support the use of geographic information systems (GIS) software and mapping technologies. To accomplish this goal, MAPS has developed and distributed user-friendly software to police departments, provides technical training and assistance, holds a mapping conference every 18 months, publishes the *Geography and Public Safety Bulletin* in conjunction with the COPS office, and has developed an e-mail discussion list (listserv) for both researchers and practitioners to foster the sharing of good ideas. Departments have benefited from NIJ's promotion of training in crime mapping, which has enabled them to more efficiently allocate resources to geographic locations where crime frequently occurs or where a small number of crime correlates are concentrated (e.g., youth activity, bars, and taverns).

NIJ has been a leader in developing and encouraging the dissemination and use of the CrimeStat program (now in its third generation). CrimeStat is being used by an increasing number of police departments and has been credited anecdotally for contributing to the crime drop. NIJ has facilitated linking police departments and producers that are creating succeeding generations of GIS software. Some of this software is used for geographic profiling. There is anecdotal evidence of the positive effect of geographic profiling, but so far no rigorous evaluation of the software has been completed.

Current Status

Although funding for the crime mapping program has diminished, NIJ is continuing to build on the previous work through its own program of intramural research, targeted publications, and training efforts. NIJ has done a good job of making GIS technologies available to criminal justice agencies, promoting their use through the crime mapping listserv, providing training (available training programs are regularly listed on the MAPS website), and encouraging user conversation. It has facilitated an expanding application of mapping technologies to an increasing number of crime control and investigation problems. The efficacy of these applications has yet to be evaluated.

The impact of the crime mapping program on the research community is less clear. Spatial analyses are used in a number of disciplines, and they had been applied to the study of a number of research questions before NIJ's efforts to promote crime mapping. In terms of criminology and criminal justice research, social environment and geography have long been important approaches to the study of crime. What has changed in the last decade or so has been the development of new GIS tools that have allowed the use of more detailed data measuring the spatial distribution of crime. These technologies have also allowed for wider use of geocoded data to address long-standing, important research questions.

NIJ's crime mapping program has facilitated the use of new crime data tracking and new law enforcement possibilities for practitioners, and it has occurred as the research community has developed a renewed interest in social environmental and geographical patterns and causes of crime. Crime mapping research also has the potential to play a role in the growing field of ecological crime research, including crime in neighborhoods and spatial effects on crime. Crime mapping technologies can be used to combine observational data and administrative data, producing rich data sets for the study of neighborhood dynamics and their relationship to crime (Fagan, 2008).

Program on Human Development in Chicago Neighborhoods

NIJ's largest investment in a single research project was to the Project on Human Development in Chicago Neighborhoods. Funded out of ORE base funds from 1990 to 2002, NIJ grants totaled $21.1 million. According to an informative 1999 memo by the project monitor, the total cost of the project exceeded $52 million.[14] Given the size of the investment, the committee recognizes that this project probably resulted in opportunity costs for other parts of the NIJ research program.

A second major source of funds for the project was the MacArthur Foundation, whose total investment was $21.9 million, exclusive of subsequent grants to the Inter-university Consortium of Political and Social Research (ICPSR) to support the distribution and use of the data collected by the project. Other major contributors to the project were the National Institute of Mental Health and the U.S. Department of Education.

[14] Internal memorandum from Christy Visher, an NIJ staff member, sent to Jeremy Travis, dated June 24, 1999, entitled "Program Review: Project on Human Development in Chicago Neighborhoods, 1990-2001" given to the committee by NIJ.

The origins of NIJ's support for the project trace back to the early 1980s. A small group of researchers, mainly from outside criminology, argued that the origins of crime and delinquency could be traced back to psychosocial influences very early in life. Over the past 30 years, this perspective, which has come to be called developmental criminology, has evolved into a dominate paradigm in criminology. The design of the project was influenced by two reports from the Justice Study Group (Farrington, Ohlin, and Wilson, 1986; Tonry, Ohlin, and Farrington, 1991) and a report from the NRC Panel on Research on Criminal Careers (National Research Council, 1986). These reports suggested the collection of longitudinal data on the developmental course of cohorts of individuals from early in their lives. Such data, it was argued, would provide the basis for empirical investigations of the early life psychosocial predictors of *career criminals.* They also advocated for an experimental component in the longitudinal data collection in order to identify interventions that would be effective in deflecting developmental trajectories leading to high-rate offending. The NRC report proposed a "criminal career model" as a context for research on developmental origins of criminality.

The NIJ–MacArthur Foundation partnership that funded about 80 percent of the program formally began in 1990. Although no recorded documentation of the origins of this partnership exists, the accounts of several participants indicate that it was brokered by key figures in the Justice Study Group who convinced NIJ leadership and senior MacArthur Foundation officials of the merits of the effort. According to former NIJ staff, the project's prospects for identifying early life predictors of high-rate offending and for providing timely and ongoing policy-relevant research on criminal careers were the basis for NIJ's support. Because there is no record of the original proposal, it is not possible to get a full accounting of the aims of the project at its outset.[15]

The program had four components: (1) a longitudinal cohort study, (2) a community survey, (3) a systematic social observation of communities, and (4) interviews with community leaders. Detailed information about the study can be found in the literature (Tonry, Ohlin, and Farrington, 1991; Earls and Visher, 1997; Inter-university Consortium for Political and Social Research, 2010). The project came to have two principal foci: (1) developmental research on the causes and consequences of individual criminality, the project's initial motivation, and (2) research on the influence of community factors on crime. Indeed, the community research came to

---

[15]The committee requested access to NIJ's working files for the project but was told that they are no longer available. We also asked to see the official grant files kept by OJP that are stored in an offsite data archive facility but were informed that these were missing.

be the dominant legacy of the project, even though it reportedly accounted for only 15 of 207 pages of the original proposal.[16]

ICPSR maintains an inventory of the research products and subsequent analyses of the data. By its count, 94 journal articles, 29 book chapters, 7 conference proceedings, and 9 dissertations are products of the Project on Human Development in Chicago Neighborhoods. Far and away the most cited is a 1997 article that appeared in *Science*. In it Sampson and colleagues introduce and provide empirical support for the concept of collective efficacy, which relates to a community's "linkage of mutual trust and the willingness [of its inhabitants] to intervene for the common good" (Sampson, Raudenbush, and Earls, 1997, p. 919). Two of the other five most-cited articles also concern collective efficacy, and all five involve the use of the community-related data sets assembled by the project.

Even though the initial motivation for NIJ's investment in the Project on Human Development in Chicago Neighborhoods was to investigate the developmental origins of high-rate offending, its dominant legacy, at least so far, is community-related research. There are several explanations for this. One is the productivity and energy of the individuals involved in the planning, design, and management of the project from 1988 to its conclusion as well as the value they placed on community research on crime. Still another factor was the decision not to make the biological correlates and determinants of crime a major design component of the longitudinal data collection. Biology and genetics since have come to be important themes in research on the developmental origins of antisocial behaviors. In addition, there are only three waves of data in the longitudinal component of the project, far fewer than in most modern longitudinal studies. This combined with the overlapping cohort design has complicated the analysis of the data. Finally, the resources were not sufficient either for data collection in more than one site or to conduct studies using experimental designs.

Current Status

NIJ and MacArthur dual support for the project ended in 2001. Research efforts are continuing and are now focused on maximizing the benefits of the investment in data collection by making data and training on its use available to the research community. The MacArthur Foundation has supported a grant to the ICPSR to promote the distribution and use of the data assembled as part of the project. NIJ currently supports secondary

[16]Internal memorandum from Christy Visher, an NIJ staff member, sent to Jeremy Travis, dated June 24, 1999, entitled "Program Review: Project on Human Development in Chicago Neighborhoods, 1990-2001" given to the committee by NIJ.

analysis of data collected through this project through its Data Resources Program (see Chapter 5 for more information).

Progress in Cumulative Knowledge Building

The preceding sections have described collections of grants across broad criminal justice categories. Our review demonstrates that NIJ has funded a number of long-term research efforts and research on very important topics. It continues to build on research in many of the areas reviewed, but research in others has ceased or has been sharply curtailed as sources of funds have dried up.

The development of cumulative knowledge requires both a data infrastructure to support studies and a stream of studies that elaborate on what is known from existing data. These collections show that often NIJ research focused on one or the other. The Project on Human Development in Chicago Neighborhoods and ADAM were efforts that produced large quantities of data, yet the use of these data has either been limited or (in the case of ADAM) eliminated. NIJ has sponsored a great deal of research on interventions, particularly in the areas of policing and violence against women. But critical longitudinal data on violence against women and data on crime trends that will help advance the field are not reflected in these collections.

The lack of stable funding has been a clear restraint on NIJ's ability to develop cumulative research. The committee also notes that other factors have affected its efforts. In developing these descriptions, we were unable to rely on documentation that described the rationale for various research activities, how a particular area of research developed, or how research findings influenced the direction of future work. It was also difficult to identify and review the products of the research. We think this lack of planning and documentation has affected NIJ's effectiveness in building knowledge and discuss these issues more fully in later chapters.

When the ORE research portfolio is viewed from the perspective of a 14-year period, the committee sees evidence of continuity of efforts that signal a significant improvement in cumulative work over what was observed in the earlier NRC review. But continuity of effort was achieved primarily in those areas in which funding was available either through congressionally mandated programs or the willingness of other OJP agencies to transfer monies to NIJ. As funds have declined, projects have been funded in an increasingly ad hoc manner and with great variety in subject matter, theory base, and intended target audience.

Program Evaluations

In our review of ORE's research programs, the committee specifically examined program evaluation activities because they represent a unique kind of research geared to a specific audience. Typically these studies ask questions: What works for whom, when, and under what circumstances? Why does it work? How does it work? The products guide practitioners and policy makers and can, when sufficiently grounded in theory, inform the science of criminology. For many decades, ORE has invested heavily in evaluations of criminal justice programs and policies. These include studies of the impact and consequences of programs, specific interventions, or changes in policy (outcome evaluations) as well as evaluations of the process of program or policy implementation. As part of our study, we reviewed ORE outcome evaluations funded between 1992 and 2008. Although many of them include process evaluation components, we did not review projects that were limited to process evaluation of operations and factors that shape successful program implementation.

Compiling a list of NIJ evaluations was challenging. NIJ's recordkeeping practices have changed over the years, and no central repository of records on its funded projects exists. As a result, our analysis relies on a report by the U.S. Government Accountability Office (GAO) on all 96 social science evaluations identified by NIJ as outcome evaluations funded between 1992 and 2002 (U.S. General Accounting Office, 2003a) and a list of 91 outcome evaluations funded between 2003 and 2008. These outcome evaluations include field-initiated studies proposed by investigators in response to NIJ program solicitations, projects undertaken as part of a mandate to NIJ to evaluate the discretionary grant programs of other OJP divisions, and legislatively mandated evaluations.

The list of 96 outcome evaluations funded between 1992 and 2002, or funded in earlier years but completed between 1997 and 2002, was compiled by NIJ for GAO in 2002. According to GAO, these evaluations included 20 larger studies with total funding of $22.8 million, 51 medium-sized studies with total funding of $11.7 million, and 25 smaller studies with total funding of $2.1 million, together totaling $36.6 million. These evaluations measured program outcomes in a wide variety of areas, including domestic violence, law enforcement, drug abuse, and juvenile justice. The evaluated programs include large national discretionary grant programs, multisite demonstration programs, and local programs or innovations.

The list of 91 outcome evaluations funded by NIJ from 2003 through 2008 was compiled by reviewing the titles of funded projects and locating projects labeled "evaluation" on the NIJ website. NIJ staff screened the preliminary list developed by the committee and identified outcome evaluations based on their knowledge of project goals and grant abstracts. Projects funded in multiple years were combined and treated as single evaluations. Evaluations that did not examine program outcomes were eliminated from the list. Available records did not permit accurate documentation of total funding of these projects, although they did indicate a range of projects, from small evaluations to large multiyear, multisite evaluations receiving large awards.

Between 2003 and 2008, programs related to youth, gangs, and violence against women or family violence were a major focus in nearly half of the outcome evaluations (44 of 91). At least four of these evaluations examined programs funded by discretionary grants from OJJDP and the Office for Violence Against Women, and funds were transferred from those offices for the evaluations. Transferred funds were heavily relied on by NIJ for other kinds of evaluation grants as well. Of the outcome evaluations we identified, more than half (52/91) were funded with transferred monies. Of the approximately $50 million NIJ awarded for outcome evaluations, only $14 million was drawn from its own base funds.

Programs of interest to specific criminal justice agencies, including police, corrections, and courts, were the major focus of two dozen outcome evaluations. A third of these evaluations looked at programs for using new technologies in criminal justice agencies. Multiple awards were also made for the evaluation of programs to combat illicit drug use and distribution, crime and violence prevention programs, programs designed to assist the reentry of prisoners, and programs to assist victims of crime. Most of the organizations conducting the evaluations were colleges and universities (just over a third) and not-for-profit research firms (over a third). Small businesses and practitioner organizations or interest groups conducted about 20 of the evaluations.

Efforts to Improve Outcome Evaluation Quality

Since 2002, NIJ has been the subject of numerous GAO reports that focus on program evaluation efforts (Ekstrand, 2002; U.S. General Accounting Office, 2002, 2003a). These reports are usually conducted at the request of Congress and reflect various members' concerns with the way NIJ is conducting business.

The GAO reviews are sharply critical of evaluation designs and procedures initially proposed by applicants; implementation procedures for the programs and the evaluation that compromised results; selection criteria for programs to be evaluated, especially the lack of representativeness of the programs; and the lack of self-assessment by NIJ of its evaluation and development efforts. These recent criticisms echo those in a 1976 report on the management of the Equipment Improvement Program of NIJ's predecessor (U.S. General Accounting Office, 1976). The GAO evaluations are discussed in more detail in the NRC report *Improving Evaluation of Anticrime Programs* (National Research Council, 2005c) and in Chapter 5.

Pressure to increase support for outcome evaluations with strong experimental or quasi-experimental designs has come from other reviews of NIJ evaluations (Sherman et al., 1997; Visher and Weisburd, 1997; Garner and Maxwell, 2000). Between 1990 and 2000, experimental evaluations comprised a small and declining portion of NIJ research (2.1 percent of all projects, 3.0 percent of all research dollars), despite a sharp rise in evaluation funds following passage of the Crime Act of 1994. The decline in support for experimentation, widely viewed as the most rigorous outcome evaluation design, was not related to funding availability, the nature of salient policy issues, implementation difficulties, average costs, or the availability of interested evaluators (Garner and Visher, 2003). It appears related to NIJ project choices.

NIJ responded to the GAO critiques and other pressures to improve their evaluation activities in several ways. The Evaluation Division was established in 2002 to provide oversight of the evaluation research portfolio. Initially freed from the task of monitoring ongoing evaluation projects, the division was charged with the task of strategic planning and development of strategies for improving evaluation research at NIJ. The Evaluation Division developed a matrix for a database classification of all evaluations. Using this database, the division initiated a semiannual review of all evaluation projects to identify projects in need of more intensive monitoring. Proactive steps to avoid funding problematic evaluations included new language in solicitations prioritizing experimental studies and funding support for preliminary studies, such as evaluability assessments, to help screen out programs that were not ready for evaluation. Many of their activities were endorsed in the report *Improving Evaluation of Anticrime Programs* (National Research Council, 2005c). Efforts to eliminate programs that were not good candidates for evaluation began immediately.

Faced with the mandate to evaluate the discretionary programs of BJP and OJJDP in FY 2002 and FY 2003, NIJ had contractors prepare evaluability assessments on 57 of the 461 BJA and OJJDP programs.[17] Standardized criteria were used to determine whether a rigorous outcome evaluation appeared feasible, what kinds of evaluation design were most viable, and how much the evaluation should cost. Results were posted on the NIJ website to provide guidance to bidders responding to competitive NIJ evaluation solicitations. Results were also used to select evaluation programs.

As noted earlier, NIJ has been highly dependent on transferred funds for

[17]The rest were screened out prior to the evaluability assessment through document review, staff interviews, and site visits as needed.

much of its research and in particular for its evaluation research portfolio. Often it has limited control over the decisions of what programs to evaluate. Evaluability assessments have been a big step forward to identify likely candidates for evaluation and provide a rationale for not proceeding with one when there is every indication the result will not be successful. Part of improving NIJ evaluations will be to establish the kind of infrastructure in which NIJ staff take an active role in defining the types of evaluations that make sense. It will also be important to ensure that NIJ has the authority to decline the responsibility for producing definitive impact evaluation results when it is not scientifically or practically feasible to produce them.

Current Status of Efforts

The Evaluation Division activities ended in December 2005, when its director and two of its three staff left the division and no attempt was made to recruit additional staff. The division was formally dissolved in July 2007 when the evaluation function was transferred to the NIJ director's office. Although NIJ advertised for two senior-level positions with evaluation expertise to advise on evaluation activities, only one of these was filled. A primary responsibility for that position was to assist ORE and OST to develop jointly offered solicitations that integrate social science research with technology implementation. NIJ has continued to fund evaluability assessments when appropriate, but these are now handled by the individual program offices. The other oversight and planning activities undertaken by the Evaluation Division were discontinued. The electronic database of evaluation activities used to track and monitor evaluation grants became inoperable and was not reinstated, and semiannual reviews of evaluation grants ceased. The result has been a decline in strategic planning around outcome evaluation and a lack of consistent record-keeping on evaluation projects. NIJ should restore its evaluation database and reinstate management practices that provide improved oversight. The committee is concerned that, without informed and continuous oversight, future ORE investments in program evaluation will experience problems that undermine the scientific quality of the studies.

Researcher-Practitioner Partnerships

ORE also sponsors evaluation research using an action research model. This is an important way ORE brings research knowledge to the practitioner. In this model, NIJ supports researchers who partner with local criminal justice agencies on issues of mutual interest. Action research is well suited for the complex world of policing. Decisions are made, then tested, and adjusted for a complex world. Such decisions cannot wait for experimental designs and statistical analysis. Yet there is a need to learn from working in this environment. Action research is a cyclical process that involves identifying a problem, planning and implementing action steps, evaluating outcomes, and repeating (Elden and Chisholm, 1993). Typically, a researcher, with an agreement to work with a criminal justice agency, develops a proposal seeking research funding and applies to NIJ. The researcher controls all steps of the research process; the agency participates by providing access to records and staff and by allowing an experiment within its operations.

However, when NIJ introduced Locally Initiated Research Partnerships in 1995 (with support from the COPS office), it changed action research. In this model, the researchers and the criminal justice agency share responsibility and collaborate on all steps of the research process, from design to interpretation of findings (McEwen, 1999).

From 1995 to 1998, NIJ funded 41 locally initiated research partnerships. These partnerships were formed across the nation and among jurisdictions ranging in population size from 2,000 to over 7 million. The partnerships addressed several issues: the organizational development and implementation of community policing, the evaluation of community policing efforts, the implementation of computer mapping, and the management of domestic violence programs (McEwen, 1999). These partnerships varied in expense, with awards ranging from $33,000 to $392,000.

The unprecedented opportunity for these partnerships in policing had its roots in the 1994 Crime Act. This legislation provided a mandate for evaluation of how police departments were using Crime Act funds. The police-researcher partnerships were a mechanism for assessing the effects of adopted solutions as well as advancing continued improvements. NIJ also used available funds to sponsor an evaluation of the partnership program conducted by the Institute for Law and Justice (McEwen, 2003).

This evaluation examined the extent to which partnerships were successful and identified the factors responsible for success (McEwen, 1999). The criteria for success included whether (1) the police department changed policies or practices as a result of the research or collaboration, (2) information systems were developed or improved, and (3) the partnership continued beyond the initial research project. The evaluation found several examples of partnerships that satisfied each of these criteria.

Building on the success of these initial partnerships and the knowledge gained from an evaluation of this program, NIJ continued to use the action research model in other partnership programs examining gun violence, such as Project Safe Neighborhoods and its predecessor. It is also collaborating with the International Association of Chiefs of Police to identify research topics of relevance to police agencies and to encourage police-researcher partnerships. This funding was renewed as recently as FY 2009.

Although NIJ continues to encourage collaborations between researchers and practitioners in its solicitation language, the committee could not find documentation after 2001 that indicated whether recent research awards supported this action research model.

In FY 2009, NIJ released the solicitation *Building and Enhancing Researcher-Practitioner Partnerships*. Funding is to support preparation of articles that describe past and current partnerships, support for a junior faculty member to conduct research, and the placement of a researcher in a criminal justice organization. A total of $1 million is being made available for up to 3 years. As of this writing, the committee does not know what, if any, proposals were funded.

The committee thinks that researcher-practitioner partnerships can be used effectively by NIJ to develop strategies for responding to pressures to improve the administration of justice. They offer two advantages: a timely response to pressing issues and an experience-grounded method of developing and testing program feasibility. The disadvantages are also twofold: the strategies are not subjected to rigorous outcome evaluation, which means they need to be positioned in a continuum of R&D activities that ensures more rigorous testing will follow, and the expense is relatively large, given that it is not clear to what extent lessons learned can be generalized to other settings. These pros and cons should be carefully weighed by NIJ as part of a broader agenda-setting process.

OFFICE OF SCIENCE AND TECHNOLOGY

NIJ, through its OST and its predecessors, has a long history of seeking solutions to law enforcement technology problems. It has done this by funding grants in key areas of law enforcement technology development, pursuing cooperative research projects with other federal agencies, developing standards for law enforcement products, and working closely with state and local public safety agencies. It was recognized early that few technology devices were ever conceived and developed specifically for law enforcement applications. NIJ has therefore taken the role of fulfilling special technology needs for state and local law enforcement and fostering technology R&D when it otherwise will not occur.

A focus on the development of new or improved technologies was included as part of the original charge to the National Institute of Law Enforcement and Criminal Justice (NILECJ) (see Chapter 2). After its inception in 1968, NILECJ began making grants in key areas of law enforcement technology, such as automatic surveillance/alarm systems, communications, and nonlethal weapons. It also began holding discussions on specific cooperative research projects with other federal agencies, including the U.S. Department of Defense, on a personal transceiver for police, riot control agents, night vision equipment, and nonlethal bullets (Law Enforcement Assistance Administration, 1969). As one might expect, given NIJ's reorganization history, frequent changes in directors, and several legislative changes (described in Chapter 2), the early efforts in science and technology bounced among offices and divisions and were often split between offices as defined by the nature of the work.

In 1995, all of NIJ's science and technology efforts were brought together with the creation of OST. OST was tasked with providing federal, state, and local law enforcement and corrections agencies with access to the best technologies available and supporting the development or adaptation of advanced technologies that will increase efficiency and effectiveness of the criminal justice system.

In November 2002, Congress mandated the establishment of OST in the Homeland Security Act of 2002. The act specified as its mission "to serve as the national focal point for work on law enforcement technology; and to carry out programs that, through the provision of equipment, training, and technical assistance, improve the safety and effectiveness of law enforcement technology and improve access to such technology by federal, state, and local law enforcement agencies."[18] The mission and duties codified in the Homeland Security Act were not unlike what OST had been carrying out previously.[19] However, it established OST as its own entity and somewhat divorced it from the oversight of NIJ.

In the past 14 years, NIJ's science and technology (S&T) research enterprise has greatly expanded. A process known as RDT&E (research, development, testing, and evaluation) undergirds OST activities, and a system of technology centers, known collectively as the National Law Enforcement and Corrections Technology Center (NLECTC) system, supports that process. The following sections, which include descriptions of the RDT&E process, the center system, and the funding and selected accomplishments of the research portfolio, aim to capture the research activities of OST. These activities can be viewed as the initial steps in the commercialization of new technologies appropriate for a federal research agency; i.e., efforts to identify technology needs and existing research gaps, to support R&D to fill those knowledge gaps, and to sponsor operational testing and demon-

---

[18]The act defined the term "law enforcement technology" to include "investigative and forensic technologies, corrections technologies, and technologies that support the judicial process."

[19]The act also specified OST's duties to include the following, among others: (1) establishing and maintaining advisory groups to assess federal, state, and local technology needs; (2) establishing and maintaining performance standards, and testing, evaluating, certifying, validating, and marketing products that conform to those standards; (3) carrying out research, development, testing, evaluation, and cost-benefit analysis of certain technologies; and (4) developing and disseminating technical assistance and training materials (U.S. General Accounting Office, 2003b).

stration of promising prototypes. Other activities which are less focused on building knowledge but more focused on disseminating knowledge and/or resources, are described in Chapter 5.

Research, Development, Testing, and Evaluation

The RDT&E process was created in response to the Homeland Security Act of 2002 and an external assessment of NLECTC system (Pymatuning Group, 1998).[20] Both the legislation and the assessment draw attention to "the need for [NIJ and its] Center system to support technology R&D for the entire criminal justice community, not just those agencies benefiting from time to time from direct technology assistance" (National Institute of Justice, 2004b, p. 10). The RDT&E process consists of five phases:

Phase 1: Determine technology needs.
Phase 2: Develop technology program plans to address those needs.
Phase 3: Perform research and development to develop solutions.
Phase 4: Demonstrate, test, and evaluate potential solutions for practice.
Phase 5: Conduct outreach and dissemination to assist practitioners in the use of new technologies.

The RDT&E process is highly touted by NIJ in its publications and by OST leadership in briefings as a way to align the S&T portfolio with the technology needs of the criminal justice community and to bring the work of the center system into a systematic process tied to strategic planning (National Institute of Justice, 2004b). In the remainder of this chapter, we examine Phases 2 and 3 through a review of OST's research portfolio in order to understand how it supports R&D of technologies for law enforcement. First, however, we introduce NLECTC, which has primary involvement in Phases 1, 4, and 5.

National Law Enforcement and Corrections Technology Center System

The NLECTC system is viewed as "an integral part of NIJ's Science and Technology program" (National Institute of Justice, 2009b). Its duties, spelled out in the Homeland Security Act of 2002, include (1) to support R&D of law enforcement technology, (2) to support the transfer and implementation of technology, (3) to assist in the development and dissemination of guidelines and technological standards, and (4) to provide technology

---

[20]For a description, see http://www.ojp.usdoj.gov/nij/topics/technology/research-development-process.htm [accessed September 9, 2009].

assistance, information, and support for law enforcement, corrections, and criminal justice purposes.

NLECTC is highly involved in Phases 1, 4, and 5 of the RDT&E process outlined above. For Phase 1, the NLECTC centers split the administration of various Technical Working Groups and maintain other links to practitioners in order to identify their high-priority technology needs. This advisory capacity is discussed in Chapter 4. In Phase 5, NLECTC activities include technology assistance, curricula development, training, standards development, certification and compliance testing, publications, conferences, and other third-party guidance for the procurement of technology. Many of these activities are illustrated in Chapter 5. Later in this chapter, we describe the Phase 4 role in implementing demonstrations and performing technology evaluations.

Initial Growth

Established in 1994, the NLECTC system was preceded by NIJ's Technology Assessment Program Information Center and to a lesser extent the Equipment Systems Improvement Program, both of which contained mechanisms for assessing the needs of the field and maintained a link to the Law Enforcement Standards Laboratory.

In 1994, Congress appropriated funds to develop a technology information exchange network and earmarked funds for the establishment of specific centers in the NLECTC system. Those centers became known as the regional centers and included NLECTC–Northeast in Rome, New York; NLECTC–Southeast in Charleston, South Carolina; NLECTC–Rocky Mountain in Denver, Colorado; and NLECTC–West in El Segundo, California. Each center was set up under the auspices of a larger institution, so it could draw on institutional resources. The existing National Center in Maryland, which administers the compliance testing program and dissemination efforts, and the existing law enforcement standards laboratory, which became known as the Office of Law Enforcement Standards, were subsumed under the umbrella of the NLECTC system. The Office of Law Enforcement Technology Commercialization, located at the National Technology Transfer Center in Wheeling, West Virginia, also became part of the NLECTC system in 1995. Additional centers were added to the system through subsequent appropriations and earmarks. These centers include NLECTC–Northwest in Anchorage, Alaska; the Border Research and Technology Center in San Diego, California, and Austin, Texas; and the Rural Law Enforcement Technology Center in Hazard, Kentucky.

The NLECTC system is not the result of top-down planning and design. It just grew. The creation and location of many of the centers were dictated by external pressure, and hence the areas of specialization and the personnel, linked closely with the host institutions, were not the careful choice of the NIJ and OST leadership.

Further Evolution

The passage of the Homeland Security Act in 2002 allowed NIJ and OST to "establish new centers through a merit-based, competitive process." In 2007, four centers of excellence (COEs) were added to the NLECTC system through a competitive proposal process, as legislatively authorized: (1) the Communications COE in Camden, New Jersey; (2) the Forensic Science COE in Largo, Florida; (3) the Sensors, Surveilance and Biometrics COE in New York City; and (4) the Weapons and Protective Equipment COE in State College, Pennsylvania. The addition of the COEs marked the first time NIJ had discretion over their number and specializations.

The NLECTC system is currently evolving. The recent addition of COEs is redefining the roles and functions of each center. Staff resources are changing, and funds are being shifted between centers. Whether or not the new COEs improve the overall function remains to be seen. Until FY 2009, funds were specifically appropriated by Congress to NLECTC; these appropriations ranged from $5-10 million in the late 1990s and rose to roughly $20 million a year for FY 2004 through FY 2008. Funding for the NLECTC system is generally much greater than the appropriations designated by Congress because the individual centers are assigned additional projects as appropriate to their expertise. The additional funding can stem from OST discretionary funds, transferred funds from other agencies, or additional earmarks.[21]

The centers existing prior to 2007 serve as the initial point of entry for technology information and generalized technology assistance. Their task is to focus on criminal justice agencies in their respective regions or domains (i.e., rural or border agencies) and to provide these agencies with access to information, both the relevant scientific and technology-related results of NIJ's RDT&E activities and the resources available from NIJ. They also work with constituents to identify unique regional technology needs. Some of these centers now play a secondary role to that of the COEs in coordinating technology demonstration, test, and evaluation activities.

The new COEs currently serve as the authoritative resource in their respective technology focus areas and handle more complicated technical

[21]For example, the NLECTC–Southeast was appropriated several million dollars over several years for the implementation of Project Seahawk, a pilot project to enhance coastal city security and law enforcement. This funding was provided for the acquisition of communications equipment, computer software and hardware technology, and R&D needed to execute the project.

problems (National Institute of Justice, 2009b). For the most part, they do not provide any new services; they have inherited or reoperationalized services previously provided by other centers or NIJ-funded entities. They are, however, looking into doing things in different ways and leveraging different facilities and expertise for conducting demonstrations, testing, and evaluations. During our 2008 site visits, the committee observed that the relationship of the centers of excellence to the regional centers was not crisply defined and that the information and work flow between them, as well as between the centers and the programmatic divisions of OST, was not at all clear. The committee further noted that the COE staff varied considerably in their qualifications in the relevant fields, a variation that NIJ staff did not appear to recognize.

In a March 2008 hearing before the House Committee on Appropriations, Subcommittee on Commerce, Justice, Science, and Related Agencies, no funding was requested for NLECTC in FY 2009. This effectively returned the roughly $20 million earmarked for NLECTC to NIJ's discretionary budget and released OST from the responsibility of managing specific centers previously mandated. For the first time in NLECTC's history, NIJ has the authority to define the locations and specializations of the entire NLECTC system. On May 21, 2009, NIJ posted three solicitations with regard to NLECTC: (1) *Criminal Justice Technology Regional Centers*, (2) *Criminal Justice Technology Center of Excellence for Information and Sensor Systems*, and (3) *Criminal Justice Electronic Crime Technology Center of Excellence*. Under the first solicitation, NIJ sought applications for funding to conduct regional outreach activities in the NLECTC system. The other two solicitations sought applicants for two new COEs. Applicants could propose, in their respective technology area of information and sensor systems or electronic crime, a plan to conduct many of the center activities described. These solicitations indicate that the applicants "should expect that the majority of their work will be on projects specifically defined by NIJ in support of the specific technology investment portfolio areas" (National Institute of Justice, 2009b).

During the course of this study, we witnessed several changes to the center assignments. The Office of Law Enforcement Technology Commercialization was discontinued early on. At the writing of this report, the 2009 solicitations were awarded. With these awards, the NLECTC system was redefined into three regional centers that represent (1) Alaska, (2) small, rural, tribal, and border law enforcement, and (3) larger criminal justice agencies in states, major cities, and counties; five COEs; and the existing NLECTC–National and the Office of Law Enforcement Standards. It appears that only one award went to a new grantee; most of the awards went to grantees who had previously administered NLECTC centers. The new awards and continuations for NLECTC in FY 2009 totaled $39 million. External assessments of the NLECTC system were conducted in the early 1990s (Pymatuning Group, 1998; Schwabe, Davis, and Jackson, 2001), and a report assessing the effectiveness of the existing center system was transmited to Congress by NIJ in 2005 (National Institute of Justice, 2004b). The new structure of centers aligned to OST's RDT&E process and assigned through merit-based, competitive awards will require a formal assessment in the coming years to measure and document any improvements from the previously mandated and loosely defined system.

Research Portfolio

From technology needs funneled up from practitioner advisory groups[22] through NLECTC, OST program managers develop multiyear program plans by considering whether technological solutions to meet those needs already exist or whether solutions need to be developed. Technology program plans are developed in collaboration with other agencies to aid in identifying existing solutions or determining if other development work can be leveraged to serve dual-use purposes.[23] One such formal arrangement is the 1401 Technology Transfer Program (see Box 3-5).

OST benefits from participation in this program. In leveraging other agencies' investment, OST is able to spend its limited money where it is needed most by law enforcement. For example, it invests less in explosive detection because there is already significant investment in it by the Department of Homeland Security and the Department of Defense; it invests more in remote weapons detection because there is not.

When critical gaps in technology development are identified, NIJ looks for ways to support such development. The committee observes that NIJ addresses practitioner-identified technology needs in four ways:

1. through research grants competitively awarded as a result of annual science and technology solicitations,
2. through research grants awarded in response to congressional earmarks,
3. through interagency agreements when R&D in other agencies can be extended to law enforcement applications, and
4. through operational testing and demonstrations primarily orchestrated by NLECTC.

---

[22]See Chapter 4 for a discussion of the Technology Working Groups and the Law Enforcement and Corrections Technology Advisory Council.

[23]"Dual use" generally refers to technologies that were developed for military purposes and can be adapted for law enforcement purposes.

BOX 3-5
1401 Technology Transfer Program

On December 2, 2002, Congress enacted legislation (Section 1401 of P.L. 107-314, the Bob Stump National Defense Authorization Act of 2003) aimed at leveraging the Department of Defense's (DOD's) technology and logistics capabilities to assist first responders. What became known as the 1401 Technology Transfer Program formalized NIJ's efforts to leverage military technology for criminal justice applications. The 1401 program is an agreement among DOD, the Department of Homeland Security (DHS), and the Department of Justice (DOJ) "to conduct a program to facilitate the transfer from the Department of Defense to the first responder community, including law enforcement responders, of technology items and equipment to enhance public safety and improve homeland security."*

DOD identifies available technologies and equipment. DHS and DOJ coordinate identifying and prioritizing first responder needs as well as communicating with first responders and facilitating awareness of available technology. The agency working groups communicate regularly to identify technology matches, to prioritize technology to be expedited, to develop plans of action, and to identify areas for collaboration in R&D and eliminate redundant and unnecessary research efforts.

The goal of the 1401 program is to provide first responders with tools needed to protect the homeland. The program provides first responders with tools in four ways.

1. First responders can purchase off-the-shelf equipment from a DOD contract.
2. DHS/DOJ will fund research to modify existing equipment for first responders.
3. DHS/DOJ will fund research to develop technology solely for first responders.
4. DOD will expedite R&D and commercialization for dual-use technologies (Lapham, 2005).

---

*A copy of the *Memorandum of Agreement among The Department of Defense, Office of the Assistant Secretary of Defense for Homeland Defense; the U.S. Department of Homeland Security, Directorate of Science and Technology; and the U.S. Department of Justice, Office of Justice Programs, National Institute of Justice Regarding the Transfer of Technology Items and Equipment in Support of Homeland Security and Public Safety,* signed November 2005, was provided to the committee by NIJ, July 2008.

OST primarily supports applied research rather than basic research, since its goal is to bring affordable and effective equipment for law enforcement and corrections to market. Supported projects often entail improving or adapting existing technologies for criminal justice applications. OST specifically looks for projects that address issues of commercialization and wide adoption into law enforcement. The ultimate goal of its research portfolio is to get effective technologies into the hands of first responders. Substantive areas of its research portfolio are listed in Box 3-1.

In order to get a clear picture of what sort of projects and agreements constitute the R&D portfolio, the committee reviewed collective information, available only for the period 2004-2008, on solicitations, grant awards, earmarks, and interagency agreements as well as FY 2006 technology program plans.

Competitively Awarded Grants

During the period FY 2005 to FY 2008, solicitations were issued for research and technology development in the following areas: biometrics, body armor, communications, concealed weapons detection, crime scene tools, defeat of improvised explosive devices, electronic crime, forensic DNA research, forensic anthropology and odontology, forensic toxicology, geospatial, general forensics, information-led policing, corrections, less lethal weapons, modeling and simulation, personal protective equipment, pursuit management, school safety, and sensors and surveillance. In addition, there were a few calls for specified technology development, such as fast capture fingerprint/palm print technology (FY 2005); quantitative research on friction ridge patterns (FY 2005); and R&D on impression evidence (FY 2006, FY 2007).

With three exceptions for the period FY 2004 to FY 2007, each solicitation produced at least one award. An average of three grants was awarded in response to a particular solicitation for technology R&D. In FY 2008, however, six solicitations[24] for technology R&D went unfunded. Total new funding for competitively awarded R&D awards amounted to $8.5 million (FY 2004); $17.4 million (FY 2005); $14.3 million (FY 2006); $19 million (FY 2007); and $13.3 million (FY 2008). Each fiscal year, there are always continuation awards to supplement or advance previously awarded research grants. With the information available, the committee was unable to separate funding amounts for continuing research grants from other OST

[24]These solicitations included *Body Armor for Law Enforcement and Corrections*; *Biometric Technologies*; *Communications Technology*; *Information-Led Policing Research, Technology Development, Testing, and Evaluation*; *Less Lethal Technologies*; *Sensor and Surveillance Technologies*.

continuations. The funds for these awards are drawn primarily from the OST base budget, the Edward Byrne Memorial Justice Assistance Grant for development and demonstration of law enforcement technologies and tools, and monies available for DNA research and development in the Justice for All Act of 2004 (President's DNA Initiative) and are supplemented by transfer funds from other federal agencies.

One example of a highly cooperative effort among federal agencies is the solicitation for fast capture fingerprint/palm print technology (FY 2005). Funds were transferred to NIJ from FBI/Criminal Justice Information Services division, the Justice Management Division, and the Department of Homeland Security to support three different technological approaches in separate grants. Each of these funded projects produced a working device suitable for testing. NIJ subsequently funded the National Institute of Standards and Technology, through an interagency agreement, to conduct an independent technology assessment using its own and FBI image and performance standards. According to one of the grantees (TBS North America), the product enabled by the $3.6 million award through NIJ is now in field tests and anticipated for production in 2010.[25]

Congressional Earmarks

OST was also tasked with managing a number of earmarks. Earmarks are designated by Congress for a specific purpose to a specific recipient.[26] The total amount in earmarks assigned to OST was about $65 million in FY 2004, $52 million in FY 2005, $38 million in FY 2006, zero in FY 2007,[27] and $16 million in FY 2008. The grants resulting from earmarks cover a broad range of activities, from academic research to knowledge applications:

- **Research projects,** such as an award to Brown University to advance nanotechnologies in an effort to miniaturize DNA testing instruments.

---

[25]See http://www.tbsinc.com/cms/front_content.php?idart=6 [accessed November 11, 2009].

[26]OMB defines earmarks as "funds provided by the Congress for projects, programs, or grants where the purported congressional direction (whether in statutory text, report language, or other communication) circumvents otherwise applicable merit-based or competitive allocation processes, or specifies the location or recipient, or otherwise curtails the ability of the executive branch to manage its statutory and constitutional responsibilities pertaining to the funds allocation process." See http://earmarks.omb.gov/earmarks_definition.html [accessed March 17, 2010].

[27]OJP did not receive any earmarks in FY 2007 (Office of Justice Programs, 2007a). However, about $6 million was awarded through OST continuations to grantees and projects previously identified in FY 2005 and FY 2006 earmarks.

- **Technology development and improvement,** such as an award to the New Jersey Institute of Technology to improve its patented dynamic grip recognition technology and move child-safe handgun technology closer to commercialization and an award to the Worcester Polytechnic Institute to develop electronic systems as part of its Precision Personnel Locator Project.
- **Integration programs,** such as the Consolidated Advanced Technologies for Law Enforcement assigned to the University of New Hampshire. In these generally collaborative efforts between researchers and law enforcement agencies, funds are provided to evaluate, demonstrate, develop, and finally deploy an advanced technology system.
- **R&D centers,** such as the Southwest Public Safety Technology Center at the University of Houston and the Steganography Analysis and Research Center.
- **NLECTC activities,** including funds specified for the administration and operation of specific centers.
- **Information clearinghouses,** such as the funds to Stetson University to manage the National Clearinghouse for Science, Technology, and Law.
- **Academic and training programs,** such as the Marshall University Forensic Science Center and the model technology-delivered training programs in DNA education tested and evaluated by the National Forensic Science Technology Center.
- **Upgraded operations,** such as the Technology Improvement Project for the Middle Rio Grande Region of Texas, which replaced communications systems to facilitate information sharing among the small and rural agencies in this region.

Interagency Agreements

Another mechanism for funding R&D is interagency agreements. Information about funded awards identified as interagency agreements is available only for FY 2007 and FY 2008; the total amounts for these years are $8.9 million and $10.8 million, respectively. About half of these monies went to the National Institute of Standards and Technology, which has a long-standing relationship with NIJ in developing standards for law enforcement equipment and conducting evaluations of prototype technologies (discussed further in Chapter 5). Other examples include agreements with the Armed Forces Institute of Pathology/Armed Forces DNA Identification Laboratory for enhancing the size, sampling, and quality of forensic mitochondrial DNA databases; with the Air Force Research Laboratory to support the operations and activities of NLECTC–Northeast; and with the

Department of Defense to expand its Cyber Crime Institute cryptographic project.

Operational Testing and Demonstrations

Funds distributed for operational testing and demonstrations round out the rest of the technology portfolio. To adequately serve practitioners, NIJ invests in understanding the capabilities and limitations of technologies. NIJ supports, often in coordination with NLECTC, the operational testing of technologies in law enforcement and correctional settings in order to capture much needed information on how devices operate in practice and how people respond to the devices. NIJ is expected to publish the findings of these tests so that all potential manufacturers may benefit, not just the vendor that supplied the technology for the testing. The goal is to provide independent evidence about how effective a technology can be in an operational environment.

Operational testing and demonstrations are generally arranged by a memorandum of understanding with vendors and funded through interagency agreements with other federal agencies or through cooperative agreements with NLECTC centers. At times, the actual testing or demonstration is then subcontracted. There have also been a few awards for operational tests in response to solicitations, since R&D solicitations often allow for the testing and evaluation of technologies.

Through our site visits to some NLECTC centers and discussions with OST staff, the committee became aware that a number of operational tests and demonstrations take place each year. The efforts that were highlighted for us include evaluation of the Safeview MMW Portal, a remote weapons detection technology, at Graterford, Pennsylvania (Bulman, 2009); evaluation of the regional Voice Over Internet Protocol pilot (Bulman, 2008); evaluation of software-defined radio technology developed by the military for public safety application in Orangetown, New York (National Institute of Justice, 2007a); and the Segway® Human Transporter Loaner and Evaluation Program (National Institute of Justice, 2004a).

However, the total number and funding for operational testing and demonstrations are impossible to discern from the financial information available.

Overview of the Total Budget

The committee received financial data with OST expenditures summarized as discretionary versus nondiscretionary as well as split into four categories (R&D; testing, evaluation, and standards; technology assistance; and capacity building). Figure 3-4 plots how rapidly the overall budget, including the total R&D budget, grew from 1994 to 2001. After 2001,

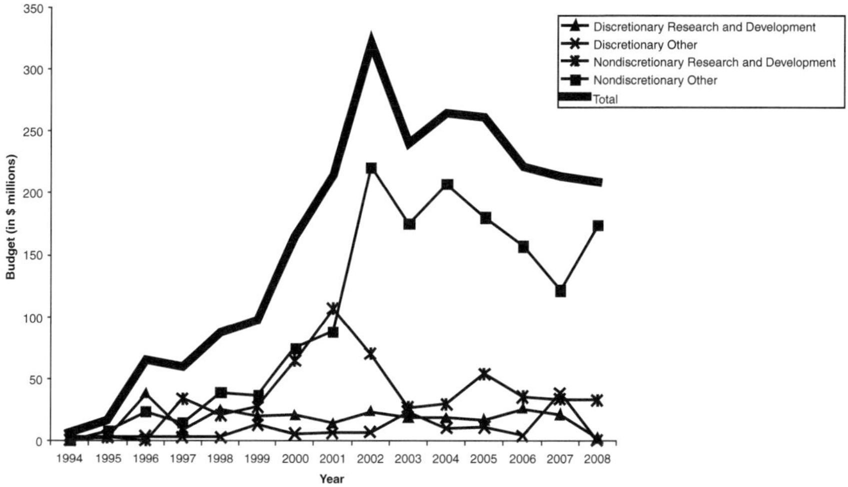

FIGURE 3-4 OST funding history, 1994-2008 (in constant 2008 dollars).
SOURCE: Adapted from figures supplied by OST.

nondiscretionary funds, primarily for capacity building, continued to rise; funds for R&D declined, then stabilized. From 1994 to 2001, the R&D budget represented roughly 50 percent of the overall budget; from 2002 to 2007, it fell to 25 percent. The figure illustrates that, as the OST budget increased, a significant portion of its funds was nondiscretionary, designated for specific programmatic uses or for specific research projects. As a result, OST had discretion for only 10-25 percent of its budget for the period 2003-2007. Although the R&D budget for developing technologies has increased greatly since 1994, OST has less control over that money and the direction of its research portfolio.

Contributions from R&D Investments

Through its investment in science and technology R&D, NIJ has made significant contributions to improving the safety as well as the efficiency of criminal justice operations. Here we highlight investments in the development of soft body armor, the advancement of DNA technology, and research on less lethal technologies. These areas were identified by NIJ leadership as among the technology programs in which NIJ has been influential. They also represent three different developments in the growth and decline of a research portfolio.

The body armor portfolio, a mainstay program for NIJ, is an example of an initiative that led to a long-term compliance testing role for the agency.

In the early 1970s, NIJ initiated R&D on body armor for law enforcement that was quickly adopted by industry. Although less involved in the R&D of body armor today, NIJ has remained active in the area through its well-regarded program for standard development and compliance testing.

The DNA technology portfolio illustrates how sustained funding over time can facilitate a long-term research agenda. Through its DNA technology portfolio, NIJ has been able to extend fruitful research in biology and medicine to forensic applications. With support from the President's DNA Initiative and other legislative initiatives, NIJ has been able to sustain a long-term research agenda in this area, which is still thriving.

The portfolio on less lethal technologies is an example of a research agenda focused on short-term solutions due to limited discretionary funding. The portfolio of less lethal technologies is illustrative of several other technology portfolios, such as those of the development of communications, corrections, information-led policing, and school safety technologies. It grew out of national controversy, makes progress by leveraging other R&D work, has covered a broad range of efforts to fill immediate knowledge gaps, and is limited from addressing priority research needs because of low funding.

Body Armor

In the early 1970s, NIJ initiated a research program to investigate the development of lightweight body armor that police could wear. The program identified several new materials with excellent ballistics-resistant properties that could be woven into a lightweight fabric. NIJ then funded the production and field testing of 5,000 vests made from Kevlar®, a ballistic-resistant fabric (National Institute of Justice, 2003d). The laboratory and field research determined that producing body armor suitable for police use was achievable, and an industry was born.

At the same time, NIJ supported a parallel effort to develop performance standards for the body armor, which is described in Chapter 5. Today, much of the investment with regard to body armor goes to support the compliance testing program and standards revisions. However, it does still contribute to the R&D of body armor when it identifies gaps in industries' R&D efforts. The research program in body armor aims to develop new testing methods that address environmental impacts, multihit capacity, and nondestructive evaluation; to advance ballistic materials towards lighter, flexible, and durable vests; and to improve the design, comfort, and coverage of vests.

Some of the recent awards include support to Cornell University and Lawrence Technical University to work on advanced body armor designs for size and gender variations and improved area coverage, respectively, and to the Office of Law Enforcement Standards at the National Institute of Standards and Technology to develop a conditioning process to test performance of body armor after significant use and to assist in the revision of NIJ's standard for ballistic resistance of body armor released July 2008 (Office of Law Enforcement Standards, 2008). Because advances in weapons and ammunition technology constantly pose new threats, the need for R&D of more effective personal body armor is ongoing.

DNA Technology

Support of DNA technology began in 1986 (National Institute of Justice, 1987, 1992; Sensabaugh, n.d.), as techniques for mapping and sequencing the human genome, developing in both basic biology and medicine, began to be seen as having applicability to forensic science. A 1987 criminal conviction in Florida based on DNA typing began the transfer of DNA analysis technologies from research laboratories to forensic laboratories and courts (U.S. Congress, Office of Technology Assessment, 1990). The quick adoption of DNA profiling, with significant consequences, created concerns about reliability and methodological standards among scientific and legal communities, as well as congressional interest. Several expert panels (U.S. Congress, Office of Technology Assessment, 1990; National Research Council, 1992a, 1996a) addressed questions regarding DNA profiling and made recommendations to Congress and federal agencies.

NIJ played a role in this national assessment of DNA profiling by providing support, in collaboration with other agencies, to several NRC studies; awarding a few research grants in new areas of DNA testing; and initiating a program to examine standards for DNA processing (U.S Congress, Office of Technology Assessment, 1990). This began what would become a significant investment in DNA technology for NIJ. As part of the 1994 Crime Act, the DNA Identification Act made monies available to NIJ to launch a research agenda as well as to assist state and local agencies more directly in building their forensic capacities (see Chapter 5 for forensic capacity-building efforts). In 1995, NIJ began a 5-year research agenda with $3-5 million a year to spend on DNA research.

In 1998, the National Commission on the Future of DNA Evidence was created at the request of Attorney General Janet Reno. The commission consisted of representatives from prosecutors, the defense bar, law enforcement, the scientific community, the medical examiner community, academia, and victims' rights organizations. Its charge was to submit recommendations to the attorney general that would help ensure more effective use of DNA analysis. In addition to an R&D working group, there were also workgroups tasked with examining crime scene investigation and evidence collection, laboratory funding, and legal issues. The R&D working group was asked to project the technical advances in the forthcoming decade and assess their expected impact on forensic DNA analysis (National Commission on the Future of DNA Evidence, 2000). These projections helped advance NIJ's research agenda for another 5 years. NIJ's support of DNA research for forensic applications continues today because of the President's DNA Initiative,[28] which has tripled its budget[29] for DNA research.

Since 1999, NIJ has released an annual solicitation, *Forensic DNA Research & Development*, seeking applications for R&D that can enhance the forensic uses of DNA technology. Over the years, its forensic DNA R&D program has drawn on the research of molecular biology, genetics, and biotechnology to develop highly discriminating, reliable, cost-effective, and rapid forensic DNA testing methods. The portfolio has contained research that supports (1) developing tools and technologies to reduce the time, cost, and labor needed for DNA analysis; (2) improving the success rate of the analysis of DNA evidence that is old, scant, damaged, degraded, or otherwise compromised; (3) identifying and characterizing genetic markers that will reveal additional information about the victim, perpetrator, or the circumstances surrounding a crime; (4) increasing the discriminatory power of DNA analysis; and (5) improving the methods for separating mixtures of DNA, especially from sexual assault evidence.[30]

Funds from the President's DNA Initiative also support a website (http://www.dna.gov [accessed March 17, 2010]) managed by NIJ. On the site, there is a database of DNA research supported by NIJ, sorted by research area, with links to the more than 100 peer-reviewed articles and reports resulting from this research. The DNA research portfolio is one of the few areas in which it would be relatively easy to track NIJ's investment and assess its accomplishments externally.

Some of the accomplishments of this research portfolio, according to NIJ, include the following:

- the development of a testing system that can generate a DNA profile from aged, degraded, or damaged samples, such as skeletal remains;

---

[28]The President's DNA Initiative is the cornerstone of the 2004 Justice for All Act. It provided over $1 billion over a 5-year period to improve the use of DNA in the criminal justice system and to ensure that this technology reaches its full potential. Under this initiative, the attorney general was asked to provide funds, training, and assistance to eliminate DNA backlogs, strengthen crime laboratory capacity, stimulate research and development, and provide training. See http://www.usdoj.gov/ag/dnapolicybooktoc.htm [accessed September 16, 2009].

[29]For example, in FY 2006, NIJ spent over $13 million from the President's DNA Initiative on DNA research and development (National Institute of Justice, 2008a).

[30]Briefing paper on DNA research and development prepared for the committee by NIJ, December 2008.

- tools to enhance the discriminatory power as well as the methods used in the analysis of mitochondrial DNA;
- building on methods used in medicine, the development of novel tools to expedite the detection and separation of sperm cells in sexual assault evidence;
- demonstration that male-specific DNA markers can be detected in sexual assault evidence collected 5 or more days after a sexual assault occurs;
- development of a method that, in a single test, performs the simultaneous assessment of total human DNA, human male DNA, DNA degradation, and the presence of inhibitors in forensic samples; and
- development of a prototype miniaturized DNA testing device that can function both in the forensic laboratory and at the crime scene.

Although NIJ research has contributed to advances in DNA technology, the recent NRC report (2009c) concluded that the level of support has fallen short of what is needed by the forensic science community. There are a number of open research questions, particularly for forensic techniques that receive less attention than DNA technologies (see National Research Council, 2009c, as well as a summary of that report's research recommendations in Appendix E). According to the report, NIJ's current awards in forensic science R&D do not appear to address these questions. The NRC report calls for the establishment of a new independent federal entity responsible for forensic science activities. Should the Congress adopt this recommendation, NIJ's role in sponsoring forensic science R&D would need to be reconsidered (see Box 3-6).

Less Lethal Technologies

Like other research areas, NIJ's research program on less lethal technologies grew out of national controversy. In the 1985 case *Tennessee v. Garner* (471 U.S. 1), the Supreme Court concluded that deadly force may not be used unless it is necessary to prevent suspect escape and an officer has probable cause to believe that the suspect poses a significant threat of death or serious physical injury to the officer or others. The decision sparked the search for weapons that would avoid injury and death but would aid in detaining fleeing suspects who posed little threat. After a 1986 national conference on less lethal weapons convened by the attorney general (Sweetman, 1987), NIJ's research program was established.

The first research award under this program was made in 1987 to assess the feasibility of a dart that could deliver a safe but incapacitating chemical to a fleeing suspect (Hart, 2002a). In the past 20 years, the program has

BOX 3-6
Creation of a National Institute of Forensic Science

The Committee on Identifying the Needs of the Forensic Sciences Community in its report, *Strengthening Forensic Science in the United States: A Path Forward* (National Research Council, 2009c), proposed the following recommendation:

> To promote the development of forensic science into a mature field of multidisciplinary research and practice, founded on the systematic collection and analysis of relevant data, Congress should establish and appropriate funds for an independent federal entity, the National Institute of Forensic Science (NIFS) . . . NIFS should focus on:
>
> (a) establishing and enforcing best practices for forensic science professionals and laboratories; (b) establishing standards for the mandatory accreditation of forensic science laboratories and the mandatory certification of forensic scientists and medical examiners/forensic pathologists—and identifying the entity/entities that will develop and implement accreditation and certification; (c) promoting scholarly, competitive peer-reviewed research and technical development in the forensic science disciplines and forensic medicine; (d) developing a strategy to improve forensic science research and educational programs, including forensic pathology; (e) establishing a strategy based on accurate data on the forensic science community, for the efficient allocation of available funds to give strong support to forensic methodologies and practices in addition to DNA analysis; (f) funding state and local forensic science agencies, independent research projects, and educational programs as recommended in this report, with conditions that aim to advance the credibility and reliability of the forensic science disciplines; (g) overseeing education standards and the accreditation of forensic science programs in colleges and universities; (h) developing programs to improve understanding of the forensic science disciplines and their limitations within legal systems; and (i) assessing the development and introduction of new technologies in forensic investigations, including a comparison of new technologies with former ones.

expanded to include a broad class of less lethal weapons that address a wide range of possible applications. These types of weapons include chemicals, conducted energy devices, directed energy devices, light and noise distractions, physical barriers such as nets and foams, blunt-force controls, as well as vehicle-stopping technologies. These weapons are used not only to stop fleeing suspects but also to control crowds and other potentially violent situations while protecting bystanders and preventing unnecessary injury to offenders and officers. As part of this research program, NIJ not only supports the development of improved devices but also encourages better understanding of the health and safety risks. The agency solicits research to identify new psychological and physiological vulnerabilities that such devices might exploit.

As a result of its investments, NIJ has assisted in the development of less lethal devices, such as the Jaycor's Pepperball System and Sticky Shocker, improved flash/bang grenades, and Capture Net.[31] In making its investments, NIJ draws on past military, civilian, and international investments in research and development of less lethal technologies.

According to information from former NIJ director Sarah Hart (Hart, 2002a), NIJ invested an average of $1.5 million per year in the program from 1993 to 2002. From 2003 to 2007, according to information supplied from NIJ,[32] the program supported awards totaling over $15 million. The projects from this later period cover a broad range of efforts.

The committee examined the list of projects provided and defined by NIJ as its less lethal technology portfolio as of July 2008 and categorized the 37 projects:

- 1 research effort on laser technology that could be potentially used in a less lethal weapon;
- 7 technology development projects that could result in prototypes (all of which were awarded in 2005 or before);
- 3 projects to develop models and simulation tools for testing;
- 7 studies on the effects that less lethal devices have on humans;
- 8 studies or reviews on the outcomes (e.g., injuries) of police use of force (some of these were funded through the ORE FY 2005 solicitation *Outcomes of Police Use-of-Force* and some were intended to assemble databases for future investigations);
- 3 projects regarding standards for less lethal devices;
- 3 field evaluations of existing less lethal devices;
- 1 demonstration;
- 1 pilot introductory course on less lethal weapons;
- 2 advisory groups to monitor the field and recommend ways to leverage efforts and avoid duplication; and
- 1 project with mixed purposes.

Despite the range of projects funded, in terms of technology development, the impact of this program on emerging weaponry is limited due to the low funding in comparison to military-sponsored R&D (Davison, 2007). With a modest budget, the less lethal technology portfolio can be characterized as leveraging past R&D of other agencies or modifying existing weapons to offer improved tools to law enforcement (National

---

[31]These less lethal technologies were identified in the 2006 program plan for the less lethal technology portfolio provided to the committee by NIJ, April 2008.

[32]Briefing paper on less lethal technology portfolio prepared for the committee by NIJ, July 2008.

Research Council, 2003a) as well as filling research gaps in examining the safety, effectiveness, and policy implications of existing weapons. In FY 2008, a *Less-than-Lethal Technologies* solicitation was posted, but no new awards were made for the program (only a few continuations were funded, totaling $1.2 million). There is no record that a *Less-than-Lethal Technologies* solicitation was posted for FY 2009.

We are surprised at the disappearance of this technology portfolio, since it is an area that is defined by law enforcement use. No one (e.g., military or public) uses less lethal weapons more widely than law enforcement. Department of Defense investments in less lethal technology still provide an opportunity to leverage NIJ resources; however, most of this technology is geared to military requirements and requires significant investment to adapt to law enforcement needs. The agency, in its current financial state, cannot contribute to the development of new technologies or the translation of military technologies; it lacks the discretionary funding necessary to implement the less lethal program needed by law enforcement.

Progress in Building Cumulative Knowledge in Technology R&D

Over the years, the technology program has grown to represent a broad range of technologies that are used or could be used by law enforcement. The program addresses R&D and testing and evaluation of such technologies; the development of equipment compliance standards; the effects on humans and the implications for policy as a result of introducing these technologies; as well as the distribution of knowledge for informed acquisition by law enforcement agencies. These are all very important efforts in the service of the nation's law enforcement. However, OST does not have the discretionary budget to adequately carry out a research program of this range. Nor, as discussed in Chapter 4, does it have the staff with the expertise necessary to adequately develop its very broad research portfolio. As a result of external priorities (i.e., nondiscretionary funding) and limited discretionary funding, OST's research portfolio has focused more on filling the voids in getting existing technologies into the hands of law enforcement and less on advancing knowledge toward effective, safer, affordable technologies for law enforcement in the future.

CONCLUSIONS

This chapter describes how NIJ has gone about fulfilling its research mission over the past 14 years. It focuses primarily on its research grantmaking role and excludes other supporting activities, such as technology assistance, capacity building, and dissemination. As part of this review, the committee analyzed funding patterns and identified funding sources. We described selected social science and technology R&D activities in which NIJ has made a considerable investment as well as other research-related activities, such as researcher-practitioner partnerships. We also examined the evaluation research portfolio that cuts across these other R&D activities separately, since this body of work has been the subject of assessment by the U.S. Government Accountability Office, and we were interested in learning the current status of efforts to improve the quality of evaluations. On the basis of this review, the committee draws several conclusions:

- **NIJ has developed research programs appropriate to its mission. It has succeeded in developing a body of knowledge in important areas that are critical to preventing and controlling crime and improving the administration of justice.**

The committee considers both the social science research and the technology research and development described in this chapter appropriate to NIJ's research mission and that both endeavors have the potential to result in useful knowledge for the criminal justice field. NIJ-sponsored research has often led the way and served as the foundation for researchers to build on and for practitioners to learn from. There is some evidence that NIJ research has influenced criminal justice practice and policy, particularly in the areas that have been sustained over time—such as hot spots policing, violence against women, drugs and crime, and crime mapping, on the social science side, and body armor, less lethal technologies, and DNA analysis, on the technology side. Cumulative knowledge has been achieved almost in spite of itself, given the inadequate or unstable resources and shifting priorities of NIJ's leadership. However, the contributions it has made over a time span of 14 years do not compensate for what the committee observes to be the increasingly ad hoc nature of the topics from year to year and the lack of systematic planning (addressed in Chapter 4).

- **NIJ has failed to summarize its accomplishments and to maintain the kinds of records of what has been funded and what findings and products have been produced.**

Several times in this chapter, we have indicated the difficulty we had in identifying NIJ's priorities and bodies of related research. With records given to the committee and available publicly, it is difficult to discern research awards from other investments (many of which are detailed in Chapter 5). It is difficult to classify specific kinds of research supported, such as impact versus process evaluations and technology R&D versus operational testing.

- **Congressional support and stable funding have been key ingredients to sustaining a research program area over time, particularly in the case of more expensive scientific endeavors, such as longitudinal studies and complex evaluations. In particular, the evaluation research portfolio is heavily dependent on transferred funds and programs of specific interest to the Office of Justice Programs.**

Once congressional support ceases, as it did for research on prison sexual assaults and drug use monitoring, or declines, as it has done for violence against women, NIJ is unable to fill the funding void with its own base funds. On the technology side, NIJ is unable to sustain research in such areas as safe school technologies, information-led policing, communications, and less lethal technologies because specific appropriations in the Crime Identification Technology Act and other inititiatives as well as targeted reimbursements from other agencies have declined or disappeared.

- **NIJ's discretion to award research grants is also on the decline.**

NIJ's discretion is impacted by the decline in its base budget and by the increase in appropriated funds that are designated for specific programmatic uses or for specific research projects. Extensive earmarking does not allow NIJ to set its own priorities or steer its own course. This substantially diminishes its ability to select research it will support on the basis of the best current science using the peer review process characteristic of strong research agencies.

Later in this report (Chapter 7) we make the case for substantially more independence for NIJ, in part to ensure that like other respected federal research agencies it set its own research agenda consistent with its mission but unencumbered by earmarks.

- **The NIJ research function is greatly diminished.**

The ORE budget, which primarily supports social science research and program evaluations, has been declining for the past 6 years. Research monies for many of the OST portfolio areas have also declined recently. Once amounting to 50-70 percent of its total budget, OST's research expenditures are now less than 25 percent, and several technologies that have been traditionally studied, such as communications, less lethal technologies, and sensors and surveillance, are no longer the focus of solicitations. The number of research and evaluation awards, roughly 150 or fewer a year, stands in stark contrast to the 50 topics areas NIJ acknowledges as addressed in its research portfolios (see Box 3-1). As such, NIJ's research program is very broad without much depth, or conversely, some of the research topics receive sustained attention while others are neglected. In addition, NIJ supports three times as many awards for program support, technology assistance, and capacity building than it does for research and evaluation.

In the next two chapters we address other aspects of NIJ's capacity to support research. In Chapter 4, the committee examines the agency's operations and staff resources for managing its research portfolios and other activities. In Chapter 5, we look at its other functions and assess how they support or detract from its primary research mission.

4

Research Operations and Staffing Resources

The history and broad outline of the research portfolio of the National Institute of Justice (NIJ) described in this report reflect frequent changes in leadership, an increased oversight role for the Office of Justice Programs (OJP), several upswings and downturns in funding, and a shift from support for a predominantly social science research program to one in which the majority of funding is expended on technology-related activities.

In an effort to better understand these changes and their ramifications, the committee examined NIJ's research operations and staffing resources. In this chapter, we first describe how NIJ plans its agenda, develops solicitations, conducts peer review, awards grants, and reviews its research reports. We examined these processes in light of three overarching issues: (1) the transparency of the processes, (2) the relationship between the research and practitioner communities and NIJ staff, and (3) the relationship between NIJ and OJP. When documentation is available, we describe how the processes changed over time.

We then describe NIJ's staffing resources and analyze staff turnover and other staffing characteristics that have affected how NIJ conducts its business. Taken together, this analysis provides an important context for understanding and assessing the current program and its evolution into the research organization of today.

RESEARCH OPERATIONS

Consistency, openness, efficiency, and fairness are characteristics associated with good research and development (R&D) project management (National Advisory Committee on Criminal Justice Standards and Goals, 1976). They are also useful as a yardstick against which one can measure the quality of a research agency's operations and determine how well they contribute to fulfilling its mission. For our analysis of research operations, the committee reviewed written OJP guidelines and policies (Office of Justice Programs, 2007c) and also relied heavily on interviews with former and current staff as to how these processes worked in reality and over time. Anyone familiar with bureaucracies knows that often there is a divide between what an official policy or process proposes and how things are actually done. In this report, we have found it necessary to distinguish the two.

We have also tried to describe the differences between the way the Office of Research and Evaluation (ORE) and the Office of Science and Technology (OST) handle various functions. As described earlier, until the late 1990s, the social science research activities dominated the science and technology ones. Consequently, the background information on operations primarily describes how social science research activities are handled. After the mid-1990s, when the OST program greatly expanded, these processes were either adopted by OST or were modified to reflect its own statutory requirements and programmatic needs. We have tried to indicate the nature of these changes and when and how they occurred.

Planning

Past Planning Activities

Traditionally, planning at NIJ has been a bottom-up process, with staff playing a major role in determining research priorities. Although there had been some attempt to use an advisory board (see Chapter 2) to solicit input from a broader audience and build support for research activities, there is no documentation that the NIJ Advisory Committee in the 1970s or the NIJ Advisory Board in the 1980s contributed to a formal research plan.

Rather than rely on an overall advisory board to advise it on long-range planning and annual priorities or on an advisory infrastructure for specific program areas, NIJ has convened topical meetings and workshops to solicit input from practitioners and researchers[1] on its social science research ac-

---

[1]Throughout our report, we use the terms "researcher" and "practitioner" to refer broadly to two groups of people who generally differ from each other in their training, expertise, and

tivities. One example of meetings aimed exclusively at practitioner groups is the 21st-century working groups convened during 1991-1993. Three separate groups of law enforcement, courts, and corrections practitioners provided informal guidance about the research agenda. The law enforcement group consisted of newly appointed and progressive police chiefs who met three or four times a year. The courts and corrections groups were convened less frequently but also assisted in identifying critical research needs.[2]

Through the years, NIJ staff have also participated heavily in conferences and meetings held by national criminal justice practitioner organizations, such as the International Association of Chiefs of Police and the American Correctional Association; research organizations, such as the American Society of Criminology and the Justice Research and Statistics Association; and meetings convened by other federal agencies, such as the Centers for Disease Control and Prevention. NIJ relies heavily on these meetings to exchange information and to generate interest in its activities.[3]

Until the mid-1990s, planning was conducted and coordinated by a director of planning who headed the Analysis, Planning and Management staff and reported directly to the NIJ director. The staff prepared budget requests for the Office of Management and Budget (OMB) and the U.S. Department of Justice, developed budgets, tracked spending, handled personnel matters, and oversaw an institute-wide planning process. The director of planning was responsible for communicating with outside groups, soliciting their input, and working closely with NIJ management and staff to develop an annual program plan.

Strategic Planning

NIJ undertook development of a long-range strategic plan in the early 1990s (National Institute of Justice, 1993). Six long-range goals were identified: (1) reduce violent crimes and their consequences; (2) reduce drug-related crimes; (3) reduce the consequences of crimes for individuals, households, organizations, and communities; (4) develop household, school, business, workplace, and community crime prevention programs; (5) improve the effectiveness of the criminal justice and service systems in responding to offenses, offending, and victimization; and (6) develop and evaluate information for criminal justice responses to changing and emerg-

---

occupation. The term "researcher" is inclusive of all people whose primary training, expertise, and occupation involve research activities regardless of where they work.

[2]E-mail from Craig Uchida, former director ORE (August 20, 2009).

[3]Memorandum to David W. Hagy, director of NIJ, from Thomas Feucht, assistant director of ORE, on practitioner consultations, August 2, 2007.

ing crime patterns and for use of new technologies. The idea was to build a body of cumulative research—both basic and applied—and to develop practitioner-oriented activities around these as well. The result of this planning was the development of a substantial number of solicitations that were issued in fiscal year (FY) 1994. A matrix was developed that could be used to monitor progress in conducting the research over a 10-year period. With the change in leadership in 1994, the plan was relegated to an open solicitation and its use was abandoned.[4]

In FY 2002, NIJ developed a 3-5 year strategic plan.[5] This plan, referenced in NIJ's submission to OMB's assessment process in FY 2005, identifies 7 broad strategic goals and 10 program areas. These same goals appear in NIJ's 2002 Annual Report to Congress and represent a change from mission statements that appear in its 1999-2001 annual reports. After 2002, no similar statement of mission or strategic goals appears in NIJ's annual report to Congress. More recently, NIJ took steps to develop a strategic plan and to obtain some feedback on its research priorities, in requesting this study from the National Research Council (NRC).

The lack of a structured strategic planning process makes NIJ even more susceptible to having its priorities set by others.[6] Sometimes these priorities are supportive of NIJ's mission, but sometimes they are questionable. On the science and technology side, for example, one program that was developed at the request of the attorney general was research on new technologies to detect concealed weapons at a distance. This line of research had never received much support from practitioners, but NIJ staff agreed that it would be useful and subsequently requested and received additional monies from the attorney general's office. A solicitation was issued and, according to NIJ staff, high-quality proposals were received. In a similar way, the school safety technology program became a priority because of congressional and departmental interest and continues to be supported today. But this priority did not engender the same kind of support from senior managers, who questioned whether the investment in new technology was an appropriate response to the spike in school homicides.

---

[4]E-mail from Carol Petrie, former acting director of NIJ, August 7, 2009.

[5]In response to the committee's request for this plan, we received a memorandum dated August 15, 2002 prepared by Sarah Hart, then director of NIJ, to Deborah Daniels, assistant attorney general. According to the memo, NIJ's initial attempt to develop a strategic plan was insufficient, and the revised plan was being submitted as part of the document. No other documentation regarding a strategic plan was uncovered by the committee.

[6]With the exception of the planning efforts by OST, there is little documentation regarding the priority-setting process across NIJ. The information on concealed weapons and the school safety program that follows was taken from staff interviews.

Annual Research Plans

Intermittently during the 1980s and 1990s, an annual NIJ research prospectus or research plan was published. It contained general descriptions of "strategic challenges" and focused almost exclusively on social science research activities, with increasing mention in the 1990s of other activities, such as crime mapping, DNA analysis, and standards development (National Institute of Justice, 1987, 1991, 1992, 1996, 1997, 1998, 1999). The documents also contained information on targeted or "directed" solicitations—for example, solicitations linked to 1994 Crime Act initiatives. After 2000, this kind of annual document signaling NIJ priorities to the research community was discontinued, until 2009, when NIJ released *High Priority Criminal Justice Technology Needs* (National Institute of Justice, 2009a), a document that describes how NIJ sets its research agenda. Unlike its predecessors, it focuses exclusively on the programs of OST.

Although no research prospectus for NIJ itself was produced during the period 2001-2008, the Violence and Victimization Research Division of ORE prepared a detailed divisional strategic plan in 2005. Covering FY 2006 "and beyond," the plan built on an earlier planning document written in 2001. It reflected the deliberations from a two-day planning meeting as well as ideas from an earlier Violence Against Women research agenda. The strategic plan contained descriptions and justifications for more than a dozen future solicitation topics.

Currently, agenda setting and planning is decentralized, and ORE and OST present their plans separately to the director. Consultation on program priorities between the director and the senior management staff is conducted on an ad hoc basis. Although several people have had responsibility for planning in the director's office since 2000, the current Planning, Budget, Management, and Administration Division does not appear to have major responsibility or oversight for institute-wide programmatic planning. Its responsibilities appear to be exclusively confined to providing financial oversight and monitoring activities, such as responding to audits and other financial inquiries, overseeing the packaging of grant proposals, and managing contracts.

Office of Research and Evaluation

Planning and agenda setting is handled differently by ORE and OST. ORE uses an ad hoc process that varies from year to year and from division to division. It relies heavily on staff expertise and consultation, primarily with practitioner groups, and policy makers through participation at professional meetings. In a listing of consultations with practitioners and policy makers for 2006-2007 prepared by ORE staff, approximately a dozen meetings were held for the purpose of planning research activities. Also listed were NIJ staff participation in research advisory committee meetings of the International Association of Chiefs of Police, and other meetings involving groups of related programs, such as the Project Safe Neighborhoods, the Multi-jurisdictional Task Force Cluster, and the Serious Violent Offender Re-entry Initiative. There were also meetings to plan research workshops (e.g., on elder abuse, sexual violence).

As mentioned earlier, ORE also sponsors periodic workshops and meetings on particular topics as the need arises. According to NIJ, it has held approximately two dozen meetings or workshops (it is unclear what distinguishes one from the other) since 2000, an average of about two a year. NIJ relies heavily on these "strategic planning" meetings to articulate new or emerging knowledge needs; to assess and evaluate a body of recently matured research findings; or to describe options and priorities for further research in a given area.[7] The list of various meetings covering 2001-2008 is available online, along with many of the meeting agendas, participant lists, and summaries.[8] Of the 27 meetings listed, 12 focused on sexual violence, victimization, and violence theory; 4 were on policing; 4 were related to forensic science, including 2 on DNA evidence; 2 were on drugs and crime; 2 were on terrorism; and single meetings were held on pretrial research, hate crime, and human trafficking. With one or two exceptions, most of the meetings involved a mix of researchers and practitioners, with the number of practitioners dominating a majority of the meetings. In general, the meeting materials reflect a broad overview of the subject, with a general listing of issues or questions needing research. With few exceptions, there appeared to be little emphasis on the science but more on what information practitioners need to do their jobs better. No further information on these meetings exists, and with few exceptions it was not possible for the committee to determine the relationship between research ideas presented at these meetings and any action taken by NIJ in response to them.

There are no standing advisory committees for ORE as a whole or for any of its divisions. Occasionally NIJ-wide working groups have been formed, but these are strictly composed of NIJ and other OJP staff with an interest in the particular area. In 2007, according to ORE, there were at least eight of these working groups, as well as other internal NIJ working groups that participate in an activity known collectively as the Innovative Assessment Program. These internal NIJ staff groups meet for the purpose

[7]Memorandum to David W. Hagy, director of NIJ, from Thomas Feucht, assistant director of ORE, on practitioner consultations, August 2, 2007.

[8]A list of NIJ's research meetings and workshops with links to available background materials is available online at http://www.ojp.usdoj.gov/nij/events/research-meetings.htm [accessed October 15, 2009].

of identifying, verifying, and assessing innovative criminal justice programs and policies.[9]

Once research topics are identified by the ORE divisions, they wind their way up to the director, following a series of meetings between staff and the ORE director. The process is not a formal one (i.e., no written guidelines or requirements). Similar meetings are held between the NIJ director and the OST director. The NIJ director then makes decisions on what particular research and programs will help accomplish the missions, with some consultation with the office directors and to some extent from senior management of OJP and the offices of the attorney general.

The interviews with current NIJ staff reveal considerable differences in their knowledge of the steps in the planning process as well as the quality of the process itself. The overriding sense of these interviews was that the process was a haphazard one. Some described the process as "intermittent," with no focus on long-range efforts. Generally, there was a sense that "hot topics" rule, and some areas are completely neglected due to scarce resources. Some staff attributed the ad hoc nature of the process to the fact that senior managers are not provided with budget numbers around which to plan. Others expressed the view that, with such limited resources, there was no incentive to plan.

Ongoing consultation with the broader research community outside more formal planned meetings or workshops appears to be very limited and dependent on individual staff initiative. According to the staff interviews, some staff contact researchers directly to obtain feedback on particular issues and to keep abreast, and other staff depend on meetings with "experts," presentations at professional association meetings, and contact with relevant Justice Department offices to provide opportunities to engage the research community.

Office of Science and Technology

In contrast to ORE, OST has had a history of working with a large and complex set of advisory and working group entities. It has relied on these groups to provide feedback on its overall program, to identify practitioner needs, and to coordinate with others conducting technology R&D (National Institute of Justice, 2009a).[10] Currently, OST relies on the Law

[9]Memorandum to David W. Hagy, director of NIJ, from Thomas Feucht, assistant director of ORE, on practitioner consultations, August 2, 2007.

[10]From 1994 to 2003, Vice-Admiral Al Burkhalter, Jr. USN (Ret.), chaired an executive panel of members with science backgrounds that advised OST and provided detailed reviews of particular programs.

BOX 4-1
Technical Working Groups (TWGs)

- Biometrics
- Body Armor
- Communications Technologies
- Community Corrections
- DNA Forensics
- Electronic Crime
- Explosives
- General Forensics
- Geospatial Technologies
- Information-Led Policing
- (Institutional) Corrections
- Less-Lethal Technologies
- Modeling and Simulation
- Personnel Protection
- Pursuit Management
- School Safety
- Sensors and Surveillance

Enforcement and Corrections Technology Advisory Council (LECTAC),[11] a group of approximately 40 senior-level representatives from federal, state, and local criminal justice agencies; labor organizations; and international criminal justice organizations. They meet once a year to review field needs developed from various technical working groups (TWGs) and make a list of the top-10 R&D priorities. Through this list of priorities, NIJ uses practitioner-based input to help shape the activities of its S&T portfolio. Although the number of active TWGs has fluctuated, in 2008, there were 17 TWGs developing high-priority needs and reporting them to LECTAC (Law Enforcement and Corrections Technology Advisory Council, 2008). See Box 4-1 for the core technology portfolios represented by these TWGs.

[11]A law enforcement advisory body, LECTAC has its roots dating back nearly 30 years before the establishment of the current TWG process (Law Enforcement and Corrections Technology Advisory Council, 2008). The Technology Assessment Program Advisory Council (TAPAC), established in the mid-1980s and consisting of more than 80 senior federal, state, and local law enforcement officials from the United States and Canada, preceded LECTAC (National Institute of Justice, 1994a). TAPAC was preceded by the National Advisory Committee for Law Enforcement Equipment and Technology, established in 1977 under NILECJ. According to David Boyd, former director of OST, LECTAC played a larger role in planning, and the TWGs began as subgroups of LECTAC.

As their titles indicate, some focus on specific technologies (e.g., body armor), some on criminal justice areas (e.g., community corrections), and others on crime problems (e.g., school safety).

Most, if not all, TWG members are criminal justice practitioners appointed by the OST deputy director and approved by the NIJ director. TWGs do not have formal policies or procedures regarding their size, management, or activities. There are no term limits on membership; members simply have to be actively employed. The TWGs meet twice a year to develop, rank, and finalize a list of priority technology needs in their respective areas. Each TWG generates about 50 priority needs, which results in a long list of roughly 900 technology needs. OST estimates that it is able to address one-sixth of them through competitive R&D and another one-sixth through operational testing and demonstration.[12] The needs that are addressed depend on budget and directives as well as gap analyses conducted by OST staff to determine that no other federal agency is investing in similar technologies.

The OST process is well regarded by the OST staff and by many practitioners who are familiar with it through their association on the TWGs. However, the current process reflects numerous deficiencies. Planning by OST does not appear to include systematic or formal outreach to the research or academic communities. Researchers are seldom included as members of either the technical working groups that develop the initial list of "technology priority needs" or on LECTAC, which selects the overall priorities. Although one might argue that technology priority needs are not meant to be the same thing as research priorities, the technology priority needs are the basis for the operational requirements that NIJ uses to provide direction for its research and development activities. According to NIJ, its solicitations for research and development of new tools and technologies for criminal justice practice are advised by TWGs and LECTAC recommendations (National Institute of Justice, 2009a).

Although the TWGs play an important role in identifying practitioner needs, and through those needs identify priorities, they do not operate like formal scientific advisory groups. With the exception of the DNA Forensics TWG, their membership does not include scientists who can use their expertise to assess the state of the art or the methodology required to move the technology forward. The absence of scientific or technical advice means that needs are developed in a vacuum, without input as to what is possible. As a result, opportunities may be missed. TWG meetings are not open, nor are their deliberations made public. The Homeland Security Act of 2002 specifically exempts the TWGs from the Federal Advisory Committee Act (FACA) rules which require notification of meetings and access by the

[12] E-mail from George Tillery, OST deputy director, May 16, 2008.

public to documents and meetings. As a result, they do not seek or elicit guidance from the broader scientific and practitioner community.

The current TWG structure is defined around the OST R&D portfolio areas and is not intended to be static. The TWGs are expected to adapt as priorities in the field change or as new technological capabilities emerge (National Institute of Justice, 2009a). However, the committee noted at least one example of a TWG (Corrections TWG) continuing to meet despite the absence of funded research awards in their respective portfolios over a number of years. OST's investment portfolios are likely to change first, because of limits on available funds or office reorganization, before the TWGs are restructured. As such, the advice coming from the TWGs often falls into a void, and it is unclear to what extent their advice and recommendations can and do result in solicitations and subsequent awards. According to OST's research, development, testing, and evaluation process (described in Chapter 3), if practitioner needs are not addressed in research and development programs because potential solutions already exist (or perhaps development is already sponsored by another agency), these needs are then addressed in Phase 4 of the process, in which NIJ considers supporting demonstrations and operational evaluations of potential solutions, or in Phase 5, in which NIJ considers publishing resource guides or standards documents that may be useful to the practitioner community. The elaborate advisory structure is used more often to inform the broader federal research community of the technology needs of criminal justice practitioners and to define NIJ's dissemination and outreach practices regarding technological capabilities than to define its technology research and development agenda.

Thus, while the OST process is standardized and more formalized than the ORE process, the OST process shares some major deficiencies. It is unclear what guidance and advice either office receives from the research community. In the case of ORE, there is some attempt to document researcher input by posting agendas and summary minutes of meetings and workshops on specific research topics on the NIJ website. But it is very unclear how final decisions about priorities are made or how these decisions in turn influence which solicitations are released. It is clear that both offices rely almost exclusively on staff judgments as to what the state of the art is, what is needed, what is feasible, and how a particular research technology or question should be approached. The committee has doubts as to whether the scientific and technical qualifications of the staff are up to the task. Consequently, the committee thinks that the advice and guidance of researchers need to be made a meaningful part of a sustained agenda-setting process.

Solicitations

Directed and Field-Initiated Solicitations

The committee heard brief descriptions of NIJ's solicitations in presentations by staff and was told that, to understand NIJ's research priorities, we should look at their solicitations. NIJ maintains an archive of solicitations from 1996 to the present.[13] From this archive, the committee reviewed the types of solicitations over the years, changes in topics, and changes in deadlines. In addition, we received from NIJ a list of titles for applications received and subsequent awards by solicitation for the period 2004 to 2007.

ORE and OST issue different kinds of solicitations to the field. ORE funds solicitations that are "directed" and describe the scope of the research or evaluation and the nature of the proposed research activity. It also issues an annual "open" or "field-initiated" solicitation. This kind of solicitation allows the researcher creative license to propose research studies on a broad array of topics. Typically $500,000 to $1.5 million is set aside for each directed solicitation and from $2.1 to $2.8 million for the annual field-initiated solicitation. However, in FY 2008, $5.4 million was awarded under the field-initiated *Crime and Justice Research* solicitation.

OST issues solicitations dealing with a specific technology area (e.g., communications, less lethal technologies, biometrics) that call for research studies and other kinds of activities to solve problems related to adoption and use of new technologies by criminal justice agencies. The solicitations are usually structured in two phases: submission of a concept paper, followed by a full proposal if the concept paper is approved. Concept papers under OST solicitations, which were introduced in 2005, differ from full proposals in that they are much shorter and do not contain detailed budgets. All concept papers and subsequent proposals are subject to review by a panel comprised of expert practitioners and technologists[14] (National Institute of Justice, 2006b).

An average of $1 million is designated for grants funded under each solicitation for targeted technology development. For some solicitations such as *Personal Protective Equipment* and *Corrections Technology*, $250,000 is set aside while up to $3 million is set aside for the *Forensic DNA Research* solicitation. OST also issues a second kind of solicitation, which calls for capacity-building activities. These are issued for such programs as the Fo-

[13]See http://www.ojp.usdoj.gov/nij/funding/expired-96-07.htm and http://www.ojp.usdoj.gov/nij/funding/expired.htm [accessed November 24, 2009].

[14]NIJ uses the term "technologist" to refer to scientists and engineers; it can include academicians. Technologists are often program managers from one of NIJ's federal partner agencies.

rensic DNA Backlog Reduction Program and the Paul Coverdell Forensic Science Improvement Program (see Chapter 5 for more details). Typically over $90 million is designated per year for grants through the eight solicitations for DNA backlog reductions and forensic lab improvements.

Between 1996 and 2009, only nine solicitations have been released regularly each year for a period of 6 years or more:

1. Crime and Justice Research (and previously titled Investigator Initiated);
2. Data Resources Program: Funding for the Analysis of Existing Data;
3. Research and Evaluation on Violence Against Women;
4. Forensic DNA Research and Development;
5. Electronic Crime and Digital Evidence Recovery;
6. Paul Coverdell Forensic Science Improvement Program (and its predecessor Forensic DNA Lab Improvement Program);
7. Forensic Casework DNA Backlog Reduction Program;
8. W.E.B. Du Bois Fellowship Program; and
9. Graduate Research Fellowship.

This list reflects a mix of sustained effort in which the criminal justice field can expect NIJ to support: (a) field-generated research, (b) knowledge accumulation in a few substantive areas (violence against women, forensic DNA analysis, and electronic crime), (c) forensic capacity building, and (d) development of the research infrastructure through fellowships (examined in Chapter 5). NIJ has regularly released about 40 solicitations since 2005, which is a doubling of the 20 solicitations released each year in the period 1996-2004.

Most of the research, development, testing, and evaluation solicitations (70 percent) in substantive areas, however, have a shelf life of 1 or 2 years. A few have been continued for 4 or 5 years, such as research on elderly abuse, terrorism, and the impact of forensic science as well as technology development in communications, information-led policing, less lethal weapons, sensors and surveillance, biometrics, and general forensics, although half of these areas have been discontinued as of the 2009 solicitations.

As noted earlier, the annual release of NIJ's research prospectus or research plan was discontinued in 2000. No other document or mechanism has filled its place that would adequately signal to the research community NIJ's upcoming research priorities. The lack of a research plan, in combination with sporadically appearing and unannounced solicitations, leaves the research community unprepared to respond competently to NIJ's changing priorities.

Annual solicitations are released in the period from October of the preceding year to May-June of the fiscal year. From 2005 to 2009, the average number of days from solicitation release to due date has remained fairly constant, 55-68 days. Solicitations available for a shorter period, 29-46 days, tend to be from OST, both for technology development and forensic capacity building. A smaller window for these kinds of grants is probably justified on the basis that technology development solicitations involve submission of a concept paper stage months prior to the solicitation deadline for full proposals and the forensic capacity-building program is a formula grant award program that requires more of a pro forma application. ORE solicitations tend to be posted for 60-100 days. For the most part, the same type of solicitation is released at a regular time of the solicitation cycle.

For example, OST calls for technology development are released around October, and its solicitations for new national technology centers were released in May. There have been a few examples of a regular solicitation lagging from its regular release date: the *Crime and Justice Research* solicitation release date has varied from October to February; the *Data Resources Program* solicitation release date has varied from November to April; and the *Social Science Research in Forensic Science* solicitation release date has varied from November to February.

In the absence of a publicly available research agenda, the timing of solicitation announcements and their posting times are critically important factors in determining the level of response from researchers. This is particularly true for studies that are either appropriate for or call for building collaborative relationships between researchers and practitioners.

In spite of a narrow window for preparation, NIJ received an average of 1,200 applications a year through its competitive solicitations for the period 2004-2007. Of these, roughly 35 percent were submitted in response to the capacity-building solicitations; many of these (58 percent) were funded. In contrast, only 15 percent of the applications under solicitations for substantive areas of research, development, or evaluation are funded. These are not unusual trends when comparing awards for formula grants with awards for research grants. However, NIJ's rate of funding research applications is noticeably lower than the 20-25 percent rate reported in recent years by other federal agencies, despite the recent financial squeezes they have experienced (Chase, 2009; Powell, 2009). With the exception of OST's capacity-building solicitations, most (about 70 percent) of NIJ's solicitations have resulted in only 1-3 funded awards per solicitation.

In FY 2008, ORE issued 11 directed solicitations[15] in addition to its field-initiated solicitation. OST issued 13 solicitations for targeted technology development.[16] Most of these solicitations were supported with funds transferred from other federal agencies (such as the Office for Victims of Crime, the Department of Homeland Security, and the Federal Bureau of Investigation) or were the result of congressional priorities (such as the Prison Rape Elimination Act, the President's DNA Initiative, the Violence Against Women Act). It is also noteworthy that in 2008 10 of these solicitations did not result in funded awards.

According to ORE, directed solicitations, the pillars of its strategic research program, are used to build empirical knowledge over a number of years.[17] Although directed solicitations end up reflecting NIJ's research priorities, for the most part they are not independently arrived at as part of a strategic planning process, and few are supported by NIJ base funds. Instead, they depend on transferred funds and the interests of the funding agencies, Congress, or both. NIJ thus plays a minor role in determining how its directed solicitations will build knowledge across projects and over time.

The annual field-initiated solicitation is intended to fund numerous exploratory research activities. These awards for the period 2005-2008 address a range of issues, from understanding criminal behavior and victimization to examining the effects of a state's program or policy. NIJ argues that open research solicitations create the most diversity and allow for innovative research and unanticipated research knowledge.[18] This objective appeared to be reflected in the FY 2008 *Crime and Justice Research* solicitation, which called for "any social and behavioral research and evaluation topic relevant to State and/or local criminal and juvenile justice policy and

[15]These included *Sexual Violence in Prisons*, *Criminal Justice Technology Evaluation*, *Social Science in Forensics*, *Justice Systems Reponses to Violence Against Women*, *American Indian/Alaskan Native Criminal Justice Systems and Criminal Justice Technology*, *Crime Prevention and Gangs*, *Pretrial and Jail Research and Evaluation*, *Research on Trafficking in Persons*, *Policing/Public Safety Research and Evaluation*, *Terrorism Research*, and *Elder Abuse Research and Evaluation*.

[16]These included *Biometric Technologies*; *Body Armor for Law Enforcement and Corrections*; *Communications Technology*; *Electronic Crime and Digital Evidence Recovery*; *Forensic DNA Research and Development*; *Geospatial Technology*; *Information-Led Policing Research, Technology Development, Testing, and Evaluation*; *Less Lethal Technologies*; *Personal Protection Equipment*; *Research and Development in Forensic Anthropology and Forensic Odontology*; *Research and Development in the Area of Controlled Substances Detection and Analysis*; *Research and Development in the Forensic Analysis of Fire and Arson Evidence*; and *Sensors and Surveillance Technology*.

[17]Unpublished paper by Thomas E. Feucht, June 2008, drafted in response to questions from the committee on how ORE selects and organizes its research programs and research investments.

[18]Unpublished paper by Thomas E. Feucht, June 2008.

practice" (National Institute of Justice, 2007b). However, two grants NIJ funded under its FY 2008 solicitation included a $1.9 million longitudinal study of policing[19] and a $995,707 grant to continue a longitudinal study of desistance by juvenile offenders in two states.[20] Changing course with the FY 2009 solicitation, NIJ directed the field to focus on the following topics: predicting crime, terrorism, human trafficking, gangs, prisoner reentry, improving the justice system, and reducing the prison population. As of this writing, it is not known whether the resulting grants will reflect these priorities.

Approval Process for Solicitations

Through the 1990s, the approval process for solicitations was a fairly straightforward one. Solicitations were signed off by the NIJ director, prepared for publication, and then disseminated by the National Criminal Justice Reference Service using its mailing lists. In some years, the solicitations were published in full or as a summary announcement in the *Federal Register*.

Currently, preparation of solicitations consumes a great deal of staff time in terms of developing them, getting them through the review process, and readying them for posting on the NIJ website. Currently, solicitations go through a lengthy review process that involves three offices in OJP: (1) the Office of the Chief Financial Officer Budget Division (OCFO-BD), (2) the Office of the General Counsel (OCG), and (3) the Office of the Assistant Attorney General. OJP guidelines advise its bureaus to allow 47 days for review and final sign-off by the assistant attorney general, OJP.

The process includes multiple reviews by OCFO-BD and OGC and the assistant attorney general, OJP. It includes an initial review by OCFO-BD prior to its being signed off by the NIJ director. We were told that the purpose of this early review is to check whether appropriate performance measures are contained in the solicitations. Since a check of solicitations from 2007, 2008, and 2009 showed that they contain standardized language regarding performance measures, the nature of the review is unclear. Once approved by the NIJ director, it is sent to OGC, where, until spring 2009, it was reviewed by one of two staff attorneys specifically assigned to NIJ.

NIJ staff explained that OGC checks to be sure the solicitation is in keeping with NIJ's legislative mission and that NIJ is not requesting an

[19]An award of $1.9 million was made to the University of Illinois, Chicago, for the project Advancing Knowledge and Practice in Policing: A Longitudinal Platform for National Research.

[20]The Pathways to Desistance study has been an ongoing effort since 1999 at the University of Pittsburgh. It was originally funded by the Office of Juvenile Justice and Delinquency Prevention and the MacArthur Foundation.

activity to be undertaken that may pose later legal issues. However, NIJ staff also reported that OGC staff also review for programmatic content and frequently raise questions or offer comments about the research objectives or activities being proposed. NIJ staff reported that on at least one occasion, an OGC attorney raised questions about the need for a particular methodological approach in a technology research solicitation. Once comments are made, staff must respond to them, and if changes are made, the documents are recirculated to the OJP offices for re-review. The whole process is handled electronically, and, in the final review stage, the various offices can sign off simultaneously.

The committee found this process to be an onerous one, and we question why this level of oversight and programmatic review by others outside NIJ is necessary or appropriate.

Peer Review and Grant Award Selection

Peer Review

NIJ developed its first peer review process in direct response to the recommendations of the earlier NRC committee (National Research Council, 1977). From the beginning the process was managed by an outside contractor that had responsibility for maintaining a list of qualified reviewers, identifying appropriate reviewers in response to a staff request, arranging for the logistics and payments associated with in-house peer-review meetings, and managing the transmission of the reviews to NIJ staff and then storing them. Numerous contractors have performed these services over the past 30 years; there has been some variation in how each contractor handled these tasks, but the basic tasks have remained the same.

Centralizing Peer Review in OJP. Over time, other program offices in OJP determined that they should also use peer-review processes for their competitive programs. To meet this need, the various offices transferred funds to NIJ in order to use its contractor. Eventually, this arrangement became an administrative burden, so the individual bureaus contracted for their own services.

In 2004, OJP determined that the peer-review process would be centralized. This decision resulted from recommendations of the OJP Business Process Improvement initiative, which was created to improve the OJP grant application process. According to the OJP order, the new policies are intended to increase the efficiency, integrity, and overall quality of the OJP peer review process.

Today, all applications for OJP competitive discretionary funding are subject to peer review, and one contractor serves the needs of all the bureaus. The peer-review contract is overseen by an OJP contracting officer's technical representative. For each solicitation, there is a subject-matter expert, usually a program manager assigned to a particular solicitation.

Description of the Process. A directive that is available on the OJP website describes responsibilities of the bureau program staff who oversee the work of the peer reviewers as well as various administrative requirements (Office of Justice Programs, 2007b). For example, it requires that peer review panels be conducted by either telephone or video conference unless a waiver is sought and approved for an in-person peer review.[21] The order also describes requirements for evaluating peer reviewer performance, the process for changing peer-review panel dates, and a standardized methodology for scoring applications. The order establishes certain guidelines regarding how often the same peer reviewers may be used and requires that program offices track the composition of peer-review panels on a yearly basis in order to "promote unique panel compositions for each review cycle; track the individual service of peer reviewers; and analyze the use of peer reviewers by skill or primary discipline." It also requires formal orientations and ongoing training for all peer reviewers. Steps in the review process include

- individual scoring by the peer reviewer prior to the convening of the panel,
- discussion of each applicant's individual score by the group,
- preparation of a final recommendation memorandum by the NIJ staff, and
- presentation of the scores and recommendation memorandum to the program office leaders with any additional analysis performed by lead program staff.

Guidance is also provided by NIJ to its peer reviewers.[22] This guidance describes in more detail the various steps leading up to the preparation of a final recommendation memorandum and includes a description of specific responsibilities before and during the peer-review panel, of the lead

---

[21]NIJ argued against this requirement when it was proposed on the grounds that video- or teleconferenced peer reviews were not as effective in discussing research applications and arriving at consensus around complex issues (memorandum to Regina B. Schofield from Glenn Schmitt, acting director, NIJ, December 21, 2005). NIJ was denied approval to hold in-person meetings from 2006 through 2008 and was required to seek a waiver for each in-person review it sought. The committee could not find out how many waivers were requested or approved. In January 2009, the acting assistant attorney general, OJP, rescinded this policy but the OJP order has not been revised as of this writing.

[22]Instructions to Reviewers for Peer Review Panels, ORE, NIJ, U.S. Department of Justice (February 2007).

technical reviewer as well as the other technical reviewers and practitioner reviewers and the NIJ program manager. Ethics and integrity, conflict of interest, and confidentiality issues are also spelled out.

According to the contracting officer's technical representative for the peer-review contract, assessment is ongoing and includes monthly monitoring of the frequency of individual peer reviewers' participation and use of first-time reviewers. Ad hoc reviews of peer-reviewer evaluations as well as the peer reviews themselves are also conducted.[23]

The committee was very interested in the details of NIJ's peer-review process because of its importance to the research enterprise. We were particularly interested in the various steps of the review process and the extent to which the recommendations of peer-review panels are followed at the division level and to what extent the recommendations are used by the NIJ director. This decision process is not detailed in the OJP grants management system, although it does exist manually in the documents forwarded to the NIJ director.

The committee did not have access to any documents associated with the review or award of grants. We were unable to assess how closely these written policies are followed by NIJ or other program offices; what, if any, latitude the program offices actually have in modifying or changing any of these policies; whether quality reviews are being undertaken; and what role the numerical rankings play in funding decisions. The last question was of particular interest, since the OJP order clearly states that "final decision makers of awards may consider application scores generated by peer-review panels in their review of applications but shall not be bound by them."[24] The OJP order explains that numerical scores are considered predecisional, for internal information only, and are not "normally" released to the applicants.

On the basis of staff interviews and the memoranda we examined, we think that centralization of peer review in OJP, as well as some of the specific practices associated with it, are problematic for NIJ and raise serious questions about the quality and integrity of the process. The U.S. Government Accountability Office (GAO) has noted that there is no uniform federal policy for conducting peer reviews and cites officials at the White House's Office of Science and Technology who believe that peer-review practices should not be dictated uniformly for every agency or for all types of federally funded research (U.S. General Accounting Office, 1999). This view was also expressed in an OMB guidance document to the effect that

[23]Telephone interview with Amy Callaghan, contracting officer's technical representative, OJP, August 7, 2009.

[24]See the section above on the grant award process for a discussion of recent findings of the U.S. Department of Justice audit of NIJ's practices.

a one-size-fits-all approach is not appropriate for agencies with different missions (U.S. Office of Management and Budget, 2004).

Issues Arising from Centralization. On the basis of our review of how solicitations are developed and applications are reviewed, the committee thinks that a centralized process limits NIJ's ability to tailor peer review to its own needs and mission. Its discretionary grants are very different from those of other OJP bureaus, which provide support for program services, training, or equipment. Applications requesting programmatic support require a different kind of expertise than applications proposing to conduct research. The former usually have more definitive goals and activities and may involve less complicated issues than research applications in which there is a need to discuss the feasibility and appropriateness of a particular research design and methodology and the need to meet accepted standards of rigor. Furthermore, the peer review for an NIJ research application may serve a more expansive purpose than one produced for another OJP program: it may be used by NIJ to modify the application, to provide guidance once the applicant is funded, and to inform the program staff of potential issues with the newly funded research, among other issues.

Because peer review is so fundamental to the scientific process, NIJ needs to have a full say in all aspects of its peer review, including how the panels are conducted, the selection of reviewers, the composition of the panel, the review criteria, and other aspects of the process. NIJ also needs the ability to make the reviews available in a timely way to the applicants and to conduct its own assessment of the quality of the process. It needs to be able to explain the process accurately and fully to all applicants. In our review of the OJP order and NIJ guidelines, the committee notes several features that deserve further scrutiny: the use of practitioners on panels, the scoring and ranking system, and the process for making individual peer reviews available. These are discussed further below.

The role of practitioners as peer reviewers is an issue that NIJ needs to address, but it will be difficult to do if the peer-review system remains centralized. Although this has been a long-standing practice of NIJ (certainly since the 1980s), the committee questions whether practitioners should be using the same review criteria as technical reviewers and should be participating in equal numbers on larger panels. (Apparently on panels of four persons or larger, the number of reviewers is evenly divided between practitioners and researchers.) Although there is no written government-wide definition of peer review, GAO points out there is concurrence among officials at research agencies that peer review is a "process that includes an independent assessment of the technical, scientific merit of research by peers who are scientists with knowledge and expertise equal to that of the researchers whose work they review" (U.S. General Accounting Office,

1999). The committee acknowledges the importance of soliciting input from practitioners as to the need and impact of the proposed research—but we suggest that such input can best be obtained as part of a two-step process or, if practitioners are included as part of the same panel meeting, they should be using different criteria to score the proposals. The practice of using practitioners on peer review panels is not mentioned in the formal guidelines and appears to have originated with NIJ directors. According to NIJ staff, some directors were more insistent on it and, in fact, one recent NIJ director believed that practitioners should not be excluded from serving as the lead technical reviewer, the person responsible for drafting the consensus review. According to staff, this was tried once or twice but proved unworkable and was abandoned.

Informing applicants of peer review results and providing them with an electronic copy of the consensus report or review summary is the responsibility of the OJP contractor after the NIJ staff person signs off on the consensus review.[25] The OJP order setting forth this policy prohibits the release of any consensus report until successful applicants receive notification of their awards. Depending on the specific solicitation, NIJ advises applicants to expect funding decisions in 4 months (e.g., DNA backlog) to 9 months (e.g., *Crime and Justice Research* solicitation). There is seldom if any feedback provided directly to applicants on their applications. All applicants, whether their applications are accepted or rejected, are notified simultaneously. They receive electronic copies of the consensus review and not the individual reviews. This practice contrasts with that of the National Science Foundation (NSF) and the National Institutes of Health (NIH), which make available electronically to all applicants the individual reviews of their applications, along with a final decision from the program officers. This kind of transparency allows the applicant to see the full range of reviews as well as to understand more fully the basis for the funding decision; this kind of visibility may also result in better quality reviews.

The committee also learned that it is not unusual for an NSF program officer to discuss peer reviews informally with applicants whose applications will not be approved but appear promising, so they can benefit from the comments and resubmit for the next known funding cycle. NIH applicants above a certain score are also informed that they should come back and resubmit for possible funding. NIJ's award cycle for all solicitations is on an annual basis, so there is no possibility that an application will be reconsidered in another year. Furthermore, a totally different panel reviews the next year's applications and does not have access to the earlier reviews.

One final point regarding the OJP process bears mentioning. In talking with NIJ staff and others who have been NIJ applicants, the committee

---

[25]E-mail from Angela Moore Parmley, acting director, ORE (October 22, 2009).

heard concerns about the standardized scoring and ranking system used by the OJP peer review process. It is not easily understood and does not appear to have a scientific basis—that is, how well scores obtained through this system reflect the overall quality of the proposal or the importance of the component parts. On one hand, the criteria are very simple and broad to accommodate any kind of proposal; on the other hand, research applications must provide very specific kinds of information that need to be assessed fully and weighted appropriately. The current scoring and ranking system does provide for different weightings of the criteria, but the committee could not determine how often this option is used or on what basis changes in weightings are made.

Although the committee is not prepared to make specific recommendations regarding the individual elements of peer review, we raise these issues to emphasize the importance of a research agency's having the authority to manage its own peer review and assess its own process to determine whether changes are warranted. It then needs to have the authority to implement them. Currently, a centrally managed peer review process under OJP does not provide NIJ with the flexibility to make changes in line with its own research program needs.

Grant Award Process

As mentioned previously, the committee was unable to view any documents relating to the peer review or grant award process, including any review memoranda proposing certain applications for award. During the period of this study, four different persons served as the final arbiter of grant award decisions at NIJ, and it is possible that each one used different criteria and a different in-house process to make his or her decision.

An example of the decision-making process was provided by an NIJ director who explained that in the FY 2008 funding cycle, he lumped all the applications from several solicitations that were recommended for funding consideration into one large pool and selected those from the pool that he had sufficient funding for and felt were most appropriate for funding.[26] Obviously, this kind of selection process sends a very mixed and confusing message to the research community, which is under the impression that it is competing against similarly themed research projects rather than against an entire pool of candidates. It also runs counter to the notion that a research institute's practices should be fair, transparent, and consistent. NIJ's grant award process should be followed for every solicitation, with full disclosure

[26]Remarks by David Hagy, director, NIJ, to the Committee on Law and Justice (October 3, 2009).

of how the process works and the roles that NIJ staff, peer reviewers, and NIJ and the OJP leadership play.

NIJ's peer-review and grant-selection processes were the focus of a recent audit by the Office of Inspector General of the Justice Department, which was requested by Senator Richard Shelby (R-AL). Released in September 2009, the audit report findings are highly critical of NIJ's grant award practices. They cite NIJ for failing to maintain adequate preaward records, for not screening persons with potential conflict of interest from peer-review panels, for having inadequate documentation of the application review process, and for failing to ensure that potential applicants disclose lobbying activities. Most importantly, the report concludes that these problems raise concerns about the fairness and openness of NIJ's competitive grant-making process. The report went on to recommend that NIJ take steps to establish policies and procedures for documenting key aspects of the preaward and award process (U.S. Department of Justice, 2009b).

Report Review

The NIJ report review process brings to full circle the research endeavor that began with agenda planning and priority setting. Grantees are required to submit a report on their research that provides a full description of the research, including the research questions, the methodology, and findings. NIJ heavily relies on final research reports to ascertain what has been accomplished and to pave the way for understanding the implications of the research for policy and practice. It relies on peer review of these reports for its assessment, in terms of both quality of the research and its utility. Peer review of ORE final reports generally consists of two outside reviews—one by a practitioner and one by a researcher, although occasionally only technical reviews will be requested. OST final reports generally receive three reviews by a combination of practitioners and technologists (refer to footnote 14 in this chapter). On the ORE side, there are separate review questions for practitioners and researchers. Most questions are common to both except that researchers are asked to comment on whether the findings are supported by the research and the appropriateness of methodology and practitioners are asked about the utility of the report.

The NIJ program monitor must also complete a review. Once the reviews are completed and a decision is made to recommend some form of dissemination other than archiving the report, the report is sent to the NIJ Editorial Review Board. A recommendation is then made to the NIJ director, who has the final approving authority. (See Chapter 5 for further discussion of NIJ's dissemination efforts.)

The report review process is straightforward up to the point at which a recommendation is made to the director. From that point on, depending on the recommendation, the director may become more or less involved in further discussions around the final production of the report and the selection of a specific kind of format. The committee heard from two NIJ directors that they were involved in editing publications. NIJ staff and former grantees also commented on the amount of time it took to produce a report once the actual peer-review process had been completed. However, the committee was not able to document the length of this process or to assess the rationale behind or the nature of the director's involvement in the process. Here it suffices to say that different directors have had their own ideas as to their level of involvement in review and dissemination of reports.

The report review process can be a critical component of a research agency's efforts to ensure that research of high quality is produced. It therefore deserves careful scrutiny in terms of the role the staff plays in assessing research reports, the quality of and utility of the peer reviews, the nature of the review itself, and the feedback that is provided to the grantee. The committee did not see actual reviews by peer-review consultants, but we were able to review the consultant task agreement that peer reviewers must sign. The committee notes the following areas of concern. Neither group receives background information on what was proposed, other than the report itself. The questions to the researcher are very general and do not get at such issues as data quality and utility. It is also unclear whether researcher and practitioner views are treated equally. In any event, such a review falls short of what would constitute a review by a peer-reviewed journal. The 1977 NRC report pointed out the inadequacy of a mail review to assess research findings (National Research Council, 1977). NIJ should assess its report review process in an effort to explore these issues. As with other research operations, NIJ needs to ask the questions: How can this process be used by NIJ to ensure quality in its research? Does this process contribute to NIJ's stature as a science agency?

Availability of Final Reports

At a minimum, all final grantee reports are supposed to be stored with NCJRS for public access. The committee undertook an analysis to determine how many final reports are actually available at NCJRS. This was a tedious task. Neither NIJ nor NCJRS could provide the committee with records that adequately identified the number of grants producing final reports or whether these final reports have been received.

However, NCJRS did provide the committee with a list of all publications received from NIJ since 1995 linked to their grant numbers. We matched these grant numbers to those in our award archive database and

TABLE 4-1 Analysis of Final Research Reports

Fiscal Year	Number of Research and Evaluation Grants[a]	Percent with a Final Report at NCJRS by December 2009	Year by Which All (or all but one) Currently Available Reports Had Been Submitted to NCJRS
1997	142	75	2004
1998	197	67.5	2004
2002	92	62	2005
2003	108	64	2009

NOTE: NCJRS = National Criminal Justice Reference Service.
[a]This number is less than what is presented in Figure 3-2. For this analysis, we removed all the Interagency Agreements (because we were sure we didn't have them all represented in our database) and all the awards continued from an earlier year.

considered the availability of final reports for 4 years: 1997, 1998, 2002, and 2003. We chose these years to allow enough time for a final report to be available and to compare years with different funding levels. We also considered only research grants (both social science and science and technology) and evaluation awards that had the potential to produce final research reports or equivalent articles in peer-reviewed journals. These grants had been awarded to a range of academic institutions, research foundations, and, to a lesser extent, local criminal justice agencies. We found the trends quite similar across each of the years. Our results are presented in Table 4-1.

The data show that 25 to 38 percent of the anticipated reports were not available in NCJRS and that this rate has increased in recent years. We were unable to determine whether missing reports were the result of grantees not turning in reports to NIJ or of NIJ not submitting final reports to NCJRS. Either way, we think NIJ should examine its final report submission processes in order to increase the percentage of final research reports that become publicly available. The average time of 3 years from grant award to availability of final report also needs consideration, especially when this average represents turnarounds from 1 to 7 years. It is noteworthy that NIJ was quite successful at short turnarounds with its 2002 grants. It is also interesting that its 1998 grants resulted in a higher number of missing reports in social science research areas. These trends can be understood only if the topics of specific grants and the context in which they were administered are examined, a task that was beyond the available resources of the committee.

Average Time from Year of Award to Year Submitted to NCJRS	Number of Grants Without a Report in NCJRS	Number of Those Missing a Report Considered Social Science Research	Number Considered Technology Development and/or Demonstration or Forensic Science Research
3.04	35	9	26
3.47	64	53	11
2.79	35	10	25
2.96	39	14	25

STAFFING RESOURCES

Dichotomy of Staff Responsibilities

Well-qualified and trained staff are important for good performance. It is also critical that they have a clear understanding of their roles and responsibilities. Similar to those of other science agencies that fund research, NIJ staff responsibilities fall into two broad and simplified categories: (1) knowledge development and (2) grant management. Knowledge development includes the activities involved in developing a research agenda and portfolio, such as identifying research needs, articulating research questions, identifying appropriate methodologies, preparing solicitations, providing input to the researcher on substantive issues, and assessing the quality of the research. Among the skills that are required to perform these tasks are substantive knowledge of a research area and research methodology. Because NIJ is a funding agency, program staff are also required to oversee the grant application and the review and award processes and, once grants are funded, to ensure that grantees comply with administrative and programmatic requirements. These kinds of activities require that staff have administrative and communication skills as well as relevant substantive knowledge of the work to be performed. There is considerable overlap between the two kinds of responsibilities required by program staff throughout the research grant process. By no means are they mutually exclusive. From management's vantage point, the ideal staff person will have a mix of skills and will handle both kinds of responsibilities equally well.

Tension arises when responsibility for developing and implementing a research portfolio becomes overwhelmed or supplanted by grant administrative responsibilities. To attract and retain staff with substantive expertise who have a primary interest in knowledge development, a research institute will need to offer a different set of responsibilities and rewards than it will need to attract persons who see themselves as good grant managers and communicators. An appropriate balance between the two kinds of roles needs to be maintained if staff who have a primary interest in knowledge development are not to be turned off by what they perceive as unnecessarily time-consuming responsibilities that are tangential to their main interests and expertise.

This dichotomy constantly asserted itself as a backdrop to the committee's review of staffing levels, staff characteristics, and organizational culture. It was very much reflected in a September 2007 NIJ staff survey conducted in-house by NIJ (results of the survey presented at the NIJ forum, January 10, 2008) as well as interviews with former and current NIJ staff conducted for this study. NIJ's staffing resources are described in the following sections and serve as an important context for this report.[27]

Staff Size Compared with Budget

NIJ's level of staffing resources has shifted dramatically in the past 10 years. From FY 1994 to FY 2000, the size of NIJ's staff mirrored the rise and fall of its budget. But when one looks at the individual program offices—ORE and OST—the size of these offices has not necessarily reflected the rise and fall of their individual budgets (see Figures 4-1 and 4-2). When one compares budget size with staffing resources for ORE and OST, the staffing of OST has remained relatively constant during a period of great influx of funding, while the staffing of ORE has continued to

[27]Information in this section has been pieced together from various sources. We relied heavily on information for the period 1994-2008 provided by the National Finance Center (NFC), the federal employee records center, which listed the names of individual staff, their position titles, and grade levels. In December 2007, ORE gave the committee a breakdown of numbers of full-time equivalents by year for the period 1994-2007, but comparable information was not available from OST. The ORE staffing information was relied on only for trend analysis. We were also given three signed NIJ organizational charts listing organizational units, names of staff (for one of the years), position titles, grade levels, and office designations. Two of these charts listed vacancies. Information on NIJ losses by separation or transfer was provided by the OJP Human Resources Division and covered the period from January 1, 2002, through November 24, 2007. We also conducted interviews with 26 current and former staff and were provided with a summary of findings from a survey of 45 nonsupervisory NIJ staff conducted in October 2007.

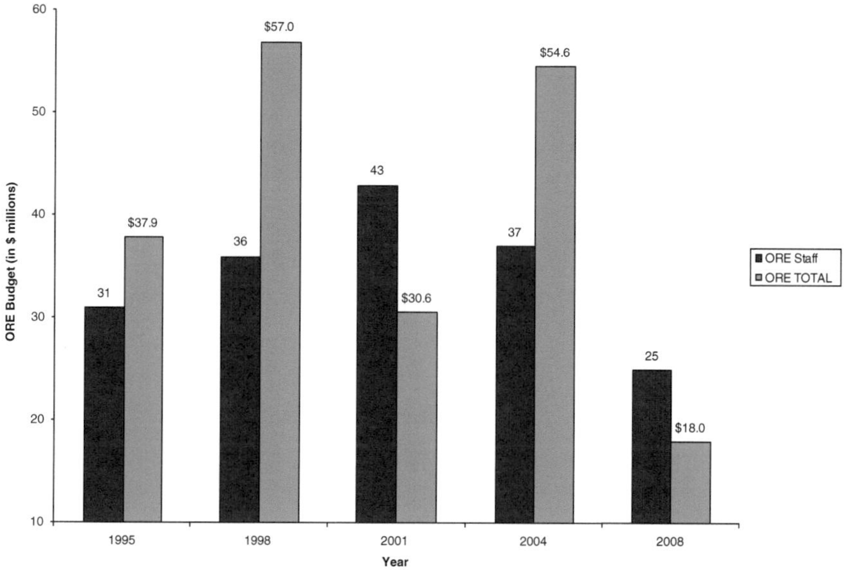

FIGURE 4-1 ORE employees and budget (in constant 2008 dollars).
SOURCE: Adapted from figures sent from National Finance Center (for staff totals) and National Institute of Justice (for budget totals).

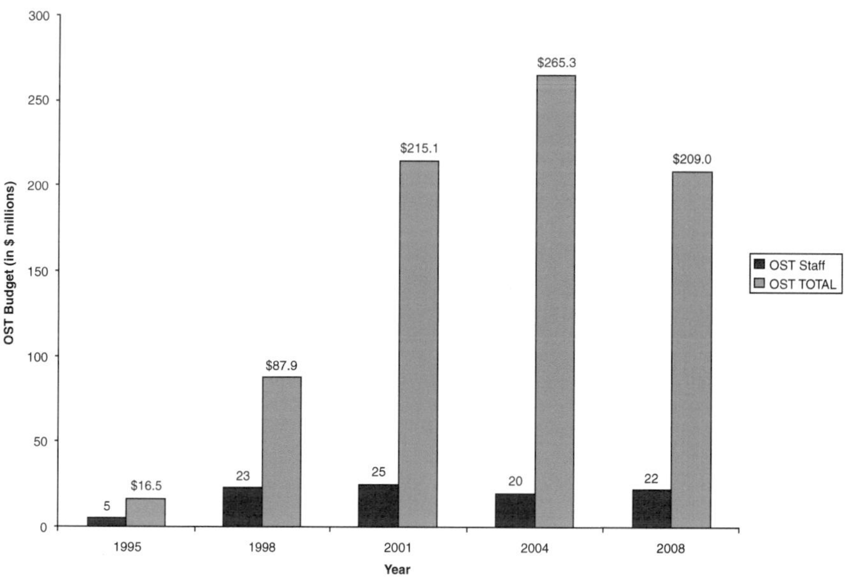

FIGURE 4-2 OST employees and budget (in constant 2008 dollars).
SOURCE: Adapted from figures sent from National Finance Center (for staff totals) and National Institute of Justice (for budget totals).

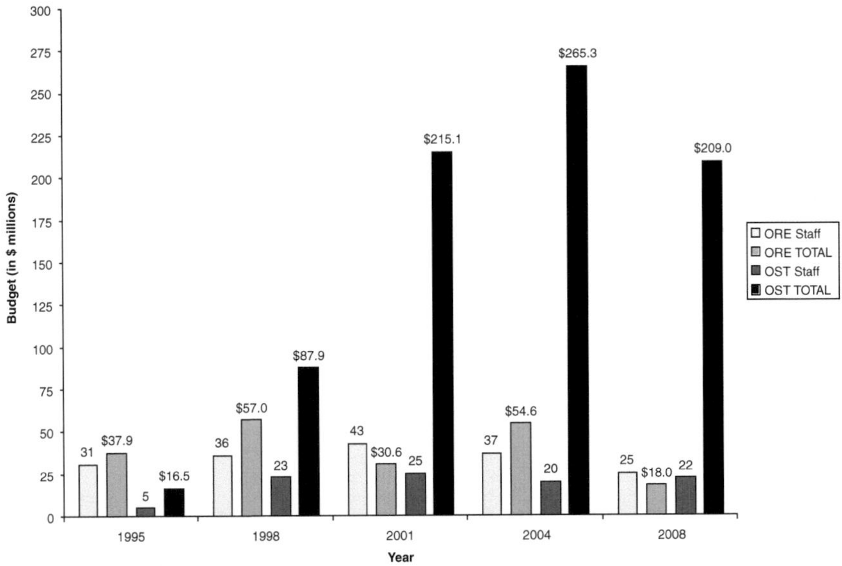

FIGURE 4-3 Number of ORE and OST employees for budget years 1995, 1998, 2001, 2004, and 2008 (in constant 2008 dollars).
SOURCE: Adapted from figures sent from National Finance Center (for budget totals) and National Institute of Justice (for staff totals).

decline, whether funds allocated to this office have increased or decreased (see Figure 4-3).[28]

Trends in Staffing

In FY 1994, the NIJ staff consisted of approximately 40 people who oversaw a total budget of $33 million (National Institute of Justice, 1994b). Of these, approximately 18 were professional staff handling nonadministrative research grant responsibilities. After the passage of the Crime Act in 1994, a large influx of transferred funds for evaluation and other specific

[28] These figures are approximate, since it is difficult to compare individual office staffing levels over time. For example, to obtain an accurate picture of staffing for OST and ORE in 2008 in comparison to the numbers provided for 1998 and 2001, one would need to count people assigned to the Planning, Budgeting, Management, and Administration Division (in the Office of the Director), who work with OST and ORE on administrative matters. As described earlier, we have relied on annual lists of NIJ employees compiled by the NFC for much of this analysis. Because we do not know whether the NFC lists of NIJ employees were compiled at the same time each year, there could be considerable variation in total numbers for any given year, depending on when people were hired or resigned.

research purposes came into NIJ. Beginning in 1995, the NIJ director recruited heavily, adding approximately 21 new program staff in 1995, 12 in 1996, and 16 in 1997. By 1998, the size of the NIJ staff had more than doubled (from 44 to 101) and the size of its total program budget had increased sixfold to $176 million. By 1999, the number of NIJ staff had reached its highest level of 111.[29]

Within two years and a changed administration, the size of staff had begun to shrink dramatically, even as funding increased as a result of the President's DNA Initiative. Between the years of 2002 and 2003, NIJ experienced its biggest turnover, with 18 staff departing. This decrease continued (except in 2005) until 2007, when approximately 58 people were identified as NIJ employees. Since 2008, the size of NIJ's staff has increased slightly.

Use of Contractors

In addition to the individuals listed in the staff rolls, NIJ relies on contractors to meet its responsibilities. Their involvement with various grant-related matters was mentioned frequently during site visits with OST grantees. Limited information was available on the extent to which contractors were used and the nature and scope of their responsibilities.[30] We learned that contractors have been heavily used since 2000 by OST for a variety of technology and research-related tasks, in addition to grant-processing activities, and to a lesser degree by other offices at NIJ for primarily administrative and grant-processing activities. The committee's strong sense is that NIJ relies on contractors for a level of experience and expertise that is not available from its staff.

For example, in 2001, NIJ oversaw the work of 45 contractors as part of what it called its Systems Engineering and Technical Assistance (SETA) staff. Approximately 25 of these were assigned to OST divisions and projects, and another 8 worked somewhere in NIJ, 3 were assigned to work offsite on National Institute of Standards and Technology activities funded

---

[29]These numbers do not include other nonfederal employees working at NIJ, who would have been hired under the Intergovernmental Personnel Act Mobility Program. This program provides for the temporary assignment of personnel between the federal government and state and local governments, colleges and universities, Indian tribal governments, federally funded research and development centers, and other eligible organizations. These individuals serve as visiting scientists and in some cases have managed specific programs, such as NIJ's International Center and OST's forensic science activities. A typical term of appointment is 1-3 years, and, unlike contractors, they can participate fully in all aspects of NIJ's work. OST has had as many as three visiting scientists on board for most of the years described.

[30]Presentation by David Boyd, deputy director, OST, to Glen Schmitt, deputy director, NIJ (August 2, 2001).

by NIJ, and 3 were assigned to the Bureau of Justice Assistance. NIJ continues to make use of SETA contractors to provide scientific and analytic services; they are used to create an expanded work capacity and quick turnaround to meet immediate program requirements. They also free up program managers, who can then respond quickly and proactively to new developments. SETA contractors are subject to certain restrictions.

Continued reliance on contractors may weaken NIJ in the short and long term. Contractors are not treated like federal employees. They cannot speak for NIJ at meetings or conferences and are not allowed to access certain types of information (e.g., the electronic grant management information system). This restriction was noted by NIJ grantees, who complained that the SETA contractors with whom they consulted were limited in their ability to handle certain grant monitoring functions. As a result, the needs of researchers may not be getting met. Also when contracts expire and are not renewed, the resulting turnover may be detrimental to NIJ's stability. In FY 2008, 75 percent of the contractors supported the Forensic Science Division, the one that handles approximately 75 percent of the NIJ budget.[31]

Staff Turnover and Vacancies

As indicated above, the past decade has been one of staff growth and decline, with very high turnover occurring at all levels of the organization. Looking at the period 1998-2008—only 21 of the original 111 NIJ staff from 1998 remained in 2008.[32] Of these 21, 15 individuals continued to have responsibility for research-related activities. Comparing two points in time—2002 and 2008—63 individuals (out of 93) who appeared on the 2002 rolls were gone by 2008, and 41 new staff were hired or transferred to NIJ in the interim and on board in 2008. According to a different source, information on NIJ staffing reflects that, during a 5-year period from January 1, 2002, to November 24, 2007, approximately 76 persons separated or transferred out of NIJ, many of whom held management positions.[33] The 76 included 12 division director positions distributed among 9 different divisions, 2 deputy director positions (OST and ORE), an NIJ director, and an NIJ deputy director.[34]

Turnover is to be expected during changes of administration. But personal loyalties do not explain such a great exodus by career staff, many of

[31]E-mail from George Tillery, acting director, OST (June 27, 2008).

[32]This figure is based on data from the NFC on NIJ staff for the years 1994-2008.

[33]The list of OJP losses by separation or transfer was provided by the OJP Office of Audit, Assessment, and Management.

[34]During our own brief tenure, the committee witnessed the resignation or transfer of one NIJ director, one deputy director, one ORE director, and one OST director. Several division chiefs have also been shifted within NIJ to vacated management positions.

whom took lateral positions at other agencies or research organizations. Of the 15 former staff whom the committee interviewed, all had left NIJ during the period 1998-2006. Among the reasons they cited for leaving were lack of leadership, lack of opportunity to use their methodological expertise, and lack of a culture in which substantive expertise was highly valued and could be nurtured (see the discussion on intramural research later in this chapter).

A presidential initiative intended to restructure the federal workforce and streamline federal agency operations may also have affected staff turnover at NIJ. Known as the A-76 strategy, after the OMB Circular A-76 for which it was named (U.S. Office of Management and Budget, 1983), it involved classifying positions as "inherently governmental" or "commercial" and opening the latter to competition. The process essentially requires that private companies and in-house personnel engaged in winner-take-all competitions for the tasks in hand. Despite numerous arguments being made by OJP offices as to certain positions being intimately related to the public interest and as such must be performed by government employees, by February 2003, 79 of 98 positions at NIJ were deemed to be "commercial" and therefore open to competition. The NIJ positions included 61 of 79 research grant-monitoring positions, as well as administrative support and information technology jobs (Consortium of Social Science Associations, 2003). In September 2004, the procurement process was initiated, and, for the next 2 years, many staff believed their jobs were in jeopardy pending the outcome of the competition. In September 2006, the Department of Justice cancelled the OJP procurement, after the congressional appropriators directed that any A-76 action related to OJP needed to be brought to them in advance and special justification submitted for any program changes that reduced the personnel of an agency by 10 percent or more (U.S. House of Representatives, 2005). But by then many senior staff had departed.

It is obviously difficult to project whether or not such a high rate of turnover will continue and what the impact might be. However, one possible indicator of future turnover among senior staff is the number of staff eligible for retirement. As of April 30, 2008, NIJ had 12 employees eligible for retirement, 7 at the grade service (GS)-14/15 level and 1 at the executive-service level.

Contrasted with these numbers is NIJ's authorized staffing allocation of 87. On February 14, 2008, 21 NIJ positions remained vacant, almost one-fourth of its full-time equivalent positions.[35] These vacancies included seven

---

[35]The committee obtained OJP-approved NIJ organization charts dated September 28, 2006; November 21, 2007; and February 14, 2008. Each showed an approved allocation of 87. Information for earlier years was unavailable. Only the organization chart dated February 14, 2008, showed vacancies.

supervisory positions (either a chief or deputy chief of every ORE division, chief of the Planning, Budget, Management, and Administration Division, and chief of one OST division). In addition, there were two senior-level social science analyst positions at the GS-14/15 level and a physical scientist at the GS-14/15 level. Prior to filling a vacancy, the NIJ director must seek approval from the assistant attorney general, OJP, through the Human Resources Division, Office of Administration. NIJ managers informed us that they were not allowed to move ahead with vacancies. It is possible that some vacancies were advertised but not filled, and we know of one position in the Office of the Director for which this was true. The committee surmises that the sheer number of vacancies reflects NIJ's inability to obtain approval to move ahead and do what is necessary to fill them.

There was consensus among the former and current staff who spoke to us that NIJ is understaffed. While many factors affect how many staff a specific program will require, the committee is unaware of any formal standards by which to judge the staffing levels of federal agencies. But agencies do use some kind of yardstick to determine approved staffing allocations; given budget constraints, one can assume that these allocations will be based on conservative estimates of what is needed. Certainly for the past three years, based on the approved allocation and the number of positions that remain unfilled, NIJ appears to be severely understaffed.

Staff Qualifications

Education Levels

Given that NIJ staff are responsible for developing and managing a research portfolio, the committee was interested in learning about the staff's educational training and whether it reflects substantive knowledge of relevant science as well as training in research methodologies. We were also interested in understanding the responses to our survey of researchers and practitioners, in which only 57 percent of the respondents were satisfied with the qualifications of staff and researchers were less satisfied than practitioners (53 versus 64 percent). (See Appendix B for a discussion of the survey and its results.)

Information on individuals' educational attainment proved almost impossible to obtain. The committee was informed that educational degrees are considered private information. The committee notes that this is not the case at selective NIH institutes that provide full staff listings including bios and degrees on their web pages.[36] The committee was provided with

---

[36]See http://www.nida.nih.gov/about/organization/despr/OffofDirHome.html [accessed April 19, 2010].

a breakdown of educational attainment by division, which was compiled by NIJ from information provided by NFC.[37] Although questions remain about the data, one can conclude that the proportionate number of programmatic staff with advanced degrees (doctorates and postdoctorates) has declined since 1995 in both ORE and OST, most dramatically in OST. In 2008, only 3 persons out of 20 with programmatic responsibilities in OST had doctorate degrees or postdoctoral training. In ORE 9 persons out of 23 had advanced degrees, a lower percentage than in 1995 or 2001. The rise in the number with advanced degrees in ORE in 2001 dovetails with the large numbers of staff recruited during the period 1995-2000. Given the high staff attrition after 2001, it is not surprising that the number of staff with advanced science training also declined.

The committee recognizes that educational attainment provides a very limited view of staff qualifications, particularly since we were unable to obtain information on the fields in which degrees were granted. Nevertheless, a research agency needs to be staffed by persons with strong academic and research credentials. Experience and freshness of that experience are also important. One specific program that several committee members reviewed and discussed with NIJ staff was the centers of excellence. On the basis of discussions with NIJ staff, review of the applicants' proposals, and meetings with center staff, the committee questions whether OST staff have the technical experience and expertise to evaluate the applicants' qualifications or the work of the centers.

Not all jobs or all responsibilities will require the kind of academic training that a doctorate or postdoctorate signifies. However, a critical mass is needed of staff with advanced training in the sciences that can be called on to provide the kind of scientific advice and guidance required and to signal to the research community that NIJ staff fully understand the nature of the research enterprise. One strategy for attracting and retaining this kind of expertise is to offer opportunities to conduct intramural research. The committee notes that other science agencies, including NIH and the National Institute of Standards and Technology, have staff actively engaged in conducting research. In the 1970s and 1980s, NIJ had a division specifically devoted to intramural research. But the function was eliminated at some point during an NIJ reorganization. In 1994, an

---

[37]NIJ worked from NFC lists of staff that divided staff education levels into 22 codes. NIJ staff worked with OJP's Office of the General Counsel to group those codes into broader categories because of concern that if the cells were too small, individual staff might be identified. NIJ also eliminated staff that were at the GS-7 level or lower and staff at the GS-9 or GS-10 level, as well as anyone who was a "technician" of some sort. People who were budget analysts or program analysts in high grades remained. No further clarification from NIJ was forthcoming regarding the specific codes and the kinds of degrees included in them. Since we were not allowed to see the raw data, we were unable to verify the information.

intramural research program was resurrected, and staff members with the interest and qualifications to conduct intramural research were specifically recruited. By 1996, 16 NIJ staff members were identified as authors of papers and reports emanating from the intramural research program (National Institute of Justice, 1996). Since then, some staff members have continued to engage in intramural research, but this activity is not offered as a selling point to attract qualified staff, nor does there appear to be any incentives for it. NIJ should consider the role of a formal intramural research program as a way to attract talented criminologists who can bring new energy and expertise to its organization. Such a program can also serve as a strong incentive to retain staff who are well qualified to manage the extramural research.

Positions and Grade Levels

Most civil service employees hold a position that is part of a job series and a grade level. Exceptions to the broad generalizations here include among others the military, commissioned officers of the Public Health Service, Bureau of Veteran Affairs medical personnel, "special government employees" who serve on committees and in other ways, persons hired through the Intergovernmental Personnel Act. Each job series contains one or more position descriptions, and each position carries with it a set of requisite skills. The grade level determines the rate of pay and amount of authority. The lowest level is GS-1 (an abbreviation for grade service-1) All jobs at GS-7 or above require some form of specialized training, by either government or the private sector. Those entering the job market who have master's degrees may qualify for GS-9 and those with a doctorate may qualify for a GS-11 position.

The majority of staff in ORE fall under the 101 job series that includes social science analysts or social science program specialists. Supervisors and persons with lead responsibility have the title of "supervisory social science analyst" or "lead social science analyst." This was the prevailing category in 1998 as well as in 2008. Typically NIJ staff are recruited for these positions at the GS-12 or GS-13 level and compete for a GS-14 level position when one is advertised, but this occurs infrequently and is in fact a source of great frustration to the career staff.

OST, however, has undergone a major change in the various job series of its staff. In 1998, OST had six staff members who held GS-14 and GS-15 positions.[38] Of these, four were classified as operational research analysts and fell under the 1515 series, which emphasizes having "competence in rigorous methods of scientific inquiry and analysis" and

[38] Supervisory positions can be at either at the GS-14 or the GS-15 level.

is geared toward those with an operations research education.[39] In 2008, eight OST staff persons were classified as GS-14 and GS-15. Only one of these is classified as a 1515 operational research analyst position; four are in the 1301 physical scientists series, one is in the 801 general engineering series, and two fall into the administrative and management 340 series. The physical scientist 1301 series is a catchall series and includes work in the physical sciences that is either not classified elsewhere or that combines physical science fields, with no single one predominant.[40] It does not include a research competency qualification. Although it is difficult to say with certainty, without knowing more about people's backgrounds and training, it does appear that there has been a shift in the staffing of OST from persons with greater research expertise to persons with more generalized science and technology knowledge or administrative experience.

It is difficult to draw exact comparisons with other federal research agencies. Both NSF and NIH have the authority under United States Code Title 42 to appoint scientific positions without regard to the provisions of Title 5, which governs federal appointments. This allows the directors considerable discretion in setting requirements for scientific positions and salaries. Typically, the health scientist administrator position at NIH, a position that most closely approximates the responsibilities of the social science analyst position at NIJ, is targeted at the GS-13 and GS-14 level and specifies a Ph.D. education level; the director has the ability to hire at the GS-14 level. The net result is that NSF and NIH have much more flexibility in recruiting specifically for persons with advanced degrees and scientific skills and in setting pay levels higher than what could be typically done by NIJ.

Organizational Culture

Staff resources serve as the foundation of any organization and can be quantified to provide a rough picture of how well equipped an organization is to carry out its mission. There are also many other nonquantifiable elements that can affect the quality of the workplace and the work that is performed, and organizational culture is certainly one of them. Although it is difficult to document the psychology, experiences, and values that comprise organizational culture, a fairly consistent picture emerged from our interviews with former and current NIJ staff as well as from a summary of findings from an in-house survey of NIJ's staff conducted in September

[39]See http://www.opm.gov/qualifications/standards/IORs/gs1500/1515.htm [accessed March 9, 2010].

[40]See http://www.opm.gov/qualifications/standards/IORs/gs1300/1301.htm [accessed March 9, 2010].

2007. Taken together, these reflect an organization in which there is considerable confusion and disagreement as to the roles and responsibilities of the top leadership, the mid-level managers, and line staff. With few exceptions, the staff faults the failure of top leadership to provide direction and sufficient responsibility to the staff. Mid-level managers are viewed as undeserving of their salaries when others are doing the "real" work of the agency. Finally, the program or line staff most heavily represented in the interviews and surveys expressed very different opinions as to what aspects of their work are or should be most important. According to the NIJ in-house survey summary of 35 current employees, respondents are described as falling into two groups: (1) those who believe program administration is at the heart of their work and most important and (2) those who believe that the substantive work of knowledge development, dissemination, and other service to the criminal justice field is most important.

In contrast, former and current NIJ staff persons who were interviewed did not express views that would identify themselves as persons strongly committed to either knowledge development or to program administration. These interviewees assigned great importance to the need for strong substantive and communication skills and the need to staff the agency with persons with strong subject-matter expertise and R&D (particularly on the technology side) experience. One plausible explanation for this difference may be that, of the 26 interviewees, 15 were former staff and 11 were current staff, and the median length of service for both groups was fairly long at 9 years for former staff and 7 for current staff. None mentioned a similar kind of conflict, nor did anyone describe day-to-day activities in the same way.

One area in which those interviewed and surveyed appeared to be in agreement was that attention to the mundane operations exceeded that spent on substantive issues. Examples of such unrelated research tasks include resolving issues of language with the NIJ website, estimating quarterly travel expenses, responding to short turnaround times on reviews of OJP documents, and resolving personnel issues.

In any assessment of an agency that involves interviews with former and current staff, one expects to hear criticism, but the extent and frequency of the critical comments went well beyond what would be considered normal complaints about a bureaucracy. Taken together, these views reflect an organization that is urgently in need of strong leadership that can resolve many staffing issues that prevent it from having a more positive work environment.

CONCLUSIONS

Three conclusions emerge from the committee's analysis of NIJ research operations and staffing resources.

- **Researchers currently play a limited role in NIJ's research operations.**

In reviewing NIJ's research operations, the committee was struck by the limited role that researchers currently play in the planning, peer-review, and report review processes. NIJ has never used an advisory infrastructure to help with planning or to provide feedback in a focused and consistent way. The lack of researcher involvement in current planning processes is particularly evident in the technology research as well in the social science research areas. Even when the advice of researchers is solicited, as it is with peer review of grant applications and report reviews, the scientific judgments of researchers do not take precedence over the judgments of practitioners, who are also being asked to assess scientific quality and to numerically rank applications using the same criteria. In the case of peer-reviewed reports, it is not clear whether scientific merit trumps other criteria, such as relevance and utility, and, unlike peer review of applications, practitioners and researchers are not brought together to discuss their concerns and to arrive at a consensus.

The committee is not aware of any science agency in which the research community is less involved in providing guidance and feedback or in which practitioners play a coequal role in assessing research proposals and research reports. One possible reason for this is the perceived need, on the part of NIJ or of OJP, to equalize the contributions made by practitioners and researchers in order to ensure that NIJ research is policy relevant. Whatever the reason, NIJ appears to have devalued the contribution of researchers and distanced itself from the research community, even to the extent that the term "researcher" is not used to describe the participants in the peer-review process.[41] This distancing is also reflected in NIJ's organizational culture, in which contact with researchers other than grantees appears very limited or avoided, on the grounds that such contact may create a competitive advantage or encourage an "old boy" network.

[41] "Proposals received under a solicitation are reviewed by independent peer panels, comprised of **technologists** (emphasis added) from academia, industry, and government organizations, along with practitioners from Federal, State and local agencies. Once reviewers have completed evaluations, NIJ Program Managers recommend individual proposals to the NIJ Director, who makes final award decisions" (from the NIJ website at http://www.ojp.usdoj.gov/nij/funding/proposal-review.htm [last updated November 15, 2007] [accessed December 10, 2009]).

- **There is a lack of transparency and consistency regarding NIJ's research operations.**

Nothing affects the stature of a research institute more than a lack of transparency as to how funding priorities are arrived at and funding decisions are made. Because the grant award process is a highly competitive one and researchers must invest considerable time and effort in preparing applications, researchers will not seek support from an institution they believe is arbitrary in its decision making. The committee heard firsthand from the NIJ leadership that the grant award process was altered from one in which individual applications on a particular topic competed against each other to one in which all applications for numerous solicitations were grouped together and considered for the same pool of funds. The change in the grant award process was not announced to applicants prior to their submitting an application, nor were NIJ staff aware that this might occur. Not being clear on how decisions are made or, worse, changing the rules in the middle of the game, has serious implications for researchers' perceptions of the fairness and consistency of NIJ's practices. Once these perceptions are formed, they are difficult to change.

The committee also encountered considerable difficulty in obtaining documentation for NIJ's research operations as well as other kinds of administrative information. While we note that most programmatic as well as administrative information is maintained by OJP, there are steps NIJ can take to document its research processes, improve its record-keeping, and become a more transparent operation.

One of these is to improve access to data through the NIJ website. Despite numerous improvements that have been made during the course of our study, the committee found it difficult to determine whether research grants had resulted in available final reports or to trace titles of existing reports or publications back to grants. Many websites of research agencies[42] have a searchable online database of research awards that allows users to search for awards by topic, principal investigator, or grantee institution. In addition, these agencies provide funding amounts, names of principal investigators, and abstracts for each award. NIJ does have an archive list of awards dating back to 1995 online that are sorted by topic and, in recent years, by solicitation as well; funding amounts and grantee institution are provided for each award listed. However, names of principal investigators ceased to be included after 2003, there are no abstracts or descriptions available for

[42]See, for example, the Institute for Education Sciences at http://ies.ed.gov/funding/grantsearch/index.asp and NSF at http://www.nsf.gov/awardsearch/ [accessed July 28, 2009].

the awards, and there is no mechanism to distinguish research grants from other types of capacity-building or technology assistance grants.

Recognizing the importance of transparency and conducting a thorough assessment of its research operations, financial, and administrative records to determine how it might be achieved are important steps for NIJ to take.

- **OJP's oversight of various aspects of NIJ's research operations and administrative functions is incompatible with NIJ's role as an independent research organization.**

The committee identified at least two research operations in which OJP plays a heavy hand: the approval of solicitations and the peer-review process. In the case of the solicitation review process, OJP appears to have created a lengthy and convoluted process in which NIJ solicitations undergo extensive review by numerous OJP offices, and the focus of the review appears to go beyond what are strictly legal or financial issues. The centralization of peer review has also resulted in several requirements that may not be best suited for a research organization. All solicitations are not equal, and NIJ needs the authority to assess the peer review process in light of its own needs and to make changes it deems necessary. Under the current system, this is difficult to do.

NIJ's staffing resources have also been greatly impacted by OJP's oversight and control. The analysis of NIJ's staffing resources paints a picture of an organization that has experienced great variations in staffing size and composition caused by high turnover during the period 1994-2008. For many of these years, NIJ has been badly understaffed because it was prevented by the OJP leadership from recruiting against its approved staffing allocation. Management positions have been particularly affected, and with two or three exceptions there is almost no one currently in a management position who held that same position at NIJ as recently as two years ago. There also appears to be a shift from NIJ staff with strong science backgrounds to those with a more generalized knowledge of technology and a continued reliance on contractors to compensate for this lack of research experience and technology expertise. While it is difficult to show cause and effect, the committee thinks that these changes have taken a great toll on NIJ's current staff, as reflected by its current organizational culture. NIJ staff interviews also reflect frustration with the lack of administrative support, and the nonresearch-related demands growing out of OJP oversight.

While remaining very understaffed, NIJ has a cadre of experienced people who expressed a strong desire to produce high-quality research and to be of service to the criminal justice field. For this to occur, NIJ needs control over its own operations, needs to undertake a thorough self-examination in an effort to improve its operations and become more transparent, and needs the authority and capacity to make the changes. Key among these is for NIJ to ensure the proper role of science in its decisions and to involve the research community in a more meaningful way in accomplishing its mission.

5

Building a Research Infrastructure and Guiding Policy and Practice

In addition to funding individual research projects, research agencies typically are also involved in building the infrastructure for research in their areas of interest and enhancing dissemination and utilization of research results. In this chapter we review and assess the efforts of the National Institute of Justice (NIJ) to improve the research infrastructure—efforts that are especially important for the development of crime and justice research—and to enhance the use of research by criminal justice practitioners and policy makers.

In 1968, when NIJ was established, the systems supporting crime and justice research were not well developed, and research efforts were underfunded and driven primarily by the interests of researchers. Few university-based researchers worked in this area, there were few doctoral programs that excelled in research training, and not-for-profit and other private-sector research capabilities devoted to these topics were almost nonexistent. In fact, included in the functions assigned to NIJ was the charge to support the growth of crime and criminal justice research and to take steps to encourage research utilization. The 1977 National Research Council (NRC) committee noted the absence of a strong crime and justice research community as one of the barriers to the success of NIJ (National Research Council, 1977). It also found few systematic efforts to translate research into practice or (where appropriate) to adopt research-based standards for practice and policy.

Building a research field and enhancing research utilization include the following types of efforts: (1) building research capacities, (2) using research to guide policy and practice, and (3) disseminating research findings to the research and practitioner communities. Throughout its history, NIJ has supported programs aimed at addressing each of these areas. In fact, as we show, in some of these areas NIJ has been a leader at the federal level.

The efforts of NIJ described in this chapter include fellowship programs, the data archive and training programs for researchers at the National Archive of Criminal Justice Data (NACJD), the equipment compliance standards program, technology assistance[1] provided to practitioners, and the communications office and its dissemination activities. In addition, we look at the function recently assigned to NIJ of administering grant programs to improve crime laboratories and reduce the backlog of DNA processing in these laboratories. We examine these forensic capacity-building grant programs as well as NIJ's technology assistance activities to determine what, if any, impact they have had on its ability to fulfill its mission as a research agency. We conclude the chapter with a description and appraisal of NIJ's dissemination efforts to provide information to its state and local constituents as well as the criminal justice research field.

BUILDING RESEARCH CAPACITIES

The field of crime and justice research has greatly expanded since the creation of NIJ. While this growth can be attributed mostly to changes in higher education, increased public interest in crime and justice, and the growth of the criminal justice system, the federal government, including NIJ, has played an important role. The Omnibus Crime Control and Safe Streets Act of 1968 that established NIJ also enacted the Law Enforcement Education Program, which provided almost $200 million in grants and loans to support the education of law enforcement officers returning to college as well as to the development of new doctoral programs as models for higher education (Jacobs and Magdovitz, 1977). The increased availability of federal funding for programmatic improvements inevitably attracted researchers to assist in program development and evaluations. NIJ's efforts to provide direction to the growing number of researchers working on crime and justice topics included strategies to reach and appeal to a wide range of disciplines in solicitations for research studies as well as support for researchers through fellowship programs and the creation of a publicly available data archive for criminal justice research.

This is most notable in the growth of criminology as a scientific discipline. Prior to 1966 there were 2 doctoral programs in the field; today

[1] "Technology assistance" is an elusive phrase intended to indicate support in many forms related to the operation of technology devices, such as radios or lab equipment. The committee develops a definition of technology assistance as it applies to NIJ's activities and services later in the chapter.

there are over 30 (Association of Doctoral Programs in Criminology and Criminal Justice, 2009). Masters programs have increased from a handful to over 1,100. Membership in the American Society of Criminology has grown from under 500 in 1970 (Morris, 1975) to over 3,000 today. In 1968 there was only a single reputable peer-reviewed journal focusing on crime and justice issues; today there are over 100. One commentator on the growth of criminology concluded that the Law Enforcement Assistance Agency (most importantly the Law Enforcement Education Program) was central to the establishment of these programs and the development of the discipline (Akers, 1992). Savelsberg, Cleveland, and King (2004) have documented how federal funding, including support from NIJ, has influenced the growth and direction of criminology as a science.

Fellowship Programs

The Omnibus Crime Control Act of 1968 calls for the institute to "carry out programs of instructional assistance consisting of research fellowships." From the beginning, it has provided support to doctoral students in their research through the Graduate Research Fellowship Program (Law Enforcement Assistance Administration, 1969) and has since expanded efforts to encourage young minority scholars to develop their research programs through the W.E.B. Du Bois Fellowship Program and to attract senior researchers and practitioners to NIJ through the Visiting Fellows Program. These programs have had as their goals increasing the number of young scholars in crime and justice research, addressing the gross underrepresentation of minority researchers in this field, and augmenting NIJ staff with short-term senior researchers and practitioners. In order to examine how successful they have been in achieving their goals, the committee had a review conducted of these programs.[2] The following is a summary of that review and the committee's assessment of the data that were gathered.

Graduate Research Fellowship Program

The Graduate Research Fellowship Program provides dissertation research support to outstanding doctoral students undertaking independent research on issues in crime and justice (Crossland, 2008). The goal of the program is to expand the pool of research talent by attracting doctoral stu-

---

[2]The committee notes with appreciation the assistance of Nicola Smith, who prepared a report that was helpful in the preparation of this chapter. She contacted current and former NIJ staff and W.E.B. Du Bois fellowship and Graduate Research Fellowship recipients to gather information on the fellowship programs with regard to history and current management, as well as information on recipients' research achievements.

dents who can contribute critical and innovative thinking to pressing crime and justice problems. Students from any relevant academic discipline may apply through their university. NIJ asks dissertation advisers to bring this program to the attention of their most promising students early in their dissertation pursuit. There is no predetermined number of awards each year. The monetary value of the award is a fixed amount ($20,000), although some applicants in the past have applied for less. Awardees are expected to complete their research in a 1-year period.

Individual award information is maintained through the OJP grant management system and budget files in the Planning, Budget, Management, and Administration Division. The program has been managed by four different staff members since 1999. This is not an unusual situation in government agencies. However, at no time have there been formal transition procedures from one program manager to another. As a result, the program history is not well documented, since records are missing or incomplete.

Fellows are monitored like other NIJ grantees, contacted on a monthly or quarterly basis via phone or e-mail, and required to make progress reports every six months using the categorical assistance progress report (Office of Justice Programs, 2006a). They are also encouraged to present their preliminary and final findings at appropriate academic meetings and conferences. Many fellows present their dissertation work at "job talks" when they enter the job market. No final report is required; the dissertation as approved by the grantee's university is the final report, along with a final progress report. Fellows are invited to present at colloquia at NIJ in special cases.

According to NIJ, there was a total of 68 recipients in the period 1998-2006. The recipients, at the time of their award, represented a variety of disciplines, but most were in criminology or criminal justice (55 percent) or sociology (18 percent) departments. Other disciplines include psychology, mental health, geography, engineering, political science, social welfare, social work, anthropology, economics, and biology. According to our review,[3] all but the recent awardees had completed their doctoral degrees and more than half are now in full-time teaching positions. More than half have published[4] since receipt of their fellowship. Of those who have

[3]Report prepared by Nicola Smith for the committee meeting January 8-9, 2009, on NIJ Fellowship Programs.

[4]On the basis of information on 51 of the recipients, 425 publications were authored, which included 287 articles in peer-reviewed journals, 69 technical reports, 61 chapters, and 8 books. And 42 of the journal articles are available in Tier 1 journals and 62 in Tier 2 journals. Less than half (48 percent) of the subsequent publications were deemed unrelated to dissertation topics of the respective authors. Journal publications were classified in tiers based on the classification of the University of Maryland College of Behavioral and Social Sciences. This tier classification is used to rank research publications: typically, Tier 1 (premier), Tier 2 (leading),

published, the average number of their publications was six. The strategy employed by the fellowship program, suggesting a list of broad topic areas of research, has had success in generating research publications on a wide range of topics.

A list of fellows provided by NIJ for our assessment suggests that adequate management and monitoring of the fellowship program were not in place. The original list included individuals as having received funding when in fact they had not. It also included administrative personnel from the universities as recipients of the fellowship but no information regarding the actual recipient.

Most awards are for a 1-year period; however, time of completion is not recorded by personnel in charge of the fellowship programs. According to our review,[5] more than half of the Graduate Research Fellow recipients contacted did not complete their research in 1 year—the range for completion was 1-7 years. This is not surprising for dissertation work. Although there are models for successfully completing and defending one's dissertation within a year of proposing the research,[6] the average criminology Ph.D. candidate takes 2-4 years to complete the written dissertation in a full-time program and 3-6 years in a part-time program.[7] The University of Maryland allows up to 4 years for completion of the dissertation once admitted to candidacy,[8] and other Ph.D. programs in criminology have similar requirements.

In summary, after making these awards, NIJ does not appear to have spent much effort to see that work was completed in a timely manner, to assess the career impacts of the award, or to continue a relationship with the awardees. The programs, while well intentioned and contributing to the growth of doctoral graduates in the criminal justice field, have not been integrated into the program plan or operations of the agency.

Tier 3 (reputable), and Tier 4 (local/others). Tier 1 journals represent the top publications in individual disciplines and for this analysis include the following publications: *Criminology*, *Journal of Research in Crime and Delinquency*, and *Journal of Quantitative Criminology*. The Tier 2 journals include *Criminology and Public Policy*, *Justice Quarterly*, *Social Science Quarterly*, *Law and Social Inquiry*, *Psicotherma*, *Journal of Health and Social Behavior*, and *Aggression and Violent Behavior*.

[5]Report prepared by Nicola Smith for the committee meeting January 8-9, 2009, on NIJ Fellowship Programs.

[6]See for example the Ph.D. timeline at the University of Missouri, St. Louis, available at http://www.umsl.edu/~ccj/pdfs/program_time_line.pdf [accessed July 16, 2009].

[7]See information on pursuing a Ph.D. program in criminology at http://www.topcriminaljusticecolleges.com/phd-program-in-criminology.html [accessed July 16, 2009].

[8]See degree program information at http://www.ccjs.umd.edu/Graduate/phd.htm [accessed July 16, 2009].

W.E.B. Du Bois Fellowship Program

The W.E.B. Du Bois Fellowship Program was undertaken to address a critical need to build the ranks of minority researchers interested in crime and justice issues. Planning of the program began in 1998-1999, with the goal of providing an opportunity for minority researchers to interact with NIJ staff and to provide their perspective on NIJ programs. Seeking the guidance of the U.S. Department of Justice (DOJ) on how to initiate such a program, NIJ staff were told the department's view that any federal program explicitly for minorities would be in violation of federal laws against discrimination and, if a suit arose challenging federal programs that were exclusively for minorities, the department would not support them.[9]

Despite this setback, plans for the program moved ahead. However, to address the department's concern, the requirement that all applicants be minority researchers was revised. New guidelines were written in such a way to appeal as much as possible to minority researchers, and race as a selection criterion was dropped. The original guidelines also included a requirement that grantees spend at least a portion of their time onsite at NIJ, where they would participate in its various activities.[10] In more recent years, terms of residence in the fellowship program have become more flexible.

The first W.E.B. Du Bois fellowship was awarded in 2000. The Du Bois fellowship complements NIJ's other fellowship programs and provides talented researchers early in their professional career with an opportunity to elevate independently generated research and ideas to the level of national discussion (Crossland, 2008). Fellowship awards have the goal of supporting projects with direct implications for criminal justice policy and practice in the United States (National Institute of Justice, 2007c).

The W.E.B. Du Bois fellows are monitored like other grant recipients. Recipients are required to submit progress reports every six months for the duration of the grant. A final report is also required. Du Bois fellows are encouraged to present at professional meetings, but NIJ has neither facilitated this nor tracked when it happens. W.E.B. Du Bois individual award information is maintained in the grant management system of the Office of Justice Programs (OJP) and budget files in the Planning, Budget, Management, and Administration Division.

Since the beginning of the program there have been four different managers. Again like the Graduate Research Fellowship Program, there are no formal procedures in place for transition of the program and the program history has not been well documented.

The committee's assessment of this program is therefore solely depen-

[9]Conversations with NIJ Staff, September 9, 2009.

[10]Conversations with NIJ Staff, September 9, 2009.

dent on what we learned about past recipients of the fellowship awards. There have been a total of nine recipients in the period 2000-2007, and the total amount awarded was $563,078. The awards ranged from $45,343 to $78,767, with an average of $70,385, being awarded per year. Recipients were selected from across the United States, with three selected from the South, two from the Midwest, two from the mid Atlantic, and one from the Pacific. The review of the current resumes of seven of the nine awardees, identified 67 publications[11] since completion of their fellowships, approximately half of which were related to their fellowships; 16 of 37 published journal articles are available in Tier 1 and Tier 2 journals.[12]

All the award recipients were located in established educational institutions and committed to the field of criminology. All have stayed in the field, becoming productive scholars and continuing work that began during the fellowship. Although there is variation in the productivity of the fellows, our review of their professional careers suggests that the fellowship stimulated their work and resulted in numerous publications. Of course we cannot determine how these individuals would have done without the award, but we note that the Du Bois fellows have contributed to the breadth of crime and justice research in terms of the range of topics related to the goals of the program. In addition, those supported by this program have become productive contributors to the crime and justice research literature.

However, NIJ currently does not have a very effective way to monitor and track research produced by fellowship recipients. Without such follow-up, there is no way to assess the extent to which the goal of increasing the number of young scholars, particularly underrepresented minorities, is being met.

Visiting Fellows Program

The goal of the Visiting Fellows Program, begun in 1969, was to bring criminal justice professionals and researchers to NIJ for a period of 6-18 months to work on research projects or the development of research-based action programs. For the most part, the fellows were established leaders in their field. The award included salary, benefits, reasonable relocation expenses, travel and supplementary costs for their project, and office expenses. Fellows were required to spend at least 80 percent of their time at NIJ. Often they were assigned to work with a particular program or organizational unit. Over time, there may have been some deviation from

[11]Publications include articles in peer-reviewed journals, books, chapters, and technical reports.

[12]Report prepared by Nicola Smith for the committee meeting January 8-9, 2009, on NIJ Fellowship Programs.

the original guidelines, depending on the research tasks undertaken and the program offices involved.

The committee could not find any systematic records on the fellows program or the contributions of the fellows. Without better documentation, we cannot determine how many applications were received, how the fellows were selected, what role they played at NIJ, or how their final reports were used by the agency. We were verbally informed that the program was discontinued in 2004 because of resource constraints. The agency did not issue a solicitation for the program for fiscal year (FY) 2005-2009. As the writing of this report, the solicitation for *NIJ's Visiting Fellowship Program* was released for FY 2010.

Our very impressionistic observation is that the program attracted many well-known criminal justice researchers and practitioners, many of the projects undertaken by the fellows have had influence on criminal justice practice and policy, and NIJ staff thought that many of the fellows played important roles in developing the agency's research plans and programs. The absence of better records on this program left the committee in a position of recognizing the potential value of this type of effort but with no way to assess that value.

Data Archiving Program

NIJ has been a leader at the federal level in recognizing the importance of collecting, archiving, and making available to other researchers the data collected as a part of the projects it funds. In 1981 NIJ began requiring research award recipients to submit the data collected in their projects. This was in part a response to the recommendation of the 1977 NRC committee that NIJ "collect and maintain a data archive that retains various general criminal justice data . . . collected by individual investigators after the original investigator has completed use of the data" (National Research Council, 1977, p. 113). This recommendation led directly to the establishment of the Data Resources Program (DRP).

In 1984, NIJ established DRP to ensure that data collected with NIJ funding are permanently preserved and are available for use by others in the research community. NIJ-sponsored researchers are required to submit their data to the DRP at the conclusion of their projects. Since 1991, NIJ data, codebooks, and other supporting documentation are deposited with the National Archive of Criminal Justice Data (NACJD) at the University of Michigan's Inter-university Consortium for Political and Social Research (ICPSR). Scholars, practitioners, policy makers, students, community activists, and any other interested parties throughout the world can freely use all NIJ-sponsored data collections for the purposes of conducting scientific research. This research can include verifying, refining, or refuting the original investigator's findings or pursuing inquiries not addressed by the other investigators by using alternative theoretical and analytical models or by combining with data collected at other sites or time periods.

With the support of NIJ, ICPSR is able to acquire and to facilitate the use of a wide variety of data in the fields of criminology, law, and justice. NIJ benefits from a number of important ICPSR roles, including (1) the perpetual preservation of its research investments and products, (2) an infrastructure on the Internet that provides worldwide dissemination of its data and related documentation to the research community, (3) added value by documenting and describing data files that aid the users of data, (4) a team of justice data specialists who have unique skills in data management and computerized mapping technical assistance needed by archive sponsors and data users, and (5) training programs to communicate quality research methods and analysis and promote the use of existing data. Funding for the archive has come from NIJ and the Bureau of Justice Statistics. NIJ has awarded approximately $6 million to ICPSR for the archive since 2001.

As with other aspects of NIJ, no systematic review has been conducted of DRP or the data archive at NACJD. In September 2003, NACJD provided a memorandum to NIJ indicating ways the program could be evaluated, but no action was taken on any of its recommendations. NACJD, however, regularly monitors submissions to the archive, uses of the archive, and feedback from its training programs. We were able to review the data assembled over the years in a report prepared for us by NACJD.[13] A summary of some of the information and analyses is provided in the subsequent sections.

Monitored Data Submissions

In 1997 web access to the data from NACJD was made available. Based on web logs from 1997 to October 2008, the number of NIJ-sponsored studies in NACJD grew from 256 to 776, a 200 percent increase. In 1997, NIJ-sponsored data comprised 43.3 percent of the studies in NACJD; in October 2008, they were 50.4 percent (see Figure 5-1). The database tracking NIJ-funded research was developed in December 1999 and therefore contains complete records from the year 2000. According to NACJD records, from January 2000 to October 2008, there was data "activity" (defined as data acquired, released, or preserved only, or designated as "no data to

[13]Our review of the data archive program included conversations with current and former staff at NIJ and the University of Michigan, responses to questions posed by the committee to archive staff, a site visit to the archive, and consideration of a report on the archives prepared by Kaye Marz and Christopher Maxwell. The committee notes with appreciation the contribution of the report prepared by Marz and Maxwell made to this section.

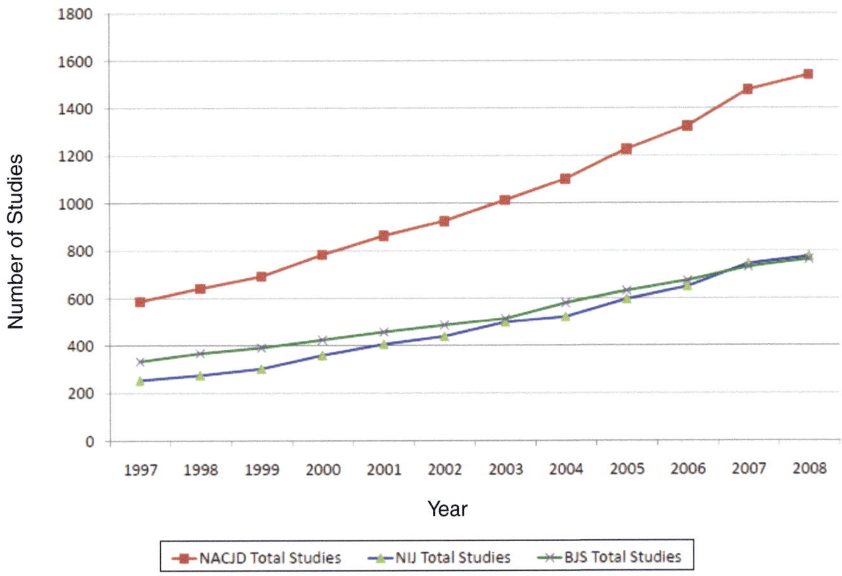

FIGURE 5-1 Total studies submitted to NACJD by year.
SOURCE: Report prepared for the committee by Kaye Marz and Christopher Maxwell, Inter-university Consortium for Political and Social Research.

archive") on 395 studies, an average of 43.9 NIJ-sponsored studies per year, ranging from a low of 28 in 2004 to a high of 80 in 2007. During the same period, NACJD released data from 320 studies, an average of 35.6 studies per year, ranging from a low of 16 in 2005 to a high of 63 in 2003; and designated 28 studies as no data to archive or storage only. Data from 47 studies remained to be processed. Note that this number of studies released or preserved does not include the 174 studies from the Project on Human Development in Chicago Neighborhoods (PHDCN) released between 2005 and 2007, for which a dedicated processor was assigned, jointly supported by NIJ and the MacArthur Foundation until March 2007.

There have been improvements in the quality of files deposited in the archive. Staff and grantee efforts to raise quality have resulted in larger numbers of data sets in the archive being judged as having higher quality and therefore ease of use, according to NACJD's data-quality measurement system, put into place in 2005. Even though data sets submitted to the archive have increased in size and complexity, their usefulness has improved as more attention has been paid to data quality. In our survey of researchers and practitioners, 75 percent of the respondents indicated that they had used the archive and 90 percent of those judged it useful to their work.

Over the years, NIJ and NACJD have sought to encourage submission of data by NIJ grantees. These efforts include special award conditions, letters to those who had not submitted data indicating the possibility of negative consequences for future funding if they did not submit their data, and new special conditions in 2008 that require awardees to deposit data and data documentation 90 days before award closeout or risk nonpayment of grant funds. These efforts combined with technological changes at the archives that make submission easier have resulted in increases in the number of data sets deposited.

What is not known is the current extent of data archiving that is occurring. One obvious measure is the proportion of completed awards that deposit complete and usable data in NACJD. This calculation is complicated by the difficulty of determining the number of awards made by NIJ and the number of those awards that produce data sets. Neither NIJ nor NACJD was able to provide us with the total number of awards that should have their data archived. However, records from NACJD as well as our own efforts to identify principal investigators in the archive database (see citation analysis in Chapter 6) indicate that a substantial number of projects that should have archived data have not done so—the estimates range from half to upward of 90 percent of all research awards since 1995. Even though we cannot precisely gauge the problem, we think that efforts must be undertaken to improve the archiving of data. An important first step to achieving this will be for NIJ to substantially improve its administrative records. We also urge NIJ to screen former NIJ grantees who are applying for grants as to whether they have complied with data archiving requirements and to withhold support until such requirements are met.

Monitored Uses of Data and Online Resources

MyData is the ICPSR user registration and authentication system for the NACJD website that collects user affiliation, institutional department, and statistical package preferences. In the years 2006-2008, roughly half of NACJD users were graduate students. Undergraduate students, faculty, and, to a lesser extent, nonacademic researchers constituted the rest of the users. Nearly half of the total users were from criminal justice or sociology departments. The remainder of users represented other disciplines.

In 1997, 4,544 data users accessed any file related to an NIJ-sponsored study on the NACJD website, representing 33 percent of the NACJD downloads for the year. By 2007, the number of similar accesses was 18,274, representing 35 percent of NACJD downloaded studies (see Figure 5-2). NACJD also keeps track of literature that cites any of the data it archives. This bibliography is publicly available online and contains links to the respective data sources and their descriptions (see Chapter 6). Over the

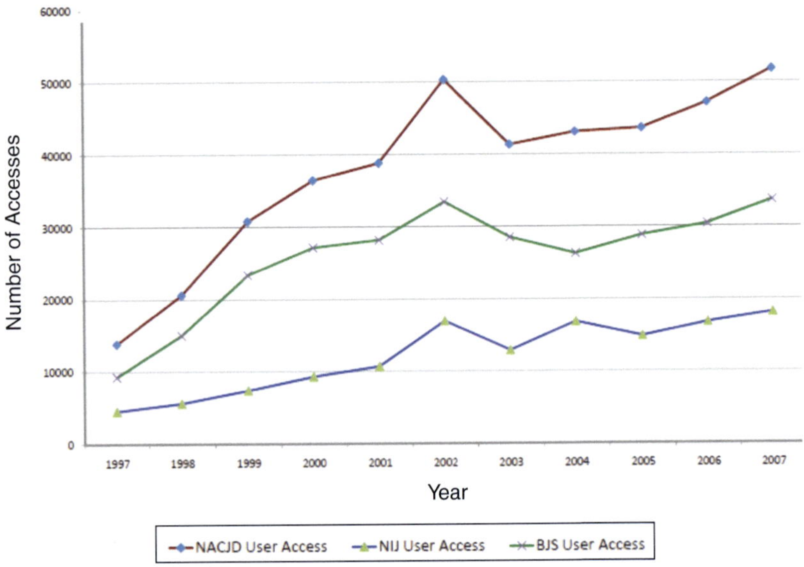

FIGURE 5-2 NACJD user access by year.
SOURCE: Report prepared for the committee by Kaye Marz and Christopher Maxwell, Inter-university Consortium for Political and Social Research.

period 1997-2007, the annual number of total publications linked to any NIJ-sponsored data housed in the archive averaged 162.

Through the DRP, NIJ not only supports an archive of data generated from the studies it sponsors, but it also funds proposals to replicate previous findings and conduct original research extending data available from the archive, as well as training programs on data acquisition and analysis.

Secondary Data Analysis

NIJ has routinely supported the use of data gathered in its earlier studies and archived at the University of Michigan in the NACJD. It has done this by issuing annual solicitations calling for secondary analysis of data to replicate findings of the original study or to test new hypotheses with existing data. In the period 2005-2008, NIJ made 16 awards under the *Data Resources Program* solicitation, an average of 4 awards per year. Most of these awards addressed effects on crime trends, such as mental illness, neighborhood dynamics, legal deterrents, and incarceration. One-third of the awards were directly related to the Project on Human Development in Chicago Neighborhoods and/or neighborhood violence.

These solicitations are generally open-ended, inviting researchers to ask compelling questions that promote understanding of crime or inform criminal justice policy and practice. However, the solicitations may suggest topics of specific interest. For example, the 2007 solicitation expressed interest in studies of crime trends in cities. The 2009 solicitation interests included analysis of data and evaluation research from PHDCN, particularly the use of experimental designs and cost-benefit analysis. Awards are generally small, with a stated limit of $35,000, but may be divided into stages for sequential funding. The award cap of $35,000 has been in place since the FY 1997 solicitation *Data Resources Program Funding for the Analysis of Existing Data.* Given the high cost of data collection required for many studies, this small initiative leverages prior NIJ investments and can provide a good return on the funding.

Sponsored Training on Data Acquisition and Use

From 1994 to 2001, DRP sponsored a one-week workshop on crime and justice data as part of the ICPSR Summer Training Program in Quantitative Methods. The program resumed in 2008 with the sponsorship of the Workshop on the Project on Human Development in Chicago Neighborhoods. Activities continued in the federal case data course in 2009. During the period when NIJ did not support the summer workshop, NACJD hosted five workshops focused on NIJ-supported data and resources. Through funding from the MacArthur Foundation, courses on the PHDCN data were held in 2005 and 2006. In addition, a workshop on spatial statistics using CrimeStat[14] was held in 2005, 2006, and 2007.

Highlighted topics and studies selected each year present substantive areas of research interest, new analytical techniques or applications, and available data on the topic from the archive. The workshops recruit expert researchers or faculty as presenters, including those who were principal investigators on the data set of interest. Workshop participants are a combination of university faculty, advanced graduate students, and criminal justice agency–based researchers or analysts. These workshops are designed to enable participants to achieve a theoretical understanding of the topic and to gain practical knowledge from using the data. Participants have consistently reported these workshops to be of high value.

[14]*CrimeStat* is a spatial statistics program for the analysis of crime incident locations, developed by Ned Levine & Associates, that was funded by NIJ grants.

GUIDING PRACTICE AND POLICY

On a wide range of fronts, there have been increasing calls for research to inform practice (Sherman, 1998; MacKenzie, 2000; Welsh and Farrington, 2001; National Research Council, 2005c; Ritter, 2007). As part of their efforts to build research infrastructures, federal research agencies have a responsibility to facilitate the transfer of research findings to policies, applications in the field, and public knowledge. This is particularly important for NIJ, since it has a mandate to improve federal, state, and local criminal justice systems. As we outline in Box 5-1, there are many possible federal-level activities aimed at guiding practice and policy at state and local levels. One of the continuing challenges facing NIJ is to support activities that are best aligned to its research mandate and to assign a lower priority or to avoid support for activities that are best assumed by other programmatic offices in OJP, such as the Bureau of Justice Assistance.

In this section, we describe three activities currently pursued by NIJ to guide practice and policy: (1) testing and evaluation, and standards, (2) technology assistance, and (3) forensic capacity building. We show how NIJ's role in guiding policy and practice has, in the past 5 years or more, consumed the agency. Note that the total sum of the funds for these three activities represents 15-35 percent of NIJ's total budget for the period 1996-2001, grew to 55-65 percent from 2002 to 2007, and represents 84 percent of the total budget in 2008 (see Figure 5-3). Grants for these activities are administered primarily out of the Office of Science and Technology (OST) and supported by funds from legislative mandates, such as the President's DNA Initiative and earmarks to the National Law Enforcement Corrections Technology Center (NLECTC), as well as from OST base funds.

Given that NIJ has a wide audience, a limited budget, and a first priority of sponsoring research aimed at accumulating knowledge, the committee grappled with the question of what assistance activities are appropriate for a federal research agency. The committee focuses the discussion here on technology development because the majority of NIJ's assistance activities are technology-related. However, our approach is appropriate for any context in which a research agency's role in the continuum from the accumulation of knowledge to its use or translation into practice is considered.

While there is a continuum from development of technology to adoption of new technology by state or local agencies, no clear thresholds exist between research, development, dissemination of knowledge from that research, and assistance in using that knowledge to acquire, conduct training on, or use new technologies. Because NIJ's charter is to conduct research and currently it is devoting considerable operational resources and funds to nonresearch or assistance activities, the committee sought to define some boundaries.

BOX 5-1
The Continuum from Development of Technologies to Adoption into Practice

As the activities fall on the continuum from technology research and development to assistance as ranked by the committee	Activities that define the federal role in supplying technology-related support to state and local agencies

Research and Development

- Sponsoring research and development
- Testing and evaluating technology and developing performance standards for technology and its use
- Providing information in the form of technology-related conferences
- Providing information in the form of technology news, including federal reports, newsletters, etc.
- Providing advice on selecting technology, such as evaluations of technology appearing in federal publication, Internet sites, etc.
- Providing technology assistance by applying federal resources and expertise to specific problems
- Providing access to available federal technology, such as a database
- Providing training in the use of technology
- Assisting with access to federally supplied technology
- Funding the acquisition of or access to equipment and/or technology

Assistance

SOURCE: Adapted from Schwabe, Davis, and Jackson (2001, pp. 6-7, 115).

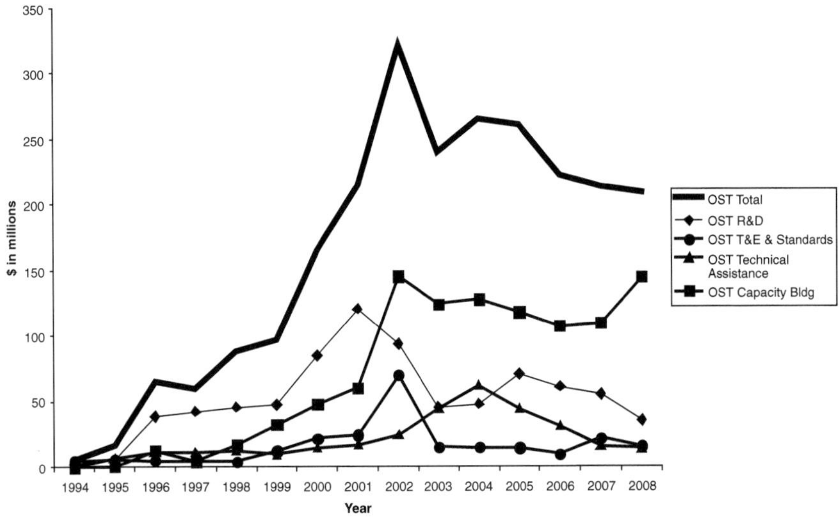

FIGURE 5-3 History of OST spending by functional efforts (in constant 2008 dollars).
NOTES: OST = Office of Science and Technology, R&D = Research and Development, T&E = Testing and Evaluation.
SOURCE: Created from figures supplied by OST.

We began by adapting a list of activities that describes the federal role in supplying "technology-related support" to state and local agencies from a 2001 RAND report[15] (Schwabe, Davis, and Jackson, 2001, pp. 6-7, 115). We then ranked the activities associated with technology-related support on a four-point scale from most appropriate to not at all appropriate for a federal research agency. The activities in Box 5-1 are ordered by the averages of the rankings from low (indicating lean toward research functions) to high (indicating lean toward assistance functions). This exercise was useful in identifying where on the continuum from technology development to adoption into practice the committee thinks NIJ's program assistance activities lie and how appropriate they are for this federal research agency.

[15]The RAND report was based on findings from the nationwide Law Enforcement Technology Survey and a similar Forensics Technology Survey, conducted in late spring and early summer 2000; interviews conducted throughout the year; focus groups conducted in autumn 2000; and review of an extensive, largely nonacademic literature. The report examined the technologies in use or needed by law enforcement agencies at the state and local levels, for the purpose of informing federal policy makers as they consider technology-related support for these agencies. The report peripherally addressed services and programs supported by NIJ, particularly those coordinated through the NLECTC system.

NIJ currently engages in all of the activities identified in Box 5-1. Its role in sponsoring research and development is discussed in Chapter 3. In the remainder of this chapter, we describe its activities to (1) develop performance standards, (2) provide technology assistance, and (3) build forensic capacity—discussing these three activities in an order that parallels their descending relevance to NIJ's research mission.

Testing and Evaluation and Standards

There is continuing need in law enforcement agencies to procure products and equipment, at reasonable cost, that can be used effectively under rigid safety standards (Law Enforcement Assistance Administration, 1969; Schwabe, Davis, and Jackson, 2001). The best way to verify the capabilities and reliability of particular products is through independent, third-party testing and evaluation in combination with recognized performance standards (McBath, 2008). Federal sponsorship of such independent, third-party testing as well as establishment of the performance standards is critical because the law enforcement market is neither large nor lucrative enough to attract sufficient private-sector R&D investment (Schwabe, Davis, and Jackson, 2001).

Through OST, NIJ administers a standards and compliance testing program to help ensure that equipment will perform at a safe, dependable, and effective level. The NLECTC system (see Chapter 3) oversees the development of standards for equipment, testing protocols, and evidence collection; the production of standard reference materials, operating procedures, and equipment guidelines; and a standard-based compliance testing program. Through its testing and evaluation and standards programs, NIJ has been able to help criminal justice agencies make informed procurement, deployment, applications, operating, and training decisions for over 35 years.

The current Office of Law Enforcement Standards (OLES) has a long history. The U.S. Department of Commerce and DOJ, through a memorandum of understanding, established the Law Enforcement Standards Laboratory in 1971 under the auspices of the National Bureau of Standards (Russell and Rice, 2000), which would later become the National Institute of Standards and Technology (NIST). The laboratory's primary roles were to develop scientific-based voluntary, commercial manufacturing standards and to certify laboratories in which equipment items could be evaluated according to those standards (Law Enforcement Assistance Administration, 1971). Although the Law Enforcement Standards Laboratory changed names[16] over the years, its role and duties have persisted.

---

[16]The Law Enforcement Standards Laboratory (LESL) became the Standards Group when NILECJ launched the Equipment Systems Improvement Program in 1972. LESL became part

Currently called the Office of Law Enforcement Standards, it once had NIJ as the primary sponsor of its projects, with additional support from the National Highway Traffic Safety Administration, the FBI, the Federal Aviation Administration, the Federal Bureau of Prisons, and the Office of Management and Budget (Russell and Rice, 2000), but in recent years a significant amount of funding has come from the U.S. Department of Homeland Security (DHS), the Science and Technology (S&T) Directorate, and Community Oriented Policing Services (COPS). In FY 2008, OLES received approximately $55 million from partnerships with NIJ, COPS, and DHS S&T (National Institute of Standards and Technology, 2009).

Support of its testing and evaluation and standards programs represents 5-10 percent of the yearly budget of OST, according to figures supplied by NIJ. Much of the budget for the NIJ standards program goes to the interagency agreement with NIST and the contract to Aspen/Lockheed to run NLECTC–National. The cost to run a compliance program is about $1 million a year, and the cost to revise a standard is also about $1 million.[17]

The first standards formulated were for ballistic resistance of police body armor and for hearing protectors used on police target firing ranges. By 1975, the standards laboratory had completed nearly 20 performance standards for protective equipment (e.g., police body armor and ballistic shields), tools (e.g., handcuffs and metal detectors), and communication equipment (e.g., radio transmitters and voice scramblers) (National Institute of Justice, 1994a). There are currently 44 NIJ standards and numerous NIJ-supported reports and guides listed online at the NIST Office of Law Enforcement Standards website (see http://www.eeel.nist.gov/oles/oles_publications.html [accessed March 17, 2010]).

Through the standards contract to NIST, OST supports the development of performance testing methods and the creation of standards for equipment and operating procedures, the testing and evaluating of existing equipment, the development of examination methods for evidentiary materials, and the production of standard reference materials.

NIJ has recently revised its standards development process and is currently creating or revising standards for the chemical, biological, radioactive, nuclear (CBRN) protective ensemble, holsters, handcuffs, and electronic monitoring. In the new standards development process, NIJ iden-

---

of NIJ's Technology Assessment Program in the mid-1980s. In 1994, the NIJ National Law Enforcement Technology Center was established to take over the functions of the Technology Assessment Program Information Center. Today, what once was LESL is now the Office of Law Enforcement Standards in the National Institute of Standards and Technology and part of the NLECTC system.

[17]Personal communication from OST deputy director, George Tillery.

tifies the requirements of practitioners, reviews any existing standards, and performs a gap analysis between those requirements and existing standards. A special technical committee is set up to define the scope of the effort and to produce the standard and related documents. An advisory working group and steering committee[18] are also established to provide guidance and oversight. Draft documents are made public for review and comment before they are approved by the steering committee and published by NIJ (Robinson, 2009).

OST also supports compliance testing based on standards and dissemination of standards and other related information through NLECTC–National. NLECTC-National oversees the equipment standards and testing program, reviews and analyzes testing data and publishes test results and consumer product reports, publishes *TechBeat*, and operates JUSTNET[19] (see Box 5-2).

NLECTC-National also administers two types of testing programs for commercially available equipment: standards-based testing and comparative evaluations. Standards-based testing is conducted at NIJ-approved independent laboratories to confirm the equipment compliance with voluntary performance standards developed by OLES. This testing is now being performed continually on ballistic-resistant body armor, stab-resistant body armor, and computer forensic tools and periodically as needed on metallic handcuffs, semiautomatic pistols, and walk-through metal detectors. Comparative evaluations field-test equipment in order to make test data available to law enforcement agencies as well as vendors. This testing has been performed on patrol vehicles; patrol vehicle tires (including testing of winter tires); replacement brake pads; and cut, puncture, and pathogen-resistant protective gloves (see http://www.justnet.org/Pages/Topic.aspx?topic=218&ct=Service [accessed March 17, 2010]).

In nearly 40 years, OLES has developed over 300 standards, equipment guides, and technical reports, and NLECTC–National has tested over 5,000 models of body armor. The first performance standard and testing program for ballistic body armor has been credited with saving thousands of lives (National Institute of Justice, 2003d). Groundbreaking work in developing forensic science standards has pioneered advances in arson, ballistics, fingerprint, and DNA analyses (National Institute of Standards and Technology, 2009). The current committee did not explore in depth NIJ's standards program, but notes that an NRC panel that assessed OLES and other offices in NIST (National Research Council, 2002) was impressed with the scope

[18]The advisory working group consists of senior-level personnel from stakeholder organizations, NIJ, and NIST/OLES. The steering committee consists of the OST deputy director, the DHS S&T Standards executive, and the NIST/OLES director.

[19]See http://www.justnet.org/Pages/Home.aspx [accessed March 17, 2010].

BOX 5-2
Descriptions of NLECTC Resources

JUSTNET is a website that provides links to the entire NLECTC system and a gateway to other technology sites in order to assist those seeking information about equipment, technology, or research findings. JUSTNET houses the body armor database, which can be searched to determine whether models are compliant with NIJ standards. It also has links to other standards documents and consumer product lists of relevance to the public safety community (see http://www.justnet.org/Pages/Home.aspx [accessed March 17, 2010]).

TechBeat is NLECTC's news magazine published four times a year. It is intended to keep practitioners up to date with technologies currently being developed by the NLECTC system, as well as other research and development efforts within the Federal Government and private industry (see http://www.justnet.org/Pages/TechBeatAbout.aspx [accessed March 17, 2010]).

InShorts are two-page documents published by NIJ through OST and often prepared by NLECTC staff. They highlight a specific technology, identify benefits and issues, and provide resources for more information.

of its work and noted that OLES products are "widely used at the federal, state, and local levels, and in other countries as well, and they form the basis for testing and certification programs throughout the criminal justice community" (National Research Council, 2002, p. 56).

OLES, in conjunction with NLECTC-National, has provided a needed and valuable service. "The consequences of inadequate equipment performance or inadequate test methods can range from inconvenient to catastrophic" (Rosendall, 2002, p. xii). Federal support for technology standards development has protected the law enforcement community from disappointment as vendors "try to sell them secondhand technology originally designed for other purposes" (Schwabe, Davis, and Jackson, 2001). Success of the standards programs has increased the call for more standards (Schwabe, Davis, and Jackson, 2001; Law Enforcement and Corrections Technology Advisory Council, 2008).

Technology Assistance

According to figures supplied by OST, funds for technology assistance, ranging in annual amounts from $8 to $54 million, have represented roughly 10-20 percent of its budget from 1996 to 2007. However, it is difficult to separate out what specific activities are included in the budget category of technology assistance. Through a review of NIJ's annual reports and legislative appropriations and comparison of various budget figures, the committee has discerned that much of the technology assistance monies go to the NLECTC system. And many of the activities conducted by NLECTC now or in the past fit the definition of "technology-related support" (Schwabe, Davis, and Jackson, 2001). Some of them, if they have a foundation in knowledge from research, are appropriate for a federal research agency, but several are better suited for an assistance agency (see Box 5-1).

NIJ defines technology assistance on its website[20] as bringing "advances in scientific research and technology closer to the frontlines through the National Law Enforcement and Corrections Technology Center (NLECTC)." The website notes that NLECTC offers "scientific and technical support to NIJ's research and development efforts; demonstration and transfer of technology that can be adopted by the field; assistance in the development and dissemination of technology guidelines and standards; [and] technology assistance, information, and support to law enforcement and corrections agencies, courts, and crime laboratories." Again, we see NLECTC in the role of primary provider of technology assistance and services that advance the research mission, but some of its services appear out of scope.

NLECTC's activities tie directly to its purpose as spelled out in the Homeland Security Act of 2002 [Sec 235]. It is interesting to note that NIJ's broadening of scope—that is, taking on functions beyond a research agency's mission—is marked in legislative shifts. The Omnibus Crime Control Act of 1968 authorized the institute "to make recommendations for action which can be taken by Federal, State, and local governments and by private persons and organizations to improve and strengthen law enforcement." Thirty-four years later with the passage of the Homeland Security Act of 2002, NIJ moved beyond making recommendations and has a current legislative mandate to "provide technology assistance, information, and support for law enforcement, corrections, and criminal justice purposes."

From funds appropriated by Congress specifically from 1995 to 2008, the NLECTC centers have been able to provide resources to law enforcement agencies, public safety personnel, and vendors. Such resources include facilities and guidance for testing and evaluating technologies

---

[20]See http://www.ojp.usdoj.gov/nij/topics/technology/assistance.htm [accessed July 28, 2009].

in operational environments; reports on findings from these operational tests; equipment standards; publications, such as *TechBeat* and consumer product reports; websites, such as JUSTNET, and online tools, such as CAPRAD, and the body armor database; training workshops; and referral services. See Box 5-2 for descriptions of some of these resources. In making these resources available to the criminal justice field at no charge, the centers support the transfer and adoption of technology into practice by law enforcement and corrections agencies, courts, and crime laboratories and stand ready to provide technology assistance, information, and support for its adoption.

A 2001 RAND report provides examples of noteworthy NLECTC early accomplishments (Schwabe, Davis, and Jackson, 2001). Of the 44 examples presented there, 13 illustrate situations in which a center served as a liaison or resource for a single law enforcement agency to gain access to or information from a particular technology in order to solve a specific case. Nine are examples of specific projects between a center and a law enforcement agency or set of agencies to develop a needed tool for a particular issue; often these were needed communication networks or information databases. There were four examples of publications and conferences produced or sponsored by the centers and four examples of training developed and administered by the centers. The remaining noteworthy accomplishments included two or three examples each of serving as a liaison in the transfer of surplus equipment to law enforcement agencies, orchestrating demonstrations of new tools and technologies, providing support for testing technologies, building alliances with groups and organizations with mutual interests, and providing referrals upon calls for assistance.

Although the examples in the 2001 RAND report are probably not representative of the centers' workloads, the abundance of examples on direct technology assistance for individual case investigations is striking. The centers have been criticized for their limited reach, often serving only criminal justice agencies near center host institutions. The committee's 2008 site visits to some of the centers confirmed that direct technology assistance and services to individual local agencies were still conducted.

For example, the Border Research and Technology Center views its role as outreach and technical assistance to the practitioner community on behalf of NIJ. One assistance effort grew out of a survey of local sheriffs' administrative assistants, when the center learned that officers needed to be able to enter or type their own reports into the computer. Center staff developed a "mobile computer lab" to take laptops into the field to the actual locations for training in word processing to facilitate data entry. As of our 2008 visit, the computer class had been taught in over 30 counties with over 300 attendees.

A federal research agency's role is to use research knowledge to influence policy and practice nationally and not just to assist individual agencies. The appropriate strategy, with limited resources, is to focus on broad dissemination and development of cost-effective training and not to provide one-time technical or training services that are tailored for a specific location or agency.

Forensic Capacity Building

NIJ's success in the research and development of DNA analysis is described in Chapter 3. As a result of this success, during the past 10 years NIJ became a "go-to" place for anything related to DNA analysis and other forensic tools. As Congress recognized the power of DNA profiling to identify perpetrators of crimes and to exonerate persons charged with or convicted of crimes they did not commit, it passed initiatives to increase the use of this technology in the criminal justice system.

The DNA Identification Act of 1994, part of the Crime Act, modified the Omnibus Crime Control Act of 1968 "by inserting provisions regulating funding of DNA analysis laboratories and authorizing the collection of an index of DNA records and samples."[21] In 1996, with funds made available under the Crime Act, OST initiated major efforts, through the Forensic DNA Laboratory Improvement Program, to assist state and local crime laboratories with upgrading their equipment and developing simpler, quicker, and more portable methods of DNA testing (National Institute of Justice, 1997). In fiscal year (FY) 2000, through congressional appropriations, the Forensic DNA Laboratory Improvement Program became the Crime Laboratory Improvement Program (CLIP) and a portion of the appropriated funds was designated for distribution to the states to reduce the backlog of DNA samples taken from convicted offenders. Subsequently, the enactment of the DNA Backlog Elimination Act of 2000 provided funds to address the backlog of samples taken from crimes for which there is no known suspect in addition to convicted offender samples. In late 2000, Congress enacted the Paul Coverdell National Forensic Sciences Improvement Act, which authorized funding to improve the quality, timeliness, and credibility of forensic science services for criminal justice purposes (Hart, 2002b). Finally, since 2004, NIJ has received a substantial amount of monies, through the President's DNA Initiative and the Justice for All Act of 2004, to fund state and local forensic laboratories to help reduce DNA backlogs as well as support the development of forensic science training and

[21]See http://www.dna.gov/funding/backlog-reduction/legislation [accessed August 11, 2009].

delivery programs and models for improving the efficiency and capacity of public forensic DNA laboratories.[22]

The appropriations for DNA backlog reduction and other forensic capacity-building efforts have resulted in NIJ awards for such efforts totaling over $680 million.[23] As is evident from congressional testimony by a former NIJ director (Hart, 2002b) and from financial information supplied to the committee for the period 2003-2006, much of the money appropriated by Congress was earmarked. For example, of the $95 million in total funding for FY 2000-2002 for CLIP, approximately $59 million, was designated for specific recipients (Hart, 2002b). The remaining discretionary funds were awarded through competitive solicitation processes out of OST.

NIJ's Forensic Capacity-Building Solicitations

Since 2002, there have been nine types of solicitations, administered through OST, to sustain congressional directives and allocations. The programs resulting from these directives include

- the Paul Coverdell Forensic Science Improvement Grants Program,
- the Forensic DNA Capacity Enhancement Program,
- Forensic DNA Unit Efficiency Improvement,
- the Convicted Offender and/or Arrestee DNA Backlog Reduction Program,
- the No Suspect Casework DNA Backlog Reduction Program,
- Solving Cold Cases with DNA,
- the Forensic Casework DNA Backlog Reduction Program,
- Using DNA Technology to Identify the Missing, and
- the Postconviction DNA Testing Assistance Program.

The Paul Coverdell Forensic Science Improvement Grants Program[24] (FY 2002-2009) provides assistance to state and local crime laboratories and medical examiners to eliminate forensic backlogs, improve the timeliness of forensic science and medical examiner services, and train and em-

---

[22]Monies from these directives were also available to support R&D awards in forensic DNA analysis (see Chapter 3).

[23]This estimate is based on totals of awards for DNA backlog reduction and forensic laboratory improvements in the award database developed from NIJ's online archive of awards 1995-2008 (see Chapter 3). The estimate was compared with award figures reported on the President's DNA Initiative website (see http://www.dna.gov/funding/ [accessed March 17, 2010]) and figures reported in NIJ annual reports.

[24]For more information, see http://www.ojp.usdoj.gov/nij/topics/forensics/nfsia [accessed March 17, 2010].

ploy personnel. Funds for this program rose from $4.9 million in 2003 to $16.1 million in 2007.

The Forensic DNA Capacity Enhancement Program (FY 2004-2006) offered states and units of local government with existing crime laboratories that conduct DNA analysis funds to improve laboratory infrastructure and analysis capacity so that DNA samples can be processed efficiently and cost-effectively. The Forensic DNA Unit Efficiency Improvement Program (FY 2008-2009) is designed to support the improvement of public forensic DNA laboratories through the development and adoption of an improved laboratory process. A major goal is to publish successful, carefully evaluated, and novel improvement methodologies as models to consider by other public laboratories.

The Convicted Offender and/or Arrestee DNA Backlog Reduction Program (FY 2000-2009) provides funds to help defray the costs of DNA testing to establish DNA identification databases, a legislative mandate in all states. This testing must be done by accredited labs and all DNA profiles must be entered into the Combined DNA Index System (CODIS).[25] By 2007, NIJ had provided more than $150 million to perform DNA analysis on samples for more than 100,000 cases and the processing of DNA samples for about 2.5 million convicted criminals (National Institute of Justice, 2007a). Although NIJ awards have been successful in eliminating backlogs of DNA samples, the ultimate goal is hard to achieve because the backlog of DNA samples is a growing target. Backlogs grow because, as DNA profiles become more useful and collection of samples more efficient, states are extending the categories of individuals qualifying for DNA profiling (e.g., arrestees) and of the crimes in which DNA analysis may be used (e.g., nonviolent crimes and misdemeanors).

The No Suspect Casework DNA Backlog Reduction Program (FY 2001 and 2003) offered an opportunity for states to apply for funding for identification, processing, and analysis of cases with no suspects, either by their own public laboratories or by qualified fee-for-service vendors. Grantees were asked to process or analyze all samples according to established procedures and protocols following the Quality Assurance Standards for Forensic DNA Testing Laboratories set by the director of the FBI and to use DNA databases to solve no-suspect crimes having DNA evidence. Approximately $25 million was available for identification, processing, and analysis of no-suspect casework in FY 2003 (National Institute of Justice, 2002).

Solving Cold Cases with DNA (FY 2004, FY 2007-2009) seeks applications from states and units of local government for funding to identify, review, and investigate "violent crime cold cases" that have the potential to be solved using DNA analysis and to locate and analyze biological evidence

---

[25]Both CODIS and the National DNA Index System (NDIS) are managed by the FBI.

associated with these cases. Advances in DNA technologies have substantially increased the successful DNA analysis of aged, degraded, limited, or otherwise compromised biological evidence. As a result, crime scene samples once thought to be unsuitable for testing may now yield DNA profiles. In addition, samples that previously generated inconclusive DNA results may now be successfully analyzed using newer methods (National Institute of Justice, 2008c). These funds allow agencies to start cold case units, hire and train personnel, or buy equipment and supplies (National Institute of Justice, 2007a).

The Forensic Casework DNA Backlog Reduction Program (FY 2004-2009) provides funding to state and local DNA laboratories to reduce the backlog of untested DNA evidence and convicted offender DNA samples that overwhelm the nation's crime laboratories. In 2004, officials estimated a backlog of over 540,000 unsolved criminal cases with biological evidence available for DNA testing (Lovrich et al., 2003).

The program Using DNA to Identify the Missing (FY 2008-2009) provides funds (1) to assist eligible entities in performing DNA analysis on unidentified human remains or reference samples to support the efforts of states and units of local government to identify missing persons and (2) to enter the resulting DNA profiles into the FBI's National DNA Index System using CODIS (National Institute of Justice, 2008d).

Under the Postconviction DNA Testing Assistance Program (FY 2007-2009), NIJ helps states defray the costs associated with postconviction DNA testing of violent crime cases in which actual innocence might be demonstrated. A number of people convicted of crimes have been subsequently exonerated through DNA analysis of crime scene evidence that was not tested at the time of trial. Such posttesting of samples is possible because newer technologies have substantially increased the successful analysis of aged, degraded, limited, or otherwise compromised biological evidence.

Assessment

As one can surmise from the above descriptions for numerous solicitations and annual programs, in addition to the monies spent over the past 5 years or more, NIJ puts a substantial amount of attention (i.e., funds, staff, administrative resources) on providing direct services and assistance to individual law enforcement agencies and crime laboratories. Furthermore, NIJ puts a lot of resources into assessing these forensic capacity-building programs. This kind of support for systematic assessment, described briefly below, does not exist for other NIJ programs.

Two audits constitute NIJ's assessment of the forensic capacity-building program: the Coverdell program and the DNA Backlog Reduction Program. Both are conducted by the National Forensic Sciences Technology Center (NFSTC), currently the grantee that administers the Forensics Science Center of Excellence (see Chapter 3). One audit review, known as External DNA Audits, grew out of the original authorizing language for the program, and funds were earmarked for this purpose. It examines operating DNA laboratories for their compliance with FBI and American Society of Crime Lab Directors standards.[26]

A second audit, known as the Grant Progress Assessment (GPA) Program, was established in 2004 by the NIJ director. The program assesses grantee progress in meeting program goals and objectives, reviews program documentation, and assesses the impact of the grant funding. As part of the audit, a random sampling of offender and casework DNA profile data is conducted to ensure the work quality is up to standards. The audit also assesses the lab's internal data review and quality control programs. This review addresses the legislative requirement that DNA profile data generated under these grants meet the quality standard for submission to the national DNA database.

Management of the DNA backlog reduction programs and the Coverdell Program has been critiqued by the DOJ Office of the Inspector General (Office of the Inspector General, 2002, 2004, 2005, 2008; U.S. Department of Justice, 2009a). The essence of the critiques is that NIJ has been lax in the management of these programs, noting (among other problems) failure to provide guidance to grantees regarding programmatic requirements or to ensure grantee compliance with these requirements, failure to effectively monitor grantee financial and programmatic activities, failure to evaluate grantee effectiveness in meeting program objectives, and failure to ensure that performance reports were submitted in a timely fashion. The most recent audit, of the Convicted Offender DNA Backlog Reduction program (U.S. Department of Justice, 2009a), made 11 recommendations, all of which were accepted by OJP with proposed or already implemented corrective actions.

DISSEMINATING RESEARCH KNOWLEDGE

Dissemination of knowledge has always been part of the NIJ mission. The Omnibus Crime Control Act of 1968 mandated that the institute "carry out a program of collection and dissemination of information pertinent to crime and justice issues." To accomplish this mission, NIJ historically has pursued a two-fold strategy: (1) put research findings into the hands of policy makers and practitioners and (2) inform and communicate

[26]For more information, see http://www.nfstc.org/assessments/external-dna-audit-program/ [accessed March 19, 2010].

with the research community about ongoing research and current state of knowledge.

NIJ views policy makers and practitioners, particularly at state and local levels, as the primary audience for its dissemination activities. But by reaching out to researchers and encouraging their discourse, a research agency invests in building a research infrastructure, fosters a scientifically competent, highly qualified community of researchers, and strengthens its own research capacity.

While it expects that many of the researchers it supports will seek to have their work privately published, and citation analysis is one performance measure in the Program Assessment Rating Tool (PART) assessment of the Office of Management and Budget, NIJ does not appear to place great importance on its research being presented in peer-reviewed journals. This judgment is based on the fact that NIJ expends few resources on tracking such data (see Chapter 6) and makes few public references (outside its PART submission) that reflect its interest in the privately published work of researchers.[27] The committee believes that publication of findings in peer-reviewed journals is a critically important dissemination product and researchers should be encouraged by NIJ to submit their reports and acknowledged when publication occurs.

While many of its dissemination products emanate from NIJ's research studies, many do not. This practice of not focusing exclusively on research findings dates back to NIJ's inception when it was required by Congress to begin research and to disseminate results simultaneously. With the criminology field in its infancy and years to go before NIJ-sponsored research would yield a sizeable body of knowledge, there simply was not much research to disseminate. With little choice, NIJ turned to what the 1977 NRC review committee called a "highly aggressive marketing approach" that involved disseminating nonresearch-based "products," an approach the committee felt was highly inappropriate for a research institute (National Research Council, 1977).

Today, the context in which NIJ operates is quite different and the field of criminology has matured. In the following sections, we provide a brief overview of the size and scope of NIJ's current dissemination activities, how its products and audiences have changed over time to reflect its current portfolio, and its efforts to assess its dissemination activities.

[27]The committee found only one public reference to the peer-reviewed publications of NIJ-supported researchers, in a presentation by Margaret Zahn at the NIJ meeting called Stimulating the Adoption of NIJ Research Results (December 12, 2008).

Size and Scope of Dissemination Activities

Budget

Dissemination is generally handled by the Communications Division located in the Office of the Director. Over the past 5 years, the dissemination budget has remained stable. In FY 2009, the Communication Division's budget totaled $4.6 million, of which $1.05 million was designated for publications; $1.7 for the National Criminal Justice Reference Service (NCJRS); $1.5 million for NIJ's annual conference; and the balance of $385,000 for two websites, one for NIJ and the DNA.gov website. In addition to the resources budgeted to the Communication Division, OST expends its own funds to support and manage certain dissemination activities. For example, about 30 percent of the NLECTC system budget, approximately $4 million, goes toward informational activities. Of that amount, NLECTC–National expends about $1.1 million a year on costs associated with an 800 Line Call Center, various publications including *TechBeat*, conferences exhibits, and JUSTNET. In addition, another $2 million is spent by the four Centers of Excellence on informational activities. Included in this budget is also the Applied Technology Conference,[28] a major showcase for NIJ technology work. OST also expends about $330,000 on its Technologies for Critical Incident Preparedness and Response Conference, a joint venture with the Department of Defense and the Department of Homeland Security.[29] Prior to 2002, the funds for dissemination have been about 10 percent of NIJ's total budget. This percentage for dissemination is reasonable for a research agency.[30] However, in the past 6 years, the percentage of NIJ's budget for dissemination has dropped to about 2-6 percent, due primarily to the dramatic increase in OST's overall budget while the total amount of funds for dissemination has remained fairly constant (roughly $10 million).

With no increase in the dissemination budget for 5 years, NIJ staff expressed the view that they were hard-pressed to keep up with major changes that are taking place in the communications field. Greater reliance on the Internet requires additional resources to support a variety of new activities, such as podcasts and video productions, writers trained to write for the web, and web analytics necessary for understanding and optimizing web usage. In some cases, it is not a matter of NIJ deciding to allocate its own

[28]See http://www.ojp.usdoj.gov/nij/events/applied-technologies/welcome.html [accessed March 17, 2010].

[29]Personal communications from George Tillery, acting director, OST.

[30]See for comparison the Institute of Education Sciences FY 2010 budget request, which notes spending about 12 percent of its FY 2008 $160 million budget for research, development, and dissemination (U.S. Department of Education, 2010).

resources but requesting and then competing against the other OJP bureaus for additional administrative funds for information-related services.

NIJ Publications and Products

Since its inception, NIJ has had to grapple with the issue of how best to serve the different information needs of many diverse groups: researchers, both academics and analysts based in criminal justice agencies; criminal justice officials and practitioners at federal, state, and local levels; policy makers; advocacy groups; and the public. During administrations of different NIJ directors, the emphasis has shifted back and forth between a greater focus on dissemination activities and publications geared to researchers and a focus on publications and activities intended to provide practical advice and guidance to the broader criminal justice practitioner community. In addition to a shift in intended audiences, a shift has also occurred in the volume of information being disseminated as well as its content.

As reflected in its annual reports to Congress, NIJ dramatically changed the scope and focus of its dissemination activities in 2002 from what it had produced during the previous 6 years.[31] During the period FY 1995-2001, NIJ published, either in hard copy or electronically, a variety of documents geared to inform the criminal justice field about the latest social science and technology research findings. Through the late 1990s, there was a heavy emphasis on producing reports based on NIJ research grants. More than eight different formats of varying lengths were used to describe research in progress and completed research studies. Some formats presented the findings in summary form only; others presented the full reports containing all the details of the research. Most focused on NIJ-sponsored research, but some described research activities being undertaken by other agencies, such as the Centers for Disease Control and Prevention and the Office of Juvenile Justice and Delinquency Prevention. In addition to reporting on findings, NIJ published documents that provided information on specific programs being conducted by state and local criminal justice agencies that appeared to be promising crime prevention or reduction efforts. It also produced and distributed videotapes of 60-minute lectures with a question and answer segment presented by well-known scholars and accompanied by a Research Preview summarizing the salient points of the discussion.

To illustrate the expanse of NIJ's prior dissemination efforts, one need only look at the materials published in FY 1999, the year between 1995

[31]This analysis is based on a review of titles of dissemination materials contained in NIJ annual report appendices. The lists appear to be inclusive until about 2004, when materials produced by NCLETC tended not to be included (see Appendix D).

and 2007 when NIJ publication activities reached their peak. That year, NIJ produced more than 75 different publications and products. Of these, approximately 61 documents were based on social science research activities and 14 on technology R&D efforts (see Box 5-3).

During this same year, NIJ produced volumes 23 and 24 of its *Crime and Justice Journal*, a series devoted to essays by leading criminal justice researchers that summarized current knowledge on topical subjects. It also produced several brochures, a videotape, three *NCLETC Bulletins*, three issues of *TechBeat*, and three issues of the *NIJ Journal*.

BOX 5-3
NIJ Publications and Products in FY 1999

A *Research in Action* report on case management in the criminal justice system (12 pp.)

18 *Research in Briefs*: summaries of recent NIJ research and evaluation findings (4-12 pp.)

16 research reports providing more detailed information on R&D projects (40-60 pp.)

10 *Research Previews*: 2- to 4-page summaries on research and evaluation findings

3 *Issues and Practices* reports on program options for criminal justice managers and administrators (50-100 pp.)

3 *Program Focus* reports highlighting specific state and local criminal justice programs (20-40 pp.)

5 publications resulting from NIJ research forums and conferences

2 guides on batteries and police body armor

2 equipment performance reports on auto-loading pistols and vehicle tires

---

SOURCE: National Institute of Justice (1999, Appendix C).

In reviewing the documents from the period 1995-2002, one is struck not only by the volume of reports but also by the degree to which various formats were tailored to specific audiences (see Appendix D). With the exception of some of the reports specifically labeled "research reports" and some equipment-related materials, such as guides, test protocols, and testing results, most were written in nontechnical language and emphasized research findings that had implications for policy and practice as appropriate.

After 2002, however, there was a sharp decline in the total number of publications and products. In the NIJ FY 2002 annual report, 20 publications and reports are listed. The numbers have increased only slightly since then, and, through 2007, NIJ produced on average about 30 products and publications exclusive of issues of *TechBeat*, *NIJ Journal*, and the newly developed *Geography and Public Safety Bulletin*, a quarterly publication produced jointly by COPS and NIJ.

There also appears to be a shift from targeting a readership made up of both practitioners and researchers to one aimed primarily at practitioners and policy makers. In 2002, NIJ abandoned several of its former report formats, including Research Previews (two-page summaries), Research in Action, and Issues and Practices. The currently named Research in Brief, a document of 16-20 pages, is the only publication specifically intended for researchers and scholars as well high-level practitioners and policy makers (National Institute of Justice, 2005) (see Table 5-1). By producing fewer documents for the research community, NIJ appears to have abandoned an important strategy for encouraging interest in criminal justice research and for keeping researchers informed about its research activities.

The committee also notes that, in 2003, NIJ discontinued its long-term support for *Crime and Justice, A Review of Research*. Begun in 1978, *Crime and Justice* was intended to be an annual volume of essays on crime and justice. The rationale behind the series was to bring together the very best thinkers to address a particular topic and purposefully look beyond their own specialty to develop a broader understanding of crime and justice. NIJ provided support for an editorial board, editors, and commissioned papers. The average cost of a volume was approximately $175,000. The staple essays presented a summary of the state-of-the-art with authors also presenting their views on the policy and research implications of what was known at that time. *Crime and Justice* has continued to be funded, most often with funding from European sources, and its content consists primarily of European topics. The committee did not discuss whether funding for such a publication should be reinstated but offers it as an example of a

TABLE 5-1 Types of NIJ Grant Products

Type	Audience	Length
Research for Practice	Practitioners and their staff	3,000-5,000 words 20-30 manuscript pages 8-16 printed pages
Research for Policy	Policy makers and their staff	500-1,000 words 4-8 manuscript pages 16-20 printed pages
Research in Brief	Researchers and scholars; high-level policy makers, practitioners, and their staffs	4,000-6,000 words 32-40 manuscript pages 16-20 printed pages
NIJ Journal	High-level policy makers, practitioners, and their staffs	500-5,000 words 3-35 manuscript pages 1-5 printed pages
Science and Technology Report	Practitioners and policy makers	Varies with content (20-500 printed pages)
Special Report	Varies with content	Varies with content (20-500 printed pages)
Web-only Document	Varies with content	Varies with content (20-500 printed pages)

research tool that was of value to the scholarly community and contributed to NIJ's stature as a research institute.[32]

With the shift in the NIJ budget to one in which technology-related research activities receive heavy support, it is not surprising that there has also been a marked shift in the number of reports that focus on technology and, in particular, forensic science. This is most dramatically reflected by the most requested documents compiled annually by the National Criminal Justice Clearinghouse. In FY 2000, of the top 24 most requested documents, 10 dealt with technology topics. For each subsequent year, the number of technology-related reports has increased. In FY 2007, 19 reports dealt with technology issues, 3 reports dealt with social science research, and the 2 remaining reports were issues of *NIJ Journal*, the semiannual periodical. The shift is also reflected in NIJ's FY 2006 and FY 2007 annual reports. In the 2006 annual report, only two of its six chapters describe social science research on victims and victimization and improving corrections programs

[32]In 2005 ISI citation analyses showed *Crime and Justice* had the highest "impact" (frequency of citation per article published) of any "criminology, criminal justice, or penology" journal. No later statistics are available because the *Crime and Justice* data were inadvertently dropped in 2006-2008 but reinstated in 2009 (Tonry, 2009).

and practices. The remaining four chapters are devoted to technology activities. The 2007 annual report devotes even fewer pages to social science research. In its five chapters, only one chapter on courts and corrections describes past and ongoing social science research activities.[33]

In addition to its own sponsored publications, NIJ also relies on other venues to disseminate useful information to the practitioner and policy maker. An example that was touted by NIJ was the regular appearance of articles authored by NIJ staff or others writing about NIJ research activities in *Corrections Today*, a monthly publication produced by the American Correctional Association with a monthly distribution of 36,000. The committee reviewed these articles because of criticism from national corrections leaders regarding NIJ's failure "to do a good job of marketing to constituents" and a failure to disseminate executive summaries of NIJ research as well as other information of use to corrections but not necessarily produced by NIJ.

Since 2003, NIJ has submitted 33 articles to *Corrections Today* for inclusion under its "NIJ Update" or NIJ "Technology Update" bylines or as a *Corrections Today* feature. (The latter publication is produced approximately 4-5 times a year.) Three topics have been the subject of multiple articles: stress reduction, reentry, and federal benefits for disabled offenders. Other articles highlight a specific research project (e.g., boot camps); describe several studies on a similar topic (e.g., drug courts); identify new technologies being developed and adapted for corrections use (e.g., duress systems in correctional facilities); and approaches to improving security (e.g., cell phone smuggling); one describes the difficulties in undertaking cost–benefit analyses. Interestingly, one article reports on an unsuccessful program, Project Greenlight, a reentry program in New York, and the possible reasons for its failure. In almost all cases, the articles provide citations and web addresses.

The committee notes the usefulness of this approach for disseminating information about NIJ activities but makes no judgment regarding the quality or usefulness of the information itself. Given the criticism we heard and the relatively low satisfaction ratings with NIJ, there do seem to be questions as to whether NIJ is providing topics of interest to the corrections field and whether the current format and content lend themselves to increased familiarity with NIJ and its activities. A systematic assessment might shed some light on these questions.

---

[33]Singled out in this chapter are activities that involve adoption of a mental health screening tool developed by an NIJ-funded researcher, an evaluation of a domestic violence field experiment, and an analysis of California's parole policy.

National Criminal Justice Reference Service

NIJ relies heavily on NCJRS, the federally supported information clearinghouse, to disseminate information about its research program and related activities. It also serves as the archive for all grantee final reports. Initiated in the mid-1970s through a competitive contract, NCJRS now serves as the information clearinghouse for 13 other federal offices and bureaus who contribute funding support. It has approximately 14,600 registered users, who can tailor the information they want to receive.[34] Throughout 2008, NIJ sought to attract more users for its information by offering direct subscription from its own website. In 5 months since e-mail alerts were offered, almost 3,000 subscribers have signed on.[35]

The activities associated with the clearinghouse include a call center, a library and abstract service, a website (see http://www.ncjrs.gov [accessed March 17, 2010]), a warehouse and fulfillment function, conference exhibits, and associated management/administration expenses. NCJRS also assists NIJ with editorial and graphics work on their publications.

Numerous changes occurred with NCJRS in the late 1990s. A major shift to electronic technologies occurred, and the warehouse was emptied out. After 2003, documents could be downloaded. This had a significant impact, with major changes in the basic operation and a shift in costs. Mailing lists needed to be developed, and priorities for other OJP offices (that were contributing to NCJRS) needed to be redefined. This process took a couple of years.

In 2002, responsibility for NCJRS was transferred to the Office of Communication in OJP. The NIJ staff member responsible for the contract was moved to that office, but, by 2007 when that person was reassigned, for the first time in NCJRS history, no one with former or current ties to NIJ was responsible for the oversight and management of NCJRS.

It is difficult to ascertain whether this change has impacted the quality or efficiency of the NIJ dissemination activities conducted by NCJRS. No records are available to compare the costs or services prior to and after OJP assumed responsibility. Former and current NIJ staff members who were interviewed reported that from time to time there are disagreements with OJP management over NCJRS policies and practices, but no details were offered.

One observation was made that OJP centralized management of NCJRS has appeared to impact NIJ in the degree to which NIJ as an organization is visible at various conferences and meetings. Since OJP assumed responsibility for the NCJRS contract, there has been an OJP policy that prohibited an

---

[34]E-mail communication from Lesley C. Flaim, NCJRS, May 22, 2009.

[35]E-mail communication from Lee Mockensturm, NIJ, May 22, 2009.

individual agency from displaying its own banner at the NCJRS conference booth if two or more OJP bureaus wanted to have a staff person there. Attendance by multiple OJP bureaus occurs frequently because many of them view attendance there as an effective way to share information about their office's activities and to communicate with the broader criminal justice community. Also, the bureaus often want to reap the benefits of sharing the costs of the NCJRS booth. Without individual banners, OJP is the focus of attention and is viewed as the developer and provider of the informational materials and activities rather than the individual bureaus, such as NIJ. As a result, NIJ's visibility as well as those of other OJP bureaus is significantly reduced.

NIJ-Sponsored Conferences

Conferences constitute a major dissemination strategy. Some of the regular conferences that highlight research sponsored by NIJ include its Annual Conference on Research and Evaluation, the Applied Technology Conference, Technologies for Critical Incident Preparedness Conference (cosponsored with the Department of Defense and the Department of Homeland Security), and a Crime Mapping Conference. In addition, NIJ sponsors electronic seminars (webinars) and symposia.

NIJ's Assessment of Its Dissemination Activities

NIJ relies on several methods to assess the quality and utility of its dissemination activities. These include direct feedback from users from a regular 800 number, flyers attached to periodicals, and occasional NCJRS user surveys and focus groups. The most recent survey of NCJRS users by an outside organization was completed by the Gallup Organization in 2000. Gallup conducted a series of three focus groups, drawing on attendees at an OJP-sponsored conference on corrections and a national meeting of forensics science directors. The survey of NCJRS users reported a high familiarity with NIJ products and services (95 percent); high satisfaction with publications and videos (89 percent); and a high rating of NIJ as an excellent or very good source of criminal justice information (81 percent). The Gallup report of the focus groups also reported great familiarity with NIJ products and services, a finding not surprising since the focus group members were drawn from the ranks of policy makers attending OJP- and NIJ-sponsored conferences. As might be expected in any survey of users, some respondents reported that the NIJ information was not concise enough and that they were more likely to read and use quick summaries. NIJ has not conducted a similar survey since 2000, instead relying on online surveys distributed randomly to its website users.

Other kinds of data compiled and used to assess the use of NCJRS and the quality of NIJ products include statistics on requests for reprints; the use of the website (characteristics of users accessing documents; numbers of documents downloaded; and customer satisfaction index ratings); and citations of NIJ documents as well as anecdotal information and communications from the field through "ASK NIJ." Finally, the NIJ considers the more than half a dozen awards for content and visual display received in 2007 and 2008 from government and private communication organizations as evidence of the high caliber of its publications.

Although NIJ conducts some assessment of its dissemination activities, its efforts are limited and are not designed to improve its targeting of the information or to assess its quality or utility. For example, data being compiled by NIJ on web usage and the distribution and accessing of documents will not reveal who is using NIJ-produced materials and to what use they are being put. It is this kind of critical look that needs to be undertaken by an outside entity to ensure proper distancing and validity.

Our survey of researchers and practitioners (see Appendix B) found very high levels of use of the major dissemination modalities supported by NIJ: 98 percent had used the NIJ website and 73 percent of those found it useful; 90 percent had used NCJRS and 89 percent of those found it useful. Practitioners (83 percent) tended to find the NIJ-sponsored workshops more useful than researchers (60 percent). Of the three NIJ conferences, 77 percent of practitioners found the NIJ Research and Evaluation Conference useful; 62 percent found the NIJ annual technology conferences useful; and 50 percent found the NIJ critical incidents conferences useful. However, only 56 percent of respondents thought NIJ did a good job of disseminating information to policy makers, and only 64 percent thought that NIJ did a good job of disseminating information to researchers.

CONCLUSIONS

The 1977 NRC committee concluded that NIJ was doing little to establish a foundation for crime and justice research and its dissemination efforts were not well developed. That group found little if anything being done by NIJ to attract new researchers to the field, make data available for secondary analysis, provide continuity to research efforts, or promote effective dissemination of research results. Over 30 years later, we have found substantial efforts and accomplishments by NIJ in each of these areas and commend it for them.

In the past three decades, NIJ has developed and sustained fellowship programs at three levels: (1) doctoral candidates, (2) young faculty, and (3) visiting fellows. The recipients of NIJ fellowships have made scholarly contributions to the criminal justice literature or to NIJ's research programs and many have remained in the criminal justice field. NIJ has supported the development and operation of a publicly available criminal justice data archive, which serves to extend research capabilities and opportunities to a broad pool of researchers. NIJ's DRP and the resulting data archive at the National Archive of Criminal Justice Data are unparalleled and have provided the community with valuable research and information resources.

NIJ has carried out its mission to guide policy and practice by pursuing a broad range of activities that include testing and evaluation and standards, technology assistance, and forensic capacity building. Since their inception, these activities have helped criminal justice agencies make informed procurement, deployment, operating, and training decisions and have enabled them to improve and expand their facilities and equipment and to process growing backlogs of DNA samples. The police body armor is the best known of the technologies that NIJ has pioneered and run through its standards process. To its credit, NIJ has continued to refine the standards development process and to expand its testing to include comparative evaluations.

Finally, NIJ has expended considerable efforts and resources to provide useful information and assistance to the field. The agency has developed and supported a series of publications, websites, workshops, and conferences aimed at different audiences. Our survey of criminal justice researchers and practitioners indicated a high level of use of NIJ resources.

The committee's review of NIJ's efforts to build a research infrastructure strongly suggests that many of its programs have been successful enough that they warrant significant continuation and expansion, although with important modifications as described below. Some functions that have been recently assigned to or taken on by NIJ (e.g., providing direct technology assistance to individual agencies and building forensic laboratory capacities), though successful to some degrees, have been shown to consume its operations. As a result, they detract from the agency's research mission.

In our review, the committee identified the following circumstances that limit NIJ's ability to fulfill its research mission.

- **The NIJ budget contains large segments designated by earmark or congressional mandate for functions that are at best minimally related to research.** These mandates include funds for the NLECTC system and associated technology assistance activities and the more recent congressional appropriations for the DNA backlog reduction and crime laboratory improvement programs. Funds for forensic laboratory capacity-building and forensic training activities, such as the Paul Coverdell, DNA Backlog Reduction, Solving Cold Cases, and Forensic DNA Unit Efficiency Improvement programs, swamp the NIJ program and now represent more than half of the

OST budget. NIJ bears the burden of administering these funds, a drain on resources that might otherwise be directed toward advancing its research mission.

- **Some of NIJ's efforts are directed toward programs that are better suited for other agencies with clearly defined technical assistance missions.** For example, management of the forensic capacity-building programs diverts a considerable fraction of NIJ's time and resources away from its research mission. Although there is potential to incorporate research questions into the capacity-building programs (asking, for example, about the impact of backlog clearance on police operations, prosecutions, and crime rates), both the legislative intent and the grantee perception is that these programs are vehicles for the distribution of funds to state and local agencies. This situation is unlikely to change, particularly in the current economic climate, as cash-strapped local forensic laboratories can be expected to look increasingly to the federal treasury for relief. Moreover, the administrative burden of these programs is likely to increase as OJP implements the recommendations encouraged by reports of the Office of the Inspector General. These considerations lead us to question whether the DNA backlog reduction and the forensic laboratory capacity-building programs properly belong in NIJ. Relocation of these programs to bureaus more accustomed to managing assistance programs to state and local agencies such as the Bureau of Justice Assistance or the Community Policing Oriented Services office would remove a major distraction from NIJ's ability to focus on its research mission.

- **NIJ's outreach activities to the research community have declined.** As a federal research agency, NIJ has a duty to transfer knowledge from research in a way that helps its constituencies improve skills and practices. NIJ's audiences include both the nation's criminal justice practitioners and its researchers. Historically, NIJ has played an important role in helping build the research field by reaching out to researchers in a wide range of disciplines, communicating useful information, and providing a variety of venues in which researchers can learn from each other. In the past 5 to 10 years, NIJ has reduced its activities and products intended specifically for the research community. Examples of such activities and products include research forums for discussing research in progress or completed research and written and electronic products that present syntheses of research or research reviews across broad topics, as was done in the *Crime and Justice* series. NIJ does not make public available information on ongoing research, such as the names of principal investigators and abstracts useful for scientific pursuit. NIJ appears to have shifted dramatically the balance of its dissemination activities to an almost exclusive focus on the information needs of practitioners and policy makers.

The committee does not intend to imply that the shift in NIJ's dissemination strategy conflicts with the goal of creating appropriate and effective mechanisms for translating research into policy and practice. The committee does not see a conflict between a strategy that is aimed at getting research findings into the hands of policy makers and practitioners and a strategy aimed at informing and communicating with the research community about ongoing research and the current state of knowledge. NIJ needs to pursue both strategies and its products and services should be tailored to each group.

- **The practitioner community appears less satisfied.** A common thread running through the presentations and interviews was the valuable contribution NIJ has made to improving criminal justice practices. NIJ was cited as being helpful in providing services for specific activities, such as those in connection with the 2002 Washington, DC, sniper investigation, Hurricane Katrina, and the 2009 presidential inauguration and in supporting crime lab improvements. But these types of anecdotal comments were offset by numerous criticisms, which the committee also heard from practitioners who had a long relationship and were very familiar with NIJ. Some commented that NIJ was no longer the go-to place for information and guidance. Leaders of the largest police and corrections agencies said that they had limited contact in the past 5 years with NIJ and that they had not been consulted on important crime-related issues despite their positions and expertise.

In our review, the committee identified numerous failings in NIJ's programs. They are highlighted below. If these failings are addressed, NIJ would be in a better position to document the successes of its programs, to determine if program goals have been achieved, and to set a program agenda that is more appropriate to its role of building a research infrastructure and enhancing dissemination and utilization of research results. Addressing these failings will lay the groundwork for more effective expansion of important programs.

- **NIJ lacks proper procedures for staff transitions.** Management of the fellowship programs has not been as efficient as one would expect. This has had an impact on NIJ's ability to effectively carry out the goals of these programs. Over the years, procedures have not been in place for a smooth transition of information and documentation regarding the fellowship programs for the NIJ personnel in charge of the programs. This has led to inaccurate documentation of basic and relevant information regarding the fellowship recipients.

- **NIJ lacks a culture of self-assessment.** NIJ does not maintain proper records for assessment. The committee notes the lack of documentation that was available to us on the activities reported in this chapter and their impact. Assessing NIJ programs was challenging, furthermore, because of the amalgamation of different types of activities in available records. NIJ has not conducted formal assessments of the fellowship programs, DRP, nor its standards program. Given NIJ's sustained support for them, they should be fully assessed and the results of the assessment made publicly available. There were extensive external assessments of NLECTC and the federal role in technology assistance, but these were both conducted at about the same time in early 2000. Very little transparent assessment is done periodically and systematically (this is discussed further in Chapter 6). This is also true of its dissemination activities. The limited efforts undertaken cannot reveal who is using NIJ products and, equally important, to what use are they being put. The regular assessments NIJ does support are conducted in conjunction with its forensic capacity-building programs and not for the programs that better reflect the research mission. In part this is due to the absence of a plan to guide these efforts, to funding problems, and to the absence of an effective advisory structure. More generally, it reflects an agency more focused on processing awards than in building a research infrastructure and enhancing research utilization.

- **NIJ's status quo management of its fellowship programs has limited its ability to build the field.** Programs aimed at supporting new and more diverse scholars working on crime and justice issues have been modest in size, not well managed, and poorly integrated into the operations of NIJ. The need for new and diverse researchers studying crime and justice issues is as critical today as it was when NIJ was founded. Expanded fellowship programs, especially ones that more effectively reach out to new disciplines, could be an important component of a federal research agency for crime and justice studies. Moreover, in being targeted to provide only

1 year of support for graduate students, typically the final year, the graduate fellowship programs offered by NIJ are compromised in their capacity to attract new scholars to criminal justice studies. Specifically, the NIJ fellowship programs do not compare well against other graduate fellowship programs, such as the multiyear programs offered by the National Institutes of Health and the National Science Foundation and the training grant programs offered by NIH.

- **NIJ has not lived up to its potential in contributing to the development of a resource database for use by the criminal justice research community.** Although a significant fraction of the data in the National Archive of Criminal Justice Data originates from NIJ grant activities, too many grantees continue to ignore requirements for submitting data generated by their grants to the data archive. Contributing to the problem, NIJ has not mounted a successful strategy to obtain compliance from research grantees or to provide the necessary support to produce quality data sets for NACJD. For example, NIJ could require applicants to designate funds in their budgets for this purpose.

Our review suggests that the data archive program is effective, well run, and making significant contributions to research. To maximize the contributions of NIJ's data archiving program, we encourage NIJ to adopt practices as outlined to NIJ in a 2003 memorandum from ICPSR/NACJD. These efforts include (1) being more diligent in making sure that all grantees with data submit it to the archive in user-friendly formats, refusing to continue or make new awards to any university or research organization whose projects have failed to submit data is a reasonable step to enforce the data submission requirement; (2) requiring grantees who generate data to include in their proposals funding to cover the costs of preparing data for archiving; and (3) expanding the summer program to cover more topics and to include researchers who are in criminal justice policy and operational agencies. These steps, combined with careful monitoring by NIJ of compliance with its own requirements and efforts already under way at ICPSR, will greatly improve this important aspect of NIJ.

6

Assessing Research Programs

The committee concluded in Chapter 5 that the National Institute of Justice (NIJ) lacks a culture of self-assessment. NIJ conducts very little transparent assessment, either periodically or systematically. This lack of assessment has limited our ability to assess not only NIJ's programs but also the influence of those programs. In this chapter, we discuss why assessing the impact of sponsored research is important and critique what NIJ has done to assess the efficacy of its research programs. We also summarize what we learned from our own limited efforts to examine the influence of NIJ-funded research and from our review of the assessment practices of other federal research agencies. All of this is presented in order to provide NIJ with initial guidance on establishing its own self-assessment practices.

THE IMPORTANCE OF ASSESSMENT

Like many federal research agencies, NIJ supports research to address a broad range of national needs and objectives. This is primarily accomplished by setting research agendas and then providing grants to investigators in regard to those agendas. This is also done by developing and funding the research infrastructure, which includes programs of education, training, and tools for the succeeding cohorts of researchers. Federal research agencies serve the role of sustaining lines of research in areas of ongoing national need, and they also have the ability to redirect support when opportunities arise in new directions for knowledge and societal benefit. Historically, the federal government can make the difference between development or stagnation of research fields (National Research Council, 2007).

Because priority-setting decisions can alter the vitality of research fields and because government has limited resources to support scientific activities, assessing progress in order to appropriately set priorities is essential. Since the need to understand progress and to set priorities is ongoing, the process of assessing progress needs to be continuous, consistent, and in accordance with an agency's mission and goals. If they were not mindful before, the passage of the Government Performance and Results Act (GPRA) in 1993 has made all federal agencies sensitive to the importance of assessing the results of their activities (Sunley, 1998). Its enactment addressed demands for accountability and demonstrated accomplishments by requiring that all federal agencies, including research agencies, develop multiyear strategic plans and evaluate and report annually on their activities.

CURRENT PRACTICES

As this report illustrates, NIJ does very little to strategically assess its performance and even less to track the influence of its research on scholarship and practice. There is very little internal management information gathered by NIJ or its component offices that focus or assess effectiveness, and what external assessments it does support are irregularly conducted, narrowly focused on a few programs,[1] and often done in response to political criticisms. What internal assessments it does conduct, such as regularly review progress reports from grantees and maintain dialogue with grantees and constituent groups, are rarely summarized for its constituents. In other words, NIJ's own processes for assessing the results of its activities are not transparent and are viewed by the committee as inconsistent or nonexistent.

PART Evaluation

The current NIJ approach to assessing the efficacy of its programs is based largely on the Program Assessment Rating Tool (PART) of the Office of Management and Budget (OMB).[2] The PART is designed to help agencies identify a program's strengths and weaknesses in an effort to inform funding and management decisions aimed at making the program more ef-

---

[1]NIJ's assessment efforts have been focused on its outreach activities and forensic capacity-building programs and not on its research portfolios.

[2]For more information, see http://financingstimulus.net/part.html [accessed March 24, 2010].

fective. NIJ first completed the PART in 2005 and has updated it annually.[3] NIJ acknowledges the limited numbers of specific long-term performance measures that focus on outcomes and reflect its mission. It attributes this to the nature of its program, consisting of basic and applied research, which have uncertain, long-term outcomes and impose measurement difficulties.[4] It also acknowledges that its program assessments do not satisfy PART definitions of scope, quality, independence, or regularity (U.S. Office of Management and Budget, 2010).

In 2005, using PART, OMB provided an assessment of NIJ and of NIJ's selection of performance measures in the areas of purpose/design, strategic planning, program management, and results/accountability. The detailed assessment is available online. OMB gave NIJ a rating of "Adequate" for its overall evaluation. Programs that are "performing" have ratings of Effective, Moderately Effective, or Adequate. Programs categorized as "not performing" have ratings of Ineffective or Results Not Demonstrated. The Adequate rating describes a program that needs to set more ambitious goals, achieve better results, improve accountability, or strengthen its management practices (see http://www.whitehouse.gov/omb/expectmore/rating.html [accessed March 17, 2010]).

Although the intent of PART is to demonstrate accountability for NIJ's work and to provide information about the results of its work for later planning, the specific performance measures included do not give much meaningful information about NIJ's operations or its influence on scholarship and practice because of the limitations described below.

Performance Measures

The PART assessment for NIJ includes the following program performance measures: average days until closed status for delinquent grants; number of new final grant reports, research documents, and grantee research documents published; total number of electronic and hard copy documents/publications/other requested; number of fielded technologies; and number of citations of NIJ products in peer-reviewed journals. See Table 6-1 for the recorded measures for the period 2003-2008. Note that these performance measures are all outputs and not outcomes, and the linkage between these and NIJ's reported strategic goals is not apparent.

---

[3]The results of NIJ's assessment can be found at http://www.whitehouse.gov/omb/expectmore/summary/10003804.2005.html [accessed June 22, 2009]. The assessment details can be found at http://www.whitehouse.gov/omb/expectmore/detail/10003804.2005.html [accessed June 22, 2009].

[4]The difficulties associated with applying PART to R&D agencies have received much attention (National Research Council, 2008b; Radin, 2008; Redburn, Shea, and Buss, 2008).

TABLE 6-1 Program Performance Measures as Reported in the PART by NIJ

Year	Target	Actual
Measure: Number of Fielded Technologies		
2001	Baseline	5
2002	N/A	6
2003	N/A	5
2004	N/A	8
2005	N/A	15
2006	Baseline	26
2007	25	21
2008	26	17
2009	28	
2010	32	
2011	35	
2012	37	
2013	39	
Measure: Number of Citations of NIJ Products in Peer-Reviewed Journals		
2003	Baseline	54
2004	55	53
2005	60	65
2006	65	176
2007	70	96
2008	70	259
2009	70	
2010	Discontinued	
Measure: Total Number of NIJ Electronic and Hard Copy Documents/Publications/Other Requested		
2003	Baseline	5,416,579
2004	5,600,000	5,616,648
2005	5,850,000	7,327,961
2006	6,080,000	3,568,919
2007	6,310,000	3,070,622
2008	7,500,000	6,953,762
2009	4,000,000	
2010	4,500,000	
2011	4,500,000	
2012	4,750,000	
2013	4,750,000	
Measure: Average Days Until Closed Status for Delinquent NIJ Grants		
2003	Baseline	511
2004	400	275
2005	200	81
2006	90	80

TABLE 6-1 Continued

Year	Target	Actual
2007	90	80
2008	90	88
2009	90	
2010	80	
2011	80	
2012	70	
2013	60	
Measure: Number of New NIJ Final Grant Reports, Research Documents, and Grantee Research Documents Published		
2003	Baseline	328
2004	182	226
2005	192	325
2006	258	257
2007	258	178
2008	259	171
2009	300	
2010	300	
2011	300	
2012	300	
2013	300	

NOTE: N/A = not applicable.
SOURCE: Created from information available: http://www.whitehouse.gov/omb/expectmore/detail/10003804.2005.html [accessed December 30, 2009].

Average Days Until Closed Status for Delinquent NIJ Grants. The first measure, days until closed for delinquent grants, is an indicator of management. Although it appears straightforward, it is unclear when a grant is considered delinquent. As long as NIJ is consistent in its definition of when a grant is delinquent across the years, this may be a useful performance measure. However, it would be more appropriate to define a management performance measure in terms that are more easily understood by a broad audience. For example, "number of months for release of data as measured by time from end of data collection to data release on Internet" or "percentage of grant award or funding decisions made available to applicants within 9 months of application receipt or deadline date" (see National Research Council, 2008b).

Number of New Research Publications. The number of new research publications seems straightforward. However, there is no information on what is meant by "NIJ and grantee research documents" or on how these figures are compiled (e.g., Are grantees reporting how many related research documents they produce? When and how often is this reported to NIJ?) Note also that the NIJ-based production of research publications is declining; a trend discussed in Chapters 3 and 5.

Number of Publications Requested. The number of requested publications also seems straightforward. But again, there is little information to the reader as to how these data are compiled. Are these requests made to NIJ directly, through the National Criminal Justice Reference Service (NCJRS), or both? Do the numbers indicate number of requests or number of publications requested? There is a sizable drop in total number for 2006 and 2007, thereby raising questions as to whether this suggests a decline in requests or perhaps a change in the way the figures were compiled for those years.

Number of Fielded Technologies. For the measure of fielded technologies, the committee obtained some information from NIJ on the nature of these data and how they were compiled. With this added information, the committee concludes that NIJ's efforts to assemble this performance measure are inconsistent and ill defined.

The committee received a listing of the 26 fielded technologies for 2006 and the 21 fielded technologies for 2007. These listings contain brief descriptions of the technologies transferred, the award numbers, the performers of the awards, and the Office of Science and Technology (OST) divisions that managed each award. Upon examination, we noted that the technologies reported to be fielded in 2006 were products of grants originating in the period 1995-2005 and those in 2007 in the period 1998-2006, thus raising the question as to when a technology is considered "fielded." Is it when the grant is closed or when the "transfer" to the field takes place? Furthermore, we determined from the lists that the fielded technologies cover a broad range of technology activities, from an actual developed and marketed product to a training CD. We were unable to ascertain what is meant by a "fielded technology."

According to the fiscal year (FY) 2009 Performance Budget Report for the Office of Justice Programs (U.S. Department of Justice, 2008), the performance data item "number of fielded technologies" represents the NIJ-developed technologies that are transferred to the field for use by criminal justice practitioners. The original measure may have been limited to counting the number of technology prototypes produced for counterterrorism,[5] interoperable communications, computer crimes, and protective equipment; however, this technology transfer measure has since been broadened and now includes publications, demonstrations, examples of commercialized

[5]It is important to note that the FY 2006 target was reset as the baseline because of the phase-out of counterterrorism funds from NIJ to DHS.

technologies resulting from research, new DNA markers,[6] and assistance for first adopters (U.S. Department of Justice, 2008).

When a performance measure covers such a broad array of outputs, it becomes difficult to demonstrate a program's efficiency and impact. An assessment of NIJ's role in preparing technologies for use by the criminal justice field and gauging their impact would require an in-depth examination of the technical aspects of these technologies as well as deliberations among researchers and criminal justice practitioners on their relevance. This kind of assessment was beyond the scope and resources of our study. From the committee's very limited review, it is fair to conclude that NIJ has initiated some work that is quite impressive[7] and befitting its role to identify and support research with specific forensic and law enforcement applications. However, NIJ has also supported some work that appears to be less cutting-edge development or to have impact limited to a specific locale as opposed to the broader field.[8]

Although NIJ seems to be engaging in relevant work in transferring technologies to the field, its inclusion of so many different kinds of activities as fielded technologies is misleading and not a useful way of measuring program outcomes. For the measure to be useful, it should be clearly defined to include a timeframe and categorization of what is being measured. Many infer "fielded technologies" to be the percentage of NIJ-sponsored projects that resulted in commercialized products currently on the market; but if that is not the case, then it should be clearly noted. As noted throughout this report, OST supports a wide range of research and other activities and often combines them together without distinguishing among its products and efforts, making assessment of its research efforts difficult. This may be the result of a lack of the necessary technology expertise to filter and categorize appropriately technology-related outcomes and products.

---

[6]A DNA marker is a gene or DNA sequence having a known location on a chromosome and associated with a particular gene or trait.

[7]For example, Brijot Imaging Systems commercialized its passive millimeter wave weapons detection camera, which is based on technology developed by Lockheed Martin with NIJ funding through an interagency agreement with the U.S. Air Force Research Laboratory. In addition, NIJ support of mini-STR typing systems has fostered a unique forensic application. The mini-STR typing system is designed to provide a DNA profile on degraded DNA (often collected at crime scenes). The system is well designed and did well in beta testing, and its commercialization by Applied Biosystems Inc. qualifies as an important success.

[8]For example, a grant was awarded and counted as a fielded technology for implementing AmberView in West Virginia school systems. AmberView is a program that assisted state law enforcement by quickly issuing a digital picture of a missing or abducted child and has since been discontinued (Kasey, 2009).

Citations of NIJ Products. The performance measure "number of citations of NIJ products" is also not useful in determining what is being measured. According to NIJ, the citation figures were obtained from different sources over the period 2003-2008. For example, in 2003-2005, the Social Science Citation Index was used; in 2006, Sociological Abstracts and Ebsco Academic Search Premier were used; in 2007, the Social Science Citation Index (SSCI) was used; and in 2008, Sociological Abstracts, SocIndex, and the Sage Publications Database were used. According to NIJ, the citation information was derived from searches using variations of NIJ's name, and the results reflect the appearance of NIJ's name in reference lists of articles, books, etc. As a result, this citation count captures only the citations of publications authored or published by NIJ and significantly underestimates the influence of NIJ-supported research on scholarship, since searches were never conducted on the works of the numerous principle investigators that NIJ supports.

Assessment Power of PART

It is impossible to draw any concrete or specific findings regarding NIJ's influence on research and practice from the PART assessment. It is unclear what the specific program performance numbers generated by NIJ indicate, since there is no information as to how the numbers were generated or whether they represent consistent figures from year to year. Criticisms have been leveled at PART, but the Obama administration is unlikely to abandon it, focusing instead on improving it.[9] NIJ should give greater attention to the identification of appropriate performance measures and the data required to track them. The committee does not consider NIJ's current effort for the PART assessment a measure of the possible use or influence of its research, and it does not compare to other approaches and efforts for generating some estimate of influence.

Other Assessments

Assessments of NIJ are acknowledged on its website (see Figure 6-1). However, the only identified ongoing effort to assess program performance is the reference to the PART. The only external assessment conducted at the request of NIJ that is identified to the public is this study by the National Research Council (NRC)—an assessment conducted 30 years after the first one by NRC in 1977. The other "assessments" have been audits conducted by the Office of the Inspector General which evaluated NIJ's operations and

[9]Statement of Jeffrey D. Zients, deputy director for management, OMB, before the Budget committee, U.S. Senate, October 29, 2009.

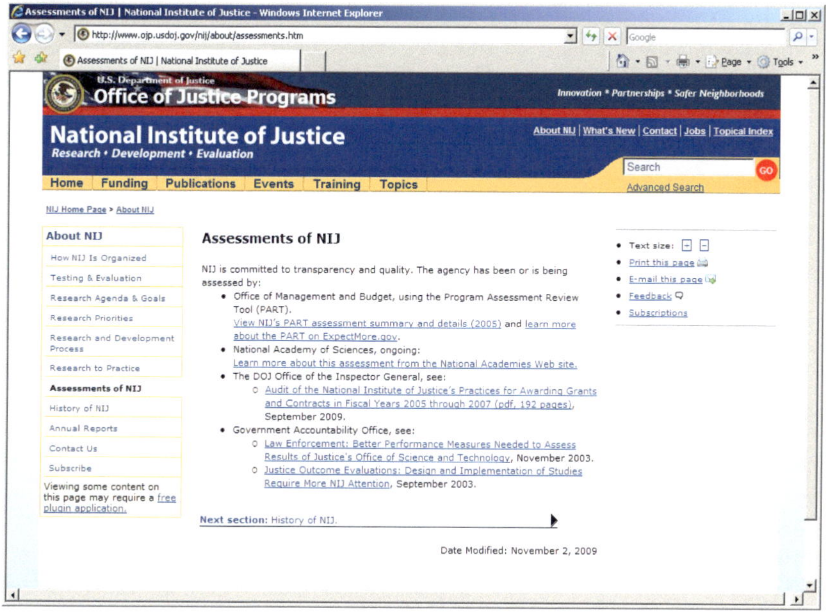

FIGURE 6-1 The limited assessment of NIJ.
SOURCE: Available: http://www.ojp.usdoj.gov/nij/about/assessments.htm [accessed February 19, 2010].

accounting practices, and programmatic reviews by the U.S. Government Accountability Office, which assessed the methodological rigor of evaluations and the quality of program monitoring for specific programs during specific periods. These assessments do not represent efforts to routinely and consistently collect data in order to assess the quality and impact of research programs.

THE COMMITTEE'S ANALYSES

Since NIJ has not conducted assessments of its research programs, we chose to make initial attempts to assess the impact of NIJ-funded research. Our data collection efforts began as a way to capture some otherwise unavailable information about NIJ's influence on scholarship and practice. Although resource constraints and the lack of information precluded more comprehensive analyses, these endeavors provide some information on NIJ's influence and, more importantly, provide an illustration of what NIJ could carry out and what information could be obtained with respect to gauging its influence on policy and practice. This section offers two exemplars of what can be learned from a limited effort to capture measures of impact of NIJ programs. It includes (1) citation analyses and (2) a survey of researchers and practitioners.

Citation Analyses

Citation analysis, although limited, offers an easily adoptable approach to gauging the influence of NIJ-sponsored research. Although it cannot tell much about effects on practice, citation analysis is a standard method for examining the impact of research literature. Because there is no clear consensus of how citation analyses should be carried out or what their precise meaning or interpretation is, the committee provides examples that may serve as an illustrative approach (among many) for NIJ to gauge its influence on scholarship.

Citation analyses count the number of times an individual piece of literature has been cited by another piece of literature. In other words, an article with 20 citations has been consulted more than an article with 1 citation, and the former article can thus be considered to be somewhat more influential than the latter article. The essence of citation analysis is that literature with a higher volume of citations is more influential than literature with a lower volume of citations. Of course, although citations to research can be both positive and critical, they provide one means of assessing the influence of that work. Citation analyses also help to understand the birthplace of certain ideas or methods. For example, a single study may be cited by 2,000 publications that subsequently carry out theoretical and empirical research that can be largely attributable to the original, influential study.

The committee carried out two different citation analyses. First, the committee selected prominent journals in the criminology and criminal justice area and journals in the forensic sciences area: *Criminology*, *Justice Quarterly*, *Criminology and Public Policy*, *Forensic Science International*, and *Journal of Forensic Sciences*. The committee then went through them manually for a period of time (1995-2008) and recorded the number of articles that mentioned NIJ-funded data or support from NIJ in some capacity (these are usually, though not always, listed in an acknowledgment section). The committee then took that subset and identified citations as one barometer of measuring impact.

Table 6-2 presents the results of this analysis. In the criminology/criminal justice journals, 126 of the 1,051 articles published (12 percent) referenced funding support from NIJ. In the forensic sciences journals, 75 of the 6,119 articles published (1.2 percent) referenced funding support from NIJ. It is worth noting that none of the 7,170 articles across the 5 journals reported using data from an earlier NIJ-funded study. This may be less of

TABLE 6-2 Publication/Citation Analysis of Articles Linked to NIJ Support in Five Journals

	Total Number of Articles	Total Number Mentioning Use of NIJ-Supported Data	Total Number Mentioning Funding from NIJ	Total Citation Count for Articles Mentioning NIJ
Criminology	439	0	53	854
Justice Quarterly	375	0	52	276
Criminology & Public Policy	237	0	21	2
Forensic Science International	3,135	0	11	15
Journal of Forensic Sciences	2,984	0	64	0
TOTAL	7,170	0	201	1,147

NOTE: With respect to the criminology/criminal justice journals, the analysis included articles, reaction essays, and comment-oriented papers. A decision was made not to include editorials or book reviews in the searches. For the forensic science journals, the following types of articles were included in the search: articles, short reports, case studies, experiments, comment papers, and announcements of population data. The analysis excluded editorials, errata, corrections, book reviews, letters to the editor, replies to letters to the editor, and technical notes.

a reflection of NIJ's impact and more of the field's limited reference to the agency originally funding the research that generated the data for additional or secondary data analysis. A citation analysis was performed for those articles which referenced funding support from NIJ. As the table shows, a total of 1,147 citations were identified for the 201 articles referencing support from NIJ. Articles appearing in the criminology/criminal justice journals were cited more often than those appearing in the two forensic science journals. Most of the highly cited articles appeared in *Criminology.* The most cited articles are identified in Box 6-1.

At first glance, this analysis indicates low visibility in these highly respected and established journals. The journals we selected undoubtedly present a limited sample, because some of NIJ's funded research may be published in other, more specialized outlets in the policing, courts, corrections, and forensic science areas or in other criminological/criminal justice/forensic science journals. Still, since NIJ is considered a leader in these areas, one would expect research projects and products emerging from a

BOX 6-1
Highly Cited Articles

- Mastrofski, S.D., Worden, R.E., and Snipes, J.B. (1995). Law enforcement in a time of community policing. *Criminology, 33*(4), 539-563 (52 citations).

- Morenoff, J.D., Sampson, R.J., and Raudenbush, S.W. (2001). Neighborhood inequality, collective efficacy, and the spatial dynamics of urban violence. *Criminology, 39*(3), 517-559 (159 citations).

- Reisig, M.D., and Parks, R.B. (2000). Experience, quality of life, and neighborhood context: A hierarchical analysis of satisfaction with police. *Justice Quarterly, 17*(3), 607-630 (58 citations).

criminal justice research agency funding stream to have more visibility in these journals. However, without any baseline information for comparison or the resources and information available to carry out a similar search for an earlier time period, no definitive conclusions can be drawn from this analysis. Since there currently exists no other independent assessment of NIJ in this regard, this approach can be considered as providing a baseline to such an undertaking.

For our second analysis, the committee compiled a list of the principal investigators for NIJ's research grants 1995-2007, and used the National Archive of Criminal Justice Data (NACJD)/Inter-university Consortium for Political and Social Research (ICPSR) online bibliography[10] to identify publications relevant to respective grants with the associated principal investigator (PI) as an author. For the purpose of this analysis, the committee focused on grants that had the potential to result in peer-reviewed literature—that is, the research grants. The committee was able to generate a sample of 2,238 research grants with PIs identified for the period 1995-2007.

Because of missing information and limitations in matching grant titles with data titles, we are unable to report verifiable statistics on the

[10]ICPSR is the host to NACJD, as discussed in Chapter 5. They maintain an online Bibliography of Data-related Literature, which is a searchable database that contains over 48,000 citations of known published and unpublished works resulting from analyses of data held in the ICPSR archive. The bibliography was developed with support from the National Science Foundation.

publications and subsequent citation of NIJ-funded research. Of the 2238 grants in the sample, only 130 of the associated principal investigators were available through the NACJD/ICPSR bibliography, that is, only 130 PIs had uploaded their data to NACJD, and as one would expect from the discussion in Chapter 5 on the data archive, most, if not all, of these emerged from the Office of Research and Evaluation awards and not Office of Science and Technology. From there, we were able to accurately link only a sample of 46 grants to data and subsequent publications, in the archive. We then identified a total of 113 related literature entries (i.e., journal articles published by the respective PIs, though not necessarily as first author, in relation to their NIJ-funded research)[11] associated with those 46 grants. A citation count was then performed on these 113 related literature entries using SSCI through Web of Science.[12] The combined citation count was 571. Although we cannot draw any conclusions from this citation analysis because of known limitations in the sample information and the absence of baseline information for comparison, we did, however, find the publicly available NACJD/ICPSR online bibliography to be a very useful tool.

This searchable database has extensive information about each data set held in the archive, including a list of resulting literature. It also has an online citation reporting feature. This feature permits the generation of a report of related literature that relied on any data supported by NIJ held in the NACJD/ICPSR archive. According to this reporting, 989 unique NIJ data collections were cited a total of 4,373 times in 3,621 publications[13] published between January 1, 2000, and August 18, 2009. This publicly available tool not only generates figures illustrative of scholarly use but also provides a bibliography of the literature citing NIJ-supported data and links to more information on those data sets. The tool can easily be used to compare data collection citation for different time periods after January 1, 2000. To our knowledge, this feature has not been used by NIJ to track the impact of its research. To the extent that more data could be archived, this will expand the pool of data available for others to use and will also improve NIJ's ability to track the use and influence of its awards.

---

[11]On occasion, there were other individuals listed as having published work based on the data listed with NACJD/ICPSR, but this portion of our analyses focused solely on the work of the NIJ PI's.

[12]The committee recognizes that the SSCI count via the Web of Science is entirely contingent on journal collection, abstraction, and reporting and this varies across journal outlets. Thus, this count should be viewed as a lower-bound, rough approximation.

[13]These publications include 320 books or book sections, 110 conference proceedings, 1,497 journal articles, 7 magazine and newspaper articles, 1,542 reports, 119 theses, and 16 documents.

Limitations of Citation Analysis

Citations mean something in assessing contributions to knowledge (and for gauging influence on academics), but they are far more problematic with regard to assessing impact on policy. They are also problematic for assessing adoption into practice; articles that describe a new technique or protocol may be rarely cited but nevertheless may find their way into many procedures manuals.

There are many other routes from research to policy and practice than publication in academic journals. As Weiss (1979) has observed, rational use of research evidence in a problem-solving mode is the least common type of use. More often research evidence is used politically, to bolster a preexisting position. That is, policy makers and practitioners who are partial to a particular course of action already are apt to use new research findings to support their position. Much of the most common use of research comes about through what Weiss (1978) refers to as "enlightenment," in which policy makers and practitioners do not necessarily have to know the published research but what they hear is the nature of findings, such as "Scared Straight doesn't work." It becomes impossible to trace the path of transmission of the information, because it is largely informal, through conversations, trade publications, magazines, the office grapevine, etc.

Thus, citation counts are likely to underestimate the influence of research. So it is reasonable to conclude that any citation information presented here represents a lower bound of influence. The committee does not conclude that a potentially low documentation of NIJ-funded data or citation count indicates that NIJ was not influencing research or criminal justice policy. The committee had neither the information nor the resources necessary to compare data with other time periods, projected goals, or other agencies, so the committee is unable to draw conclusions.

When conducted accurately and consistently, citation analysis can be one barometer (among several) to track progress over time. Citation analysis can be worthwhile for evaluating publication records of individual scientists or research products, as long as some of the limitations are sufficiently considered. However, citation analysis should always be considered as one of several evaluation criteria (Schoonbaert and Roelants, 1996).

Survey of Criminal Justice Researchers and Practitioners

Another possible source of information for the purpose of assessment is periodic surveys of constituent communities aimed at identifying the consideration, use, and implementation of research findings. In November 2008, the committee conducted a survey to learn about the views of criminal justice researchers and practitioners. The committee wanted to know how familiar respondents were with NIJ's activities and what they thought about the quality and impact of these activities. The committee was also interested in overall perceptions of NIJ as an independent science agency. A summary of what was learned is presented below. More details on the survey can be found in Appendix B.

Survey Results

The survey sample, a quota sample, included 347 researchers and 162 practitioners (21 percent of those originally contacted by e-mail). The target researcher sample consisted of members of the American Society of Criminology. The target practitioner sample consisted of leaders and key staff in well-known organizations with an interest in criminal justice issues.[14] Despite the limitations of survey findings (presented below), the survey results gave the committee insight into areas of relative strength and weakness in NIJ performance as well as into differences in the perceptions of researchers and practitioners and offer an otherwise unavailable window on the views of the field.

The results paint a picture of respondents who feel strongly that there is a current need for a federal research agency dedicated to crime and justice issues. Researchers were more likely than practitioners to express a critical need for such an institution. NIJ can fill this need; however, the vast majority of respondents recognize that many of the agency's operations must be improved.

The respondents were very familiar with NIJ. They report a high use of NIJ's products, such as publications and websites, and events, such as conferences and workshops. The respondents gave high marks to the usefulness of NIJ resources. NIJ data resources (such as NCJRS and NACJD) were more widely used by the researchers. The practitioners were more likely to have attended NIJ workshops and conferences. About a third considered NIJ a primary funding source for their work or had served on one of NIJ's peer-review panels or advisory groups. Nearly all of the researchers had used or had cited NIJ-sponsored research in their own work. This high level of familiarity underscores the importance of NIJ to the field and lends credibility to the survey findings.

Respondents were asked to rate their satisfaction with NIJ's performance in a number of different areas. Satisfaction was rated on a five-

[14]See Chapter 4, footnote 1, for an explanation of how the terms "researcher" and "practitioner" are used in this report. We recognize that because of our available sample pool we were only able to reach a limited population of researchers. In addition, a small percentage of our practitioner sample (14 percent) would have been considered researchers if we had the ability to separate them out. They were affiliated with our target practitioner organizations but work as researchers in government agencies.

point scale from very positive to very negative. Percentages are reported to indicate the number of respondents indicating positive or very positive satisfaction. In interpreting the responses, the committee relied on the 50 years of opinion research experience of the survey firm conducting the survey and their judgment of percentage scores. "Based on other studies of performance using similar measures, scores in the 90 percent or higher range are considered outstanding. Organizations with scores at this level are usually growing and have a high level of retention [in terms of staff and customers]. Scores in the 70-80 percent range indicate some good points and some areas for improvement. Scores below 70 percent are indicative of more serious problems" (see Appendix B). NIJ's satisfaction scores in many areas were 60 percent or less.

The results reveal a number of areas in need of improvement to increase respondent satisfaction including qualifications of the staff, consultation with the researcher and practitioner communities, and NIJ leadership. In addition, many of the respondents pointed to the inadequacy of NIJ resources (i.e., only 27 percent rated the adequacy of resources positively). Researchers were less satisfied than practitioners in several areas: qualifications of the staff, NIJ leadership, adequacy of resources, and consultation with the researcher community. Practitioners reported more satisfaction than researchers with NIJ's overall performance; however, both are still low ratings (69 versus 50 percent).

Researchers and practitioners were asked about satisfaction with NIJ specifically in the areas of their particular interest. Among the researcher sample, satisfaction with NIJ performance is considered moderate to low in such areas as dissemination, funding, and research agenda setting. However, researchers tended to be more satisfied with the dissemination of findings to the research community than to policy makers and practitioners. Recipients of NIJ grants expressed low levels of satisfaction with the grant process and project monitoring in such areas as ease of applying and quality of feedback. Awardees are most satisfied with staff responsiveness, fairness, and competence. They expressed the least satisfaction with the transparency of the award process. Unsuccessful grant applicants in our sample also expressed similar low satisfaction with the ease of applying, the quality of feedback, the quality of funding decisions, and the transparency of the award process. Those in our sample who never applied to NIJ for funding did not do so more often because they thought they were unlikely to get funded.

Among the practitioner sample, satisfaction with NIJ performance is considered moderate in the areas of disseminating relevant research knowledge to practitioners and policy makers, identifying research and technology needs, and maintaining fairness and openness in practices. Practitioners appear to be more satisfied than researchers with NIJ's dissemination as well as its commitment to fairness and openness. Practitioner satisfaction with NIJ performance is considered relatively low in other areas: development of affordable and effective tools and technologies, improvement of forensic laboratories, technical assistance, testing of existing and new technologies, and development of equipment standards.

Respondents were asked about the independence of NIJ. Our sample was split on the issue of independence. A third indicated that it does not have the necessary independence, while a third indicated it does, and another third was not sure. More practitioners than researchers believe it does have the necessary independence. Researchers, asked to judge political considerations impacting NIJ, believe NIJ has been most impacted in setting research priorities and selecting proposals for funding and less so in disseminating research findings.

The open-ended comments are reflective of what respondents believe the impact of political considerations, whether external or internal to the agency, are on NIJ. Over a third of the 509 respondents offered comments. Areas of concern described in the mostly negative comments include inappropriate political influence on NIJ (6 percent), lack of continued research funding (4 percent), the need for NIJ to operate independently (3 percent), the desire for NIJ to develop an unbiased grant process (3 percent), and an interest in diversifying the research to include topics other than DNA analysis, technology, and terrorism (3 percent).

Limitations of Survey Findings

To accomplish its mission, NIJ needs to interact effectively with two key audiences: (1) criminal justice practitioners and (2) researchers conducting studies related to crime and justice. A web-based survey was chosen as a cost-effective strategy for collecting information on NIJ's effectiveness from large numbers of these key stakeholders. This survey has some limitations that must be considered in interpreting the findings.

One limitation derives from the population eligible for interview. For this survey, the researchers eligible for the sample were limited to members of the American Society of Criminology, and such membership hardly covers all researchers conducting studies related to crime and justice. Scientists whose primary focus is on hard sciences, such as forensic sciences or equipment development, may be less likely to join than social scientists. Some researchers do not choose to join or join other criminology professional groups. It was even more challenging to define operationally the population of criminal justice practitioners, encompassing truly vast numbers of individuals engaged in a wide range of jobs. For this survey, eligible practitioners were limited to individuals who held leadership roles in a range of national professional organizations during the prior decade. As leaders of national organizations, eligible respondents may have had more exposure to NIJ's role at a broad level but perhaps less experience with day-to-day effects on practice. Despite these exclusions, the sampled populations constitute audiences for large numbers of NIJ presentations and key target audiences for NIJ.

More serious limitations stem from the low response rates that characterize this—and most—web-based surveys. The reader is urged to remember that the views expressed are those of respondents who have e-mail addresses, were motivated to respond, and completed the survey in time to be included in the results. Thus it is difficult to know, or even estimate, the extent to which different results would have been obtained from interviews with all individuals in the population. To assist in the proper interpretation of this web-based survey, the results are presented in terms of ranges and compared with results of similar surveys.

BEST PRACTICES OF OTHER AGENCIES

The regular review of research programs is important not only to retrospectively determine an agency's accomplishments but also to inform the strategic planning of its research programs. Other granting agencies employ both internal and external mechanisms for assessing their influence on scholarship and practice and to use these data to advance their agency's goals (U.S. General Accounting Office, 2003c). In reviewing how other federal research agencies[15] address the issue of assessing influence, the committee reached a number of conclusions. First, many research agencies are struggling with defining quality and then constructing a process to assess it (National Research Council, 2007). This is especially true in assessing the impact of research or research outcomes as a measure of quality. Second, scientists outside the agency are heavily relied on, either individually or as peer reviewers, to assess the impact of research. Third, a combination of approaches for collecting information is used to define an agency's influence from its investment in research.

There are two generic strategies for assessing scientific progress and setting research priorities: (1) analytic techniques, such as citation analysis, and (2) deliberative processes, such as those of expert review panels. (National Research Council, 1999a, 2000, 2001a, 2005d, 2008b, 2009b). Often it is the information and data from the former that informs the latter, resulting in a report of accomplishments and strategic recommendations.

Information and data in the form of metrics and performance measures

[15]The committee received briefings from agency directors and program division directors of several federal research agencies (see Chapter 1).

BOX 6-2
Examples of Performance Measures

Quantifiable
- Research grants awarded
- Percentage of awards peer reviewed
- Time between awards and final reports
- Data sets produced by supported PIs
- Publications and products produced by the agency, staff, and supported PIs
- Presentations by staff and supported PIs
- Distributions and citations of such works as a proxy for use of publications and products
- Tools, technologies, and models produced
- Conferences and workshops supported by the agency and attendance at such
- The demographics of participants

Qualitative
- PI-submitted descriptions of contributions and collaborations within and across disciplines
- Testimonial letters
- Surveys of constituents
- External reviews, which can take the form of workshop summaries, program evaluations, or advisory reports

SOURCES: National Research Council (2008b), National Science Foundation (2009).

are indicators and statistics that are used to gauge progress with respect to stated goals. The associated metrics and performance measures may be quantitative or qualitative (National Research Council, 2005d). Box 6-2 lists a number of examples of quantifiable and qualitative information that have been collected to help assess the impact of research.

Although space constraints preclude a listing of all assessment efforts of other research agencies, the committee does highlight some efforts made by the Division of Behavioral and Social Research of the National Institute on Aging and the National Science Foundation (NSF) that appear promising.[16]

[16]The National Institutes of Health (NIH) also undertakes several different types of internal and external evaluations regarding their research program. Specifically, it has a Performance

National Institute on Aging

The National Institute on Aging conducts periodic and broad review of its divisions to assess their overall performance and the appropriateness of the future research being considered. Its Division of Behavioral and Social Research (BSR) was reviewed in 2008 by a committee of 16 distinguished scientists. In conducting its review, the committee received background material[17] to assist them in their deliberations, participated in three 90-minute conference calls prior to the full 2-day review meeting, and participated in a 45-minute conference call to finalize its report.

The review was guided by the five overarching areas for consideration (National Institute on Aging, National Advisory Council on Aging, Division of Behavioral and Social Research Review Committee, 2009):

1. What promising areas for future research should be encouraged?
2. Has BSR been supporting a balanced, high-quality, and innovative portfolio of research? Are there significant gaps? What areas are weaker than they should be, and which, if any, might now be deemphasized?
3. Is the branch structure appropriate to the science? Is BSR adequately staffed?
4. How can BSR promote training and development of new scholars in fields that are becoming increasingly interdisciplinary? Is BSR attracting adequate numbers of high-quality individuals to pursue research careers in fields of relevance to BSR, and can their professional development be sustained?
5. What can be done to ensure appropriate review of high-risk, interdisciplinary research projects and program projects?

In addition, nine subcommittees were formed to consider research areas that represent important, burgeoning areas or areas needing extra attention that may be perceived as being deficient or potentially critical for progress.

Assessments Office, in the Division of Program Coordination, Planning, and Strategic Initiatives (DPCPSI), which coordinates all NIH program performance activities, which include monitoring and assessing NIH-level program performance through several federally mandated reporting mechanisms. These mechanisms include GPRA, OMB PART, and the Performance and Accountability Report (PAR). Although several reporting mechanisms exist, many assess progress and performance through specific GPRA goals (see http://nihperformance.nih.gov/ [accessed July 2, 2009]).

[17]Such background materials include the 2004 review committee report, the BSR response to the 2004 review, the BSR organizational chart, BSR funding trends over time (as proportion of NIA total, by mechanism, by portfolio area, and by branch), a BSR memorandum on structure and staffing, BSR-relevant press releases for the period 2004-2008, background briefing papers by staff on certain research areas, and BSR media mentions for the period 2006-2008.

Each subcommittee was tasked with preparing a short briefing paper highlighting achievements and shortcomings in their respective research areas. These subcommittee papers and materials, provided by BSR staff, served as the primary basis of deliberations of scientific directions.

The review committee found that BSR has been highly responsive to the recommendations in a previous 2004 review report and has made excellent progress. The review committee felt that BSR has been substantially transformed in just 4 years with a number of notable accomplishments (National Institute on Aging, National Advisory Council on Aging, Division of Behavioral and Social Research Review Committee, 2009). Although there is seldom a clear line between performance and congressional action, it appears possible that as a result of this positive review, the FY 2010 budget request for BSR reflected an increase of $1.9 million from its FY 2009 funding level (Consortium of Social Science Associations, 2009).

National Science Foundation

NSF also uses a committee of outside advisers periodically to conduct reviews of its programs every three years, referred to as the Committee of Visitors. Among the activities it may examine are the program's health, its direction, the responsiveness of the funding process to the agency's goals and mission, research results, and future research ideas. The Committee of Visitors carries out its responsibilities by closely examining a random sample of grants and all information related to the grants: the processing routines, the average number of reviews, and the success rate. After review, the written report is posted on the NSF website.[18] This process is noteworthy because of the level of detail and because it examines not only the quality of research portfolios but also the process around creating those portfolios. It assesses staff as well as researchers and is a very transparent process.

In addition, NSF performs three ongoing tasks aimed at yielding information from which to assess the influence of its research program. First, NSF undertakes a "development of people outcomes," in which the agency tracks the research careers (publications, citations, and awards) of the individuals they fund. Second, like the National Institutes of Health, NSF has developed a "top discoveries" feature on their website that highlights "discoveries that began with NSF support."[19] Third, NSF has a performance

[18]See http://www.nsf.gov/od/oia/activities/cov/covs.jsp [accessed July 10, 2009].

[19]The Discoveries tab on the NSF website lists the top discoveries as a result of NSF investment (see http://www.nsf.gov/discoveries/ [accessed June 25, 2009]). NIJ does identify significant impacts that have emerged from its research, but these accomplishments are scattered throughout their website, products, and publications and are not contained in one easily accessible location.

accountability tab on their website that provides information on internal and external performance assessments designed to provide "stakeholders and taxpayers with vital information about the return on their investments." These performance assessments are guided by GPRA and NSF's own strategic plan, which include tracking performance and impact and developing various metrics. NSF has an oversight group, referred to as the Advisory committee for GPRA Performance Assessment, formed in 2002 to provide advice and recommendations to the NSF director regarding the Foundation's performance. It meets annually and assesses NSF's overall performance with respect to its strategic outcome goals.

CONCLUSIONS

The committee concludes that NIJ does not have any mechanism in place for monitoring on a regular basis the impact of the research it funds or the accumulation of useful knowledge for science and for affecting public policy. It has not adopted an assessment approach by qualified staff that integrates quantitative metrics (e.g., number of citations, publications produced and requested, and technologies commercialized) and qualitative reviews (e.g., narrative descriptions of research accomplishments and survey results). We found no evidence of deliberative and transparent assessment practices. We found no record of systems appropriate for tracking accomplishments and performance measures. The performance measures NIJ currently compiles are vague, inconsistent, and largely incomplete. They are not easily understood by a broad audience or sufficiently accurate to be credible and have not been durable to remain relatively constant over the years. As such, they are not easily linked to its mission and strategic goals.

We recognize there are no easy solutions to measuring the extent to which research has informed what is known about crime and crime prevention. It is even more difficult to determine the impact of research on how researchers conduct future inquiries and how policy makers and practitioners think about criminal justice issues. Because research does not exhibit immediate, short-term effects, its impact is usually measured and assessed over the long term. In addition, research does not operate in a vacuum, and it is often influential only when timing, political agendas, financial resources, and empirical facts converge. Hence, establishing the influence of research is a difficult and imprecise undertaking (Petersilia, 1987).

NIJ's task is further complicated by the lack of clarity regarding the kinds of research it supports. As discussed in Chapters 2 and 3, NIJ's research program has swung back and forth between basic and applied research. Sometimes applied research is characterized as policy-relevant research; however, even basic research can have implications for policy and practice. The committee recognizes that all fit within NIJ's research mission, particularly when one considers the specific needs of the criminal justice community that might not be addressed in research funded by other federal research agencies. Even though most scientists "know it when they see it" (National Research Council, 2005d), the definitions of basic, applied, and policy-relevant research are not consistently articulated. NIJ can make a significant contribution by promoting the dialogue necessary to clarify these kinds of research in the context of criminal justice needs. This in turn will help it determine appropriate metrics for measuring its impact. The adoption of thoughtful metrics or performance measures as part of a routine approach to assessing the progress of its scientific investments is essential for a strong, more viable research organization.

7

Recommendations

The National Institute of Justice (NIJ) is the only federal research agency devoted to the control of crime and the administration of justice, which are a central component of national identity. Since its establishment as part of the emerging federal role in assisting state and local officials in these important issues, NIJ has been the central research arm of the U.S. Department of Justice (DOJ). The charge to this committee, detailed in Chapter 1, was to assess the performance of this agency and to identify changes in the agency that would allow it to better achieve its mission.

Our review has demonstrated that NIJ is central to the better understanding of how to control crime and its impact on citizens and communities and how to ensure that the system of justice is fair and effective. No other federal, state, local, or private organization can do what NIJ was created to do. During the past 40 years, no other agency has contributed more to the understanding of crime and justice efforts than NIJ. This report has documented many of these accomplishments, including in the areas of crime mapping and hot spot policing, violence against women, the role of firearms and drugs in crime, drug courts, and forensic DNA analysis, as well as the success of the data archives, fellowships, and other outreach programs. Despite the many shortcomings of NIJ that are demonstrated in this report, the nation needs an NIJ—but one that functions better than the current one. We are convinced that a "new" NIJ, defined by the recommendations that follow, will better serve the nation and instill increased confidence in its justice system operations. We encourage Congress and the executive branch to provide the funding that the tasks assigned to NIJ require.

As this report demonstrates, few major initiatives in criminal justice during the past 40 years have occurred without significant involvement of research developed and sponsored by NIJ.

These contributions are in part noteworthy because they have occurred in an agency that, as documented in this report, has lacked the level of independence, appropriate leadership, funding, and operational practices that characterize much more successful federal research agencies. The appropriate level of independence is important to ensure that a research agency has the authority to set agendas through planned deliberations with the research and practitioner communities. Otherwise, its mission, decisions, and results can be influenced by nonscientific goals and objectives, and it loses credibility with these communities. Although NIJ has had periods of good leadership, it has never had leadership with experience and prestige in the research community. This not only reinforces the problems associated with limited independence, but it also results in leadership that cannot exercise independent scientific judgment and credibly involve the research community in its work. We have demonstrated that, given its mission, the funding of NIJ has been seriously inadequate, far too variable, and too subject to earmarks that remove funding decisions from peer review and scientific standards. We also have demonstrated that basic operations at NIJ—that is, agenda setting, peer review, report review and assessment—have not been consistent with those at other successful federal research agencies. These aspects of NIJ are unlikely to be greatly improved without attention to the issues of independence and resources.

The committee gave considerable attention to the issue of how best to achieve the appropriate level of independence for NIJ. Two basic approaches were considered: (1) moving NIJ out of the Office of Justice Programs (OJP) and (2) retaining NIJ in OJP and giving it a level of independence similar to other federal research agencies. In considering these options, the committee reviewed other federal research agencies, consulted with former directors of NIJ and OJP, and raised the issue with many others who offered guidance to the committee.[1] We also included a question about NIJ's independence on our survey of researchers and practitioners. In addition, the committee considered the recommendations of two other NRC committees that issued reports on related topics during our deliberations—the report on the needs of the forensic science community (National Research Council, 2009c) and the report on BJS (National Research Council, 2009a). After careful consideration of all the evidence the committee concluded that maintaining NIJ in OJP but with substantially increased levels of independence secured by Congress offered the greatest likelihood of NIJ achieving its mission. The

[1]Most instructive were the views of Jeremy Travis and James K. Stewart, former directors of NIJ (Travis, 2008; Stewart, 2009).

committee considered whether the independence NIJ needs to be an effective science agency can be achieved in other ways (e.g., an attorney general order or an OJP policy) and concluded that nonlegislative options could not be as effective. Only Congress can provide the requisites of increased independence and the necessary oversight to ensure that specific authorities cannot be easily retracted or eroded.

Strengthening Forensic Science in the United States: A Path Forward recommended that a new federal agency should be developed outside DOJ to address all the needs of the forensic science community. The primary rationale for this approach was the belief that placing such activities in a law enforcement agency could result in science being actually biased or perceived to be biased towards law enforcement agencies.[2] In *Ensuring the Quality, Credibility, and Relevance of U.S. Justice Statistics*, the recommendation was to move the Bureau of Justice Statistics (BJS) out of OJP into a new agency in DOJ that would report directly to the Attorney General. This recommendation was based on the conclusion that political influences from OJP had and could in the future bias BJS findings and reports.

The committee concluded that the concerns that prompted these recommendations were not major reasons for the problems we have described at NIJ. We also concluded that forensic science research fits within NIJ's research mission. Furthermore, the committee received information that convinced us that having NIJ report directly to the attorney general was not likely to reduce potential political influence; that it is unlikely that a new research and statistical agency in DOJ would be established given the costs of doing so; that moving NIJ out of OJP would make linking research and action programs less likely; and that such a move would make it less likely for Congress and the administration to move funds from action agencies to NIJ as has happened in the past and is specified in the OJP current appropriations bill. The committee concluded that keeping NIJ in OJP but with increased independence and greater involvement of the research and practitioner communities has a better chance to result in an agency that can gain the trust and confidence of Congress, the administration, and the criminal justice community. If the changes we recommend are not implemented within 5 years or if they are and the problems we have identified persist then we recommend that the idea of moving this research function should be carefully revisited.[3]

Furthermore, the committee concluded there are a number of substan-

[2]As described in Chapter 3, should Congress adopt the recent recommendation of the National Research Council (NRC) (2009c) and establish a new independent federal entity responsible for forensic science activities, NIJ's future role in sponsoring forensic science research and development activities would need to be defined accordingly.

[3]Currently, Congress is considering establishing a national crime commission. If it is formed, then it would be the natural body to conduct this review.

tive reasons for retaining NIJ within OJP. Foremost is that this relationship allows NIJ to be organizationally closest to those for whom its research is eventually intended. This does not mean that specific research projects will have immediately useful findings. However, unlike other federal research agencies, such as the National Institutes of Health (NIH) institutes and the National Science Foundation (NSF), NIJ's mission includes a greater focus on development and evaluation activities designed to bridge research and practice. Being in OJP provides an opportunity for NIJ to advise and participate in the development of OJP-sponsored programs and to be in a position to evaluate those programs. Because criminal justice policy makers and practitioners are much more closely tied to OJP than NIJ, NIJ can use its OJP relationship as a bridge to the field. NIJ can then use these connections to better target its research to the needs of the field, to involve practitioners and their agencies more directly in research activities, and to increase the likelihood that its research will eventually have an impact on criminal justice practices and policies.

Because of the importance of the overall OJP program to the field and to DOJ, as well as the unprecedented levels of federal funding that have been made available in recent years, the OJP Assistant Attorney General is in a position to assist NIJ in making a compelling case for a well-designed and funded research program with the Office of Management and Budget (OMB), DOJ, and Congress. The need for research is particularly apparent given the expanded scope of OJP and DOJ program efforts, their partnerships with state and local criminal justice agencies and the expectations of Congress for well-designed, evidence-based programming.

Of course, leaving NIJ in OJP means that the relationships between these agencies need to be clearly specified in the authorizing legislation for each. NIJ should be able to set its own research agenda, determine the awards it makes, set monitoring and oversight procedures for its grantees, control publication and dissemination decisions, hire and supervise its allotted personnel, present its budget to the Attorney General and Congress, and interact with appropriate DOJ and congressional entities. When OJP provides some limited centralized services, it should be done in full cooperation with NIJ and without the level of interference in research decisions and operations that have occurred too often during the history of NIJ.

To address these issues the committee makes five recommendations: (1) to ensure NIJ's independence and improve governance, (2) to strengthen its research mission, (3) to bolster the crime and justice research infrastructure, (4) to enhance the scientific integrity and transparency of its operations, and (5) to establish a culture of self-assessment. Our analysis strongly suggests that if these recommendations are implemented, NIJ can be a great leader in national efforts to reduce crime and improve the administration of justice.

ENSURE INDEPENDENCE AND IMPROVE GOVERNANCE

RECOMMENDATION 1: The committee recommends that Congress provide for the requisite independence and authority of the National Institute of Justice (NIJ) while retaining its organizational placement within the Office of Justice Programs and the U.S. Department of Justice. Among the key issues to be considered in pursuit of this goal are a statutory advisory board, a set term of office and minimum qualifications for the NIJ director, and clear authority for NIJ to make awards and control its budget and resources.

NIJ's efforts to fulfill its research mission to build a research infrastructure and produce a body of knowledge that can contribute to a greater understanding of crime and society's response have met with mixed success. Much of this is due to the deficiencies that have continued to persist since the last review. To become a more effective agency, NIJ needs control over its research and development (R&D) management operations. Like the prior review by the the NRC (1977), we recognize the need for independence, improved governance, and authority to conduct its work.

Need for Independence

The issue of independence for research and statistical agencies has been hotly debated for years. The 1931 Wickersham Commission, the 1967 President's Crime Commission on Law Enforcement and Administration of Justice, and participants at the 30th Anniversary Symposium of the President's Crime Commission held in 1997 all grappled with it.

The 1977 NRC report pointed out that the location of NIJ in the Law Enforcement Assistance Administration had not served it well. Its lack of independence and political constraints prevented the institute from fulfilling its mission of building knowledge about crime. The report warned that unless its present form was changed to an independent research agency within DOJ, with final approval authority over all awards as well as control over its administrative budget, personnel, and detailed program review, it was unlikely to become a "significant and quality-oriented research agency" (National Research Council, 1977, p. 3). In many respects, this prophecy could be made today exactly as it was more than 30 years ago.

As this report shows, the history of NIJ reflects diminishing authority and resources, not only as a result of congressional action, but also from actions taken by its oversight agency, OJP.

From our review of other federal research agencies, we are well aware that independence is an essential attribute shared by all of them. Conducting rigorous and objective research requires freedom from control by policy makers and others who have a stake in the research findings and their implications for policy, programs, and practice. Independence does not necessarily imply that all federal research organizations need to be free-standing, like NSF, whose single purpose is "to promote the progress of science." What it does imply is that clear lines of separation need to be made from the policy-making organization, with a balance maintained between independence and responsiveness to problems a parent agency is addressing. This appears to be best accomplished in mission-oriented agencies when program services (funding of direct or indirect services) are separated but related to the research unit. In addition, in these situations, the research agency should report to the parent agency's top leadership to ensure that it receives the best scientific advice on issues of concern.

An effective research organization needs to have the independence to conduct its work. The key components of independence include authority to (1) establish research and evaluation priorities; (2) control the grant-making process, from solicitation through grant approval; (3) make budgetary recommendations to the highest level of the parent agency; (4) make staffing decisions, including recruitment and hiring; and (5) issue reports and other dissemination activities. An important aspect of these powers is the ability to avoid earmarks in the budgeting process. In order to achieve the level of independence necessary for a trusted crime and justice research agency, the new NIJ that we propose will need a strong advisory board, terms of service for a qualified director, and grant-making, budgetary, and staffing authority.

Governance

Advisory Board

While advisory boards have been used in different ways over the years at NIJ, the committee concludes that they have never functioned as a scientific advisory board should—to set agendas, review the integrity of the research operations, and assess the accomplishments of the agency with the standards of science as the guiding principles. As described in Chapter 2, these groups were a disappointment to their respective NIJ directors. Neither was able to build support for NIJ by gaining the attention of Congress, nor was it able to serve as a buffer against what was regarded as a highly politicized environment in which everyone had a different take on crime and what was needed to combat it. There was never any sustained attempt to involve the members in a policy-making or priority-setting role.

Although scientific advisory boards are used in different ways by different federal research organizations, they appear to be central to the effective operation of these agencies. Advisory boards provide oversight, assist in setting research agendas, may have approval authority for certain awards, and conduct reviews of agency operations. Federal research agencies may have one or more boards; if they have more than one, a distinction is made between ongoing oversight boards and those created periodically to assess performance. In all instances that the committee reviewed, scientific advisory boards are overwhelmingly comprised of research scientists but also may include a small number (perhaps 25 percent of membership) of those practicing in the field. Boards are usually nominated by the research agency and approved by the head of the agency that houses the research agency or a designee. They report only to the director of the research agency or if they are advisors to a subunit, to the head of that research component.

The experience with the NIJ advisory board differs markedly from that of other research agencies, including many with an operational mission. For example, the Environmental Protection Agency (EPA) has an overall Science Advisory Board to guide its various science programs as well as individual program boards, such as the Clean Air Scientific Advisory Committee. These science boards are distinct from policy boards and each has a separate role to play in guiding the agency's operational and technology programs. The U.S. Department of Education (DoEd) has a 15-member research advisory board that works with the assistant secretary for educational research and improvement to develop the agency's long-term research and development agenda. The board's membership includes some policy officials, especially local school officials, but most of its members are scientists.

The two most prominent research agencies, NSF and NIH, have advisory groups that play a major role advising on policies and a wide range of research activities, approving priorities, soliciting advice from the field, suggesting how the research can be strengthened, and assessing the work of their respective organizations. The members of both these boards are appointed by the president, have set terms that are staggered, and are selected for their preeminence in research, a particular field of scientific endeavor, or public service.

Among the 27 institutes and centers that constitute NIH, 20 of them have some kind of advisory council, committee of counselors, or panels, and several have more than one kind of advisory group.[4] The most common form of advisory group is the advisory council composed of 12-18 members, who are appointed by the secretary of health and human services in consultation with the institute director and serve 4-year terms. The National Advisory Council on Drug Abuse has 18 members, of whom

[4]For example, the National Cancer Institute has five advisory groups: (1) the President's Cancer Panel, (2) the National Cancer Advisory Board, (3) the Director's Consumer Liaison Group, (4) the Board of Scientific Advisors, and (5) the Board of Scientific Counselors (see http://getinvolved.nih.gov/advisory_councils.asp [accessed March 17, 2010]).

12 are experts in scientific fields and 6 are knowledgeable members of the public.[5] The National Institute on Alcohol Abuse and Alcoholism (NIAAA) has 15 members, of whom 10 represent health and scientific fields (including not less than 2 individuals who are leaders in the fields of public health and the behavioral or social sciences) relevant to the activities of NIAAA.[6] The remaining one-third are selected from the public and include leaders in the fields of public policy, law, health policy, economics, and management. These councils approve scientific review group or peer-review recommendations. They also provide advice on research opportunities, guidance on ways to improve approaches to stimulating research, and ideas for working more closely with constituent groups and consumers of the research. Although these councils do not make policy, there is a tradition of their advice being heeded by the institute administrators.

Similarly, in addition to the presidentially appointed National Science Board, which provides overall guidance and oversight of the National Science Foundation, each of its seven directorates also has its own advisory committee. The Directorate of Social, Behavioral & Economic Sciences (SBE) is the principal source of federal support for fundamental research on human cognition and behavior and social structures and social interaction, as well as research on the intellectual and social contexts that govern the development and use of science and technology. It has an 18-member advisory committee that meets semiannually to review and advise on the impact of programs in the disciplines and fields encompassed by the directorate, provides oversight of overall program management and performance, and advises on the impact of NSF-wide policies on the SBE scientific community. A typical agenda includes briefings on recent scientific discoveries and activities, review of human capital and succession planning issues, a discussion with representatives of professional research member organizations, and review of program assessment reports produced by committees of visitors (described in Chapter 6).[7]

Our committee discussed whether the Office of Research and Evaluation (ORE) and the Office of Science and Technology (OST) should also have advisory boards and concluded that NIJ is currently too small to warrant such an elaborate advisory board structure. However, subcommittees of the proposed NIJ advisory board could be designated for more specific oversight of ORE and OST, for specific grants or contracts, or for both.

In proposing an advisory board for NIJ, the committee considered

[5] Available: http://www.nida.nih.gov/about/organization/NACDA/NACDAHome.html [accessed March 17, 2010].

[6] Available: http://www.niaaa.nih.gov/AboutNIAAA/AdvisoryCouncil/default.htm [accessed March 17, 2010].

[7] Available: http://www.nsf.gov/sbe/advisory.jsp [accessed March 17, 2010].

the number of NIJ constituencies and decided 15 members was a reasonable number to cover all functions and perspectives. Given the scope of the agency and the responsibilities we have outlined for the advisory committee, it would be difficult to have a smaller membership. In determining who should be the appointing authority for the advisory board, the committee carefully considered three alternatives: appointment by the president, appointment by the attorney general, and appointment by the NIJ director. NIJ's size (organization as well as resources) seemed to preclude it as being suitable for a presidential appointed advisory board. The committee thought that giving the NIJ director authority to appoint might provide too much power and give the perception that the members were in some way beholden to the director. The prior experience of having the attorney general as the appointing authority seemed to work well. Previous advisory boards appointed by the attorney general contained a mix of highly regarded and nationally recognized researchers, practitioners, and policy makers who were familiar with NIJ and supportive of its mission.

Using the experiences of these other federal agencies as a guide, the committee suggests the following structure for the NIJ advisory board:

a. Membership
   i. 15 members appointed by the attorney general for 5-year staggered terms.
   ii. A slate of nominees will be recommended to the attorney general by the NIJ director following consultation with institutional groups representing important research and practitioner communities. Interested parties may also recommend nominees either via the NIJ director or to the attorney general directly.
   iii. Ten board members will be experienced researchers; five members will be from the practitioner and policy communities. Their interests and expertise should be broadly representative of criminology and criminal justice and of issues of importance to both NIJ's social science and technology research programs.
   iv. Additional persons from other federal research agencies as well as NIJ leadership may be invited by the advisory board to serve as ex officio members as appropriate.

b. Governance and Scheduling
   i. The chair and vice chair should be elected by the board for terms of 2 years.
   ii. The board should meet at least semiannually.
   iii. The board will report directly to the director, NIJ.

c. Powers and Responsibilities:
   i. Advise on policies involving grant selection and administration.
   ii. Advise on the development and implementation of research priorities.
   iii. Review and advise on appropriate procedures for technical and scientific peer review.
   iv. Review and advise on NIJ's dissemination strategy.
   v. Review and advise on NIJ's quality assurance activities.
   vi. Review all grants and contracts exceeding $1 million prior to their award.
   vii. Biannually prepare a report to the attorney general on NIJ's progress.

Given the powers and responsibilities described above, the committee suggests in Box 7-1 an array of topics that might conceivably be included in meeting agendas.

Leadership

Since 1979, the NIJ director has been a presidential appointee. But the original legislation says little about the requirements for that position, does not set terms, and does not provide for a careful transition from one director to another. Traditionally this role has been seen as one requiring familiarity with legal institutions, crime trends, crime policy, and the criminal justice system but not experience in directing or conducting crime and

BOX 7-1
Possible NIJ Advisory Board Meeting Topics

- Critical research gaps relevant to NIJ's mission
- Development of a cumulative research strategy
- Need and realities of balancing basic and applied research
- NIJ's research activities vis-à-vis the work of other federal agencies
- Creation of an advisory infrastructure
- Feasibility of expanding efforts to build research infrastructure (e.g., graduate fellowships or the data archive)
- Transparency in the peer review and grant award processes
- NIJ's role in translating knowledge to policy and practice (e.g., training, commercializing new technologies, and/or dissemination products)
- Objective performance metrics for measuring strategic performance

justice research. In short, there has never been a premium placed on having as the director of NIJ a criminal justice researcher and in its 40-year history no NIJ director can be described as such.

Successful research agencies are characterized by leaders who are recognized scientists in their field and staff who are researchers with experience and expertise in areas of their specialization. Success in the application of the science or in related areas cannot substitute for scientific accomplishments. In situations in which the research unit is in a parent organization dealing with intense political issues, terms of appointment that are fixed and that minimize the influence of political factors in retention decisions are critical (e.g., a fixed term of appointment that overlaps presidential elections).

This is in sharp contrast to other federal research agencies, such as the Institute of Education Sciences (IES), in which the director is appointed for a 6-year term designed to overlap presidential administrations. The most common terms of office are 4- and 6-year terms. The director of NSF also has a 6-year term. The head of Congress's Office of Technology Assessment has a 6-year term, and the head of the U.S. Government Accountability Office has a 12-year term. Terms of office do contribute to a longer period of sustained professional management and decrease the likelihood of shifting priorities and interests that a new director might bring to the job.

The NRC has conducted numerous assessments of federal research programs similar to this one (e.g., National Research Council, 1992b, 2000, 2008c). These assessments have been unequivocal about the need for a top science official. In a study of EPA's Office of Research Development, the report noted "the lack of a top science official is a formula for weak scientific performance in the agency and poor scientific credibility outside the agency" (National Research Council, 2000, p. 5). The leaders of the NIH institutes, the NSF directorates and divisions, and IES are all drawn from the scientific community. In the case of the latter, this requirement is legislatively mandated and calls for the director to be "[a] highly qualified authorit[y] in the fields of scientifically valid research, statistics or evaluation in education as well as management within such areas" (U.S. House of Representatives, 2002).

For these reasons, we recommend that Congress should set science requirements for the director and a renewable fixed term of service of 6 years. An appropriate director for NIJ shall have had experience in directing crime and justice research, be recognized as a highly qualified authority in the fields of crime and justice research (including evaluation research), and have demonstrated success in managing substantial crime and justice research efforts. A term of 6 years means that appointments will overlap presidential elections but allows for change in leadership as the requirements of the position may change. Also, during the most recent congressional reorganization of a major research operation (DoEd), a 6-year term was deemed preferable.

Grant Sign-off, Budget, and Staffing Authority

NIJ's authorizing legislation provided for sign-off authority for grants. The committee strongly believes that this authority be retained. Earlier in the report, we note that this authority has not always been recognized by the leadership of OJP. The committee reiterates the point that this authority is essential for a science agency, and any attempts to weaken or eliminate it deserve immediate attention and action.

The committee also stresses the importance of giving NIJ the authority to present its budget to DOJ and for NIJ to have its own budget line item in the departmental budget that is considered by the Office of Management and Budget (OMB) and congressional appropriation committees. Unlike other science agencies, NIJ does not have its budget separately reviewed or discussed by congressional appropriators. As a result it is constrained in its ability to advocate for its program directly with Congress. Reaching out to legislative and funding bodies to describe its research activities and useful findings should be part of any federal research agency's advocacy strategy. This is a change from former practice. In 2003, the House appropriations subcommittee noted that DOJ had merged seven different accounts into one larger "justice assistance" heading and requested that the former accounting system be reinstated (U.S. House of Representatives, 2003, p. 36). This attempt to consolidate OJP funding into a single pool has continued in each subsequent year. Regarding submissions for fiscal year (FY) 2009, Senate appropriators commented that "the Committee again rejects the Department's proposed merger of all OJP programs under this heading and instead has maintained the previous account structure" (S. Report 110-397, p. 64, as cited in National Research Council, 2009a, p. 235). During the FY 2009 appropriations hearings, the congressional appropriators focused their attention on OJP's request to consolidate state and local law enforcement assistance programs. Despite numerous references by the acting OJP administrator regarding the utility of research and data, neither the NIJ budget nor that of the Bureau of Justice Statistics came up for discussion (Consortium of Social Science Associations, 2008).

The committee recommends that NIJ should be given authority for staffing, including staffing allocations and independent hiring authority. One way to exert political interference is to control the numbers of authorized staff, grade levels, and the ability to fill vacancies. Allocations are currently made across six OJP programmatic offices, and NIJ must compete with the others for them. Prior to 1979, NIJ had this authority; it also handled the substantive aspects of the recruitment and hiring process, including candidate screening and selection. In the committee's view, this model should be restored. NIJ needs to strengthen the scientific and technical qualifications of its staff. By having greater authority for its staffing, including recruitment, NIJ will have more flexibility to determine job and position series, grade levels, and other staffing options including fellowships to attract and hire talented and scientifically trained people. NIJ needs staff who can manage awards but also who are recognized as leaders in their areas of concentration and have the requisite scientific and technical ability to develop, manage, and assess research activities.

STRENGTHEN THE SCIENCE MISSION

RECOMMENDATION 2: To strengthen its science mission, the National Institute of Justice (NIJ) should direct its efforts toward building a body of cumulative knowledge that will assist the criminal justice field in its effort to prevent and control crime and improve the criminal justice system; sponsoring research that will improve and upgrade current scientific methods used to study crime; and supporting new areas that have heretofore been neglected due to NIJ's incapacity to commit resources required to support projects of long duration, great complexity, and substantial expense. To improve NIJ's ability to support research, the committee recommends that Congress remove responsibility for forensic capacity-building programs and reinstate them in other U.S. Department of Justice and Office of Justice Programs agencies, such as the Bureau of Justice Assistance and the Community Oriented Policing Services office, that have a clearly defined technical assistance mission, are closely linked to state and local criminal justice agencies, and have larger financial reserves to draw on.

NIJ has succeeded in developing a body of knowledge in important areas that are critical to preventing and controlling crime and improving the administration of justice. For the most part, however, these efforts have been heavily dependent on congressionally mandated programs or the transfer of funds from other OJP or DOJ offices. These requirements have been made without a strong science foundation.

This conclusion is particularly true of NIJ's evaluation research portfolio. Part of its mission is to determine if proposed criminal justice innovations work. Ideally, such innovations would have a strong research base, but innovations are frequently prompted by policy and operational determinations that are only minimally derived from strong research. The extreme diversity of the ORE outcome evaluations—in topic, theory, focus, and method—points to a lack of programmatic focus on systematic knowledge building or problem solving. One reason for the lack of programmatic focus is that NIJ frequently has had limited control over decisions of what programs to evaluate. It is often placed in the role of evaluating programs selected and funded by other offices in OJP or programs adopted by localities that do not have adequate (or any) preliminary evidence of effectiveness or grounding in scientific theory. A second and related reason has been NIJ's failure to engage in long-term strategic planning.

NIJ-funded programs designated by earmark or congressional mandate are at best minimally related to research and detract from its research mission. In its discussion of the OST program, the committee differentiates between what it deems appropriate for a research agency (e.g., technology development) and what is inappropriate (e.g., the forensic laboratory capacity-building and forensic training activities) such as the Paul Coverdell, DNA Backlog Reduction, Solving Cold Cases, and Forensic DNA Unit Efficiency Improvement programs. These are awards to provide direct assistance to individual agencies and have nothing to do with NIJ's research function. They now represent more than half of the budget of OST. The research mission of NIJ is being overwhelmed by these activities, and its standing as a science agency has been negatively affected. If these essentially formula grant programs are removed from NIJ, then NIJ can more effectively focus on its research mission.

As a science agency, NIJ should play a central role in efforts to develop research-based, effective strategies for preventing and treating criminal behavior in the United States in the 21st century. Its primary mission is not to evaluate OJP programs and in the process neglect the fostering of a robust program of more "basic" kinds of research. Basic research as well as applied research offers the possibility of clarifying the nature of crime and documenting aspects of the justice system. Nor is NIJ's primary mission to advise OJP and DOJ on policy, build the capacity of line agencies, or disseminate information that is not science based. As a science agency, NIJ should set priorities for its work that are based on an accurate assessment of the research needs and possibilities at any point in time. NIJ should take an active role in defining the types of research that make sense. Among the possibilities are interdisciplinary efforts with other federal research agencies whose work has implications for solving crime and justice problems. In the description of NIJ's research portfolio, the committee notes several examples of interagency cooperation in Chapter 3, and we think that such efforts should be encouraged and facilitated. As part of its science role, NIJ should also work with other program offices within OJP and DOJ to advise them on their program development activities, develop a strategy for identifying appropriate programs for evaluation, inform them of the policy and practice implications of their research, and identify the research needs of the field. To play this central role will require the agency to make longer term commitments of funds and staff to solving problems in specific areas of criminal justice practice, to engage more actively with the research community in selecting priority areas and testing the feasibility of ideas as they develop, and to make multiyear commitments to researchers to work through the development process. This will entail significant organizational commitment to the goals and development of management and practices that support the process.

The committee was charged with recommending a research agenda for NIJ. Our approach to this task is to note the many recommendations that other NRC panels have made to guide the NIJ research agenda (see Appendix E), and to emphasize the need for a science-based process to set agendas, select awardees, and monitor performance. We have not specified a specific research agenda because we became convinced that proper governance and transparent processes should be established first within the agency in order to set the agenda and to resolve such issues as the levels of support for basic and applied research and for social science research and technology development. An NIJ with the autonomy and type of leadership we propose will use a strong advisory board and the many research recommendations it has already received to set both its long- and short-term agenda and priorities.

The NIJ advisory board should be one component of a broader advisory infrastructure that provides for outside scientific advice and feedback for particular programs of research as well as individual large-scale grants, as appropriate to the role of a research agency. NIJ should have a program of research to improve scientific methods in crime and justice research, including work on how to make sure experimental designs, longitudinal studies, and long-term observational research are appropriately supported.

NIJ should be provided with the authority and resources necessary to devote sustained attention to more long-term research activities appropriate for a research institute. In 1977, the NRC Committee on Research on Law Enforcement and Criminal Justice concluded that extensive knowledge about crime and criminal behaviors and the operation of the criminal justice system was necessary in order to develop fair and effective governmental responses. The need to identify questions that will advance theory, research methods, science, and practices around important issues—such as crime control theory, the etiology of criminal behavior, the factors that influence desistance from criminal behavior, and the emergence of new opportunities for crime in the face of social and technological change—remains as strong today as it was 30 years ago. NIJ will also be in a better position to justify and support research to improve scientific methods and other kinds of studies, such as surveys and longitudinal studies that have been neglected because of their duration, complexity, and expense.

BOLSTER THE RESEARCH INFRASTRUCTURE

RECOMMENDATION 3: The National Institute of Justice should undertake efforts to nurture and grow the pool of researchers involved in criminal justice research as well as activities that support the research endeavor itself. These efforts should include increasing the resources devoted to supporting graduate education for persons pursuing a career in criminology and criminal justice studies and other disciplines engaged in research and teaching on criminal justice topics, such as the Graduate Research Fellowship Program and the W.E.B. Du Bois Program, and enhancing the Data Archive Program.

Improving research on crime and justice will require more and better trained researchers in all of the sciences on which NIJ depends, most especially criminology and other social sciences and the forensic sciences. NIJ's support for graduate students and rising academics has been effective but modest. In the past three decades, NIJ has developed and sustained a number of fellowship programs. The recipients of NIJ doctoral and young faculty fellowships have made scholarly contributions to the criminal justice literature or to NIJ's research programs and many have remained in the criminal justice field.

Currently, NIJ lacks the resources or administrative oversight to effectively expand these programs. The committee observes that, over the years, there has been inaccurate documentation of basic and relevant information regarding the fellowship recipients. In addition, no external formal assessments of NIJ's fellowship programs have been conducted to date. We make suggestions for enhancement of these efforts in Chapter 5.

Similarly, NIJ has operated a very effective program of archiving and disseminating data needed for crime and justice research. It has been a leader at the federal level in recognizing the importance of collecting, archiving, and making available to other researchers the data collected as a part of the projects it funds. Since 1981, NIJ has included some kind of special requirement in its research awards for grantees to submit the data collected. But too many grantees continue to ignore such requirements and NIJ has failed to monitor compliance with its requirements that grantees submit their data sets or risk nonpayment of funds or to develop a strategy that would provide the necessary support to produce quality data sets to the National Archive of Criminal Justice Data. Again, Chapter 5 outlines steps that could be taken to increase the number and quality of data submissions.

ENHANCE THE SCIENTIFIC INTEGRITY AND TRANSPARENCY OF RESEARCH OPERATIONS

RECOMMENDATION 4: The National Institute of Justice (NIJ) should revise its research operations to allow for greater transparency, consistency, timeliness, and appropriate involvement of the research and practitioner communities. In particular, NIJ should make information about its research operations and activities publicly available, easily understood, and consistent with the highest standards found in other high-quality federal research agencies

Recommendation 1 reflects our view that NIJ does not have sufficient independence, authority, or resources to fulfill its mission. We think it will take congressional and executive action to change this. But the quality of key research agency activities, such as agenda setting and making awards, does not depend on the organizational location of a research agency or the size of its budget but on good leadership. NIJ does not have proper R&D management processes in place to ensure that good planning occurs, that all research proposals are subject to high-quality peer review, that fair and impartial funding decisions are made, that reports receive careful assessments, and that the agency is doing everything it can to ensure that its research operations are of the highest quality and in keeping with its mission. In addition, NIJ's efforts to involve researchers and practitioners in an advisory capacity have not always been consistent or appropriate, given their expertise and training.

With regard to how NIJ can improve the quality of its research operations and enhance the trust and confidence of the research community, a central element is greater transparency in processes and decisions. Current levels of transparency are not sufficient and contribute to the opinions noted in our survey results that NIJ decisions are not made on the basis of scientific criteria. From early announcement of award cycles, to greater information on proposal reviews and decisions, to improved easily available data on awards and award completion, NIJ will need to be better understood by the research and practitioner communities.

Improving Research Operations

Agenda Setting and Planning

NIJ lacks a formal and centralized strategic planning process. Agenda setting and planning are handled differently by ORE and OST, with neither well understood by its own staff or by the broader research community.

NIJ should revise its program planning and grant selection processes in ways that reflect adherence to established criteria and well-established scientific practices. The committee urges the new NIJ to establish a clear and timely planning process that includes the following elements:

1. A structured agenda-setting process with full participation of staff and broad outreach to researchers in the planning process for both social science and technology research.
2. Engagement of practitioners in the planning process to identify needs and to build support for the conduct of research as well as the adoption of findings by criminal justice agencies.
3. More open, transparent, and collaborative approach to identifying areas and topics for long-term funding.
4. Development of a strategic plan that identifies these areas and topics.
5. Making the strategic plan publicly available in a timely way.
6. Consistent and extensive oversight by external, independent, scientific reviewers.

There are numerous models of agenda setting employed by other federal research agencies that NIJ can turn to for guidance. The individual institutes of NIH engage in a very structured process that is well documented, involves the full participation of staff, and engages the research community through their participation as members of standing advisory committees and as experts in particular areas. Although there is considerable variety in the specifics, the overall process is similar and is designed to result in a strategic plan. The purpose of the strategic plan is to announce to researchers the near-term priorities—priorities that focus on "the greatest need and promise for scientific advancement" (National Institute on Alcohol Abuse and Alcoholism, 2006).

Several NIH institute division directors met with the committee, shared information about their planning processes, and described the various roles of senior leadership, program staff, and researchers. Detailed written information was also received from the Division of Epidemiology and Prevention Research (DEPR) at the National Institute on Alcohol Abuse and Alcoholism (NIAAA) that proved very helpful in fleshing out the particulars of its planning experience (see Box 7-2).

Two things stand out about the DEPR process. There was broad input from the science field at every stage, including the final review meeting of NIAAA's Extramural Advisory Council. Ad hoc experts from several federal agencies, universities, research centers, and medical centers attended this meeting, commented on the priorities, and responded to questions. There

BOX 7-2
Planning at the Division of Epidemiology and Prevention Research

One of four divisions of NIAAA, the Division of Epidemiology and Prevention Research was newly created in 2004. Its responsibilities are similar to those of NIJ in that it plans, conducts, and supports epidemiological studies; it supports clinical programs; it analyzes ecological and situational factors related to its particular subject area; it collaborates with outside organizations; it collaborates on studies with a broad array of organizations; it sponsors scientific conferences; and it supports a wide range of grants, including research and research training.

As part of its 2-year strategic planning process, division staff developed a mission statement; identified critical issues; reported on trends and related areas impacting on the problem being studied; reviewed relevant research findings; analyzed its current portfolio; described pertinent methodological issues; developed contextual background information and information on other relevant initiatives sponsored by the broader agency; and undertook a financial analysis of funding allocations within the division. This planning process culminated with the adoption of its strategic plan that received approval by the NIAAA National Advisory Council.

was also full documentation of the process, of the analyses that had been undertaken, and of decisions reached. Upon review by NIAAA's National Advisory Council in February 2007, the strategic plan and all written materials were posted on the NIAAA website, where it remains today.

In comparison to the DEPR description of a formal process, NIJ's agenda planning activities have varied over time and, particularly in the case of ORE, are not well developed or formalized. NIJ should take immediate steps to develop a formal, unified, and structured planning process. It should include broad participation of the research community at various stages and in different capacities. NIJ should base its agenda on a thorough understanding of the state of the art, an analysis of its own past and current research portfolio, and extensive consultation with the science community. Only by having such a process is NIJ likely to encourage creative and innovative thinking about both research issues and methodologies.

Signaling of Research Solicitations

NIJ has not been consistent in signaling the research community about its solicitations and proposed submission dates. NIJ should provide more predictable levels and timing of funding and as much advance notice as possible about solicitations. Other federal research agencies, such as NSF, provide notice of solicitations well in advance of their deadline dates. In the case of the Law and Science Program at NSF, submission dates occur semiannually at the same time of the year. NIJ should aim for regularly timed solicitation cycles. This makes it much easier for applicants to plan around these deadlines and, in the event they apply and are not successful, to have sufficient time to revise their proposal and resubmit for the next round of funding.

Peer Review and Grant Selection Process

Much has been written about peer review and the requisites of a high-quality scientific peer-review system (National Research Council, 1992b, 2000; U.S. General Accounting Office, 1999; U.S. Office of Management and Budget, 2004). In a review of peer-review processes being used by agencies that fund education research, NRC identified the following attributes (National Research Council, 2004d):

- flexibility in designing peer-review systems to meet the individual needs of an agency;
- independence of the project officer from the peer-review process;
- nonparticipation of practitioners in assessment of research expertise; if included, their role is to assess relevance, significance, applicability, and impact of the proposal;
- a strong infrastructure: knowledgeable staff, systems for managing the logistics of peer review, technologies to support review and discussion of proposals, clear mechanisms for providing feedback, and standing panels when research priorities are clearly stable;
- predictable levels and timing of funding for the process itself;
- clearly delineated scoring systems and the meaning of the scoring levels defined and understood;
- training on scoring for reviewers as well as training on what the peer-review process entails and how to be an effective reviewer;
- qualified peer reviewers who have the research experience and expertise to judge the theoretical and technical merits of the proposals they review; and
- systematic evaluation of peer review based on intended outcomes and the public reporting of the evaluation.

Measured against these attributes, the NIJ peer-review process is very weak. The committee notes the current practice of having both researchers and practitioners serve as peer reviewers and assess proposals using the same criteria. We view this as highly inappropriate given that the purpose of peer review is to assess scientific merit and arrive at consensus.

NIJ's ability to adapt or change its peer-review process to meet its own needs is constrained because peer-review services are managed and overseen centrally under OJP. Scoring systems are not understood and do not appear to have a scientific basis. NIJ has not undertaken a systematic evaluation of its peer-review processes. Having a good scientific peer review and grant selection process in place is a critical requirement for a high-quality research program. In the federal government, although peer review is used for many purposes, its primary use is to assess the scientific merit of competitive and noncompetitive proposals. There is no written government-wide definition of peer review, but there is general acceptance that it is an "independent assessment of the technical, scientific merit of research by peers who are scientists in knowledge and expertise equal to that of the researchers whose work they review" (U.S. General Accounting Office, 1999).

Proper peer review is integral to the work and reputation of a science agency. NIJ's authority to conduct and manage its own peer review should be clearly established and protected. NIJ should follow standards of practice for peer review reflective of a science agency. NSF and NIH are excellent models of scientific peer review. These models have been in place for many years, and although the NIH peer-review process has recently undergone a major overhaul to improve what was perceived as its shortcomings, it still retains the basic infrastructure and approach (see Box 7-3).

Grant Award Process

During the course of our study, four different persons served as the final arbiter of grant award decisions at NIJ, and it is possible that each one used different criteria and a different in-house process to make the decision. NIJ staff themselves seemed unclear as to how decisions were made. According to the perceptions of Congress reflected in recent appropriation bills and the majority of researchers who responded to the committee's survey, the NIJ process appears to be flawed.

A research institute's reputation is based not only on the quality of its work but also on the perception that its grant award process is fair, consistent, and transparent. NIJ needs to reestablish its credibility by signaling clearly to the research community as much information as it can regarding its funding, the amount it anticipates providing, the selection criteria it will use, and the role of the various participants in the process—in short, the basis on which research support is being provided. Documenting and

BOX 7-3
Peer-Review Models

The NIH Peer-Review Model

Responsibility for peer review across NIH resides with the Center for Scientific Review (CSR), an organization under the Office of the Director of NIH. CSR is usually the initial point of contact for applications, and it also manages the review process for most of the grant applications from the 27 NIH institutes. For grant applications, there is a two-step review process: (1) a review by a Scientific Review Group (SRG) under CSR's direction and then (2) assignment to at least one NIH institute for potential funding. This SRG usually contains 15-18 scientific experts who meet three times a year. One of the members, designated as the chair, leads the discussion. The initial or first-level review evaluates the scientific and technical merits of the application.

The second review is done by the national advisory council for the particular institute. These councils are composed of 12 or more members drawn from the scientific and lay communities. They review the initial judgments of the proposals and make recommendations for funding in light of relevance to the program and to the institute's overall mission. In practice, the councils make few changes in the priority rankings from the initial review. Sometimes applications for funding bypass the CSR review process and are submitted directly to the individual institutes, where they undergo review by standing committees that are formed for a very specific purpose. In this case, they fall under an institute's individual Office of External Research. Once through this stage of review, they go on to the particular national advisory council of that institute for a funding decision. It is important to note that this process involves not only grants and cooperative agreements but also contracts.

NIH is currently in the implementation phase of a multiyear process to improve its peer-review process. The goals of this effort are to engage the best reviewers; to improve the quality and transparency of review; to ensure balanced and fair reviews across scientific fields and career stages and reduce administrative burden; and to provide for a continuous review of peer review. It is an activity that NIJ would do well to emulate as it seeks improvements to its own peer-review process.

The NSF Model

Peer review is conducted differently at NSF than at NIH but it reflects the same core values of scientific competence, fairness, timeliness, and integrity. The division within NSF that most closely approximates NIJ in terms of the kinds of research it sponsors is the Law and Social Science program, one of 16 individual programs with the Social and Economic Sciences (SES). The SES is located within SBE, one of seven Directorates at NSF.

Proposals received by the NSF Proposal Processing Unit within the Division of Grants and Agreements are assigned to the appropriate NSF program for acknowledgement and, if they meet NSF requirements, for review. All proposals are carefully reviewed by a scientist, engineer, or educator serving as an NSF Program Officer, and usually by three to ten other persons outside NSF who are experts in the particular fields represented by the proposal. Proposers are invited to suggest names of persons they believe are especially well qualified to review the proposal and/or persons they would prefer not review the proposal. These suggestions may serve as one source in the reviewer selection process at the program officer's discretion. Program Officers may also obtain comments from assembled review panels or from site visits before recommending final action on proposals. Senior NSF staff further review recommendations for awards. Each Division has its own Advisory Panel that is comprised of scholars from multiple disciplines (anthropology, criminology, economics, political science, psychology, sociology). In the case of the Law and Social Science Advisory Panel, eleven members serve a 2-year rotation and provide written reviews that supplement the external reviews. The Panel meets to discuss proposals and propose the ranking and within that a further breakdown for actual funding. It provides advice as to whether the proposal is competitive. The program officer makes the recommendation to the Division Director as to which ones to recommend and can disagree with the Panel's guidance. Normally final programmatic approval occurs at the division level. NSF relies on the judgment of program officers to make funding recommendations that address NSF strategic goals.

One important way in which the NSF peer-review system differs from that of the NIH is the amount of discretion the program officers have. Peer review at NSF still receives high marks because of other features it has and its overall transparency. For example, all applicants have access to an electronic system called FastLane in which they can track the progress of their applications and can view the individual peer reviews and scores as well as any summary reports, site visits, or other documents that constitute their application file. Second, NSF program officers are highly qualified researchers and academicians who see their role as encouraging good research that is responsive to NSF priorities and who work with applicants to shape them accordingly. Staff also communicate with applicants in a timely way regarding their submission and provide useful feedback that often allows unsuccessful applicants to revise pro-

continued

BOX 7-3 Continued

posals in time for the next round of applications. Third, the system is perceived as responsive to researcher needs. Detailed information on the process is available to any applicant on the NSF website. The NSF electronic system can accommodate changes in an application prior to the final submission date. Submission dates for many programs are set in advance, frequently on a semiannual schedule. Finally, there is a check on peer review in the form of program reviews that are undertaken periodically by the Committee of Visitors. This quality assurance process examines technical as well as managerial oversight of the program. In doing so, it holds program officers' accountable for their recommendations but also serves as check on the quality of reviews, the basis for the program officers' recommendations.

maintaining consistency in the award decision process is an important first step to rebuilding trust and confidence in NIJ.

Report Review

Although NIJ regards the dissemination of research findings as a part of its mission, the review process that supports its own dissemination process is very weak. There seems to be a lack of clarity about what NIJ expects from its grantees regarding final reports. Like agenda setting and peer review, the report review process is not well understood by researchers, who are critical of the amount of time it takes for NIJ to release research reports or research findings publicly.

This situation prevails despite the fact that interest in making scientific research available to the public has never been greater. Recently, particular attention has focused on the ability of scientists working in the federal government to communicate with the media and the public. The Union of Concerned Scientists, a public interest advocacy group that investigates the extent to which scientists have been thwarted in their efforts to release their findings, has been very involved in bringing to the public's attention various cases in which research findings had been suppressed or altered (Union of Concerned Scientists, 2007). It also proposes a model media policy that outlines responsibilities for public affairs officers as well as researchers and other staff. This policy provides that employees have the right to review, approve, and comment publicly on the final version of any proposed publication that significantly relies on their research, identifies them as an author or contributor, or purposes to represent their scientific opinion (Union of

Concerned Scientists, 2008). GAO has also assessed several research agencies' practices regarding release of information and recommended that policies be in place to guide researchers and public affairs officials in their efforts to disseminate research to the scientific community (U.S. Government Accountability Office, 2007).

Our examination of other federal research agencies indicates that they either have complete authority over reports issued in their name or they rely on researchers publishing independently. NIJ needs to improve its research report review process as well as to support efforts of researchers to publish in peer-reviewed journals.

Achieving Transparency

A common theme running through our assessment of NIJ's research operations is the importance of transparency. Transparency implies openness, communication, and accountability. It means that the decisions of research agencies regarding agendas, award decisions, and impact (in the form of research findings and reports) should be apparent to the research community and the public. In our examination of NIJ's research operations and comparison with the practices of other federal research agencies, the committee found a lack of transparency, which is reflected in the limitations of the information made available to grant applicants, grant awardees, and the public. It is also reflected in our interviews with NIJ staff, in which many of them explained that they did not know how funding decisions are made or the basis for them. The lack of transparency and quality of information were apparent to the committee as we attempted to access directly or be provided with certain information for this study. Despite the facts that our study meets the necessary privacy and confidentiality requirements and it was requested by NIJ itself, our efforts to gather data were often unsuccessful, either because the data did not exist, they existed in an unusable form, or barriers to obtaining the data could not be overcome by NIJ staff or leadership.

Several members of Congress have voiced concerns about the lack of transparency, raising questions about conflicts of interest and questionable practices. As mentioned in Chapter 4, the most severe criticism has come from the Department of Justice's Office of Inspector General, which concluded that NIJ's failure to document key aspects of its preselection and grant award process called into question the fairness and openness of its competitive grant-making process (U.S. Department of Justice, 2009b).

The lack of transparency is also reflected in the views of criminal justice researchers we surveyed. In the absence of information and feedback on how decisions are made and the criteria that are used to reach them, it is reasonable to attribute these decisions to political considerations.

In order to achieve transparency, a research organization needs the capability, authority, and resources to maintain records of its own activities that are accurate, easily retrievable, and accessible to the public within limits of the law. The committee acknowledges that NIJ is very dependent on OJP's centralized grant management information system and the resources provided by the Office of the Chief Information Officer. However, NIJ should take responsibility for documenting its decision-making processes, and in instances in which the information is not being generated by OJP, it should develop its own documentation and records. At a minimum these records should include

- Information on the life cycle of a grant, from award to final report and resultant publications. At a minimum, titles, grant amounts, principal investigators, and grant abstracts should be a part of this information.
- Information on individuals who have received funding and their research records, products, citations, and professional recognition.
- Financial information for all NIJ organizational units that is consistent and includes appropriated funds and expenditures and breakdowns between various categories of restricted and discretionary funds, and program topics. This information should be compiled in a way that it can be used to present a historical picture of funding.
- Information on new staff hires and vacancies that indicates grade level, position, and education levels. Such information should be compiled annually.

Involving the Research and Practitioner Communities

Another theme throughout our deliberations on NIJ's research operations is the need to clarify the important but separate roles that the research and practitioner communities should play in the research program. These roles are reflected in the proposed composition of the NIJ advisory board, in the qualifications of the NIJ director, and in the improvements that the committee recommends regarding agenda setting and planning, peer review, and report review.

NIJ should increase its efforts to involve researchers and to seek their advice in the development, implementation, and assessment of its research activities. Their advice is critical to identifying and shaping the kind of science needed to accumulate enough knowledge to answer critical policy questions. The question "What works?" requires a multilayered response and a probing into what led to success as well as what led to failure. Researchers are uniquely trained to pose these questions and seek the answers.

Practitioners also have an important role to play and through their training and expertise can provide broad policy direction to address research concerns. As consumers of the research, practitioners can also advise as to its need and relevance.

ESTABLISH A CULTURE OF SELF-ASSESSMENT

RECOMMENDATION 5: The National Institute of Justice should measure the influence of its programs on research and practice and assess the quality of operations and program-level technical and managerial matters.

NIJ's efforts to promote or conduct assessment activities have been extremely limited. With the exception of the 1977 NRC study and this current one, there has been no other independent review of its body of work. Research on particular topics has been discussed as part of more general substantive NRC reviews (see Appendix E), but, with the exception of the NRC report on violence against women (National Research Council, 1996b, 2004a), NIJ's own research has generally not been singled out. The committee saw little evidence of regularly scheduled systematic reviews of the ongoing research portfolio as part of a planning process or ongoing monitoring activities.

Ensuring quality in a research organization through careful monitoring is a particularly complex undertaking. It needs to take into account the quality of the research as well as the many different processes that support the research enterprise. At its highest level, assessment activities can be directed to assessing the broad influence of a program or its major achievements or to more narrow programmatic goals or benchmarks. They can include assessments of various processes and of the products themselves as well as customer satisfaction. They can also include assessment of staff performance.

NIJ will not be able to conduct these kinds of assessments without better records and a willingness to provide access. Throughout this report, we note difficulties in obtaining documentation of research operations as well as other kinds of administrative information. Some of the problem lies with the centralization of records under OJP, which is not tailored to the needs of NIJ. NIJ should take responsibility for creating record systems that will allow for detailed analyses of administrative and program funding, administrative and personnel matters, and all programmatic activities. These records need to be consistent across all NIJ offices. Most critically, it should create a basic mechanism to track usage and influence of funded research in scholarship and practice.

Considering how other federal research agencies address the issue of assessment is instructive. First, many research agencies struggle with defining quality and then constructing a process to assess it. This is especially true in assessing the impact of research or research outcomes as a measure of quality (National Research Council, 2008b). Second, scientists outside the agency are heavily relied on, either individually or as peer reviewers, to assess quality. Peer review has many other purposes than proposal review. Many federal research agencies rely on individual peer reviewers or peer-review panels to set priorities, develop programs, and even conduct personnel evaluations. Third, individual processes, such as peer review of proposals and the report review process, should include an evaluation component that provides useful feedback on efficiency and quality. Like other well-managed federal agencies, NIJ should establish self-assessment as an ongoing activity and use it to constantly improve its operations. Furthermore, to ensure transparency, it should make the results of such assessments publicly available. This is unlikely to happen, however, unless our recommendations on leadership and independence are implemented.

NIJ is the only federal agency devoted to crime and justice research. Despite the problems noted in this report, it has accomplished much in its short history. Our assessment of NIJ supports its continuation and growth, but with legislation and actions by the executive and congressional branches that will allow it to fulfill its role as the nation's center for improvements in crime control and prevention. When those changes happen, we are confident that NIJ's self-assessments and periodic external assessments will describe an agency that is science driven and that is making even greater contributions to the understanding of crime and the improvement of justice.

References

Akers, R.L. (1992). Linking sociology and its specialties: The case of criminology. *Social Forces, 71*(1), 1-16.

Anonymous. (1979). Debate over a National-Institute-of-Justice. *Judicature, 62*(6), 296-300.

Armbrust, E.A. (1978). *Federal Law Enforcement Assistance—Alternative Approaches.* NCJ #051182. Washington, DC: U.S. Department of Justice.

Association of Doctoral Programs in Criminology and Criminal Justice. (2009). *2009 Survey Report.* Available: http://www.adpccj.com/documents/2009_ADPCCJ_Survey_Report.pdf [accessed March 2010].

Blumstein, A., and Petersilia, J. (1994). NIJ and its research program. In National Institute of Justice, Office of Justice Programs, U.S. Department of Justice, *25 Years of Criminal Justice Research* (pp. 9-42, NCJ #151287). Washington, DC: U.S. Department of Justice.

Boisseau, R. (2009). FY 2010 House Appropriations Bill, Department of Education. *FYI: The AIP Bulletin of Science Policy News*, 100, July 28. Available: http://www.aip.org/fyi/2009/100.html# [accessed March 2010].

Braga, A.A., and Weisburd, D.L. (2006). *Police Innovation and Crime Prevention: Lessons Learned from Police Research over the Past 20 Years* (NCJ #218585). Paper presented at the National Institute of Justice Policing Research Workshop: Planning for the Future, November 28-29, Washington, DC. Available: http://www.ncjrs.gov/pdffiles1/nij/grants/218585.pdf [accessed February 2010].

Braga, A.A., Weisburd, D.L., Waring, E.J., Mazerolle, L.G., Spelman, W., and Gajewski, F. (1999). Problem-oriented policing in violent crime places: A randomized controlled experiment. *Criminology, 37*(3), 541-579.

Brock, K. (2004). *When Men Murder Women: An Analysis of 2002 Homicide Data.* Washington, DC: Violence Policy Center. Available: http://www.vpc.org/studies/wmmw2004.pdf [accessed February 2010].

Buerger, M. (1998). The politics of third-party policing. *Crime Prevention Studies, 9*, 89-116. Available: http://www.popcenter.org/library/crimeprevention/volume_09/ThirdParty Policing.pdf [accessed December 2009].

Bulman, P. (2008). Communicating across state and county lines: The Piedmont Regional Voice Over Internet Protocol Project (NCJ #224087). *National Institute of Justice Journal,* (261), 24-27.

Bulman, P. (2009). Using technology to make prisons and jails safer (NCJ #225764). *National Institute of Justice Journal,* (262), 38-41.

Bureau of Alcohol, Tobacco and Firearms. (1997). *Crime Gun Trace Analysis Reports: The Illegal Youth Firearms Market in Seventeen Communities* (NCJ #166583). Washington, DC: U.S. Department of the Treasury. Abstract available: http://www.ncjrs.gov/App/Publications/Abstract.aspx?ID=166583 [accessed May 2010].

Bureau of Justice Assistance. (2010). *Residential Substance Abuse Treatment.* Washington, DC: U.S. Department of Justice. Available: http://www.ojp.usdoj.gov/BJA/evaluation/program-substance-abuse/rsat-index.htm [accessed March 2010].

Bureau of Justice Statistics. (2007). *Homicide Trends in the U.S.: Long-Term Trends.* FBI, Uniform Crime Reports, 1950-2005. Available: http://bjs.ojp.usdoj.gov/content/homicide/tables/totalstab.cfm [accessed March 2010].

Burt, M.R., Zweig, J.M., Scarcella, C.A., Van Ness, A., Parikh, N., Uekert, B.K., and Harrell, A.V. (2001). *2001 Report: Evaluation of the STOP Formula Grants to Combat Violence Against Women.* Washington, DC: Urban Institute.

Campbell, J.C., Webster, D., Koziol-McLain, J., Block, C.R., Campbell, D., Curry, M.A., Gary, F., McFarlane, J., Sachs, C., Sharps, P., Ulrich, Y., and Wilt, S.A. (2003). Assessing risk factors for intimate partner homicide (NCJ #196547). *National Institute of Justice Journal,* (250). Available: http://www.ncjrs.gov/pdffiles1/jr000250e.pdf [accessed May 2010].

Caulkins, J.P. (1995). *Estimating Elasticities of Demand for Cocaine and Heroin with Data from the Drug Use Forecasting System* (NCJ #173823). Washington, DC: National Institute of Justice. Abstract available: http://www.ncjrs.gov/app/Search/Abstracts.aspx?id=173823 [accessed May 2010].

Chase, M. (2009, April). *Cancer Research Projects May Grow 25 Percent from Federal Funds.* Available: http://www.bloomberg.com/apps/news?pid=20601124&sid=aLUz9pBOzOcQ [accessed November 2009].

Cohen, J., and Ludwig, J. (2003). Policing crime guns. In P.J. Cook and J. Ludwig (Eds.), *Evaluating Gun Policy: Effects on Crime and Violence* (pp. 217-250). Washington, DC: Brookings Institution.

Consortium of Social Science Associations. (2003). Justice research and statistics agencies face competitive sourcing. *COSSA Washington Update, 22*(3), 5.

Consortium of Social Science Associations. (2008). OJP request for consolidation of programs draws skepticism. *COSSA Washington Update, 27*(5).

Consortium of Social Science Associations. (2009). Special edition: Proposed FY 2010 budgets for social and behavioral science. *COSSA Washington Update, 28*(11).

Crossland, C.R. (2008). *NIJ Graduate Research and W.E.B. DuBois Fellowship Programs: An Overview and Tips in Developing and Submitting Program Proposals.* Presentation at the 60th Annual Meeting of the American Society of Criminology, November, St. Louis, MO. Available: http://www.asc41.com/Annual_Meeting/2008/2008PrintProgram.pdf [accessed March 2010].

Davison, N. (2007). *The Development of "Non-Lethal" Weapons During the 1990's.* Bradford Nonlethal Weapons Research Project, Department of Peace Studies, University of Bradford, UK, Occasional Paper No. 2. West Yorkshire, UK: University of Bradford.

Doyle, C. (2001). *Terrorism: Section by Section Analysis of the USA PATRIOT Act.* CRS Report for Congress, RL31200. Washington, DC: Congressional Research Service.

Earls, F.J., and Visher, C.A. (1997). *Project on Human Development in Chicago Neighborhoods: A Research Update* (NCJ #163603). National Institute of Justice Research in Brief. Available: http://www.ncjrs.gov/pdffiles/163603.pdf [accessed May 2010].

Early, B.H., and Burger, W.E. (1972). National Institute of Justice proposal–Foreword. *West Virginia Law Review, 74*(3), 226-259.

Eck, J.E. (1993). The threat of crime displacement. *Criminal Justice Abstracts, 25*, 527-546.

Eck, J.E., and Wartell, J. (1999). *Reducing Crime and Drug Dealing by Improving Place Management: A Randomized Experiment* (NCJ #184380). Washington, DC: U.S. Department of Justice. Abstract available: http://www.ncjrs.gov/app/Search/Abstracts.aspx?id=184380 [accessed May 2010].

Ekstrand, L.E. (2002). *Statement of Laurie E. Ekstrand, Director, Justice Issues, Office of Justice Programs, before the Subcommittee on Crime, Committee on the Judiciary, House of Representatives, Regarding Problems with Grant Monitoring and Concerns about Evaluation Studies, March 7*. Washington, DC: U.S. Government Accountability Office. Available: http://www.gao.gov/new.items/d02507t.pdf [accessed February 2010].

Elden, M., and Chisholm, R. (1993). Emerging varieties of action research: Introduction to the special issue. *Human Relations, 46*(2), 121-142.

Fagan, J. (2008). Crime and neighborhood change. In National Research Council, *Understanding Crime Trends: Workshop Report* (pp. 81-126). Committee on Understanding Crime Trends, A.S. Goldberger and R. Rosenfeld, Eds. Committee on Law and Justice, Division of Behavioral and Social Sciences and Education. Washington, DC: The National Academies Press.

Falkin, G.P., Strauss, S., and Bohen, T. (1999). Matching drug-involved probationers to appropriate drug interventions: A strategy for reducing recidivism. *Federal Probation, 63*(1), 3-8.

Farrington, D.P., Ohlin, L.E., and Wilson, J.Q. (1986). *Understanding and Controlling Crime: Toward a New Research Strategy*. New York: Springer-Verlag.

Feucht, T.E., and Kyle, G.M. (1996). *Methamphetamine Use Among Adult Arrestees: Findings from the Drug Use Forecasting Program* (NCJ #161842). National Institute of Justice Research in Brief. Available: http://www.ncjrs.gov/pdffiles/meth.pdf [accessed May 2010].

Finn, P., and Lee, B.N.W. (1987). *Serving Crime Victims and Witnesses* (NCJ #97673). Prepared by Abt Associates, Inc. for the National Institute of Justice, Washington, DC. Abstract available: http://www.ncjrs.gov/app/Search/Abstracts.aspx?id=97673 [accessed May 2010].

Fisher, B.S., Cullen F.T., and Turner, M.G. (1999). *Extent and Nature of the Sexual Victimization of College Women: A National-Level Analysis* (NCJ #179977). Paper prepared for the National Institute of Justice, Washington, DC. Available: http://www.ncjrs.gov/pdffiles1/nij/grants/179977.pdf [accessed May 2010].

Fox, J.A., and Zawitz, M.W. (2004). *Homicide Trends in the U.S.* Trends by Gender, see statistical table, Victim-Offender Relationship by Victim Gender, 1976-2002. Washington, DC: U.S. Department of Justice, Bureau of Justice Statistics. Available: http://bjs.ojp.usdoj.gov/content/homicide/homtrnd.cfm [accessed February 2010].

Garner, J.H., and Maxwell, C.D. (2000). What are the lessons of the police arrest studies? (NCJ #206405). *Journal of Aggression, Maltreatment and Trauma, 4*(1), 83-114.

Garner, J.H., and Visher, C.A. (2003). The production of criminological experiments (NCJ #206436). *Evaluation Review, 27*(3), 316-335. Abstract available: http://www.ncjrs.gov/app/Search/Abstracts.aspx?id=206436 [accessed May 2010].

Goldstein, H. (1979). Improving policing: A problem-oriented approach (NCJ #56240). *Crime and Delinquency, 25*(2), 236-258.

Greenwood, P., Chaiken, J., and Petersilia, J. (1977). *Criminal Investigation Process*. Lexington, MA: D.C. Heath.

Groff, E., and McEwen, T. (2006a). *Exploring the Spatial Configuration of Places Related to Homicide Events, Final Report*. Alexandria, VA: Institute for Law and Justice. Available: http://www.ilj.org/publications/docs/Spatial_Configuration_Places.pdf [accessed May 2010].

Groff, E.R., and McEwen, T. (2006b). *Visualization of Spatial Relationships in Mobility Research: A Primer* (NCJ #214255). Alexandria, VA: Institute for Law and Justice. Abstract available: http://www.ncjrs.gov/App/Publications/abstract.aspx?ID=235787 [accessed May 2010].

Guerin, P. (2002). *Outcome Evaluation of the New Mexico Corrections Department Genesis Residential Substance Abuse Treatment Program for State Prisoners, Final Summary Report* (NCJ #203277). Summary report prepared for the National Institute of Justice, Washington, DC. Available: http://www.ncjrs.gov/pdffiles1/nij/grants/203277.pdf [accessed May 2010].

Haile, E.S. (2006). *Without a Trace: How the Gun Lobby and the Government Suppress the Truth About Guns and Crime*. Washington, DC: Brady Center to Prevent Gun Violence.

Harcourt, B.E., and Ludwig, J. (2007). Reefer madness: Broken windows policing and misdemeanor marijuana arrest in New York City, 1989-2000. *Criminology and Public Policy, 6*(1), 165-181.

Harrell, A., Mitchell, O., Merrill, J., and Marlowe, D. (2003). *Evaluation of Breaking the Cycle* (NCJ #205002). Report prepared for the National Institute of Justice, Washington, DC. Available: http://www.ncjrs.gov/pdffiles1/nij/grants/205002.pdf [accessed May 2010].

Harris, L.N. (1978). *Response Time Analysis: Executive Summary* (NCJ #46852). Prepared by the Kansas City, Missouri, Police Department for the National Institute of Law Enforcement and Criminal Justice. Newark: University of Delaware. Abstract available: http://www.ncjrs.gov/app/Search/Abstracts.aspx?id=46852 [accessed May 2010].

Harrison, L.D., and Martin, S.S. (2000). *Residential Substance Abuse Treatment (RSAT) for State Prisoners Formula Grant: Compendium of Program Implementation and Accomplishments, Final Report* (NCJ #187099). Research report prepared for the U.S. Department of Justice, Washington, DC. Available: http://www.ncjrs.gov/pdffiles1/nij/grants/187099.pdf [accessed May 2010].

Hart, S. (2002a). *Statement of the Honorable Sarah V. Hart, Director, National Institute of Justice, Office of Justice Programs, before the Subcommittee on Aviation, Committee on Transportation and Infrastructure, U.S. House of Representatives, Regarding Less Lethal Weapons, May 2*. Washington, DC: U.S. Department of Justice. Available: http://www.ojp.usdoj.gov/nij/speeches/aviation.htm [accessed September 2009].

Hart, S. (2002b). *Statement of the Honorable Sarah V. Hart, Director, National Institute of Justice, Office of Justice Programs, before the Subcommittee on Crime and Drugs, Committee on the Judiciary, U.S. Senate, May 14*. Washington, DC: U.S. Department of Justice. Available: http://www.ojp.usdoj.gov/nij/speeches/dnatest.htm [accessed August 2009].

Inciardi, J.A. (1996). A *Corrections-Based Continuum of Effective Drug Abuse Treatment* (NCJ #152692). National Institute of Justice Research Preview: Research in Progress Seminar Series. Available: http://www.ncjrs.gov/pdffiles/contdrug.pdf [accessed May 2010].

Inter-university Consortium for Political and Social Research. (2010). *Project on Human Development in Chicago Neighborhoods*. Available: http://www.icpsr.umich.edu/PHDCN/about.html [accessed March 2010].

Jacobs, J.B., and Magdovitz, S.B. (1977). At LEEP's End?: A review of the Law Enforcement Education Program. *Journal of Police Science and Administration, 5*(1), 1-18.

Kansas City (Missouri) Police Department. (1980). *Directed Patrol Project, 1979, Kansas City (MO): Final Evaluation Report, January-December 1979*. Washington, DC: National Institute of Justice.

Kasey, P. (2009, August 7). *AmberView Discontinued: West Virginia High Technology Consortium Foundation to Seek Alternate Funding*. WOWK TV 13 News. Available: http://www.wowktv.com/story.cfm?func=viewstory&storyid=64310 [accessed August 2009].

Kelling, G.L. (1988). Police and communities: The quiet revolution. *Perspectives on Policing*, (1). Washington, DC: U.S. Department of Justice. Available: http://www.ncjrs.gov/pdffiles1/nij/109955.pdf [accessed April 2010].

Kelling, G.L., and Sousa, W.H. (2001). *Do Police Matter?: An Analysis of the Impact of New York's Police Reform*. Civic Report No. 22, Center for Civic Innovation at the Manhattan Institute. Available: http://www.manhattan-institute.org/pdf/cr_22.pdf [accessed March 2010].

Kelling, G.L. and Wilson, J.Q. (1982, March). Broken windows. *The Atlantic*. Available: http://www.theatlantic.com/doc/198203/broken-windows [accessed December 2009].

Kelling, G.L., Pate, A., Dieckman, D., and Brown, C.E. (1974). *The Kansas City Preventive Patrol Experiment: A Summary Report* (NCJ #42537). Washington, DC: Police Foundation. Available: http://www.policefoundation.org/pdf/kcppe.pdf [accessed May 2010].

Kennedy, D.M. (1997). Pulling levers: Chronic offenders, high crime settings, and a theory of prevention (NCJ #169596). *Valparaiso University Law Review, 31*(2), 449-484. Abstract available: http://www.ncjrs.gov/app/Search/Abstracts.aspx?id=169596 [accessed May 2010].

Koper, C.S., Woods, D.J., and Roth, J.A. (2004). *Updated Assessment of the Federal Assault Weapons Ban: Impacts on Gun Markets and Gun Violence, 1994-2003* (NCJ #204431). Report prepared for the U.S. Department of Justice. Available: http://www.ncjrs.gov/pdffiles1/nij/grants/204431.pdf [accessed May 2010].

Laney, G.P. (2005). *Violence Against Women Act: History and Federal Funding*. CRS Report for Congress, RL30871. Washington, DC: Congressional Research Service.

Lapham, D. (2005). *Section 1401 Transfer of DoD Technology and Equipment to First Responders*. Available: http://www.zyn.com/flcfw/05meeting-recap/presentations/lapham.don-Monterey.pdf [accessed March 2010].

Law Enforcement and Corrections Technology Advisory Council. (2008). *Law Enforcement and Corrections Technology Advisory Council Annual Report, 2008*. Rockville, MD: National Law Enforcement and Corrections Technology Center.

Law Enforcement Assistance Administration. (1969). *Annual Report of the Law Enforcement Assistance Administration Fiscal Year 1969 Ending June 30, 1969* (NCJ #2157). Submitted to the President and Congress of the United States. Available: http://www.ncjrs.gov/pdffiles1/nij/2157.pdf [accessed May 2010].

Law Enforcement Assistance Administration. (1971). *3rd Annual Report of the Law Enforcement Assistance Administration Fiscal Year 1971* (NCJ #2306). Washington, DC: U.S. Government Printing Office. Available: http://www.ncjrs.gov/app/Search/Abstracts.aspx?id=2306 [accessed May 2010].

Law Enforcement Assistance Administration. (1973). *LEAA Activities July 1, 1972 to June 30, 1973* (NCJ #12300). Washington, DC: U.S. Government Printing Office. Available: http://www.ncjrs.gov/app/Search/Abstracts.aspx?id=12300 [accessed May 2010].

Lipton, D.S. (1995). *The Effectiveness of Treatment for Drug Abusers Under Criminal Justice Supervision* (NCJ #157642). Washington, DC: National Institute of Justice. Available: http://www.ncjrs.gov/pdffiles/drugsupr.pdf [accessed May 2010].

Lipton, D.S. (1996). Prison-based therapeutic communities: Their success with drug-abusing offenders (NCJ #184889). *National Institute of Justice Journal*, (230), 12-20. Available: http://www.ncjrs.gov/pdffiles/nijj_230.pdf [accessed May 2010].

Loo, D.D., and Grimes, R-E.M. (2004). Polls, politics, and crime: The "Law and Order" issue of the 1960s. *Western Criminology Review*, 5(1), 50-67.

Lovrich, N.P., Pratt, T.C., Gaffney, M.J., Johnson, C.L., Asplen, C.H., Hurst, L.H., and Schellberg, T.M. (2003). National Forensic DNA Study Report, Final Report (NCJ #203970). Washington, DC: U.S. Department of Justice.

MacKenzie, D.L. (2000). Evidence-based corrections: Identifying what works. *Crime & Delinquency*, *46*(4), 457-471.

Maxson, C.L., Hennigan, K., Sloane, D., and Kolnick, K.A. (2005). *Can Civil Gang Injunctions Change Communities? A Community Assessment of the Impact of Civil Gang Injunctions* (NCJ #208345). Final report submitted to the U.S. Department of Justice. Available: http://www.ncjrs.gov/pdffiles1/nij/grants/208345.pdf [accessed December 2009].

McBath, D. (2008). New NIJ standard for CBRN protective equipment: A time to speak up. *Police Chief*, LXXV(9). Available: http://policechiefmagazine.org/magazine/index.cfm?fuseaction=display_arch&article_id=1600&issue_id=92008 [accessed August 2009].

McEwen, T. (1999). NIJ's locally initiated research partnerships in policing—Factors that add up to success (NCJ #180068). *National Institute of Justice Journal*, (238), 2-10. Available: http://www.ncjrs.gov/pdffiles1/jr000238.pdf [accessed May 2010].

McEwen, T. (2003). *Evaluation of the Locally Initiated Research Partnership Program* (NCJ #204022). Evaluation prepared for the U.S. Department of Justice. Available: http://www.ncjrs.gov/pdffiles1/nij/grants/204022.pdf [accessed May 2010].

McGarrell, E.F., Hipple, N.K., Corsaro, N., Bynum, T.S., Perez, H., Zimmermann, C.A., and Garmo, M. (2009). *Project Safe Neighborhoods—A National Program to Reduce Gun Crime: Final Project Report* (NCJ #226686). Available: http://www.ncjrs.gov/pdffiles1/nij/grants/226686.pdf [accessed December 2009].

Mieczkowski, T. (1995). *Hair Analysis as a Drug Detector* (NCJ #156434). National Institute of Justice Research in Brief. Available: http://www.ncjrs.gov/pdffiles/hair.pdf [accessed May 2010].

Mieczkowski, T. (1997). *Hair Assays and Urinalysis Results for Juvenile Drug Offenders* (NCJ #184390). Washington, DC: U.S. Department of Justice. Available: http://www.ncjrs.gov/pdffiles/hair.pdf [accessed May 2010].

Mieczkowski, T., Mumm, R., and Connick, H.F. (1995). Use of hair analysis in a pretrial diversion program in New Orleans (NCJ #158028). *International Journal of Offender Therapy and Comparative Criminology*, *39*(3), 222-241. Abstract available: http://www.ncjrs.gov/app/Search/Abstracts.aspx?id=158028 [accessed May 2010].

Moore, M.H., Trojanozicz, R.C., and Kelling, G.L. (1988). Crime and policing. *Perspectives on Policing* (2). Washington, DC: National Institute of Justice, U.S. Department of Justice. Available: http://www.ncjrs.gov/pdffiles1/nij/111460.pdf [accessed April 2010].

Morris, A. (1975). The American Society of Criminology: A history, 1941-1974. *Criminology*, *13*(2), 123-167.

National Advisory Committee on Criminal Justice Standards and Goals. (1976). *Criminal Justice Research and Development: Report of the Task Force on Criminal Justice Research and Development*. Washington, DC: U.S. Government Printing Office.

National Commission on the Future of DNA Evidence. (2000). *Future of Forensic DNA Testing: Predictions of the Research and Development Working Group* (NCJ #183697). Washington, DC: National Institute of Justice. Available: http://www.ncjrs.gov/pdffiles1/nij/183697.pdf [accessed May 2010].

National Institute of Justice. (1987). *National Institute of Justice 1986-87* (NCJ #160881). Washington, DC: U.S. Department of Justice. Abstract available: http://www.ncjrs.gov/App/Search/SearchResults.aspx?txtKeywordSearch=160881&fromSearch=1 [accessed May 2010].

National Institute of Justice. (1990). *Drugs and Crime in America* (NCJ #122225). Washington, DC: U.S. Department of Justice. Abstract available: http://www.ncjrs.gov/app/Search/Abstracts.aspx?id=122225 [accessed May 2010].

National Institute of Justice. (1991). *NIJ Annual Report 1990-1991* (NCJ #133967). Washington, DC: U.S. Department of Justice. Available: http://www.ncjrs.gov/pdffiles1/nij/133967.pdf [accessed May 2010].

National Institute of Justice. (1992). *1991-1992 Annual Report* (NCJ #141398). Washington, DC: U.S. Department of Justice. Available: http://www.ncjrs.gov/pdffiles1/nij/141398.pdf [accessed May 2010].

National Institute of Justice. (1993). *NIJ Program Plan 1993* (NCJ #141638). Washington, DC: U.S. Department of Justice. Abstract available: http://www.ncjrs.gov/app/Search/Abstracts.aspx?id=141638 [accessed May 2010].

National Institute of Justice. (1994a). *25 Years of Criminal Justice Research* (NCJ #151287). Washington, DC: U.S. Department of Justice. Available: http://www.ncjrs.gov/pdffiles1/nij/151287.pdf [accessed May 2010].

National Institute of Justice. (1994b). *National Institute of Justice Program Plan, 1994-1995* (NCJ #147530). Washington, DC: U.S. Department of Justice. Abstract available: http://www.ncjrs.gov/app/Search/Abstracts.aspx?id=147530 [accessed May 2010].

National Institute of Justice. (1996). *Searching for Answers Criminal Justice Research, Development and Evaluation: National Institute of Justice 1995 Annual Report to Congress* (NCJ #162042). Washington, DC: U.S. Department of Justice. Available: http://www.ncjrs.gov/pdffiles/nijann95.pdf [accessed May 2010].

National Institute of Justice. (1997). *Annual Report to Congress 1996* (NCJ #166585). Washington, DC: U.S. Department of Justice. Available: http://www.ncjrs.gov/pdffiles/166585.pdf [accessed May 2010].

National Institute of Justice. (1998). *Annual Report to Congress 1997* (NCJ #171679). Washington, DC: U.S. Department of Justice. Available: http://www.ncjrs.gov/pdffiles1/171679.pdf [accessed May 2010].

National Institute of Justice. (1999). *Annual Report to Congress 1998* (NCJ #177617). Washington, DC: U.S. Department of Justice. Available: http://www.ncjrs.gov/pdffiles1/nij/177617.pdf [accessed May 2010].

National Institute of Justice. (2000). *Annual Report on Drug Use Among Adult and Juvenile Arrestees, 1999* (NCJ #181426). Washington, DC: U.S. Department of Justice. Available: http://www.ncjrs.gov/pdffiles1/nij/181426.pdf [accessed May 2010].

National Institute of Justice. (2002). No *Suspect Casework DNA Backlog Reduction Program (FY2003) Solicitation*. Washington, DC: U.S. Department of Justice.

National Institute of Justice. (2003a). *Arrestee Drug Abuse Monitoring: Annual Report, 2000* (NCJ #193013). Washington, DC: U.S. Department of Justice. Available: http://www.ncjrs.gov/pdffiles1/nij/193013a.pdf [accessed May 2010].

National Institute of Justice. (2003b). *National Institute of Justice Annual Report 2001* (NCJ #195076). Washington, DC: U.S. Department of Justice. Available: http://www.ncjrs.gov/pdffiles1/nij/195076.pdf [accessed May 2010].

National Institute of Justice. (2003c). *National Institute of Justice Annual Report 2002* (NCJ #200338). Washington, DC: U.S. Department of Justice. Available: http://www.ncjrs.gov/pdffiles1/nij/200338.pdf [accessed May 2010].

National Institute of Justice. (2003d). NIJ's bullet-resistant vest standard reaches milestone (NCJ #200906). *National Institute of Justice Journal,* (249), 24-28. Available: http://www.ncjrs.gov/pdffiles1/jr000249.pdf [accessed May 2010].

National Institute of Justice. (2004a). *National Institute of Justice Annual Report 2003* (NCJ #205944). Washington, DC: U.S. Department of Justice. Available: http://www.ncjrs.gov/pdffiles1/nij/205944.pdf [accessed May 2010].

National Institute of Justice. (2004b). *Report to Congress on the National Law Enforcement and Corrections Technology Centers.* Washington, DC: U.S. Department of Justice.

National Institute of Justice. (2005). *NIJ Author Guidelines and Editorial Style.* Washington, DC: U.S. Department of Justice. Available: http://www.ncjrs.gov/pdffiles1/nij/nijauguide_edstyle.pdf [accessed March 2010].

National Institute of Justice. (2006a). *Drug Courts: The Second Decade* (NCJ #211081). NIJ Special Report. Washington, DC: U.S. Department of Justice. Available: http://www.ncjrs.gov/pdffiles1/nij/211081.pdf [accessed May 2010].

National Institute of Justice. (2006b). *Solicitation: Communications Technology FY2007* (SL# 000775). Washington, DC: U.S. Department of Justice. Available: http://www.ncjrs.gov/pdffiles1/nij/sl000775.pdf [accessed March 2010].

National Institute of Justice. (2007a). *2007 NIJ Annual Report* (NCJ #223597). Washington, DC: U.S. Department of Justice.

National Institute of Justice. (2007b). *Solicitation: Crime and Justice Research FY2008* (SL #000820). Washington, DC: U.S. Department of Justice. Available: http://www.ncjrs.gov/pdffiles1/nij/sl000820.pdf [accessed March 2010].

National Institute of Justice. (2007c). *W.E.B. DuBois Fellowship Program 2007* (SL #000753). Washington, DC: U.S. Department of Justice. Available: http://www.ncjrs.gov/pdffiles1/nij/sl000753.pdf [accessed March 2010].

National Institute of Justice. (2008a). *National Institute of Justice Annual Report 2006* (NCJ #218970). Washington, DC: U.S. Department of Justice. Available: http://www.ncjrs.gov/pdffiles1/nij/218970.pdf [accessed May 2010].

National Institute of Justice. (2008b). *Paving the Way for Project Safe Neighborhoods: SACSI in 10 U.S. Cities* (NCJ #216298). National Institute of Justice Research in Brief. Available: http://www.ncjrs.gov/pdffiles1/nij/216298.pdf [accessed May 2010].

National Institute of Justice. (2008c). *Solicitation: Solving Cold Cases with DNA* (SL #000828). Washington, DC: U.S. Department of Justice. Available: http://www.ncjrs.gov/pdffiles1/nij/sl000828.pdf [accessed March 2010].

National Institute of Justice. (2008d). *Solicitation: Using DNA Technology to Identify the Missing* (SL #000832). Washington, DC: U.S. Department of Justice. Available: http://www.ncjrs.gov/pdffiles1/nij/sl000832.pdf [accessed March 2010].

National Institute of Justice. (2009a). *High-Priority Criminal Justice Technology Needs* (NCJ #225375). Washington, DC: U.S. Department of Justice. Available: http://www.ncjrs.gov/pdffiles1/nij/225375.pdf [accessed May 2010].

National Institute of Justice. (2009b). *Solicitation: Communications Technology Center of Excellence* (SL #000897). Washington, DC: U.S. Department of Justice. Available: http://www.ncjrs.gov/pdffiles1/nij/sl000897.pdf [accessed March 2010].

National Institute of Justice. (2009c). *Solicitation: Crime and Justice Research FY2009* (SL #000869). Washington, DC: U.S. Department of Justice. Available: http://www.ncjrs.gov/pdffiles1/nij/sl000869.pdf [accessed March 2010].

National Institute of Standards and Technology. (2009). *Electronic and Electrical Engineering Laboratory: Programs, Activities, and Accomplishments.* Washington, DC: U.S. Department of Commerce.

National Institute on Aging, National Advisory Council on Aging, Division of Behavioral and Social Research Review Committee. (2009). *BSR Review Committee Report*. Washington, DC: National Institute on Aging. Available: http://www.nia.nih.gov/NR/rdonlyres/C319B2BF-A647-4BE8-8E2A-C887B2902060/12047/2008BSRReviewReport11182008FINALwithoutAppendix2.pdf [accessed July 2009].

National Institute on Alcohol Abuse and Alcoholism. (2006). *Report to the Extramural Advisory Board*. Division of Epidemiology and Prevention Research Strategic Planning Document. Washington, DC: Author.

National Research Council. (1977). *Understanding Crime: An Evaluation of the National Institute of Law Enforcement and Criminal Justice*. S.O. White and S. Krislov, Eds. Committee on Research on Law Enforcement and Criminal Justice. Assembly of Behavioral and Social Sciences. Washington, DC: National Academy Press.

National Research Council. (1986). *Criminal Careers and "Career Criminals"* (Vol. 1). Panel on Research on Criminal Careers, A. Blumstein, J. Cohen, J.A. Roth, and C.A. Visher, Eds. Committee on Research on Law Enforcement and the Administration of Justice. Commission on Behavioral and Social Sciences and Education. Washington, DC: National Academy Press.

National Research Council. (1992a). *DNA Technology in Forensic Science*. Committee on DNA Technology in Forensic Science. Board on Biology. Commission on Life Sciences. Washington, DC: National Academy Press.

National Research Council. (1992b). *Research and Education Reform: Roles for the Office of Educational Research and Improvement*. R.C. Atkinson and G.B. Jackson, Eds. Committee on the Federal Role in Education Research. Commission on Behavioral and Social Sciences and Education. Washington, DC: National Academy Press.

National Research Council. (1996a). *The Evaluation of Forensic DNA Evidence*. Committee on DNA Forensic Science: An Update. Commission on DNA Forensic Science: An Update. Washington, DC: National Academy Press.

National Research Council. (1996b). *Understanding Violence Against Women*. Panel on Research on Violence Against Women. N.A. Crowell and A.W. Burgess, Eds. Committee on Law and Justice. Commission on Behavioral and Social Sciences and Education. Washington, DC: National Academy Press.

National Research Council. (1999a). *Evaluating Federal Research Programs: Research and the Government Performance and Results Act*. Committee on Science, Engineering, and Public Policy and Policy and Global Affairs Division. Washington, DC: National Academy Press.

National Research Council. (1999b). *Pathological Gambling: A Critical Review*. Committee on the Social and Economic Impact of Pathological Gambling. Committee on Law and Justice. Commission on Behavioral and Social Sciences and Education. Washington, DC: National Academy Press.

National Research Council. (1999c). *Transnational Organized Crime: Summary of a Workshop*. Committee on Law and Justice. P. Reuter and C. Petrie, Eds. Commission on Behavioral and Social Sciences and Education. Washington, DC: National Academy Press.

National Research Council. (2000). *Strengthening Science at the U.S. Environmental Protection Agency: Research-Management and Peer-Review Practices*. Committee on Research and Peer Review in EPA. Board on Environmental Studies and Toxicology. Commission on Geosciences, Environment, and Resources. Commission on Life Sciences. Washington, DC: National Academy Press.

National Research Council. (2001a). *Implementing the Government Performance and Results Act for Research: A Status Report*. Committee on Science, Engineering, and Public Policy, Policy and Global Affairs Division. Washington, DC: National Academy Press.

National Research Council. (2001b). *Informing America's Policy on Illegal Drugs: What We Don't Know Keeps Hurting Us.* Committee on Data and Research for Policy on Illegal Drugs. C.F. Manski, J.V. Pepper, and C.V. Petrie, Eds. Committee on Law and Justice and Committee on National Statistics. Commission on Behavioral and Social Sciences and Education. Washington, DC: National Academy Press.

National Research Council. (2001c). *What's Changing in Prosecution? Report of a Workshop.* Committee on Law and Justice. P. Heymann and C. Petrie, Eds. Division of Behavioral and Social Sciences and Education. Washington, DC: National Academy Press.

National Research Council. (2002). *An Assessment of the National Institute of Standards and Technology Measurement and Standards Laboratories: Fiscal Year 2002.* Board on Assessment of NIST Programs. Division on Engineering and Physical Sciences. Washington, DC: National Academy Press.

National Research Council. (2003a). *An Assessment of Non-Lethal Weapons Science and Technology.* Committee for an Assessment of Non-Lethal Weapons Science and Technology. Naval Studies Board. Division on Engineering and Physical Sciences. Washington, DC: The National Academies Press.

National Research Council. (2003b). *Elder Mistreatment: Abuse, Neglect, and Exploitation in an Aging America.* Panel to Review Risk and Prevalence of Elder Abuse and Neglect. R.J. Bonnie and R.B. Wallace, Eds. Committee on National Statistics and Committee on Law and Justice. Division of Behavioral and Social Sciences and Education. Washington, DC: The National Academies Press.

National Research Council. (2003c). *Measurement Problems in Criminal Justice Research: Workshop Summary.* J.V. Pepper and C.V. Petrie. Committee on Law and Justice and Committee on National Statistics. Division of Behavioral and Social Sciences and Education. Washington, DC: The National Academies Press.

National Research Council. (2003d). *The Polygraph and Lie Detection.* Committee to Review the Scientific Evidence on the Polygraph. Division of Behavioral and Social Sciences and Education. Washington, DC: The National Academies Press.

National Research Council. (2004a). *Advancing the Federal Research Agenda on Violence Against Women.* Steering Committee for the Workshop on Issues in Research on Violence Against Women. C. Kruttschnitt, B.L. McLaughlin, and C.V. Petrie, Eds. Committee on Law and Justice., Division of Behavioral and Social Sciences and Education. Washington, DC: The National Academies Press.

National Research Council. (2004b). *Fairness and Effectiveness in Policing: The Evidence.* Committee to Review Research on Police Policy and Practices. W. Skogan and K. Frydl, Eds. Committee on Law and Justice. Division of Behavioral and Social Science and Education. Washington, DC: The National Academies Press.

National Research Council. (2004c). *Forensic Analysis Weighing Bullet Lead Evidence.* Committee on Scientific Assessment of Bullet Lead Elemental Composition Comparison. Board on Chemical Sciences and Technology. Division on Earth and Life Studies. Washington, DC: The National Academies Press.

National Research Council. (2004d). *Strengthening Peer Review in Federal Agencies That Support Education Research.* Committee on Research in Education. L. Towne, J.M. Fletcher, and L.L. Wise, Eds. Center for Education. Division of Behavioral and Social Sciences and Education. Washington, DC: The National Academies Press.

National Research Council. (2005a). *Assessment of Department of Defense Basic Research.* Committee on Department of Defense Basic Research. Division on Engineering and Physical Sciences. Washington, DC: The National Academies Press.

National Research Council. (2005b). *Firearms and Violence: A Critical Review*. Committee to Improve Research Information and Data on Firearms. C.F. Wellford, J.V. Pepper, and C.V. Petrie, Eds. Committee on Law and Justice. Division of Behavioral and Social Sciences and Education. Washington, DC: The National Academies Press.

National Research Council. (2005c). *Improving Evaluation of Anticrime Programs*. Committee on Improving Evaluation of Anti-Crime Programs. Committee on Law and Justice. Division of Behavioral and Social Sciences and Education. Washington, DC: The National Academies Press.

National Research Council. (2005d). *Thinking Strategically: The Appropriate Use of Metrics for the Climate Change Science Program*. Committee on Metrics for Global Change Research. Climate Research Committee. Board on Atmospheric Sciences and Climate. Division on Earth and Life Studies. Washington, DC: The National Academies Press.

National Research Council. (2007). *A Strategy for Assessing Science: Behavioral and Social Research on Aging*. Committee on Assessing Behavioral and Social Science Research on Aging. I. Feller and P.C. Stern, Eds. Center for Studies of Behavior and Development. Division of Behavioral and Social Sciences and Education. Washington, DC: The National Academies Press.

National Research Council. (2008a). *Evaluating Research Efficiency in the U.S. Environmental Protection Agency*. Committee on Evaluating the Efficiency of Research and Development Programs at the U.S. Environmental Protection Agency. Committee on Science, Engineering, and Public Policy and Policy and Global Affairs. Board on Environmental Studies and Toxicology, Division on Earth and Life Studies. Washington, DC: The National Academies Press.

National Research Council. (2008b). *Parole, Desistance from Crime, and Community Integration*. Committee on Community Supervision and Desistance from Crime. Committee on Law and Justice. Division of Behavioral and Social Sciences and Education. Washington, DC: The National Academies Press.

National Research Council. (2008c). *Rebuilding the Research Capacity at HUD*. Committee to Evaluate the Research Plan of the Department of Housing and Urban Development. Center for Economic, Governance, and International Studies. Division of Behavioral and Social Sciences and Education. Washington, DC: The National Academies Press.

National Research Council. (2009a). *Ensuring the Quality, Credibility, and Relevance of U.S. Justice Statistics*. Panel to Review the Programs of the Bureau of Justice Statistics. R.M. Groves and D.L. Cork, Eds. Committee on National Statistics and Committee on Law and Justice. Division of Behavioral and Social Sciences and Education. Washington, DC: The National Academies Press.

National Research Council. (2009b). *Principles and Practices for a Federal Statistical Agency, Fourth Edition*. Committee on National Statistics. C.F. Citro, M.E. Martin, and M.L. Straf, Eds. Division of Behavioral and Social Sciences and Education. Washington, DC: The National Academies Press.

National Research Council. (2009c). Str*engthening Forensic Science in the United States: A Path Forward*. Committee on Identifying the Needs of the Forensic Science Community. Committee on Science, Technology, and Law. Policy and Global Affairs. Committee on Applied and Theoretical Statistics. Division on Engineering and Physical Sciences. Washington, DC: The National Academies Press.

National Research Council and Institute of Medicine. (2001). *Juvenile Crime, Juvenile Justice*. Panel on Juvenile Crime: Prevention, Treatment, and Control. J. McCord, C. Spatz Widom, and N.A. Crowell, Eds. Committee on Law and Justice and Board on Children, Youth, and Families. Washington, DC: National Academy Press.

National Research Council and Institute of Medicine. (2003). *Deadly Lessons: Understanding Lethal School Violence.* Case Studies of School Violence Committee. M.H. Moore, C.V. Petrie, A.A. Braga, and B.L. McLaughlin, Eds. Division of Behavioral and Social Sciences and Education. Washington, DC: The National Academies Press.

National Science Foundation. (2009). *FY 2008 Annual Performance Report.* Arlington, VA: Author. Available: http://www.nsf.gov/pubs/2009/nsf0922/fy2008_annual_performance_report.pdf. [accessed July 2009].

Office of Justice Programs. (1990). *Office of Justice Programs Annual Report, Fiscal Year 1990* (NCJ #129099). Washington, DC: U.S. Department of Justice. Abstract available: http://www.ncjrs.gov/App/Publications/abstract.aspx?ID=129099 [accessed May 25, 2010].

Office of Justice Programs. (1999). *Office of Justice Programs Fiscal Year 1999 Program Plan.* Washington, DC: U.S. Department of Justice.

Office of Justice Programs. (2001). Office of Justice Programs Annual Report: Fiscal Year 2000 (NCJ #187027). Washington, DC: U.S. Department of Justice. Abstract available: http://www.ncjrs.gov/App/Publications/abstract.aspx?ID=187027 [accessed May 25, 2010].

Office of Justice Programs. (2006a). *Financial Guide.* Washington, DC: U.S. Department of Justice.

Office of Justice Programs. (2006b). *Strategic Plan Fiscal Years 2007-2012.* Washington, DC: U.S. Department of Justice.

Office of Justice Programs. (2007a). OJP Annual Report to Congress Fiscal Year 2007. Washington, DC: U.S. Department of Justice. Available: http://www.ojp.usdoj.gov/newsroom/pdfs/07_ojp_annual_report.pdf [accessed May 25, 2010].

Office of Justice Programs. (2007b). *OJP Grant Application Peer Reviews, Order O 4060.1.* Washington, DC: U.S. Department of Justice.

Office of Justice Programs. (2007c). *OJP's Grant Manager Manual.* Washington, DC: U.S. Department of Justice. Available: https://grants.ojp.usdoj.gov/gmsHelp/index.html [accessed March 2010].

Office of Law Enforcement Standards. (2008). *Ballistic Resistance of Body Armor NIJ Standard-0101.06* (NCJ #223054). Rockville, MD: National Law Enforcement and Corrections Technology Center. Available: http://www.ncjrs.gov/pdffiles1/nij/223054.pdf [accessed May 2010].

Office of National Drug Control Policy. (2002). *Drug Use Trends Fact Sheet* (NCJ #190780). Rockville, MD: Drug Policy Information Clearinghouse. Available: http://www.ncjrs.gov/App/publications/Abstract.aspx?id=190780 [accessed May 2010].

Office of the Inspector General. (2002). *The Office of Justice Programs Convicted Offender DNA Sample Backlog Reduction Grant Program* (Report No. 02-20). Available: http://www.justice.gov/oig/reports/OJP/a0220/index.htm [accessed March 2010].

Office of the Inspector General. (2004). *The No Suspect Casework DNA Backlog Reduction Program* (Audit Report No. 05-02). Available: http://www.justice.gov/oig/reports/OJP/a0502/index.htm [accessed March 2010].

Office of the Inspector General. (2005). *Review of the Office of Justice Programs' Forensic Science Improvement Grant Program* (I-2006-002). Evaluation and Inspections Division. Washington, DC: U.S. Department of Justice.

Office of the Inspector General. (2008). *Review of the Office of Justice Programs' Paul Coverdell Forensic Science Improvement Grants Program* (I-2008-001). Evaluation and Inspections Division. Washington, DC: U.S. Department of Justice.

Petersilia, J. (1987). *The Influence of Criminal Justice Research* (NCJ #150371, #106799). Santa Monica, CA: RAND.

Petersilia, J., and Turner, S. (1993). Intensive probation and parole. In M. Tonry (Ed.), *Crime and Justice: A Review of Research, Vol. 17* (pp. 281-335). Chicago, IL: University of Chicago Press.

Pierce, G.L., Braga, A.A., Koper, C., McDevitt, J., Carlson, D., Roth, J., and Griffith, R.E. (2003). *Characteristics and Dynamics of Crime Gun Markets: Implications for Supply-Side Focused Enforcement Strategies* (NCJ #208079). Washington, DC: National Institute of Justice. Available: http://www.ncjrs.gov/pdffiles1/nij/grants/208079.pdf [accessed May 2010].

Powell, A. (2009, October). *Stimulus Funds Provide Welcome Research Boost: Jobs, Knowledge Promoted by Federal Economic Push.* Boston, MA: Harvard Office of News and Public Affairs. Available: http://www.harvardscience.harvard.edu/culture-society/articles/stimulus-funds-provide-welcome-research-boost [accessed November 2009].

President's Advisory Board, National Institute of Justice. (1983). *Too Much Crime, Too Little Justice: The Police, Court, and Corrections Officials Who Administer America's Criminal Justice System Speak Out for Change.* A Report of the President's Advisory Board, National Institute of Justice. Washington, DC: U.S. Department of Justice.

President's Commission on Law Enforcement and the Administration of Justice. (1967). *The Challenge of Crime in a Free Society.* Washington, DC: U.S. Government Printing Office.

Pymatuning Group. (1998). *Infrastructure and Governance Planning for the NLECTC Network* (NCJ #174192). Washington, DC: U.S. Department of Justice. Available: http://www.ncjrs.gov/pdffiles1/nij/174192.pdf [accessed May 2010].

Radin, B.A. (2008). *Should PART Be Continued?* Paper prepared for the Office of Management and Budget Watch Government Performance Workshop, October, Washington, DC.

Redburn, F.S., Shea, R.J., and Buss, T.F. (Eds.). (2008). *Performance Management and Budgeting: How Governments Can Learn From Experience.* Armonk, NY: M.E. Sharpe.

Rhodes, W., Scheiman, P., Pittayathikhun, T., Collins, L., and Tsarfaty, V. (1995). *What America's Users Spend on Illegal Drugs, 1988-1993* (NCJ #153852). Cambridge, MA: Abt Associates.

Ridgeway, G., Pierce, G.L., Braga, A.A., Tita, G., Wintemute, G., and Roberts, W. (2008). *Strategies for Disrupting Illegal Firearm Markets: A Case Study of Los Angeles.* Los Angeles: RAND.

Riley, K.J. (1997). *Crack, Powder Cocaine, and Heroin: Drug Purchase and Use Patterns in Six U.S. Cities* (NCJ #167265). Washington, DC: U.S. Department of Justice. Available: http://www.ncjrs.gov/pdffiles/167265.pdf [accessed May 2010].

Ritter, N. (Ed.). (2007). LAPD Chief Bratton speaks out: What's wrong with criminal justice research—and how to make it right. *National Institute of Justice Journal*, (257), 28-30.

Robinson, C. (2009). *NIJ Standards and Testing Program: Standards Development Process.* Presentation at the International Association of Chiefs of Police Conference, November, San Diego, CA.

Roehl, J. (1998). Civil remedies for controlling crime: The role of community organizations. *Crime Prevention Studies, 9*, 241-259. Available: http://www.popcenter.org/Library/CrimePrevention/Volume_09/CivilRemediesCommunity.pdf [accessed December 2009].

Rosendall, G. (2002). *2003 Model Year Police Vehicle Evaluation Program.* Lansing: Michigan State Police. Available: http://www.justnet.org/Lists/JUSTNET%20Resources/Attachments/398/msp2003report.pdf [accessed March 2010].

Roth, J.A. (1998). *The Detroit Handgun Intervention Program: A Court-Based Program for Youthful Handgun Offenders.* National Institute of Justice Research Preview. Washington, DC: U.S. Department of Justice.

Roth, J.A., and Koper, C.S. (1999). *Impacts of the 1994 Assault Weapons Ban: 1994–1996* (NCJ #173405). National Institute of Justice Research in Brief. Available: http://www.ncjrs.gov/pdffiles1/173405.pdf [accessed May 2010].

Russell, T.J., and Rice, K.D. (2000). NIJ sets standards with Office of Law Enforcement Standards. *Corrections Today, 62*(5).

Sampson, R.J., Raudenbush, S.W., and Earls, F. (1997). Neighborhoods and violent crime: A multilevel study of collective efficacy. *Science, 277*(5328), 918-924.

Savelsberg, J.J., Cleveland, L.L., and King, R.D. (2004). Institutional environments and scholarly work: American criminology, 1951-1993. *Social Forces, 82*(4), 1275-1302.

Schoonbaert, D., and Roelants, G. (1996). Citation analysis for measuring the value of scientific publications: Quality assessment tool or comedy of errors? *Tropical Medicine & International Health, 1*(6), 739-752.

Schram, D.D. (1978). *Forcible Rape: Final Project Report* (NCJ #043524). Washington, DC: U.S. Government Printing Office. Abstract available: http://www.ncjrs.gov/App/publications/abstract.aspx?ID=43524 [accessed May 2010].

Schwabe, W., Davis, L.M., and Jackson, B.A. (2001). *Challenges and Choices for Crime-Fighting Technology: Federal Support of State and Local Law Enforcement.* Santa Monica, CA: RAND.

Sensabaugh, G.F. (n.d.). *Genetic Analysis of DNA in Biological Evidence: Final Report* (NCJ #150730). Washington, DC: National Institute of Justice. Abstract available: http://www.ncjrs.gov/app/Search/Abstracts.aspx?id=150730 [accessed May 2010].

Sharps, P., Campbell, J.C., Campbell, D., Gary, F., and Webster, D. (2003). Risky mix: Drinking, drug use, and homicide (NCJ #196546). *National Institute of Justice Journal,* (250). Available: http://www.ncjrs.gov/pdffiles1/jr000250d.pdf [accessed May 2010].

Sheley, J.F., and Wright, J.D. (1998). *High School Youths, Weapons, and Violence: A National Survey* (NCJ #172857). National Institute of Justice Research in Brief. Available: http://www.ncjrs.gov/pdffiles/172857.pdf [accessed May 2010].

Sherman, L.W. (1998). *Evidence-Based Policing* (NCJ #177319). Washington, DC: Police Foundation. Available: http://www.policefoundation.org/pdf/Sherman.pdf [accessed May 2010].

Sherman, L.W., and Berk, R.A. (1984). *The Minneapolis Domestic Violence Experiment.* Police Foundation Reports Series. Washington, DC: Police Foundation.

Sherman, L.W., and Rogan, D.P. (1995). Effects of gun seizures on gun violence: Hot spot patrols in Kansas City. *Justice Quarterly, 12*(4), 673-693.

Sherman, L.W., and Weisburd, D. (1995). General deterrent effects of police patrol in crime "hot spots": A randomized, controlled trial (NCJ #167663). *Justice Quarterly, 12*(4), 625-648. Abstract available: http://www.ncjrs.gov/app/Search/Abstracts.aspx?id=167663 [accessed May 2010].

Sherman, L.W., Gottfredson, D., MacKenzie, D., Eck, J., Reuter, P., and Bushway, S. (1997). *Preventing Crime: What Works, What Doesn't, What's Promising: A Report to the United States Congress* (NCJ #165366). Washington, DC: National Institute of Justice. Available: http://www.ncjrs.gov/docfiles/wholedoc.doc [accessed May 2010].

Starnes, R. (1969). Think tank gives crime a whirl but study gets kiss of death. *The Pittsburgh Press,* January 26, Section 2, p. 1.

Stewart, J.K. (2009). Response to Jeremy Travis's open letter to ASC. *The Criminologist, 34*(3), 6-8. Available: http://www.asc41.com/Criminologist/2009/2009_May-June_Criminologist.pdf [accessed March 2010].

Substance Abuse and Mental Health Services Administration. (2007). *Results from the 2006 National Survey on Drug Use and Health: National Findings.* Office of Applied Studies, NSDUH Series H-32, DHHS Publication No. SMA 07-4293. Washington, DC: U.S. Department of Health and Human Services.

Sunley, J.S. (1998). Assessing the value of research at the National Science Foundation. In National Research Council, *Assessing the Value of Research in the Chemical Sciences: Report of a Workshop* (pp. 107-111). Chemical Sciences Roundtable. Board on Chemical Sciences and Technology. Commission on Physical Sciences, Mathematics, and Applications. Division on Engineering and Physical Sciences. Washington, DC: National Academy Press.

Sweetman, S. (1987). *Report on the Attorney General's Conference on Less Than Lethal Weapons* (NCJ #105195). Washington, DC: U.S. Department of Justice. Abstract available: http://www.ncjrs.gov/app/Search/Abstracts.aspx?id=105195 [accessed May 2010].

Tita, G.E., Riley, K.J., Ridgeway, G., and Greenwood, P.W. (2005). *Reducing Gun Violence: Operation Ceasefire in Los Angeles* (NCJ #192378). Washington, DC: U.S. Department of Justice. Available: http://www.ncjrs.gov/pdffiles1/nij/192378.pdf [accessed May 2010].

Tjaden, P., and Thoennes, N. (1998). *Stalking in America: Findings from the National Violence Against Women Survey* (NCJ #169592). National Institute of Justice Research in Brief. Available: http://www.ncjrs.gov/pdffiles/169592.pdf [accessed May 2010].

Tjaden, P., and Thoennes, N. (2000). *Full Report of the Prevalence, Incidence, and Consequences of Violence Against Women: Findings from the National Violence Against Women Survey* (NCJ #183781). Research Report. Washington, DC: National Institute of Justice and the Centers for Disease Control and Prevention. Available: http://www.ncjrs.gov/pdffiles1/nij/183781.pdf [accessed May 2010].

Tjaden, P., and Thoennes, N. (2006). *Extent, Nature, and Consequences of Rape Victimization: Findings from the National Violence Against Women Survey* (NCJ #210346). Washington, DC: National Institute of Justice and the Centers for Disease Control and Prevention. Available: http://www.ncjrs.gov/pdffiles1/nij/210346.pdf [accessed May 2010].

Toborg, M.A., and Bellassai, J.P. (1988). *Background and Description of the Urine-Testing Program* (NCJ #116900). Washington, DC: National Institute of Justice. Abstract available: http://www.ncjrs.gov/app/Search/Abstracts.aspx?id=116900 [accessed May 2010].

Toborg, M.A., Yezer, A.M.J., and Bellassai, J.P. (1988). *Analysis of Drug Use Among Arrestees* (NCJ #116902). Washington, DC: National Institute of Justice. Abstract available: http://www.ncjrs.gov/app/Search/Abstracts.aspx?id=116902 [accessed May 2010].

Tonry, M. (2009). Preface. *Crime and Justice, 38*(1), vii-ix.

Tonry, M., and Wilson, J.Q. (Eds.) (1990). *Drugs and Crime: Crime and Justice, A Review of Research* (Vol. 13). Chicago, IL: The University of Chicago Press.

Tonry, M., Ohlin, L.E., and Farrington, D.P. (1991). Human development and criminal behavior: New ways of advancing knowledge. In A. Blumstein and D.P. Farrington (Eds.), *Research in Criminology*. New York: Springer-Verlag.

Travis, J. (2008). *Open Letter to the American Society of Criminology*. Available: http://www.asc41.com/Travis_NIJ.pdf [accessed March 2010].

Union of Concerned Scientists. (2007). *Atmosphere of Pressure: Political Interference in Federal Climate Science*. Available: http://www.ucsusa.org/assets/documents/scientific_integrity/atmosphere-of-pressure.pdf [accessed March 2010].

Union of Concerned Scientists. (2008). *Freedom to Speak? A Report Card on Federal Agency Media Policies*. Available: http://www.ucsusa.org/assets/documents/scientific_integrity/Freedom-to-Speak.pdf [accessed March 2010].

U.S. Congress, Office of Technology Assessment. (1990). *Genetic Witness: Forensic Uses of DNA Tests* (OTA-BA-438). Washington, DC: U.S. Government Printing Office.

U.S. Department of Education. (2010). *Institute of Education Sciences Fiscal Year 2010 Request*. Available: http://www2.ed.gov/about/overview/budget/budget10/justifications/y-ies.pdf [accessed March 2010].

U.S. Department of Justice. (2008). *FY 2009 Performance Budget*. Available: http://www.usdoj.gov/jmd/2009justification/pdf/fy09-ojp.pdf [accessed July 2009].

U.S. Department of Justice. (2009a). *U.S. Department of Justice Audit of the Convicted Offender DNA Backlog Reduction Program* (Audit Report 09-23). Washington, DC: Author.

U.S. Department of Justice. (2009b). *U.S. Department of Justice Audit of the National Institute of Justice's Practices for Awarding Grants and Contracts in Fiscal Years 2005-2007* (Audit Report 09-38). Washington, DC: Author.

U.S. General Accounting Office. (1976). *The Program to Develop Improved Law Enforcement Equipment Needs to Be Better Managed* (LM099971). Washington, DC: Author.

U.S. General Accounting Office. (1999). *Peer Review Practices at Federal Science Agencies Vary* (GAO/RCED-99-99). Washington, DC: Author.

U.S. General Accounting Office. (2002). *Justice Impact Evaluations: One Byrne Evaluation Was Rigorous; All Reviewed Violence Against Women Office Evaluations Were Problematic* (GAO-02-309). Washington, DC: Author.

U.S. General Accounting Office. (2003a). *Justice Outcome Evaluations: Design and Implementation of Studies Require More NIJ Attention* (GAO-03-1091). Washington, DC: Author.

U.S. General Accounting Office. (2003b). *Law Enforcement: Better Performance Measures Needed to Assess Results of Justice's Office of Science and Technology* (GAO-04-198). Washington, DC: Author.

U.S. General Accounting Office. (2003c). *Program Evaluation: An Evaluation Culture and Collaborative Partnerships Help Build Agency Capacity* (GAO-03-454). Washington, DC: Author.

U.S. Government Accountability Office. (2007). *Policies Guiding the Dissemination of Scientific Research from Selected Agencies Should Be Clarified and Better Communicated* (GAO-07-653). Washington, DC: Author.

U.S. House of Representatives. (2002). *Education Sciences Reform Act of 2002*. [H.R. 3801, Title I, Part A, Sec. 114, 107th Congress]. Available: http://www2.ed.gov/policy/rschstat/leg/PL107-279.pdf [accessed March 2010].

U.S. House of Representatives. (2003). *Departments of Commerce, Justice, and State, The Judiciary, and Related Agencies Appropriations Bill, Fiscal Year 2004*. [House Report No. 108-221, 108th Congress to accompany H.R. 2799]. Washington, DC: U.S. Government Printing Office.

U.S. House of Representatives. (2005). *Making Appropriations for Science, the Departments of State, Justice, and Commerce, and Related Agencies for the Fiscal Year Ending September 30, 2006, and for Other Purposes*. [House Report No. 109-272, 109th Congress to accompany H.R. 2862]. Washington, DC: U.S. Government Printing Office.

U.S. Office of Management and Budget. (1983). *Performance of Commercial Activities* (Circular No. A-76). Washington, DC: Author. Available: http://www.whitehouse.gov/omb/circulars/a076.pdf [accessed March 2010].

U.S. Office of Management and Budget. (2004). *Final Information Quality Bulletin for Peer Review*. Memorandum for heads of departments and agencies, Bulletin M-05-03. Washington, DC: Author. Available: http://www.whitehouse.gov/omb/memoranda/fy2005/m05-03.pdf [accessed March 2010].

U.S. Office of Management and Budget. (2010). *Program Assessment: National Institute of Justice*. Washington, DC: Author. Available: http://www.whitehouse.gov/omb/expectmore/summary/10003804.2005.html [accessed April 2009].

Visher, V.A., and Weisburd, D. (1997). Identifying what works: Recent trends in crime prevention strategies. *Crime, Law and Social Change, 28*(3-4), 223-242.

Weisburd, D., and Green, L. (1995). Policing drug hot spots: The Jersey City drug market analysis experiment. *Justice Quarterly,* 12(4), 711-735.

Weisburd, D., McNally, A.M., Mastrofski, S.D., Greenspan, R., and Willis, J.J. (2003). Reforming to preserve: Compstat and strategic problem solving in American policing. *Criminology and Public Policy,* 2(3), 421-455.

Weiss, C.H. (1978). Research for policy's sake: The enlightenment function of social research. In H.E. Freeman (Ed.), *Policy Studies Review Annual*, Vol. 2. Beverly Hills, CA: Sage. Abstract available: http://www.ncjrs.gov/App/publications/Abstract.aspx?id=51647 [accessed May 2010].

Weiss, C.H. (1979). The many meanings of research utilization. *Public Administration Review, 39*(5), 426-431.

Welsh, B.C., and Farrington, D.P. (2001). Toward an evidence-based approach to preventing crime. *Annals of the American Academy of Political and Social Science, 578*, 158-173.

Wintemute, G.J. (1998). *Predicting Criminal Behavior Among Authorized Purchasers of Handguns* (NCJ #185550). Washington, DC: U.S. Department of Justice. Available: http://www.ncjrs.gov/pdffiles/fs000198.pdf [accessed May 2010].

Woolley, J.T., and Peters, G. (2010). *Lyndon B. Johnson, Remarks to the Members of the President's Commission on Law Enforcement and Administration of Justice, September 8, 1965.* The American Presidency Project. University of California, Santa Barbara. Available: http://www.presidency.ucsb.edu/ws/?pid=27242 [accessed November 2009].

Wright, J.D., and Rossi, P.H. (1986). *Armed and Considered Dangerous: A Survey of Felons and Their Firearms.* New York: Aldine Transaction.

Zimring, F.E. (2007). *The Great American Crime Decline.* New York: Oxford University Press.

Appendix A

Unavailable or Incomplete Information Requested by the Committee

Table A-1 is a sample of materials requested by the committee that the National Institute of Justice (NIJ) was unable to provide or provided only in part. The committee did receive a number of documents from NIJ with useful information. However, many of these were currently in the public domain or had significant limitations (e.g., information available for only a short time period or for a partial set of program activities). This sample is presented to enable the reader to understand the limits on the committee's analyses. Of critical importance is the fact that we were not allowed access to grant applications, peer-review documents, or the agency's electronic grant management system. As a result of our inability to access some types of data, we were restricted in our ability to analyze and assess the quality of NIJ's grant award process, funding decisions, and award monitoring. In addition, the limitations in the data we received curtailed our ability to examine the historical trends of NIJ's funding sources, programs, and accomplishments.

TABLE A-1 Unavailable or Incomplete Information Requested by the Committee

Data Item/Information Requested	Status	Comment
1. Budgetary Information		
Annual National Institute of Justice (NIJ) spring budget call submissions.	Not available.	
Annual Office of Justice Programs (OJP) budget submissions to Office of Management and Budget.	Not available.	
Information NIJ provided to Office of the Inspector General (OIG) for years 2005-2007 on competitive and noncompetitive grants.	Partial list of items provided but not the materials themselves.	This was an attempt to obtain information already provided to OIG for its study of NIJ's grant-making activities so that NIJ would not have to prepare budget or programmatic information in a new form.
NIJ funding history by functional area or major program, including publication and dissemination and OJP management and administrative support for years 1994-2008.	Unavailable data for ORE funds by functional area as listed on their website; breakdown of discretionary and nondiscretionary funds by functional areas not available; breakdown by such categories as research and evaluation, basic and applied also not available.	Data system for identifying and tracking evaluation grants no longer operational.
Breakdown of Office of Science and Technology (OST) and Office of Research and Evaluation (ORE) budgets by research versus program support; pass-through versus appropriation to NIJ; and earmarks and other nondiscretionary spending.	OST provided a breakdown of discretionary and nondiscretionary funds available for research category but not for other functional categories, such as testing and evaluation, technical assistance, and capacity building.	

Breakdown of grants and other financed activities that involve partnering of NIJ with other agencies.	Congressionally mandated funds were identified but not funds that had been transferred from other agencies at their discretion, e.g., funds from Office of Juvenile Justice and Delinquency Prevention or Bureau of Justice Assistance for evaluations of their programs.	
List of interagency agreements.	OST and ORE interagency agreements for 2008 only.	
List of FY 2009 grants (awarded 9/30/09).	Not provided as of 12/10/2009.	
2. ***Organization/Staffing***		
OJP-approved staffing charts of full-time equivalents (FTEs) by organizational unit, title, job series, and grade level for years 1994-2008.	Three signed OJP staffing charts obtained from NIJ date 2/14/2008, 11/21/2007, 9/28/2006.	Other years unavailable from either NIJ or OJP's human resources department.
Actual staffing chart of FTEs by organizational unit, titles, grades, vacancies, staff names by position, and noted vacancies.	Only one staffing chart for 2/14/2008 identified names of staff and vacancies.	
Educational level of staff, years of service, current position held.	Aggregate information on staff degrees presented by major office and grouped into 22 categories for years 1995, 1998, 2001, 2004, 2008.	Current educational levels and years of service available in aggregate form only; no information available on area of concentration for graduate work; only federal service available not service at NIJ.

continued

TABLE A-1 Continued

Data Item/Information Requested	Status	Comment
Staff turnover and reason for separation.	Available for period January 1, 2002, through November 2007 only.	Reason for separation not available; does not include names of staff who transferred out of NIJ but stayed in federal service.
Eligibility for retirement.	Current eligible dates available in aggregate for 2008 only.	
FTEs vs. contract employees per year.	Not available.	Human resources department does not keep FTE information by year. Office of General Counsel (OGC) advised that all information on contract employees confidential.
Previously posted electronic staff listings from NIJ website.	Not provided.	An OGC lawyer opined that once staff left NIJ, needed to have their permission to release this information; names of contractors would need to be redacted.
3. Peer-Review Process		
Peer-review reports, peer-review panel reports.	Not available.	According to NIJ, OGC indicates that no specific peer-review information can be provided to anyone other than the designated applicant without the applicant's permission.
4. Grant Award Process		
Applications submitted for the Centers of Excellence program.	Not available from NIJ.	OGC advised the committee to submit a Freedom of Information Act (FOIA) request.

Winning proposals for the Centers of Excellence.	Not available from NIJ.	Winning proposals provided by OGC via FOIA or grantee with staff names and budget removed.
5. Management Information Systems		
Description of Grant Management System infrastructure and other databases.	Not available.	Approval by OJP provided but not communicated in time to be useful.
6. Dissemination Process		
Requests for research reports by practitioner organizations.	Total quantities ordered for the 30 most requested documents 1997-2007 but no breakdown as to kind of requestor.	
7. Program Files		
Grant files on Program on Human Development in Chicago Neighborhoods.	Some random working files provided by NIJ staff. No official files stored at NIJ.	A request was made to the OJP File Archives; it was reported that the official grant files were missing.
8. Miscellaneous Information		
Written documentation of Department of Justice and OJP policies that prevented the following information from being provided: a. grant-monitoring documents/progress reports, b. proposals from unsuccessful applicants, c. proposals from successful applicants, d. staffing and budgetary information on funded proposals.	Not provided.	OGC was asked to provide documentation as to why the committee was unable to have access to certain documents.

NOTE: This list does not represent the entirety of the committee's requests, but only those documents that were not received or were incomplete.

Appendix B

Survey of Researchers and Practitioners

The Committee to Assess the Research Program of the National Institute of Justice (NIJ) asked HCM Marketing Research to conduct a survey in order to learn about the views of criminal justice researchers and practitioners. The committee wanted to know how familiar they were with NIJ's activities and what they thought about the quality and impact of these activities. The committee was also interested in overall perceptions of NIJ as an independent science agency.

METHODOLOGY

Between November 20 and December 4, 2008, a total of 509 self-administered questionnaires were completed using an online survey technique. There were 347 questionnaires completed by researchers and 162 completed by practitioners. The sample, provided by the committee, included 2,603 e-mail addresses supplied by professional organizations.

The target researcher sample consisted of members of the American Society of Criminology. The target practitioner sample consisted of leaders and key staff in well-known organizations with an interest in criminal justice issues: the American Academy of Forensic Scientists, the American Correctional Association, the American Probation and Parole Association, the International Association of Chiefs of Police, the Justice Research Statistics Association, the National Association of Drug Court Professionals, the National Association of Sentencing Commissions, the National Center for State Courts, the National Criminal Justice Association, the National District Attorneys Association, and the Police Executive Research Forum. The sample pool was such that a small percentage of "practitioner" respondents (14 percent) would have been considered researchers if it had been possible to separate them out. They were affiliated with the target practitioner organizations but work as researchers in a government agency.

Quotas for the study were set proportional to the number of researchers and practitioners provided in the sample. A quota of 500 completed interviews had been set in advance, but a light excess was due to multiple respondents completing the survey at the same time. An initial email invitation was sent on November 19, 2008, and one reminder email was sent during the course of the data collection period. Excluding 212 email addresses that bounced back as undeliverable, the overall response rate for the Internet survey is 21 percent, with nearly equal response among researchers (21 percent) and practitioners (22 percent). In order to qualify for the survey, respondents had to have some level of familiarity with NIJ. Only 13 respondents did not qualify and were terminated from continuing the survey. In addition, 73 respondents dropped out of the survey midway; had these surveys been completed, the response rate would have been 23 percent.

Data from the online interviews were captured using Kinesis interviewing software. The data were cleaned and responses to open-ended questions were coded and classified by similar responses. Cross-tabulations of the data were prepared showing replies to all questions for the entire sample as well as by multiple subgroups, including researchers, practitioners, years in field, current position, type of contact with NIJ, years of association with NIJ, field of training, respondent age, and gender. Since the cross-tabulations contain more information than can be readily assimilated, it should be regarded as the database for the study, of which this appendix is a summary.

When a question was answered by a small number of respondents (30 or less), results are not as statistically reliable as those answered by larger groups, and results should be viewed with caution or for directional purposes only.

RESULTS

Familiarity with NIJ

NIJ is well known to criminal justice researchers and practitioners. Most of those interviewed (70 percent) said that they are very familiar with NIJ; only 13 of the potential respondents were dropped because they were unfamiliar with NIJ. This high level of familiarity underscores the importance of NIJ to the field and lends credibility to the survey findings.

Familiarity with NIJ was higher among researchers than practitioners:

74 percent of the researchers said they were very familiar with NIJ compared with 61 percent of the practitioners. Many researchers actively use NIJ information resources, cite NIJ research findings in their work, and participate in NIJ's grant process.

- Nearly all researchers (98 percent) have made use of or have cited NIJ-sponsored research in their own work, including 87 percent who have done so three or more times.
- Among available sources of research funding, researchers most frequently named state or local governments (43 percent), followed by NIJ (31 percent), as their source of funding within the past 5 years.

The types of contact with NIJ varied among respondents. A majority (75 percent) have used NIJ's products and services. Over half said they had attended a NIJ conference or workshop or applied for a research grant (53 percent each). Roughly two in five have applied for and received a grant (43 percent). A third (33 percent) have been a peer reviewer, and over a quarter (26 percent) have been a participant in an advisory group. Only 8 percent said they have not been associated with NIJ in any of these types of roles. Of the 92 percent of respondents who have been associated with NIJ in some type of role, nearly all (91 percent) reported contact with NIJ since 2001.

Image and Perceptions of NIJ

Respondents believe that NIJ is an important government agency dedicated to the funding and dissemination of research on crime control and criminal justice issues, and many feel the need for NIJ has become more critical over the past decade. Furthermore, they believe that NIJ has impacted the policy and practices in many areas of criminal justice.

- Nearly all (99 percent) of respondents believe it is important to have a government agency, such as NIJ, dedicated to funding and disseminating research on crime control and criminal justice issues.
- More researchers than practitioners believe such an agency is very important (94 versus 85 percent).
- Two-thirds (67 percent) of respondents feel the need for NIJ has become more critical over the past 10 years. Nearly a quarter (23 percent) feel the need has remained the same, and 5 percent feel the need has become less critical over the past 10 years. Another 5 percent were unsure.

While deemed important and influential, some respondents questioned whether the agency has the necessary independence required to operate objectively, consistently, and fairly to best meet field needs.

- Respondents were equally likely to say that NIJ does not have the independence necessary to be a research agency as to say that it does (37 percent doesn't have independence versus 36 percent has independence). Over a quarter are not sure if NIJ does or not (27 percent).
    - More practitioners than researchers believe NIJ has the necessary independence (44 versus 32 percent).
- Areas in which researchers believe political considerations have impacted NIJ are setting research priorities (85 percent), selecting proposals for funding (73 percent), and disseminating research findings (60 percent). Open-ended comments indicated that respondents believe that political considerations, whether external or internal to the agency, are too influential in establishing research priorities and in selecting proposals for funding.
- NIJ commitment to fairness and openness in disseminating research findings was rated positively by 65 percent of the researchers, but only half as many researchers gave positive ratings to NIJ commitment to fairness and openness in establishing research priorities (37 percent) and selecting proposals for funding (36 percent).

One measure of NIJ influence is the percentage of respondents saying that NIJ has an impact on policies and practices. Ratings of NIJ influence range from moderate to low for each of 15 areas listed in the questionnaire, as described below.

- Areas in NIJ seen as having the greatest impact are crime mapping (75 percent), law enforcement (66 percent), forensics and investigative science (66 percent), forensic laboratory enhancement (62 percent), and program evaluation (60 percent).
- Other areas of impact reported by more that half of the respondents include technology research and development (59 percent), courts (59 percent), violence against women and family violence (59 percent), corrections (59 percent), crime prevention (53 percent), victims (53 percent), juvenile justice (51 percent), and drugs and crime (51 percent).
- Over a quarter (28 percent) indicated that NIJ has impacted policies and practices in areas other than these 15.

Performance on Key Measures

Overall satisfaction is a key measure of how respondents feel about their experience with NIJ. Satisfaction was rated on a five-point scale from very positive to very negative with the midpoint of three indicating neither satisfied nor dissatisfied (answer wording varied by question). These scores were reclassified to indicate the percentage with positive or very positive satisfaction ratings. Based on other studies of performance using similar measures, scores in the 90 percent or higher range are considered outstanding. Organizations with scores at this level are usually growing and have a high level of retention. Scores in the 70 to 80 percent range indicate some good points and some areas for improvement. Scores below 70 percent are indicative of more serious problems.

The results reveal opportunities for improvements to increase satisfaction with NIJ. Fewer than 60 percent of all respondents (57 percent) rated NIJ's overall performance positively. This includes 19 percent who rated NIJ overall performance as excellent. About a quarter (23 percent) gave a neutral rating and 20 percent gave a low rating, including 7 percent who rated it poor. Practitioners are more satisfied than researchers with NIJ's performance (69 versus 50 percent).

Respondents were asked to rate five key aspects on their importance to NIJ performance. Staff qualifications, adequacy of resources, and consultation with the researcher community were rated as important by over 90 percent of the respondents. A large majority also rated leadership (89 percent) and consultation with the practitioner community (87 percent) as important.

However, respondent satisfaction with NIJ performance for the same five key aspects is low. Over half of respondents are satisfied with the qualifications of the staff (57 percent) and consultation with the researcher and practitioner communities (51 percent each). And 40 percent are satisfied with NIJ leadership and 27 percent with adequate resources. Researchers are less satisfied than practitioners in several areas: qualifications of the staff (53 versus 64 percent), NIJ leadership (33 versus 56 percent), adequate resources (22 versus 37 percent), and consultation with the researcher community (47 versus 60 percent).

The open-ended question elicited comments from over a third (34 percent) of the 509 respondents. Areas of concern described in the mostly negative comments include inappropriate political influence on NIJ (6 percent), lack of continued research funding (4 percent), the need for NIJ to operate independently (3 percent), the desire for NIJ to develop an unbiased grant process (3 percent), and an interest in diversifying the research to include topics other than DNA, technology, and terrorism (3 percent).

Separate questions for researchers and practitioners further probed for opinions on NIJ performance related to their areas of interest, as described below.

Researcher Satisfaction with Key Measures

Researchers reported low to moderate levels of satisfaction with NIJ performance.

- Dissemination of findings to the research community was rated positively by nearly two-thirds (64 percent) of researchers, while over half (56 percent) are satisfied with the dissemination of research findings to policy makers and practitioners.
- Levels of researchers' satisfaction are lower in funding high-quality research (44 percent), establishing research priorities that are policy relevant (44 percent), encouraging top flight researchers to apply for funding (37 percent), communicating research priorities to the field (37 percent), developing affordable and effective tools and technologies (36 percent), establishing research priorities that are coherent, important, and cumulative (33 percent), and developing and financially supporting future researchers (25 percent).

Recipients of NIJ grants (44 percent of the researchers interviewed) expressed low levels of satisfaction with the grant process and project monitoring, with the exception of some moderate levels of satisfaction with NIJ staff.

- Just over half (53 percent) of grantees are satisfied with NIJ's monitoring of research activities.
- Less than half are satisfied with the review of research products (46 percent), ease of applying (44 percent), dissemination of research products (43 percent), and the quality of feedback/reviews (41 percent).
- Fewer grantees are satisfied with the quality of funding decisions (38 percent) and transparency of the award process (28 percent).
- Levels of researchers' satisfaction are moderate for the staff's responsiveness (70 percent), fairness (69 percent), and competence (66 percent) but lower for the staff's scientific knowledge (56 percent).

Unsuccessful grant applicants (56 percent of researchers interviewed who had ever been denied a grant after applying) rated NIJ somewhat lower than grantees. The percentage satisfied with NIJ was quite low in the areas of ease of applying (44 percent), quality of feedback/reviews (33 percent), quality of funding decisions (24 percent), and transparency of the award process (22 percent).

Over a third (35 percent) of researchers had never applied to NIJ for a grant for a variety of reasons. The most frequently given reasons were that they thought it was unlikely that they would get funding (55 percent), research opportunities were not in their field of expertise or interest (45 percent), and they had insufficient notice to prepare an application (24 percent).

Practitioner Satisfaction with Key Measures

Practitioner satisfaction with NIJ performance in four key areas is moderate:

1. Dissemination of relevant research knowledge to practitioners and policy makers (72 percent).
2. Excellence and integrity in the conduct of NIJ activities (68 percent).
3. Identification of research and technology needs of criminal justice agencies and practitioners (66 percent).
4. Commitment to fairness and openness in practices (61 percent).

Practitioner satisfaction with NIJ performance for six other areas is low:

1. Development of developing affordable and effective tools and technologies (55 percent).
2. Improvement of forensic laboratories (53 percent).
3. Technical assistance (51 percent).
4. Testing of existing and new technologies (51 percent).
5. Development of equipment standards (48 percent).
6. Training of new scientists (28 percent).

NIJ Information Resources

NIJ supports a number of activities designed to communicate information on criminal justice research to researchers and practitioners. NIJ data resources are used more widely by researchers, while NIJ sponsored workshops and conferences are attended more widely by practitioners. Many of those who use these resources find them to be useful.

- The NIJ website has been used by nearly all (98 percent) and is useful to three-quarters of them (73 percent).
- The National Criminal Justice Reference Service has been accessed by 90 percent of the researchers and is useful to most (89 percent) of them.
- The University of Michigan data archive has been used by 75 percent of the researchers and 90 percent of them find it useful.
- NIJ-sponsored national conferences have been attended by about half of the researchers (51 percent) and about two-thirds (62 percent) of attendees found them useful.
- NIJ-sponsored workshops have been attended by more practitioners (65 percent) than researchers (43 percent), and more practitioner participants (83 percent) than researcher participants (60 percent) found them useful.
- NIJ Criminal Justice Research and Evaluation Annual Conferences have been attended by more than a third (37 percent) of the practitioners, and over three-quarters (77 percent) of attendees found the conference useful.
- NIJ Annual Technology Conferences have been attended by 27 percent of practitioners, and nearly two-thirds (62 percent) of attendees found them useful.
- The NIJ Critical Incidents Conference was attended by 5 percent of practitioners, and half (50 percent) of the attendees found it useful.

Researcher and Practitioner Profiles and Demographics

The practitioner sample consisted of leaders and key staff in well-known organizations with an interest in criminal justice issues. Most of these respondents work full-time (89 percent) and are very experienced, with most (70 percent) having more than 20 years in the field. While nearly half (44 percent) were trained in social sciences, a number were trained in law (23 percent) and science and technology (17 percent). Nearly a quarter are currently criminal justice practitioners (24 percent) or government officials (24 percent), and 1 in 7 is a researcher in a government agency (14 percent). Demographically, practitioners are middle-aged with a median age of 52, more likely to be male than female (73 versus 27 percent), and to have an advanced degree (40 percent master's, 21 percent M.D./J.D./D.D.S., 21 percent doctorate).

The researcher sample consists of members of the American Society of Criminology and includes a broader range of age groups and experience levels. Nearly all researchers work full-time (97 percent) and are quite experienced, with half (47 percent) having more than 20 years in the field. Nearly all (92 percent) were trained in social sciences, and most (80 percent) currently work as an academic. Compared with practitioners, researchers are younger, with a median age of 48, more likely to be female (37 percent), and more likely to have a doctorate degree (86 percent).

Corrections and program evaluation were the topics most often named by researchers and practitioners as an area of interest. The primary area of interest was corrections and law enforcement for both researchers and practitioners. In addition, a fair number of practitioners focus on forensics and investigative sciences and courts.

Respondent Segment Differences

Differences in satisfaction found in the examination of the detailed tabulations are summarized below.

- Respondents with longer experience in criminal justice had more different kinds of contact with NIJ and are more satisfied with its performance than respondents who have worked in the field for shorter periods. Research applicants with over 10 years in the field who had ever been denied a grant were significantly less satisfied with the grant process than denied applicants who are less experienced.
- Opinions and perceptions of NIJ of those who have been in contact with NIJ since 2001 were compared with those who have not been in contact as recently. Both groups rated overall satisfaction with NIJ and the importance of NIJ similarly; however, respondents with recent contact were less satisfied with the leadership and having adequate resources.
- Compared with researchers with only earlier contact, researchers with recent contact since 2001 are more satisfied with the NIJ grant process, but are less satisfied with some other service aspects of NIJ.
  - Researcher satisfaction with the quality of funding decisions during the grant process and the quality of feedback and reviews if denied a grant is higher among those with recent contact than among those with only earlier contact.
  - Researcher satisfaction with NIJ's leadership and resources is lower among those with recent contact than among those with only earlier contact.
  - Researcher satisfaction with the coherence, importance, and cumulativeness of research priorities is lower among those with recent contact than among those with only earlier contact.

- Practitioners with recent contact since 2001 appear less satisfied with NIJ than those who have not been in contact as recently.
    - Practitioner satisfaction with excellence and integrity in the conduct of NIJ activities, the dissemination of research findings, and the utility of NIJ-sponsored activities is lower among those with more recent contact with the agency than those with only earlier contact.
- There are some differences in NIJ ratings between men and women. Female respondents place greater importance on NIJ and feel its impact on policy and practice has been greater in some areas than do men. Ratings for overall performance are similar among men and women, but women are more likely than men to believe the NIJ staff is qualified. Female grantees gave much higher ratings to the grant process than male grantees, but ratings among those denied a grant were similar between the two genders.

Appendix C

Legislation Impacting NIJ

This appendix summarizes legislation having significant impact on the programs and operations of the National Institute of Justice (NIJ) and documents changes in its mission statements over time. Box C-1 presents mission statements from different years to underscore these changes. We start with a description of the purpose and authorities originally given to NIJ's predecessor agency through the Omnibus Crime Control and Safe Streets Act of 1968 and then note how these authorities changed over time with the passing of subsequent legislation. We also note the appearance and disappearance of a legislated advisory board as well as of articulated research areas needing attention.

1968

The **Omnibus Crime Control and Safe Streets Act of 1968** (P.L. 90-351, Part D, Sec. 402) established, within the U.S. Department of Justice (DOJ), the Law Enforcement Assistance Administration (LEAA) as well as a National Institute of Law Enforcement and Criminal Justice (NILECJ), which would later become NIJ. Established under the general authority of LEAA, the purpose of the institute was to encourage research and development to improve and strengthen law enforcement. In this act, law enforcement referred to all activities pertaining to crime prevention or reduction and enforcement of the criminal law. No specific topic areas of research requiring attention were identified in the act. An advisory board was not established under the act.

NILECJ was authorized to make recommendations for action that can

BOX C-1
Mission Statements for 1973, 1996, 2002, and 2008-2009

1973 Mission Statement for the National Institute of Law Enforcement and Criminal Justice

The Institute's mission is threefold:

1. Responsibility for the agency's research program, which is designed to support the overall goal of reducing crime and delinquency and improving the quality of justice.
2. [Responsibility for] program development-making recommendations for actions which can be taken by federal, state, and local governments and private citizens and organizations to improve and strengthen law enforcement.
3. [Responsibility for] [t]echnology transfer—the Institute's third major function—communicates ideas between researchers and the criminal justice community. Central to this function are programs facilitating actual adoption of new techniques.

SOURCE: Law Enforcement Assistance Administration, 1973, *LEAA Activities July 1, 1972 to June 30, 1973.*

1996 Mission Statement for the National Institute of Justice

Established by Congress as the major Federal agency for criminal justice research, NIJ is authorized to:

be taken by federal, state, and local governments and by private persons and organizations to improve and strengthen law enforcement. In order to do so, NILECJ was authorized to carry out a number of research efforts through "grants and contracts with public agencies, institutions of higher education, or private organizations." These efforts, as defined in the act (P.L. 90-351, Part D, Sec. 402), included

- research, demonstrations, or special projects pertaining to the purposes described in this title;

(1) conduct and sponsor basic and applied research in the causes and prevention of crime;
(2) sponsor evaluations of major Federal anti-crime initiatives;
(3) support research and demonstrations to develop new approaches, techniques, systems, and equipment to improve law enforcement and the administration of justice;
(4) make recommendations to federal, state, and local governments on crime-related issues;
(5) sponsor conferences and workshops for criminal justice policy makers and professionals; and
(6) collect and disseminate domestic and international criminal justice information obtained by the Institute or other federal agencies.

SOURCE: National Institute of Justice (1997).

2002 Mission Statement for the National Institute of Justice

NIJ [continues] to provide objective, independent, evidence-based knowledge and tools to enhance the administration of justice and public safety.

SOURCE: National Institute of Justice (2003c).

2008-2009 Mission Statement for the National Institute of Justice

Advance scientific research, development, and evaluation to enhance the administration of justice and public safety.

SOURCE: http://www.ojp.usdoj.gov/nij/about/welcome.htm (accessed December 9, 2009).

- the development of new or improved approaches, techniques, systems, equipment, and devices to improve and strengthen law enforcement;
- studies and programs of research that addressed the effectiveness of projects or programs carried out under this title;
- programs of behavioral research designed to provide more accurate information on the causes of crime and the effectiveness of various means of preventing crime, and to evaluate the success of correctional procedures;

- programs of instructional assistance consisting of research fellowships and special workshops for the presentation and dissemination of information resulting from research, demonstrations, and special projects; and
- a program of collection and dissemination of information.

1979

The **Justice System Improvement Act of 1979** (P.L. 96-15) established NIJ, which replaced NILECJ as well as the Office of Justice Assistance, Research and Statistics (OJARS) in DOJ to provide staff support to and coordinate activities of the National Institute of Justice, the Bureau of Justice Statistics (BJS, also established by this act), and the Law Enforcement Assistance Administration (LEAA) (reauthorized in this act). NIJ was now under general authority of the U.S. attorney general and headed by a director appointed by the president "who shall have experience in justice research." The director was given "final authority over all grants, cooperative agreements, and contracts" (Part B, Sec. 202). Although NIJ's general authorities to support research efforts remained the same, the act expanded its purpose and authorizations as well as detailed areas of research attention as delineated further below. The act also established an advisory board for NIJ, consisting of "21 members who shall represent the public interest and be experienced in the criminal or civil justice systems (state and local)." The NIJ director would be a nonvoting member, and the LEAA administrator, the BJS director, and the administrator of the Office of Juvenile Justice and Delinquency Prevention (OJJDP, an office established by the Juvenile Justice and Delinquency Prevention Act of 1974), would serve as ex officio nonvoting members. The board was to recommend policies and priorities; create where necessary formal peer-review procedures over selected categories of grants, cooperative agreements, and contracts; and recommend to the president candidates for director vacancies (Part B, Sec. 204). NIJ was also authorized to appoint technical or other advisory committees (Part H, Sec. 814).

The purpose of NIJ's efforts to provide for and encourage research and demonstration was now spelled out in the legislation (Part B, Sec. 201) as:

1. improving federal, state, and local criminal justice systems and related aspects of the civil justice system;
2 preventing and reducing crimes;
3. insuring citizen access to appropriate dispute-resolution forums;
4. improving efforts to detect, investigate, prosecute, and otherwise

combat and prevent white-collar crime and public corruption; and

5. identifying programs of proven effectiveness, programs having a record of proven success, or programs which offer a high probability of improving the functioning of the criminal justice system.

The act also specified the following areas for multiyear and short-term research and development (Part B, Sec. 202):

- alternative programs for achieving justice system goals (including those authorized by Section 103, Office of Community Anti-Crime Programs, of this title);
- causes and correlates of crime;
- causes and correlates of juvenile delinquency;
- improvements toward functioning of criminal justice system;
- new methods for (i) prevention and reduction of crime; (ii) reduction of parental kidnapping; (iii) apprehension of criminals; (iv) fair disposition; (v) improvement of police and minority relations; (vi) the conduct of research into problems of victims and witnesses; (vii) participation of victims in criminal justice decision-making; (viii) reduction of court resolution in civil disputes; (ix) development of adequate and effective corrections facilities and programs; and
- programs and projects to improve and expand the capacity to respond to, combat, and prevent white collar crime and public corruption.

In addition to what was previously authorized for NILECJ, NIJ was given the authority in this act (Part B, Sec. 202) to:

- serve as a national and international clearinghouse for the exchange of information;
- submit a biennial report to Congress on state of justice research;
- make recommendations, in consultation with appropriate state and local agencies, for the designation of programs and projects which will be effective in improving the functioning of the criminal justice system; and
- encourage, assist, and serve in consulting capacity to federal, state, and local justice system agencies.

1984

The **Justice Assistance Act of 1984** (P.L. 98-473) eliminated LEAA and OJARS but retained NIJ and BJS. The act established the Bureau of Justice

Assistance (BJA) as well as the Office of Justice Programs (OJP). OJP "shall be headed by an Assistant Attorney General appointed by the President, by and with the advice and consent of the Senate." Among the duties and functions of the assistant attorney general, OJP, was "to provide staff support to coordinate the activities" of NIJ, BJS, BJA, and OJJDP (Chapter VI, Part A, Sec. 101, 102). This reauthorization act repealed NIJ's legislative advisory board and directed the NIJ director to report to the attorney general through the OJP assistant attorney general (Sec. 604). However, NIJ was given the authority to appoint advisory committees, which would be subject to the Federal Advisory Committee Act (FACA) (Sec. 807). Many of NIJ's authorizations were retained, except attention to white-collar crime and public corruption was removed from its purpose, and reference to the Office of Community Anti-Crime Programs and parental kidnapping was deleted from identified research areas. In addition, the authority to submit a biennial report to Congress on the state of justice research was struck from its legislation (Sec. 604).

1988

The **Anti-Drug Abuse Act** (P.L. 100-690) directed NIJ to:

1. develop guidelines, in cooperation with BJA, to assist state and local units of government to conduct the program evaluations as required by section 501(c) of this part; and
2. conduct a reasonable number of comprehensive evaluations of programs funded under section 506 (formula grants) and section 511 (discretionary grants) of this part.

The NIJ director was directed to annually report to the president, the attorney general, and Congress on the nature and findings of the evaluation and research and development activities. NIJ was appropriated additional funds to carry out the functions designated by this act for fiscal year 1989-1992.

1994

The **Violent Crime Control and Law Enforcement Act** (known as the Crime Act) (P.L. 103-322) was passed in response to the rising level of violent crime. In 1995, the Violence Against Women Grants Office (later to become the Office on Violence Against Women, OVW) was created within OJP and the Office of Community Oriented Policing Services (COPS) was created as an independent agency within DOJ to manage the grants authorized by this act. [Note: the COPS office is headed by a director appointed by the attorney general.] In 2003, OVW became an independent office within DOJ, headed by a presidentially appointed director who reports to the attorney general (P.L. 107-283). The act included a number of major provisions regarding the criminal justice system and an appropriation of $4.5 billion a year for 5 years, little of which was directed toward crime and criminal justice research. However, NIJ's budget did rise dramatically as a result of this act, because of transferred funds and additional appropriations. NIJ's research portfolio on drug courts, community policing, law enforcement family support, DNA identification, and violence against women (with particular attention to sexual assault, battered women's syndrome, and domestic violence) was supported with Crime Act funds.

1998

The **Crime Identification Technology Act** (CITA) (P.L. 105-251) primarily provided assistance to states to establish or upgrade criminal justice information systems and identification technologies. Under this legislation, OJP had the authority to coordinate programs of technology development with other federally funded information technology programs, such as the Local Law Enforcement Block Grant program (P.L. 105-119). As a result, significant funds were transferred to NIJ to support its technology development efforts.

2002

The **Homeland Security Act of 2002** (P.L. 103-322) is the authorizing legislation for the U.S. Department of Homeland Security. The act "abolished" the existing office of science and technology in NIJ and established a "new" Office of Science and Technology (OST). The mission and duties codified in the Homeland Security Act were similar to what OST had been carrying out previously. However, the act established OST as its own entity and divorced it from the oversight of NIJ. The act placed OST under the general authority of the assistant attorney general, OJP, and dictates that the office "shall be headed by a director, who shall be an individual appointed based on approval by the Office of Personnel Management." The act allows OST to establish and maintain advisory groups, exempt from the provisions of FACA, "to assess the law enforcement technology needs of Federal, State, and local law enforcement agencies." The act provides that decisions concerning publications issued by OST "shall rest solely with its Director." The act places control for the National Law Enforcement and Corrections Technology Center under OST and allows for the creation of new centers "with a merit-based, competitive process." It also requires that all OST research and development "be carried out on a competitive basis." The act specified (but did not limit OST to) the following areas for its research and development efforts (Subtitle D, Sec. 232):

> (A) weapons capable of preventing use by unauthorized persons, including personalized guns; (B) protective apparel; (C) bullet-resistant and explosion-resistant glass; (D) monitoring systems and alarm systems capable of providing precise location information; (E) wire and wireless interoperable communication technologies; (F) tools and techniques that facilitate investigative and forensic work, including computer forensics; (G) equipment for particular use in counterterrorism, including devices and technologies to disable terrorist devices; (H) guides to assist State and local law enforcement agencies; (I) DNA identification technologies; and (J) tools and techniques that facilitate investigations of computer crime.

2004

The **Justice for All Act** (P.L. 108-405) enacted the President's DNA Initiative. The act also expanded the Paul Coverdell Forensic Sciences Improvement Grant Program. The act called for:

- eliminating the substantial backlog of DNA samples collected from crime scenes and convicted offenders;
- improving and expanding the DNA testing capacity of federal, state, and local crime laboratories;
- increasing research and development of new DNA testing technologies;
- developing new training programs regarding the collection and use of DNA evidence; and
- providing post-conviction testing of DNA evidence to exonerate the innocent.

The responsibility for all these efforts and the subsequent appropriations were given to NIJ through the attorney general and OJP. The act also created a National Forensic Science Commission in DOJ that had responsibility through NIJ to "disseminate best practices concerning the collection and analyses of forensic evidence to help ensure quality and consistency in the use of forensic technologies and techniques to solve crimes and protect the public." The commission was also charged with identifying "potential scientific advances that may assist law enforcement in using forensic technologies and techniques to protect the public." (Sec. 306). The commission's recommendations were useful for guiding NIJ's forensic science research agenda.

2005

The **Violence Against Women and Department of Justice Reauthorization Act** (P.L. 109-162) established the Edward Byrne Memorial Justice Assistance Grant (JAG) Program, which was a merger of former programs, the Edward Byrne Memorial State and Local Law Enforcement Assistance Programs, and the Local Government Law Enforcement Block Grants program. Under the JAG program, the attorney general reserved "not more than $20 million for use by [NIJ] in assisting units of local government to identify, select, develop, modernize, and purchase new technologies for use by law enforcement." The Act provided for a "national baseline study to examine violence against Indian women in Indian country to be conducted by [NIJ] in consultation with [OVW]."

Appendix D

Types of NIJ Materials Published

TABLE D-1 Types of NIJ Materials Published

Kinds of Reports	1995	1996	1997	1998	1999	2000
Research in Action	x	x	x	2	1	
Research in Brief (2003-2007 ones are 12-20 pp.)	x	x	x	8	18	16
Research reports (comprehensive report on NIJ-sponsored R&D project)	x	x	x	11[a]	16[b]	15
Research in Progress videotapes	x	x	x	3	1	
Research Previews (2-4 pp.)	x	x	x	12	10	
Progress report						
Research reviews						
Issues and Practices	x	x	x	2	3	1
Program Focus	x	x		10	3	
Research forum				1	5	5
Research for Policy/ Practice (7-21 pp.)						
Research reports (10-40 pp.)						3
Special reports (30-100 pp.)						
In-Shorts (2-5 pp.) (S&T only)						
Final grant report						1
Standards						6
Training						
Test results						
Reports to Congress						
CD ROMS						
NIJ guides						5
NIJ Journal				3	3	3

2001	2002	2003	2004	2005	2006	2007
13	2	1	3	2	2	2
12	6					
	1					
1						
4						
1	3					
		8	4	6	3	2
3		2[c]	0	2	1	0
		3	3	5[d]	2	3
			3	2	3	7
		1[e]			3[f]	
7		1				
		1			1	1
	1	4	4	3	12	
1				1	2	1
		2		1	2	1
	5	4				
3	1	1	2	1	3	3

continued

TABLE D-1 Continued

Kinds of Reports	1995	1996	1997	1998	1999	2000
NIJ Journal articles included as individual items on specific topics						
Miscellaneous: brochure, violence against women research compendium, 9/11 guide for families, lessons from 9/11, 200				7	1	1[g]
National Institute of Law Enforcement and Criminal Justice bulletins					3[i]	
Miscellaneous technology reports				8[j]	8[k]	
Total number of documents[l]				51	72	61[m]

[a]7 of the 11 reports are annual Arrestee Drug Abuse Monitoring reports on different topics.

[b]9 of the 13 reports were Weed and Seed case studies (40-60 pp.).

[c]One report, *Satisfaction With Police—What Matters*, is 10 pp. Also included is the 2000 *Arrestee Drug Abuse Monitoring Annual Report* (221 pp.).

[d]All on S&T topics: crime mapping, forensics, nonlethal weapons, body armor (2).

[e]*Recruitment and Retention in Intimate Partner Violence* (72 pp.).

[f]*I-Safe Evaluation; Exploring Spatial Configurations of Places Related to Homicide* (Groff and McEwen, 2006a) (222 pp.); *Visualization of Spatial Relationships in Mobility Research* (Groff and McEwen, 2006b) (65 pp.).

[g]2000 Research Plan.

[h]*Mental Health Screens for Corrections* (24 pp.); reports on two research projects: 2000IJ-CX-0044 and 2001-IJ-CX-0030.

2001	2002	2003	2004	2005	2006	2007
				x	x	x
	1	5		3	1	2[h]
57	20	34	24	26	33	32

[i]Topics: electronic monitoring; patrol car tests, 1999 model year patrol vehicle testing.

[j]These appeared separately under the heading Technology Reports and included 3 research reports, 1 research in action, 3 research in brief and 1 research preview.

[k]These included 2 equipment performance reports, an evaluation of a forensic method; 2 guides, 1 test protocol, 1 brochure, and 1 videotape.

[l]The chart does not include *TechBeat*, a quarterly magazine produced by the National Law Enforcement and Corrections Technology Center since October 1994. It focuses exclusively on technology news for criminal justice practitioners.

[m]Not included are 5 documents available online that appear to be unclassified grant products but may not have been published with National Criminal Justice Reference Service accession numbers.

Appendix E

Research Recommendations in Previous National Research Council Reports

The 1977 National Research Council (NRC) report, *Understanding Crime*, recommended that the National Institute of Law Enforcement and Criminal Justice, having been in existence for only eight years, pursue a course that would maximize its capacity to produce useful knowledge about crime problems and their control and to better inform criminal justice policies. That report encouraged the institute, the forerunner of the National Institute of Justice (NIJ), to organize its research portfolio around program areas, noting that they should be "designed on the assumption that producing reliable and useful knowledge is a cumulative process" (National Research Council, 1977, p. 110). Furthermore, program areas should be defined by fundamental efforts to control crime and not by the current funding streams.

For the past 12 years, NIJ has funded a standing body at the NRC, the Committee on Law and Justice (CLAJ), to hold meetings, workshops, and seminars on crime and justice topics of mutual interest to the committee and NIJ. In addition, NIJ has, by itself or with others, funded a number of major NRC studies in such areas as firearms and violence, ballistics, forensic sciences, and policing. Other sponsors have supported NRC studies on illegal drugs, juvenile crime, school violence, violence against women, and elder abuse. In addition, several workshops have offered important ideas in neglected areas of research.

Research recommendations from 19 NRC reports on various topics are summarized below. This list is not intended to be exhaustive or exclusive; it is intended to be illustrative of the areas in which NIJ has done work and can continue to do so and for which recommendations for research agendas are available. In addition, we have included four recommendations that CLAJ has repeatedly identified as having high priority for a crime and justice research agenda: (1) racial disparities, (2) mass incarceration, (3) deterrence and the death penalty, and (4) crime trends.

Rather than listing the research agendas by report, broad categories needing research attention are listed, and relevant recommendations from various reports are described. There are eight categories:

1. understanding the nature of crime and what influences criminal behavior;
2. the effect of crime on victims;
3. deterring criminal behavior through policy, policing, community actions, and safety technologies;
4. detecting criminal behavior and threats to personal and global security;
5. enhancing the collection and forensic analysis of evidence;
6. advancing the application of justice;
7. developing effective practices for recidivism and desistance; and
8. improving criminal justice research, assessment, and evaluation.

References to the relevant studies are provided for each recommendation. All referenced reports can be found on the National Academies website, http://www.nationalacademies.org.

UNDERSTANDING THE NATURE OF CRIME AND WHAT INFLUENCES CRIMINAL BEHAVIOR

This category includes recommendations calling for baseline data collection, basic research to ascertain numerous factors, including demographic and situational ones that influence criminal behavior; risk factors for juvenile offending; extended examination of known influences, such as drugs and gambling; and the availability of firearms. These recommendations call for research on the following topics and issues:

1. Development and maintenance of new data collection systems for gun violence (National Research Council, 2005a).
2. Individual-level studies of the association between gun ownership and violence as well as individual-level studies of the link between firearms and both lethal and nonlethal suicidal behavior to determine whether a causal link can be firmly established (National Research Council, 2005a).
3. Role of factors in prenatal, perinatal, and early infant development on mechanisms that increase the likelihood of healthy develop-

ment, as well as the development of antisocial behavior through longitudinal studies (National Research Council and Institute of Medicine, 2001).

4. Effects of interactions among various risk factors. In particular, the effects of differences in neighborhoods and their interactions with individual and family conditions should be expanded (National Research Council and Institute of Medicine, 2001).
5. Etiology, life course, and societal consequences of female juvenile offending (National Research Council and Institute of Medicine, 2001).
6. Role of childhood experiences, neighborhoods and communities, and family and individual characteristics as well as the role of psychiatric disorders in the etiology of female juvenile crime (National Research Council and Institute of Medicine, 2001).
7. Nature and causes of school violence, including seriousness of behavior, motivation of perpetrators, and the role of recognized gangs, crews, and cliques or informal social groups inside and outside the school in both crime and other antisocial behavior, such as serious bullying (National Research Council, 2003d).
8. Illegal gun carrying by adolescents, especially carrying a gun to school. This research should examine the circumstances and motivations related to illegal gun carrying, the sources of and ease of access to guns, socialization to illegal gun use, and the relationship, if any between legal and illegal gun use by adolescents (National Research Council, 2003d).
9. Measurement of the prevalence of developing mental illness in young adolescents (National Research Council, 2003d).
10. Nature and causes of crimes committed against teachers in middle school and high school (National Research Council, 2003d).
11. Effects of rapid change in increasingly affluent rural and suburban communities on youth development, socialization, and violence (National Research Council, 2003d).
12. Identification and analysis of parental styles of supervision for youth in grades 6-10 when parents are at work or when their children are away from home (National Research Council, 2003d).
13. Identification of the situational contexts and dynamic interactions that lead to violence against women, with special attention given to the processes underlying victim selection, location selection, and victim-offender interaction patterns (National Research Council, 2004b).
14. Analysis of demographic factors among census tracts or small neighborhoods, police precincts or districts, or other theoretically meaningful social area aggregations and their influence on the vari-

ation in violence against women, including which features of area composition influence rates and types of violence against women (National Research Council, 2004b).

15. Nature and frequency of transnational organized crime and white-collar crimes (National Research Council, 1999c).

KNOWING THE EFFECT OF CRIME ON VICTIMS

This category includes recommendations calling for basic research on victimization of the elderly and persons with physical and mental disabilities, new methods and surveys for obtaining this information, and expanded research on violence against women.

1. Integration of federally funded research on violence against women with efforts to determine the causes, consequences, prevention, treatment, and deterrence of violence more broadly (National Research Council, 2004b).
2. Expansion of the research on the violent victimization of women to include other kinds of relationships than intimate partner violence (National Research Council, 2004b).
3. Linkage of existing data sets on violence against women and the information from these data sets with findings from clinical research. This effort should include creating a framework for developing standard definitions to overcome the lack of conceptual and operational clarity, comparable samples, and interview protocols (National Research Council, 2004b).
4. Basic research on the phenomenology of elder mistreatment (National Research Council, 2003c).
5. Development of operational definitions and validated and standardized measurement methods for the elements of elder mistreatment (National Research Council, 2003c).
6. Development of improved household and geographically referent sampling techniques as well as new sampling and detection methods to detect elder mistreatment in the community and in institutional settings, including hospitals, long-term care, and assisted living situations (National Research Council, 2003c).
7. Population-based surveys of elder mistreatment (National Research Council, 2003c).
8. Development and testing of measures for identifying elder mistreatment (National Research Council, 2003c).
9. Design and fielding of national prevalence and incidence studies of elder mistreatment. These studies should include both a large-scale,

independent study of prevalence and modular add-ons to surveys of aging populations (National Research Council, 2003c).

10. Longitudinal investigations, including follow-up studies of the clinical, social, and psychological outcomes of elder mistreatment cases (National Research Council, 2003c).
11. Nature and extent of crimes against victims, including situational contexts with developmental disabilities (National Research Council, 2001b).
12. Personal, behavioral, and developmental characteristics of victims and perpetrators (National Research Council, 2001b).
13. Impacts (e.g., physical, psychological) on victims with developmental disabilities or mental retardation (National Research Council, 2001b).
14. Identification of risk factors for personal and financial victimization (National Research Council, 2001b).

DETERRING CRIMINAL BEHAVIOR THROUGH POLICY, POLICING, COMMUNITY ACTIONS, AND SAFETY TECHNOLOGIES

This category includes recommendations calling for an understanding of a wide range of policies and their impacts, such as firearms policies, sanctioning policies for violence against women perpetrators, police practices involving discretion, school policies, illegal drug policies, and organized crime and international crime policies. It also includes the impact of safety technologies.

1. Studies of the link between firearms policy and suicide (National Research Council, 2005a).
2. Effects of different safety technologies on violence and crime (National Research Council, 2005a).
3. Examination of the covariation of individual and social area factors with the responses of both victims and offenders to legal sanctions and social interventions directed at violence against women (National Research Council, 2004b).
4. Folding of deterrence research on violence against women into broader efforts to study the decision making of potential perpetrators and the deterrence of criminal behavior generally (National Research Council, 2004b).
5. Examination of how social stigma for acts of violence against women is generated and either sustained or eroded (National Research Council, 2004b).

6. Generation and implementation of sanctions and how perceptions of these sanctions affect future offending (National Research Council, 2004b).
7. Impact of policy on levels of violence against women in specific cities or states rather than research on the average response across all cities and states (National Research Council, 2004b).
8. Collection and analysis of systematic data on the lawfulness of police activities, including the extent of police compliance, associated practices to promote lawfulness, and organizational mechanisms that foster police rectitude (National Research Council, 2004a).
9. Experiences of crime victims, individuals stopped by the police, and the public, focusing on practices in policing that support or undermine public confidence (National Research Council, 2004a).
10. Evaluation of police performance programs and other practices designed to ensure crime control effectiveness and public legitimacy (National Research Council, 2004a).
11. Police organization, innovation processes, and organizational change, and particularly more research on police training (National Research Council, 2004a).
12. Development of measures that better document at the jurisdiction level the nature and extent of nonenforcement services delivered by police (National Research Council, 2004a).
13. Evaluation of new crime information technologies in local police agencies (National Research Council, 2004a).
14. Evaluation research on citizen review boards, assessing their impact on a range of police practices (especially features that are frequent targets of citizens' complaints) that go beyond examining the effect of civilian review on complaints filed and consider other data sources (National Research Council, 2004a).
15. Effects of school policies and pedagogical practices, such as grade retention, tracking, suspension, and expulsion on delinquency, educational attainment, and school atmosphere and environment (National Research Council and Institute of Medicine, 2001).
16. Evaluation studies on school shooting prevention programs, including security measures and police tactics and police protocols that have been developed to uncover and respond to plans for rampages in schools (National Research Council and Institute of Medicine, 2003).
17. Effects of elder mistreatment interventions, including reporting practices and the effects of reporting as well as adult protective services interventions (National Research Council, 2003c).
18. Impact of interdiction and domestic enforcement activities on drug production, transport, and distribution (National Research Council, 2001c).

19. Declarative and deterrent effects, costs, and cost-effectiveness of sanctions against the use of illegal drugs, with particular attention to the relationship between severity of prescribed sanctions and conditions of enforcement and the rates of initiation and termination of illegal drug use among different segments of the population (National Research Council, 2001c).
20. Study of inaccurate responses in the national drug use surveys and development of methods to reduce reporting errors to the extent possible (National Research Council, 2001c).
21. Effects of drug prevention programs implemented under both normal conditions and outside the boundaries of the initial tightly controlled experimental tests; the effects of different combinations of prevention programs; and the extent to which experimentally induced delays in tobacco, alcohol, and marijuana use yield reductions in later involvement with cocaine and other illegal drugs specifically and long-term effects of prevention programming more generally (National Research Council, 2001c).
22. Nature of the adverse consequences of various forms of transnational organized crimes, including impact on national security and international treaties (National Research Council, 1999c).
23. Extent to which transnational organized crime increases crime and drug-related mortality and morbidity in the United States (National Research Council, 1999c).
24. Development of mechanisms for collecting better estimates of illicit goods and illegal immigrants smuggled across U.S. borders and identifying the conditions, including vulnerabilities in industries, that facilitate the development of transnational organized crime (National Research Council, 1999c).
25. Development of systematic classification of enforcement activities geared to transnational national crime and measurement (National Research Council, 1999c).
26. Development of measures to assess enforcement activities beyond the apprehension and sanctioning of the targeted individuals and organizations (National Research Council, 1999c).

DETECTING CRIMINALS AND THREATS TO PERSONAL AND GLOBAL SECURITY

1. Methods for detecting and deterring major security threats, including efforts to improve techniques for security screening (National Research Council, 2003b).

ENHANCING THE COLLECTION AND FORENSIC ANALYSIS OF EVIDENCE

This category includes recommendations calling for basic research to advance the field of forensics and to improve existing forensic capabilities.

1. Studies on the impact and effectiveness of the Local National Integrated Ballistic Information Network (National Research Council, 2008b).
2. Development of a mechanism for validating and documenting future changes to the Federal Bureau of Investigation laboratory's analytical protocol once it is revised to contain the plasma-optical emission spectroscopy procedure and to provide a better basis for the statistics of bullet comparison (National Research Council, 2004c).
3. Development of new technical methods or in-depth grounding for advances developed in the forensic sciences disciplines (National Research Council, 2009b).
4. Development of scientific bases demonstrating the validity of scientific methods (National Research Council, 2009b).
5. Development and establishment of quantifiable measures of the reliability and accuracy of forensic analyses (National Research Council, 2009b).
6. Development of quantifiable measures of uncertainty in the conclusions of forensic analyses (National Research Council, 2009b).
7. Development of automated techniques capable of enhancing forensic technologies (National Research Council, 2009b).

ADVANCING THE APPLICATION OF JUSTICE

This category includes recommendations calling for assessments of the quality, effectiveness, and transparency of decision making and the processes used to move juveniles and adults through the criminal justice system as well as the conditions of their confinement and operational impacts. It also includes research on mass incarceration, racial disparities, and deterrence and death penalty research—three of the four topics identified as research priorities by CLAJ.

1. Effect of targeting policing and sentencing aimed at firearms offenders (National Research Council, 2005a).
2. Ability of victims with disabilities to provide court testimony and useful and legal accommodations to assist them to be effective witnesses (National Research Council, 2001b).

3. Evaluation of the viability of prosecution against persons with disabilities as a hate crime and the deterrent effect of legislatively mandated special sentencing for hate crimes (National Research Council, 2001b).
4. Impact of police decisions and current police practices on number, type, and outcomes of juveniles in the system (National Research Council and Institute of Medicine, 2001).
5. Evaluation of the American Correctional Association standards for juvenile detention and correctional facilities to ensure that the needs of juveniles in these facilities are met (National Research Council and Institute of Medicine, 2001).
6. Long-term effects of transferring juveniles to adult court and incarcerating them in adult facilities as well as the effect of using informal sanctions for juveniles committing first offenses if they are not serious crimes (National Research Council and Institute of Medicine, 2001).
7. Unwarranted racial disparity in the juvenile justice system to include a focus on multiple decision-making points and processing stages; the role of organizational policy and practice in the production of juvenile arrest, adjudication, and confinement rates; and the organizational policy/practice and the decisions of individual officials (National Research Council and Institute of Medicine, 2001).
8. Racial disparities in the criminal justice system to include investigation of the selectivity of certain minority groups to be overrepresented; the effects of such a negative outcome for minorities; analysis of individual development in community context; and an examination of the social policies and process that lead to disparate treatment (CLAJ).
9. Causes in the explosion in incarceration rates since the 1980s; the role played by incarceration in the decline in crime rates since the mid-1990s; alternatives to incarceration that would better serve public safety at less cost; the role that deep unaddressed social divisions and issues of social justice in American society has played in mass incarceration (CLAJ).
10. Risk of error in death penalty cases and identification of methods to determine potential rates of error as well as questions regarding the deterrent effect of the death penalty on homicide and the reasons for differing conclusions about deterrence; the fairness of the death penalty; the need for the death penalty when there is a parole alternative; the benefits of the death penalty, whatever they may be and their costs; and the arbitrariness of the death penalty. Also the impact of death penalty prosecutions on priority-setting for

homicide prosecutions and on levels of punishment for noncapital homicides and deterrence (CLAJ).

11. Approaches to overcome methodological limitations of much existing research on racial disparity in the juvenile justice system, including sample selection biases and traditional emphasis on black-white differences and a focus on primarily urban jurisdictions (National Research Council and Institute of Medicine, 2001).
12. Data on charging decisions, conviction rates, and police arrest rates to increase their transparency (National Research Council, 2001a).
13. Development, enforcement, and impact of special initiatives in prosecutors' offices (National Research Council, 2001a).
14. Assessment of "decisions to prosecute" policies and activities for reviewing adherence to policies (National Research Council, 2001a).
15. Role that theory or empirical evidence plays in prosecutorial decision making (National Research Council, 2001a).
16. Evaluation of community prosecution outcomes that looks at individual offenders and neighborhood welfare (National Research Council, 2001a).
17. Role of prosecutorial discretion in high-crime versus low-crime periods (National Research Council, 2001a).
18. Impact of other innovations, such as special units and applications of technology, and procedural innovations, such as prosecution-initiated waivers of juveniles to adult court (National Research Council, 2001a).
19. Role that prosecutors' perceptions of constituents plays in their actions (National Research Council, 2001a).
20. Impact of victims' movement on the politics of prosecution (National Research Council, 2001a).
21. Criminal justice system responses to victims with developmental disabilities, including identification of barriers to access and eligibility and how can they be eliminated and improvement of system coordination (National Research Council, 2001b).
22. Management of prosecution offices, including how decisions are made, impact of various organizational structures, coordination with other players, witness notification and cooperation, case review, and performance monitoring (National Research Council, 2001a).
23. Nature and extent of abuse of prosecutorial discretion (National Research Council, 2001a).

DEVELOPING EFFECTIVE PRACTICES FOR RECIDIVISM AND DESISTANCE

This category includes recommendations calling for well-designed evaluations that look at the impact of specific factors and the effectiveness of interventions on future offending behavior.

1. Effectiveness of such programs as the use of secure detention and secure confinement as well as community-based alternatives for delinquent youth (National Research Council and Institute of Medicine, 2001).
2. Nature of decisions made in juvenile court by key actors and the impact of the decisions on subsequent juvenile behavior as well as on the system (National Research Council and Institute of Medicine, 2001).
3. Identification of appropriate treatments for female juveniles. Long-term outcomes for well-designed interventions that have shown short-term promise for reducing risk factors for delinquency (National Research Council and Institute of Medicine, 2001).
4. Evaluation of interventions with perpetrators of violence (National Research Council, 2004b).
5. Examination of whether access to local services can affect localized rates of intimate partner violence and consideration of implications for planning and locating preventive services (National Research Council, 2004b).
6. Impact of community supervision on desistance of crime and development of standard measures of desistance (National Research Council, 2008a).
7. Evaluation of interventions to include cost-effectiveness studies (National Research Council, 2008a).
8. Evaluation of cognitive-behavioral approaches that take into account implementation issues (National Research Council, 2008a).
9. Evaluation of the effectiveness of promising mental health treatments (e.g., cognitive-behavioral and pharmacotherapy treatments) (National Research Council, 1999b).
10. Evaluation of the extent of unmet needs and what barriers contribute to compulsive gambling, such as lack of insurance coverage, stigmatization, or the unavailability of treatment (National Research Council, 1999b).
11. Assessment of the effects on pathological gambling of remote access to gambling (e.g., Internet gambling), new gambling machines, and gambling while alone (National Research Council, 1999b).

IMPROVING CRIMINAL JUSTICE RESEARCH, ASSESSMENT, AND EVALUATION

This category includes recommendations calling for activities that will improve the quality of criminal justice research, including identification of selection criteria for subjects of evaluations, development of specific kinds of studies, development of methodological approaches, and creation of and improved use of data sources and surveys.

1. Feasibility or design studies that include site visits, pipeline studies, piloting data collection instruments and procedures, and evaluability assessments prior to conducting a full impact study (National Research Council, 2005b).
2. Adaptation of impact evaluation designs for criminal justice applications—for example, development and validation of effective applications of alternative designs, such as regression discontinuity, selection bias models for nonrandomized comparisons, and techniques for modeling program effects with observational data (National Research Council, 2005b).
3. Development and improvement of new and existing databases that expand the repertoire of relevant outcome variables and knowledge about their characteristics and relationships for purposes of impact evaluation (e.g., self-reported delinquency and criminality, official records of arrests, convictions, and the like, measures of critical mediators) (National Research Council, 2005b).
4. Reliability and validity of self-report surveys (National Research Council, 2003c).
5. Comparison and contrast of the understanding of crime and victimization in self-report and official data (National Research Council, 2003c).
6. Assessment of whether differential validity for African American males in surveys exists and, if so, its source and magnitude and identification of techniques for eliminating it (National Research Council, 2003c).
7. Measurement of the effect size of repeated measures and its sources and the identification of methods to reduce its threat to the validity of self-reported data in longitudinal studies (National Research Council, 2003c).
8. Methodological studies designed in a cross-cutting fashion so that reliability and validity, improved item selection, and panel bias can be investigated simultaneously (National Research Council, 2003c).

9. Feasibility and cost-effectiveness of longitudinal studies on violence against and by women in U.S. populations (National Research Council, 2004b).
10. Theoretical integration of economic and criminological perspectives around the issue of crime trends; development and testing of substantive explanation of crime trends; testing a variety of models and estimation strategies to describe trends, to illuminate the causes of fluctuations, and to provide forecasts of future trends; and analysis of local crime trend data to determine its reliability and utility in developing and forecasting neighborhood-level crime trends (CLAJ).

NRC REPORTS INCLUDED IN THIS SUMMARY

Committee on Law and Justice Reports

1. *Ballistic Imaging* (2008)
2. *Parole, Desistance from Crime, and Community Integration* (2007)
3. *Improving Evaluation of Anticrime Programs* (2005)
4. *Advancing the Federal Research Agenda on Violence Against Women* (2004)
5. *Fairness and Effectiveness in Policing: The Evidence* (2004)
6. *Firearms and Violence: A Critical Review* (2004)
7. *The Polygraph and Lie Detection* (2003)
8. *Deadly Lessons: Understanding Lethal School Violence* (2003)
9. *Measurement Problems in Criminal Justice Research: Workshop Summary* (2003)
10. *Elder Mistreatment: Abuse, Neglect, and Exploitation in an Aging America* (2002)
11. *Crime Victims with Developmental Disabilities: Report of a Workshop* (2001)
12. *Informing America's Policy on Illegal Drugs: What We Don't Know Keeps Hurting Us* (2001)
13. *Juvenile Crime, Juvenile Justice* (2001)
14. *What's Changing in Prosecution? Report of a Workshop* (2001)
15. *Pathological Gambling: A Critical Review* (1999)
16. *Transnational Organized Crime: Summary of a Workshop* (1999)

Other NRC Reports

1. *Strengthening Forensic Science in the United States: A Path Forward* (2009)

2. *Forensic Analysis: Weighing Bullet Lead Evidence* (2004)
3. *Existing and Potential Standoff Explosives Detection Techniques* (2004)

NRC REPORTS CONSIDERED BUT NOT INCLUDED

Committee on Law and Justice Reports

1. *Understanding Crime Trends: Workshop Report* (2008)
2. *Education and Delinquency: Summary of a Workshop* (2000)
3. *Assessment of Two-Cost Effectiveness Studies on Cocaine Control Policy* (1999)
4. *Understanding Violence Against Women (1996)*
5. *Violence in Urban America: Mobilizing a Response* (1994)
6. *Understanding and Preventing Violence*, 4 Volumes (1993-1994)
7. *Criminal Careers and "Career Criminals,"* 2 Volumes (1986)
8. *Research on Sentencing: The Search for Reform* (1983)

Other NRC Reports

1. *Surveying Victims: Options for Conducting the National Crime Victimization Survey* (2008)
2. *Assessment of Millimeter-Wave and Terahertz Technology for Detection and Identification of Concealed Explosives and Weapons* (2007)
3. *Ethical Considerations for Research Involving Prisoners* (2006)
4. *Technological Options for User-Authorized Handguns: A Technology-Readiness Assessment* (2005)
5. *Owner-Authorized Handguns: A Workshop Summary* (2003)
6. *An Assessment of Non-Lethal Weapons Science and Technology* (2003)
7. *Assessment of Two Cost-Effectiveness Studies on Cocaine Control Policy* (1999)
8. *The Evaluation of Forensic DNA Evidence* (1996)
9. *Pathways of Addiction: Opportunities in Drug Abuse Research* (1996)
10. *Understanding Child Abuse and Neglect* (1993)
11. *DNA Technology in Forensic Science* (1992)

Appendix F

Biographical Sketches of Committee Members and Staff

Charles F. Wellford (*Chair*) is professor of criminology and criminal justice at the University of Maryland. He was chair of the Department of Criminology and Criminal Justice (formerly Institute of Criminal Justice and Criminology) from 1981 to 1995 and from 1999 to 2004. From 1992 to 1998 he was director of the Office of Academic Computing Services in the College of Behavioral and Social Sciences. He also served as acting dean of graduate studies and research, acting dean of continuing education, director of the Office of International and Executive Programs, and director of the Maryland Justice Analysis Center. He serves on numerous state and federal advisory boards and commissions. He is a past president (1995-1996) of the American Society of Criminology (ASC) and in 1996 was elected an ASC fellow. In 2001 he was selected to be a national associate of the National Research Council (NRC) of the National Academies. At the NRC, he chaired the Committee on Law and Justice from 1998 to 2004 as well as its panel on research on pathological gambling and panel on research on firearms. He currently serves on the Maryland Sentencing Policy Commission. From 1976 to 1981 he served in the Office of the U.S. Attorney General, where he directed the Federal Justice Research Program. The author of numerous publications on criminal justice issues, his most recent research has focused on the determinants of sentencing and the correlates of homicide clearance. He has a B.A. from the University of Maryland and a Ph.D. from the University of Pennsylvania.

George F. Sensabaugh, Jr. (*Vice Chair*) is professor of biomedical and forensic sciences in the School of Public Health at the University of California,

Berkeley, and a member of the Graduate Group in Forensic Science at the University of California, Davis. His research interests include genetic variation and evolution in human and microbial populations and application of the biosciences in forensic science. His current lines of research include the comparative population genetics of the *Staphylococci* and the use of biological evidence in sexual assault investigation. He is also exploring the potential of microbial community profiling as a tool in forensic science. At NRC, he served on two Committees on DNA Technology in Forensic Science, in 1988-1992 and 1994-1996. He has held postdoctoral research positions at the University of California, San Diego, and at the National Institute of Medical Research in London. In 1993 he was awarded a Fulbright scholarship. He is a fellow of the American Academy of Forensic Sciences, from which he received the Paul Kirk Award, Criminalistics Section, in 1987. He has a B.A. from Princeton University and a doctor of criminology from the University of California, Berkeley.

Charles E. Anderson, Jr., is director of the Engineering Dynamics Department in the Mechanical and Materials Engineering Division of the Southwest Research Institute. His expertise is in penetration mechanics, warhead mechanics, and hypervelocity impact; he has been recognized for his technical contributions and leadership in combining numerical simulations with experimental data to develop advanced models of the response of materials to shock, impact, and penetration. He has authored numerous reports for government and has served on a number of governmental advisory committees. He is a founding board member and the first president of the Hypervelocity Impact Society; a senior institute fellow of the Institute for Advanced Technology; and the regional editor (North America) of the *International Journal of Impact Engineering*. He received the Distinguished Scientist Award in 2000 and was elected a fellow of the American Physical Society in 2005. He has a Ph.D. in physics from Rensselaer Polytechnic Institute.

Betty M. Chemers (*Study Director*) is a senior project officer at NRC, which she joined in May 2005, after spending 30 years in the public and nonprofit sectors working on criminal justice and juvenile justice issues. She served as study director of the committee that issued the report *Protecting Individual Privacy in the Struggle Against Terrorism* in 2008. Previously she held numerous positions at the U.S. Department of Justice, including director of the evaluation division of the National Institute of Justice (NIJ) and deputy administrator for discretionary programs at the Office of Juvenile Justice and Delinquency Prevention, where she oversaw its research, demonstration, and training and technical assistance activities. Her nonfederal service includes directing the planning and policy analysis division of the Maryland Department of Public Safety and Correctional Services and consulting on strategic planning, finance, and management issues with nonprofit organizations. She has an M.A. in history from Boston University and a B.A. in education/sociology from the University of Maryland.

Robert D. Crutchfield is professor and chair of the Department of Sociology and adjunct professor in the Department of American Ethnic Studies at the University of Washington. Previously he was acting associate dean of the Graduate School there. His current research focuses on social inequality as a cause of crime and racial inequality in the criminal justice system. Prior to his academic career, he was a juvenile probation officer and an adult parole officer in Pennsylvania. He also served on the Washington State Juvenile Sentencing Commission. He is a past vice president of the American Society of Criminology. He received the Fellows Award from the Western Society of Criminology in 2006. He has M.A. and Ph.D. degrees from Vanderbilt University.

Joel S. Engel is president of JSE Consulting and a member of the National Academy of Engineering. His expertise includes the theory and design of cellular telecommunications systems, wireless communications, high-speed data communications, video compression, and interactive video. He is also a senior executive with over 40 years of experience in the communications industry. He is a retired former chief technology officer of one of the regional Bell companies, where he was responsible for all aspects of the specification and management of the network technology. Prior to that, he spent 20 years at Bell Laboratories, where he headed the team that developed the first cellular telephone system architecture. For this achievement, he has been awarded the Alexander Graham Bell Medal of the Institute of Electrical and Electronics Engineers and the National Medal of Technology. He has a B.S. in electrical engineering from the City College of the City University of New York, an S.M. in electrical engineering from the Massachusetts Institute of Technology, and a Ph.D. in electrical engineering from the Polytechnic Institute of Brooklyn.

John L. Hagan is the John D. MacArthur professor of sociology and law at Northwestern University and codirector of the Center on Law and Globalization at the American Bar Foundation in Chicago. His research with a network of scholars spans topics from causes of crime to war crimes and human rights. Hagan is a former president of the American Society of Criminology and received Guggenheim, German Marshall Fund, and Russell Sage Foundation Fellowships, as well as the C. Wright Mills, Albert Reiss, and Michael J. Hindelang Awards. In June 2009, he received the Stockholm Prize in Criminology. He is the editor of the *Annual Review of*

Law and Social Science. At NRC, he served on the Panel on Juvenile Crime: Prevention, Treatment, and Control and the Panel on High-Risk Youth. He has a B.A. from the University of Illinois at Chicago, and an M.A. and Ph.D (in sociology) from the University of Alberta.

Adele V. Harrell, an independent consultant, is the retired founding director of the Justice Policy Center at the Urban Institute. Her research over the past 35 years has focused on criminal justice responses to drug abuse and domestic violence. She served as codirector of the Evaluation of the Judicial Oversight Demonstration, a multisite longitudinal evaluation of court and community services to reduce intimate partner violence. Other large-scale experimental and quasi-experimental studies she has directed include evaluations of Children at Risk, a community-based drug prevention program, Breaking the Cycle Demonstration, a system-wide intervention for drug-involved felony defendants, the Superior Court of the District of Columbia's Drug Intervention Program, and the Brooklyn Treatment Court, which provides drug court services for female offenders. She is a fellow of the Academy of Experimental Criminology, a member of the District of Columbia Sentencing Commission, and a former member of the National Advisory Panel for the Office of National Drug Control Policy. She has a Ph.D. in sociology from George Washington University.

David D. Jensen is associate professor in the Department of Computer Science and director of the Knowledge Discovery Laboratory at the University of Massachusetts, Amherst. Previously he served as an analyst in the Office of Technology Assessment (OTA), an analytical agency of the U.S. Congress. At OTA, he evaluated the potential of artificial intelligence technologies to detect money laundering and other kinds of fraud. His research focuses on machine learning and knowledge discovery in complex data sets, with applications to social network analysis and fraud detection, as well as causal inference techniques, computing and public policy, and research methods in computer science. He serves on the Executive Committee of the Association for Computing Machinery's Special Interest Group on Knowledge Discovery and Data Mining and on the program committees of the International Conference on Machine Learning and the International Conference on Knowledge Discovery and Data Mining. He is an associate editor of *ACM Transactions on Knowledge Discovery from Data*. He was a member of the 2006-2007 Defense Science Study Group, and he currently serves on the Information Science and Technology Group of the Defense Advanced Research Projects Agency (DARPA). He has M.S. and D.Sc. degrees from Washington University in St. Louis.

Tracey L. Meares is deputy dean and Walton Hale Hamilton professor at Yale Law School. Previously, she was Max Pam professor of law and director of the Center for Studies in Criminal Justice at the University of Chicago Law School. She has held positions clerking for the Honorable Harlington Wood, Jr., of the U.S. Court of Appeals for the Seventh Circuit and as a trial attorney in the Antitrust Division of the U.S. Department of Justice. At NRC, she has served on the Committee on Law and Justice since 2004. Her teaching and research interests focus on criminal procedure and criminal law policy, with a particular emphasis on empirical investigation of these subjects. Her legal research and writings on such issues as crime prevention reflect a civil society approach to law enforcement that builds on the interaction among law, culture, social norms, and social organization. She has a B.S. in general engineering from the University of Illinois and a J.D. from the University of Chicago Law School.

Edwin Meese III is distinguished fellow and holder of the Ronald Reagan chair in public policy at the Heritage Foundation. He served as the 75th attorney general of the United States from February 1985 to August 1988. Previously he was counselor to the president from 1981 to 1985. In this capacity he functioned as the president's chief policy adviser, with management responsibility for the administration of the cabinet, policy development, and planning and evaluation. Formerly, he served as Governor Reagan's executive assistant and chief of staff in California from 1969 through 1974 and as legal affairs secretary from 1967 through 1968. Before joining the governor's staff in 1967, he served as deputy district attorney of Alameda County, California. His expertise centers on the U.S. legal system, law enforcement and criminal justice, intelligence and national security, and the Reagan presidency. His current interests focus on the criminal justice system, federalism, emergency response management, and terrorism. He is also a distinguished visiting fellow at the Hoover Institution, a member of the Board of Regents of the National College of District Attorneys, a distinguished senior fellow in the Institute for United States Studies at the University of London, and a member of the boards of directors of the Capital Research Center and the Landmark Legal Foundation. He is a graduate of Yale University and has a J.D. from the University of California, Berkeley.

Daniel S. Nagin is the Teresa and H. John Heinz III university professor of public policy and statistics in the Heinz School of Carnegie Mellon University. His research focuses on the evolution of criminal and antisocial behaviors over the life course, the deterrent effect of criminal and noncriminal penalties on illegal behaviors, and the development of statistical methods for analyzing longitudinal data. His work has appeared in such diverse outlets as the *American Economic Review*, the *American Sociological Review*, the *Journal of the American Statistical Association*, the *American Journal of Sociology*, the *Archives of General Psychiatry*, *Criminology*, *Child Development*, *Psychological Methodology*, the *Law and Society Review*, the *Crime and Justice Annual Review*, *Operations Research*, and the *Stanford Law Review*. Nagin is an elected fellow of the American Society of Criminology and of the American Society for the Advancement of Science. He is the 2006 recipient of the American Society of Criminology's Edwin H. Sutherland Award (for research contributions) and is a 1985 recipient of the Northeastern Association of Tax Administrators Award for excellence in tax administration. He has a Ph.D. in urban and public affairs from Carnegie Mellon University.

Carol Petrie (*Director, Committee on Law and Justice*) was director of the Committee on Law and Justice until her retirement in 2009. In this capacity since 1997 she has developed and supervised a wide range of projects resulting in reports on juvenile crime, pathological gambling, transnational organized crime, prosecution, crime victimization, improving drug research, school violence, firearms, policing, and forensic science. Previously she served as the director of planning and management at NIJ, where she was responsible for policy development, budget, and administration. In 1994, she served as the acting director of NIJ. Throughout her career she has worked in the area of criminal justice research, statistics, and public policy at NIJ and the Bureau of Justice Statistics. She has conducted research on violence and public policy and managed numerous research projects on the development of criminal behavior, domestic violence, child abuse and neglect, and improving the operations of the criminal justice system. She has a B.S. in education from Kent State University.

Alex R. Piquero is professor in the College of Criminology and Criminal Justice at Florida State University. During preparation of this report, he was a professor in the Department of Criminology and Criminal Justice at the University of Maryland. Previously he was on the faculty of the John Jay College of Criminal Justice, the City University of New York, the University of Florida, Northeastern University, and Temple University. His areas of research have included criminal careers, juvenile violence, community policing, and criminal justice research methods. He has served on numerous committees, including the National Consortium of Violence Research, the MacArthur Foundation Research Program on Adolescent Development and Juvenile Justice, and the National Science Foundation Panel on the Future of Race and Crime. He is currently an investigator on the MacArthur Panel Study of Pathways to Desistance. His honors include the University of Florida Teacher of the Year Award and the American Society of Crimi nology Young Scholar Award. He is executive counselor with the American Society of Criminology and also coeditor of the *Journal of Quantitative Criminology*. He has a Ph.D. in criminology and criminal justice from the University of Maryland.

Charles H. Ramsey is commissioner of the Philadelphia City Police Department. Previously he was chief of the Metropolitan Police Department of Washington, DC, from 1998 to 2006. A native of Chicago, he joined the Chicago Police Department as an 18-year-old cadet in 1968 and served in progressively more responsible positions for 30 years. While in Chicago, Ramsey was instrumental in designing and implementing the Chicago Alternative Policing Strategy, the city's nationally acclaimed model of community policing. A nationally recognized innovator, educator, and practitioner of community policing, in Washington, DC, he refocused the force on crime fighting and crime prevention through a more accountable structure, new equipment and technology, enhanced strategy of community policing, and, since 9/11, new approaches to homeland security and counterterrorism. He has served as an adjunct professor at Lewis University and Northwestern University. A graduate of the FBI Academy, he has a B.A. and an M.A. (criminal justice) from Lewis University in Romeoville, Illinois.

Mary Ann Saar, an independent consultant, is the former secretary of the Maryland Department of Public Safety and Correctional Services. In this position, she supervised 12,000 employees from 12 agencies, including the Division of Corrections, and had responsibility for a budget exceeding $1 billion. Previously she served as state director for U.S. Senator Barbara A. Mikulski, associate commissioner for juvenile services for the Maine Department of Corrections, and secretary of the Maryland Department of Juvenile Services. She is an attorney by training, and her experiences with both adult and juvenile corrections as well as her familiarity with prosecutorial decision making have made her knowledge of criminal justice broad as well as deep. She received the E.R. Cass Award in 2007 from the American Correctional Association, the highest award nationally for a corrections practitioner. Her elected positions include president of the Council of Juvenile Correctional Administrators (2000) and Board of Governors, American Correctional Association (2002-2006). She has a B.A. in criminology/sociology from the University of Maryland, and an L.L.B. from the University of Maryland Law School.

Julie A. Schuck (*Research Associate*), has worked in the Division of Behavioral and Social Sciences and Education of NRC for over 7 years. She has provided research support for a number of projects and workshops, including ones on improving undergraduate instruction in science, technology, engineering, and mathematics; understanding the technical and privacy dimensions of information for terrorism prevention; and developing metrics for the U.S. Department of Homeland Security Science and Technology Directorate. Previously she was a research support specialist at Cornell University. She has an M.S. in education from Cornell University and a B.S. in engineering physics from the University of California, San Diego.

Jay A. Siegel is professor and chair of the Department of Chemistry and Chemical Biology and director of the Forensic and Investigative Sciences Program at Indiana University–Purdue University. His research interests include analysis of ink dyes, fibers, and cosmetic products. Currently, he is a member of the External Advisory Committee of the Deakin University Forensic Science Course (Victoria, Australia), and a fellow of the American Academy of Forensic Sciences. In 2005 he was awarded the Paul Kirk Award, Criminalistics Section, by the American Academy of Forensic Sciences. He has also served as president of the Council of Forensic Science Educators of the American Chemical Society. He has authored and coauthored numerous book chapters and articles on such subjects as textile fibers, forensic identification, and forensic science. At NRC, he currently serves on the Committee on Identifying the Needs of the Forensic Science Community. He has M.S. and Ph.D. degrees from George Washington University.

Carol H. Weiss is the Beatrice B. Whiting professor emerita of policy research at the Harvard University Graduate School of Education. She was a pioneer in the fields of evaluation methods, including theory-based evaluation, and the influence of research and evaluation on decisions. She has written many books, articles, and book chapters dealing with evaluation, uses of research in policy making, cross-national comparisons of research influence, legislative and bureaucratic obstacles to reliance on research, and media reporting of research. Her most recent research was a study of decision making by school districts about the choice of drug abuse prevention programs and the influence of evidence from evaluation studies on those decisions. One surprising finding was the frailty of the evaluation evidence on which many decisions were made. At NRC, she has served on 10 committees, including ones on NASA's Elementary and Secondary Education Program, on assessing behavioral and social science research on aging, and on the federal role in education research. She is currently serving on the Committee on Field Evaluation of Behavioral and Cognitive Sciences-Based Methods for Intelligence and Counter-Intelligence. She has been a fellow at the Center for Advanced Study, a senior research fellow at the U.S. Department of Education, and a guest scholar at the Brookings Institution. She has a Ph.D. in sociology from Columbia University.